Guillem Balagué is a well-known football pundit and a regular commentator on the BBC, after twenty years on Sky Sports. He is also a frequent contributor to various magazines, newspapers, blogs, podcasts and radio stations in Spain and in the UK.

Also by Guillem Balagué

A Season on the Brink
Pep Guardiola: Another Way of Winning
Messi
Brave New World

CRISTIANO RONALDO

THE BIOGRAPHY

GUILLEM BALAGUE

WEIDENFELD & NICOLSON

To R.

I did say you were not going to appear in the book . . .

A W&N Paperback

First published in Great Britain in 2015 by Orion
This paperback edition published in 2018 by Weidenfeld & Nicolson,
an imprint of Orion Books
Carmelite House, 50 Victoria Embankment,
London EC4Y 0DZ

An Hachette UK company

1 3 5 7 9 10 8 6 4 2

Copyright © Guillem Balagué 2015, 2016, 2018

Main researcher: Maribel Herruzo
Additional research: Luis Miguel García
Translation: Marc Joss and Hugo Steckelmacher
Copy-editing: Richard Collins
Proofreading: William Glasswell and Simon Fox

A CIP catalogue record for this book is available
from the British Library.

ISBN 978 1 4746 1156 5

Printed and bound in Great Britain by Clays Ltd, Elcograf S.p.A.

www.weidenfeldandnicolson.co.uk
www.orionbooks.co.uk

CONTENTS

LIST OF ILLUSTRATIONS

10. Signing for Madrid. (Sipa Press/REX)
11. I presented a couple of events with Ronaldo. (Christopher Lee/ Getty Images for Nike)
12. José Mourinho was more foe than friend over the years. (Jasper Juinen/Getty Images)
13. So close, so far apart. (Reuters/Ruben Sprich)
14. Celebration at the end of the 2014 Champions League final. (Lars Baron/Getty Images)
15. With Irina Shayk. (Christof Koepsel/Getty Images)
16. Jorge Mendes has been another father figure. (EPA)
17. Ronaldo's third Ballon d'Or, at which his son stole the show. (Fabrice Coffrini/AFP/Getty Images)
18. Sent off for fouling Edimar in January 2015. (Gonzalo Arroyo Moreno/Getty Images)
19. With Gareth Bale. (Dani Pozo/AFP/Getty Images)

AUTHOR'S NOTE

All quotations taken from secondary sources have been numbered in the text, with a full list provided in the bibliography. All other quotations, unless otherwise stated in the text, have been taken from interviews I have conducted or from statements at press conferences, post-match interviews and the like. All other insights have come about as a result of the extensive investigations that I have carried out for this book.

Guillem Balagué
September 2015

PROLOGUE

WHAT WE ARE, WHERE WE ARE, WHERE WE ARE GOING

'News is circulating that I allegedly made offending remarks regarding Lionel Messi. This is absolutely false and I have assured my lawyer takes action to sue those responsible. I have the utmost respect for all my professional colleagues, and Messi is obviously no exception.'

Cristiano Ronaldo on Facebook, 11 November 2014

Ronaldo, or whoever writes his Facebook content, was referring to statements of his that I had included in my book entitled *Messi* (Orion, 2013), the first authorised biography of the Argentinian footballer.

When I found out about his reaction on Twitter, I decided to take a step back. Clearly there was going to be uproar.

■ ■ ■

According to Manu Sainz, a journalist who was Ronaldo's spokesperson over those controversial days, the Portuguese's anger while on international duty with his country was 'rife'. And the player wanted to respond as soon as possible in the most public way.

Had he not done so, the accusation, defamation or comment (depending on how you viewed it) could have gone unnoticed.

Ronaldo was attempting to crack a nut with a sledgehammer and did so by sending the above message to his one hundred million followers. Why? He would be crossing paths with Messi in a friendly match in Manchester in the coming days. He could meet him face to face and deny the allegation. My allegation. The story I was told by people very close to Cristiano.

In reality, the 'offending' paragraph had been in the public domain for eleven months.

Why was there such a dramatic reaction almost a year after the publication of his rival's biography?

That week, with no domestic matches to report on and only international games, the *Daily Telegraph* chose to publish two extracts from the paperback edition of *Messi* which had just been published. In fact, the English daily newspaper selected two excerpts already featured in the hardback eleven months earlier (Arsenal's attempt to sign Leo and the relationship between Messi and Ronaldo) and it all kicked off.

The media (initially in Spain, but then the social networks got hold of it and it quickly spread to all corners of the globe) grabbed hold of one word, took it out of context, twisted it and, in Spain, translated it incorrectly. Could that word define the most distinguished rivalry in the history of football? My career was judged and debate ensued over whether or not such things are said in a dressing room full of adrenalin-infused warriors.

The word was 'motherfucker'.

That is how I said Ronaldo referred to 'the Flea' in front of his team-mates in the dressing room.

■ ■ ■

By that point, I had already begun research on my next book. This one.

I had spoken to Cristiano regarding the possibility of chatting about his life, his way of thinking, his past. 'Yes, of course, no problem,' he told me on four separate occasions. I had also conversed with his agent Jorge Mendes, who agreed to collaborate just ten days before that Facebook post, although both of us questioned whether or not it was a good idea. I will explain why later.

I went to the Derbyshire Peak District in order to take advantage of the international break. While out jogging, I could not stop asking myself what made him respond in that way. Was a legal threat necessary?

Other people are better suited to such conflicts than me. Johan Cruyff used to say that he wanted to know where the line separating those who loved him and hated him lay, just so he would know who to fight against. Frank Rijkaard once told me that he would feel awful if he found out that even one person hated him. I know what you mean, Frank.

I spent plenty of time around the English countryside over those days. I started focusing on the colours, aromas, the sound of the branches cracking, but all that was blurred by the new questions swirling around my head.

What can we learn about Ronaldo if we study his reaction? Was I changing my perception of him and my desire to study him? What would happen to the collaboration that had been discussed? For a start, I was unaware that my influence was such as to prompt him to react with such opprobrium. The media circus had gone to town. It was another one of those storms that surge when the names Messi and Ronaldo are uttered in the same sentence. Especially during an international break with the resultant paucity of football news.

What else was happening at the time for him to feel compelled to write such a message? There had to be more to it, something that set his alarm bells ringing.

It finally hit me some time later: there were ten days to go before voting for the Ballon d'Or closed, an award that Ronaldo was the favourite to win for the third time.

Surely his Facebook post was not just a way to prevent people from changing their vote in that year's Ballon d'Or. Or was it?

And what to say about the media's reaction?

The subject became big news and received what I consider disproportionate coverage in sports sections in newspapers and on the radio, especially in Spain. On the very night of Ronaldo's post, I spoke about the issue on Onda Cero, the radio station I work for. I did not want to do it; I wanted the Messi book to speak for itself. But I had just been involved in an interview with Real Sociedad president Jokin Aperribay for the radio programme *Al primer toque* and the presenter, Héctor Fernández, to whom I still owe various favours, convinced me to say something, whatever it might be.

I came out with what I have repeated ever since: 'It's all in the book.' This is what you can read in *Messi*:

Ronaldo, perhaps as a symptom of the immaturity that marks so many footballers, thinks it necessary to put on a brave face in front of his team-mates, not be scared of Messi and to rise to the challenge. All very macho; very false. And that is why, according to some Real Madrid players, CR7 has a nickname for him: 'motherfucker'; and if he sees someone from the club speaking to Leo, he also ends up being baptised 'motherfucker'. In that environment, Ronaldo usually compares their relationship with that between the Republic of Ireland and the United Kingdom. And the Madrid players, with their less than subtle dressing-room sense of humour, have a long list of jokes that include Messi as Ronaldo's dog or puppet, or kept in a designer handbag belonging to the Portuguese player. And much worse.

It became clear that not many people had actually read the book, nor did any of them find the time to seek out and analyse the paragraph concerned until I posted it on Twitter on the night of the Facebook post.

All that says little in favour of my weight in the Spanish media circus: almost nobody felt compelled to read my book, even though it was the first authorised one of 'the Flea'. It also reflects the speed with which news is generated and consumed.

On returning to reality after my isolation in the Peak District, I began going over the various reactions.

A man whom I admire dearly, Paco González, had given me a rap on the knuckles on his programme on COPE radio. He stated that there are things that need not be told, dressing-room talk that should remain there. But part of his own success, aside from being a marvellous communicator, is the way in which he manages the information that reaches him from the dressing room.

A handful of journalists performed the selfless role of 'Ronaldistas', defending the player in the face of accusations because that is what their job consists of: being a transmission chain for the footballer.

It was not pleasant to be put under the microscope, but it gave me some idea of what players experience when they are judged by supporters for ninety minutes once or twice a week. And then again the next day by the media. Relentlessly.

■ ■ ■

Did it make sense to include that word, that paragraph, that dressing-room chit-chat in the Messi book? A year-long piece of work involving hundreds of hours of conversations and thoughts assembled in 600 pages about 'the Flea' had turned into controversy because of one word. Did it improve it? Did it add much to Leo's story?

Maybe it did not contribute much. In reality, it said more about Ronaldo than it did about Messi, about the Portuguese's need to show off to his peers.

Maybe I should have left it out.

But, essentially, had I done anything wrong?

That last question did have an answer: everything that I publish is checked thoroughly, especially on a subject such as this one, especially in a biography. Furthermore, all books are scrutinised by the publisher's lawyers. The context, which was and continues to be ignored, was crucial: Ronaldo and Messi respect each other because of their similar footballing paths; they mix respect with feelings that you have for your nemesis but, importantly, they react to each other's success differently. Cristiano is a warrior from the moment he leaves his home, when he gets dressed, speaks or behaves like a player. He is afraid of no one. Plus, he can show no sign of weakness. On the contrary.

While I repeatedly mulled over the situation, everyone else was focusing on breaking other news: Sergio Ramos had said something or other about certain Spanish internationals' commitment. The message was implicitly understood as a jibe at Cesc Fàbregas and Diego Costa, who had withdrawn from Vicente del Bosque's latest Spain squad. One controversial story was replaced by another.

Forty-eight hours in the eye of a hurricane. Only forty-eight, but it seemed much longer.

One question remained fixed in my head: does the truth save you?

■ ■ ■

PROLOGUE

I could not stop thinking about the role of sports journalism both in England and Spain, the two countries where I know it well.

As sports writers, we only tell a portion of what we know. In fact there are almost always two conversations with our sources or interviewees: one with the microphone on and another with it off. Many stories are known but do not come out for a plethora of reasons: be they good (insufficient sources, waiting for the right moment . . .) or bad (so as not to annoy a friend, lose a source or the fear of isolation that always accompanies breaking an exclusive).

Only part of the truth is told. Whatever we think will be of interest. Or whatever we think will sell best.

One can, or, rather, one *must*, be accurate, fair and unbiased when it comes to data. The way a story is presented and treated must be honourable, but being objective is an impossibility from the moment one word is chosen over another to describe something.

We are answerable to an ethical code, of course. And to our bosses, now more so than ever, now that work is so precarious. The person who pays calls the shots.

In fact, the person who pays defines the parameters of what is and is not true. And information is bought and sold because it is now no more than a product and even more so in the showbiz world of professional football.

Plus very powerful people make huge efforts to ensure they can influence what is written. I know that an important club president in Spain tried – unsuccessfully – to get the head of a major sports newspaper sacked for not sharing his ideas in a ploy to prevent criticism. He used personal accusations and other pressure tactics in his attempt. I shall not reveal who was involved. I will only tell you half the story for the time being.

You see? Journalism is not simply a recounting of events.

■ ■ ■

During an appearance of journalist Manu Sainz on the television show *El chiringuito de jugones* he spoke about his relationship with Ronaldo just after the player was sent off for aggressive conduct against Córdoba in La Liga:

> Cristiano is exemplary even when he makes a mistake. [. . .] The other day, he was on the team bus minutes after the match against Córdoba and he told me: 'I want you to write a few things for me. I haven't had time to apologise and want you to write something.' I was going to do it but I did not because the club later said it was better to do it on Twitter.[1]

Write things on behalf of a player? Some people were incensed. Some labelled it terrible journalism. 'Manu is just Ronaldo's scribe,' retorted others. That is, however, the reality of how a large part of the industry works: a certain level of submission is exchanged for information. What I had never previously heard so clearly was the 'he gave me a few sentences to write down' concept.

In England, many journalists also defend coaches or players because they are friends. I shall not reveal who. I have a soft spot for Rafa Benítez, I've seen him take training and how he works; I know many of the reasons behind his decisions and his way of thinking. I defend him over and above my journalistic duties because I feel that he is unfairly treated. There is a sort of crusade behind my statements about Rafa, who was not helped by the way he disrupted the status quo in the Premier League with his challenging of Sir Alex Ferguson, Manchester United, referees, the FA, even José Mourinho. I always thought if he were English he would be a national hero.

But is that journalism?

Is that intellectual corruption or are we the consequence of how the industry is set up?

I, for one, will never be able to nor shall I try to be objective when it comes to Cristiano Ronaldo. But I promise the following: read on.

■ ■ ■

You may be familiar with Oliver Sacks, perhaps the most famous professor of neurology of the twentieth century, physician, best-selling author and chronic introvert. He was curious about the world and our minds, but unable to have meaningful conversations or relationships with most people, as he explained in his beautiful autobiography *On the Move*.

Sometimes, though, he would be so astonished by the thrill of observation and could not help sharing:

> I almost never speak to people in the street. But some years ago, there was a lunar eclipse, and I went outside to view it with my little 20x telescope. Everyone else on the busy sidewalk seemed oblivious to the extraordinary celestial happening above them, so I stopped people, saying, 'Look! Look what's happening to the moon!' and pressing my telescope into their hands. People were taken aback at being approached in this way, but, intrigued by my manifestly innocent enthusiasm, they raised the telescope to their eyes, 'wowed' and handed it back. 'Hey, man, thanks for letting me look at that,' or 'Gee, thanks for showing me.'

I don't promise objectivity, but a total commitment to the curiosity that we all have for a life like Ronaldo's and especially his journey.

■ ■ ■

There is another issue that can endanger the relationship with the subject of a biography.

Let us imagine that I convinced Cristiano to sit down and tell me how he has got where he is using new words, unknown stories and the required sincerity. Maybe he would say: 'I may seem arrogant, but I'm not because of this, that and the other.' Or maybe he would admit that he is, but refuse to accept others judging him. Maybe he would say that he wants everyone to love him. Maybe he would say that he does not fancy going to work in the morning. Or that sometimes he doesn't enjoy playing football.

But who is capable of being so brutal, open and sincere?

We all have black marks, weaknesses, issues, thoughts which we are ashamed of, chapters from the past that we try to keep under wraps, and, if they do come out, we cover them up. Even more so if we are in the public eye.

That is the limit which the biographer battles against: interviewing the subject in question does not guarantee access to the whole truth. It guarantees *the subject's* truth.

Furthermore, Cristiano Ronaldo has been the main protagonist in a crucial image campaign since 2012, when he realised that the world did not understand him.

Jorge Mendes, the brains behind GestiFute, the most renowned agent in the football world, instigated the campaign. More doubts began circling in my head. Did I want to tell the GestiFute version of the Ronaldo story? ▪ ▪ ▪

Around that time, I went out for a bite to eat with a very famous player. He was a top star of a legendary team during a spell of historic title wins and now earns his living as a coach. He has been in the business for over thirty years.

'You know you can't tell the truth, right?' he told me while discussing the limits of the exercise that I had undertaken. 'They will want to control you. It is only normal they would do that.'

■ ■ ■

I had a missed call on my mobile phone from an unfamiliar Portuguese number two weeks before the whole Facebook saga. Could it have been Jorge Mendes? I had been trying to see him since the previous Christmas, which I had spent in Dubai after accepting his invitation to the Globe Awards which he has been organising for seven years.

This is an event to celebrate the success of the Mendes empire. In the one I attended, Deco, who was represented by the Portuguese agent, won the player of the decade award while Xavi Hernández, who was offered an all-expenses-paid trip to Dubai for a few days with his family, received the award for best player over the last ten years. Seriously. The titles of the awards change depending on who is in attendance. But the networking is of the highest calibre, as you would expect.

I only had a Spanish number for Mendes, who spends most of his time in Madrid and, as I say, I had been waiting for his call since that Christmas. We had exchanged a few messages and it seemed that the definitive conversation, which would determine our relationship in the subsequent twelve months when I would be writing the book, was about to take place.

From the moment the Real Madrid communications department directed my requests to interview president Florentino Pérez and the players to Mendes, and when I was told that in order to arrange a chat with Ronaldo I had to speak to his agent, I knew that everything would be decided during a difficult and possibly one-off phone call. Mendes does not beat about the bush; there are no pauses in his conversations. Bang, bang, bang and that is it. That is how you speak to Mendes. Or, more like, how he speaks to you.

I had already been to Funchal (Madeira) and Lisbon. I had spoken to Real Madrid players. I had spent time in Manchester and shared long conversations with many people who were part of Cristiano's life. I had plenty of information. My experience with Ronaldo (interviewing him for Sky Sports, presenting some of his commercial events) added something extra. I could do the book with the information already available to me.

But I remained determined to speak to Mendes despite the doubts about the expected fight for control of what would be written.

'Speak to people who know me, Jorge. You'll find out what type of writer and person I am.'

'I'm not after an authorised book, but we could chat and you could come with me on this journey.'

I was sending him text messages of that ilk. I was receiving either negative responses or silence.

As part of my research, I read a biography of Ronaldo by Mario Torrejón, a colleague on SER radio, who collaborated with Mendes. Mario, who communicates his ideas very well in what is his first book, was able to interview the agent, Ronaldo and the Real Madrid president. I feel he did have to pay a price, however. It seems to me that many of the stories told in that biography have the GestiFute stamp on them.

I called the Portuguese number back. I thought that, if it was Mendes, I would see where the conversation took me, without committing to anything.

It was Mendes.

'Look,' he told me, without first exchanging pleasantries, 'I've decided I'm going to help you, but don't screw with me! I've spoken to people who tell me you're a good guy.'

I later found out that Mendes had asked, among others, *Marca* director Oscar Campillo for reports and was given glowing references.

'The problem is I don't know what you're going to write. You've done the Messi book. With Mario [Torrejón], we knew what he wanted to do and what he was writing from the first minute. I don't really know how I can help you. I want to help you, but I don't really know how.'

In the very first minute we were heading down a dead-end street. It was now a battle for the upper hand.

– I don't know what you're going to write, I don't know who you're going to speak to.

– Do you want to know who I'm speaking to? I can tell you . . .

– No, you can do whatever you want.

– But everybody tells me to speak to you.

– The club should take greater responsibility. But I don't know if we'll speak because I don't know what you're doing and what you're going to write.

– We can sit down and talk it over, I'll tell you the angles I'm covering.

I explained to him that, before knowing what I was going to write, I had to do a few more interviews and the format of the book would start to take shape a few months down the line. That was not entirely true, but it gained me some time in case I needed it to finally reach an agreement with him.

Ronaldo's entourage has understood that in order to keep him happy, and also to feed the competitive beast that he is, he must be given absolute guarantees that everybody and everything, sporting institutions included, are at his service. They must keep criticism at a distance, or control it, create the narrative and keep him on his pedestal. That helps him win more Ballons d'Or and trophies. It is good for business, too.

One question remained unanswered. What happens if we disagree on something? 'We'll discuss it,' he told me.

I thought: let's take Ronaldo's transfer to Real Madrid, for example. I know what took place, I have seen the contracts, but what if Mendes does not want to explain the whole saga, including the offer he got from Manchester City that he seemed happy to consider? How can we explain from Ronaldo's point of view the story of him taking the only locker opposite a mirror in the Manchester United dressing room? Is it treated as a triviality or a reflection of a vain personality? Can we discuss narcissism? Would they let me analyse the presence (and absence) of an alcoholic father who refused help towards the end of his life?

'Just so you know,' insisted Mendes, 'this is fully my responsibility. Some people in my camp are telling me not to work with you, but I understand that you're a decent guy and we're going to work together, we're going to do this together, but you can't screw me.'

We could not get away from that. He was telling me that he did not know how to help me because he did not know how to control me. I was offering him a certain level of supervision, but not complete.

I have not spoken to Mendes since the Facebook controversy.

■ ■ ■

In fact, after the Facebook post, Mendes made a few calls to the opinion makers of the Spanish media. If Ronaldo is upset, Mendes multiplies it by twenty. He wanted his friends in the media to deny the story but also to question my credibility.

■ ■ ■

Portugal and Argentina met in a friendly at Old Trafford on 18 November 2014. The build-up to the game centred around the relationship between Ronaldo and Messi. Plenty was written about their relationship and every now and then the infamous word from my book was mentioned. It had been taken out of context, planted somewhere else and allowed to grow.

I had planned to go to Manchester, but did not want to bump into either player. I could imagine Ronaldo ignoring me in front of my colleagues when, previously, he would have stopped to say hello and chat. I could imagine Messi shaking my hand, talking to me as he sometimes does. That would be enough – I thought – for somebody to reignite the story. Why open another potential can of worms?

I was also aware that the situation was probably not that serious, but my sensitivity had increased, as had my paranoia.

■ ■ ■

The Facebook post ended the debate with Mendes about controlling the content of this book, and I genuinely felt an overwhelming sense of freedom.

For Real Madrid, Mendes or Ronaldo's version, there are official books or ones on which they have collaborated.

I prefer not to participate in the construction of that legend. But, in truth, I have no other choice.

What you will read here is my version of Ronaldo's journey, what has influenced him, which Madeiran traits remain with him, how he developed at Manchester United and what Real Madrid have done for him. I will discuss his arrogance and vanity, which will constitute the debate over whether or not his battle to be the best requires those two elements. Why does he feel the need to be acknowledged as the best? And constantly so? What drives him? Why does he work so much harder than anybody else?

While thinking about his addiction to his job and self-improvement, I read a magnificent Marco Ruiz interview in *AS* with Arrigo

Sacchi, AC Milan's legendary coach from the eighties:

– Your players speak highly of you, but they say: 'He was a workaholic.'

– There's an Italian poet who used to say: 'There's no art without obsession.' If you don't put much in, you don't get much back. In his book, Carlo [Ancelotti] said: 'Arrigo was so determined and convinced that we said: we have to carry on.' It was almost a matter of fanaticism. I saw that quality in all great coaches: Lobanovsky, Michels, Guardiola, Kovacs . . . They gave everything they could give. I retired after tweny years of hard work. I couldn't cope with that pace. I was spent. Only one certainty drove me: that you could always do better. My Milan side won the European Cup, European Super Cup and Intercontinental Cup in the space of a few months. Baresi said to me: 'Now we're the best in the world.' I answered him: 'Yes, until midnight tonight.'[2]

These are also the qualities that make Ronaldo who he is.

There are more Cristianos than the obsessive one. Take the cocky and generous one, for example. The one who has evolved on the pitch, the one who made himself, the one who was alone as a teenager. The one who protects his family, becoming a rock in the process. The one who celebrates his work in controversial ways. The one who gives away his bonuses.

I travelled far and wide to discover as many angles as possible. However, I discovered a certain level of mistrust in Madeira, and Portugal in general, when it came to discussing Ronaldo or Mendes. Why so afraid? Why is the only possible relationship with either of them a submissive one?

Would it be possible to explore all of this if the final version had to be signed off by Jorge Mendes?

I discovered that a fascinating culture shock had taken place at the Carrington training ground in Manchester. Many people were part of the creation of Ronaldo (or so they say) and many others wanted to change him as they did not believe he would become half the player he is today. Some even lost faith in him, given his obsession with individual play over the requirements of the team. Maybe they did eventually change him, but not all of them would admit that Cristiano also transformed the culture of one of the most famous footballing institutions in the world.

It was going to take some scraping away to remove the layers of paint that cover the Ronaldo that his circle is trying to sell to the world nowadays, while remaining conscious of human strengths and weaknesses. Will my version be better than others'? The truth is, it does not matter. One thing is for sure, though – I will try to make it different.

Everybody takes photographs of the Eiffel Tower, but the key lies in taking the one that nobody has seen before.

Maybe it will not be the Ronaldo that you all want to see, or the Ronaldo that he wants you to see, or the Ronaldo that Mendes wants to portray, or even the Ronaldo that he really is. Or the Ronaldo that his critics 'know' so well. What follows is based on research, analysis, studies, twenty-five years of journalistic experience, on chats with people who know him, psychologists, sociologists, players with whom he has shared the dressing room, club directors, some of his coaches, as well as conversations that I had with him and his circle before the controversy . . . Both on and off the record.

Ronaldo has let the world explore his life. He often offers interviews and lets the cameras in behind the scenes at trophy presentations. CNN were granted open access to his home for a chat in 2012 and so on. That is how the image of a winner is gradually created.

It will not be easy to find the real person.

■ ■ ■

By the way, for those who wonder, no, I never did get a call from Ronaldo's lawyers.

ONE

MADEIRA

A SMALL ISLAND, LIKE ALL THE OTHERS

When we are born, we are the consequence of four elements of which we have no choice: our mother, our father, our siblings and the place where we are born. What else is there? Our passion, what motivates us. After that we only have the superfluous, the decorative. I know you will not all agree.

While we wait to see what drives an unborn Cristiano Ronaldo, who deserves the first pages, the mother, the family or the place where he was born? What should we write about first?

Dolores Aveiro is the mother who still lives alongside Cristiano and who looks after his son as if she were his mother, rather than his grandmother. She is also the woman who let her twelve-year-old son leave home in order to pursue his dream of becoming a footballer. It hurt, but she did let him go at such a young age. Maybe because it was the best option, or the only one. Or maybe because something similar happened to her. It is often said that in life lessons, virtues and defects are repeated from generation to generation: Dolores's father walked out on her, although he did it in a different way, without the kindness that she packed into Cristiano's suitcase when he flew to Lisbon. I get the impression that there is an invisible thread linking both experiences.

Anyway, you simply cannot understand Ronaldo without going through Dolores's life.

We need to set the scene by pinpointing the place where Dolores and Cristiano were born, grew up and from where they eventually escaped. We need to go to Funchal.

Funchal is . . .

The capital of the Portuguese island of Madeira, off the northwest coast of Africa.

The extremely verdant island is filled with the spirits of departed inhabitants and present-day residents on the verge of departing.

A prison without doors.

A crossroads.

A springboard.

And it was discovered by accident.

Let us go back to the beginning of the Age of Discovery in the early fifteenth century. Henry the Navigator, Infante of Portugal and the first Duke of Viseu, moved around the Portuguese king's court with freedom. Henry, the son, brother and uncle of monarchs, had hooded eyes but a determined voice and skilfully obtained the monopoly over the exploration of the African coast. He put together the best navigators and cartographers in the country, and, by definition, in the world at the time. He sent them to discover new lands with square-riggers, three masts and limited resources: an astrolabe, an hourglass and a compass. Little else.

The winds off the African coast were treacherous and new to the young captains, João Gonçalves Zarco and Tristão Vaz Teixeira, who lost their way. Days went by without any sight of land, before the discovery of a small island with golden beaches that they named Porto Santo. Having charted the waters, the navigators returned to Portugal to report on their findings.

'Thank you,' said Infante Enrique. 'Now go back and colonise the island. Keep looking for new horizons, too.'

It was the year 1419.

Back in the area, not very far from Porto Santo, towards the south, the explorers witnessed a vast cloud formation that anyone who has been to Madeira knows is as characteristic of the island as its steep roads and wine.

Every nautical mile into unexplored waters was a step into the unknown, a repudiation of superstition and fear. They had to battle against the Atlantic waves and the harsh weather conditions to get from Porto Santo to the Bay of Machico, the gateway to Madeira.

The navigators finally dropped anchor on the biggest of the four islands in the volcanic archipelago, 400 kilometres from the Canary Islands and located on the same latitude as Casablanca, Morocco. They left the small and unpopulated Desertas and Savage Islands, both current World Heritage Sites, for a later date.

Madeira was discovered.

Henry the Navigator sent families, principally farmers, from the Algarve to colonise the new lands soon after. There are almost 270,000 people living there today.

The Portuguese empire was formally dissolved in 1975 with Madeira remaining as a trace of that golden era, but also a distant cousin the family back in Portugal struggles to accept.

■ ■ ■

I stopped off in Lisbon ahead of my first trip to Funchal. I went out for dinner with some friends at Clube de Jornalistas, a venue that one might imagine is a breeding ground for intellectual and sensitive discussion. Not when it comes to Madeira: 'The Madeiran people,' they informed us, 'not only have a strange accent, but they are strange, too. I imagine you've heard about the latest paedophilia scandal over there and the poverty swamping the island. It's a small dictatorship with the longest-standing leader in the country. It's not Portugal, it's something else.

And the tourist area?

'For lower-class English people,' we were told by a man who continued to volunteer such details despite the fact he had never set foot on Madeira. Nor did he need to, he said.

After landing at the tiny airport in Funchal, I noticed that the statue of Zarco still stood in the town centre, looking over the descendants of the families from the Algarve who, six centuries earlier, colonised the island of dense, volcanic rock. And, as the explorers had found, we were welcomed by low-lying clouds that you could almost touch, fulsome and round, reminiscent of a painting by John Constable.

As it was May, at the close of another exhausting football season, my visit to Madeira was intended for relaxation purposes, as well as making contact with people linked to the main protagonist of my new book. I looked for a good hotel and a rental car, without knowing quite how big an engine was needed to comfortably negotiate the steep roads with more than a 30-degree gradient.

I plunged myself into Funchal and went on the hunt for my first sources of information. I interviewed some renowned local journalists who painted a surprising picture of Ronaldo, who seemed distant whenever he went back to Funchal, had forgotten Madeira, according to them, and had little interest in what he had left behind. It reminded me of what they say about the Beatles in Liverpool: it hurts Liverpudlians that John, Ringo, George and Paul never felt grateful to the city in which they were born.

There was more: Ronaldo had gone into business with some very affluent people who tried to take advantage of him, by asking him for money without keeping to the promises that had been made. Meanwhile, they told me, Cristiano had become very friendly with the island's ruling clique, one of the guaranteed ways to be looked after on the island.

Let us put this into context. The former president of the autonomous region of Madeira, Alberto João Jardim, enjoyed thirty-seven years in power before tendering his resignation in January 2015. A fine politician, benefactor and leader for the Madeiran cause for some, the perfect representative of the establishment for the rest. During his farewell speech to journalists on the day he left office, he said: 'I didn't plan to hurt anyone, but if someone is unfair to me, they'll pay for it.'

Jardim, who was surrounded by associates with more power than sense, was a man with whom you needed to be on good terms.

An initial glance reveals two types of Madeiran. Those, like Jardim, for whom Madeira is the world, and those, like Zarco, the founding father, who left to conquer new worlds, although he kept a house on the island. The fact is that no Madeiran ever truly leaves . . .

The first settlers worked the land and, even today, cultivating smallholdings is the biggest economic activity on the island. There were many bad harvests, however, and the land had to be split up to cope with the growing number of inhabitants, making survival much more difficult. People had to emigrate, though most did so in the hope of returning someday.

Being a tiny island at the crossroads of Europe, America and Africa, the big continents beckon. That is why large communities of Madeiran people grew in places as far away as South Africa and Venezuela, with most of them quickly becoming leading figures in their professions soon after landing in their new territories: builders, factory workers, lawyers or hotel and catering entrepreneurs. There is no point leaving your homeland unless it is to conquer another world. Now, 750,000 self-proclaimed Madeirans, spread across the globe, like to boast about their origins. Does it not remind you of Ronaldo?

■ ■ ■

On that first journey to Cristiano's homeland, I had time to wander around the area where he was born, the humble Quinta do Falcao, built into a mountainside and defined by two steep roads, modest housing, clothes drying outside the windows, one lone shop and a bar with a plastic roof and a raised terrace situated on a block of uneven cement. Cristiano's house was demolished less than ten years ago in order to build more council houses.

Grants from the European Union have allowed for an increase in prosperity in the area, but, although the autonomous government wants to hide it, the island is actually floating on a sea of economic inequality. The autonomous government speaks of only about 2 per cent living below the poverty line in a bid to protect tourism, while the charitable organisation União das IPSS puts that figure at 20 per cent. Unemployment is widespread and state benefits do not reach everybody. More than 28,000 citizens must rely on the authorities for subsidised food.

The very wealthy, meanwhile, comprise 10 per cent of the population.

The turn of the century generated an interesting transformation. Madeira has been closely linked to the United Kingdom since the seventeenth century, when it became a port of call for British traders on their long transatlantic journeys. British soldiers even occupied Madeira on a couple of occasions during the Napoleonic Wars to prevent the French from colonising it. Some decided to set up shop on the island in order to begin developing farms and the wine trade.

During the Victorian age, ladies with unmistakably British surnames such as Blandy and Leacock would spend the mornings drinking Madeiran wines and the afternoons sipping tea in the salons of their luxurious mansions.

The Second World War signalled the beginning of the end of British influence and the strategic importance of the port. The new generations, facing economic decline, sold the residences that had been homes to their families for centuries and returned to the United Kingdom. Barely 200 British residents remain, but the idea persists among Madeiran inhabitants, or even the Portuguese in general, that the British lifestyle represents an enviable and better way of life.

So, after three centuries under British rule, the colonial style was replaced by a new generation of businessmen. They were descendants of Portuguese expatriates who had made their money in South Africa or Venezuela. This group, families like the Pestanas, the Roques, the Berardos, returned to consolidate their wealth and set about improving the island's infrastructure and stabilising the unsteady economy.

From the top of the hill where my hotel is located, you can see some spectacular residences, but also the huts built in the gaps left by the mountain, half-built houses on dry wasteland and rubbish on the street.

And many tired-looking, elderly people wandering around aimlessly.

■ ■ ■

On the last day of my stay, I bumped into Ricardo Santos, son of the president of Andorinha, Cristiano's first club. The same age, he had been a team-mate of his, both at the club and in the street games. They were close friends. But he insisted, with a shy look, that part of his life means little to him now.

On the way to the airport, I called Fernando Egídio, a well-known sociologist who lives in Funchal. He refused to speak about Ronaldo. He was not the only one.

I got the feeling that many Madeirans have an excessive respect for the player, and even that he divides opinion. Of course, envy surrounds his achievements, but at first glance there was minimal evidence of the almost religious devotion that many, for example, have for Lionel Messi in Rosario or Diego Maradona in Buenos Aires.

Maybe that is just a reflection of the way football is experienced in each country.

■ ■ ■

Cristiano, contrary to what some of his compatriots say, does care about Madeira and have real interest in what goes on there. He chose the island as the location of the first hotel in his CR7 chain, which opened in summer 2016; the next ones to open will be in Lisbon and Madrid. He has a house on the coast and has built another one nearby for his mother. He donated generously towards flood relief on the island in 2010 when excessive flooding caused forty deaths and more than one hundred injuries. Such involvement has helped his homeland (including free advertising campaigns) strengthen Madeira's position as a tourist destination.

In December 2013 he opened a museum that houses 155 of his trophies and medals, twenty-seven match balls signed by team-mates after hat-tricks and well-known photos that tell his story. Or part of it at least. As the *Daily Telegraph* put it in an article in May 2014: 'Pelé, the greatest of them all, needed three World Cups, 1,281 goals and another 31 years after his career finished before anyone felt it necessary to open a museum in his name.'[3] The entrance, which boasts two sliding doors across which a larger-than-life photo of Ronaldo suddenly divides, leads the visitor into a 'thoroughly modern Aladdin's cave of a shrine' containing evidence of his greatest successes.

As the Catalan poet Salvador Espriu said, the mirror of the truth is broken into minuscule fragments. All the one thousand visitors that the museum welcomes in a typical week are delighted to buy one of those pieces, the one that recreates the fairy tale that the Ronaldo family want you to know. Espriu also said that each of the pieces contains a glimmer of light. Ronaldo's trophies are certainly real, but just as real is the difficult background that the Santos Aveiro family endured and ultimately overcame.

■ ■ ■

Maria Dolores Aveiro was born in Caniçal, Madeira, where life was tough in the 1950s. Her brother had been born a year earlier, but wasn't officially registered until the birth of Dolores. In poverty, official documentation is both a foreign language and a nuisance.

From then on, Ronaldo's mother's story is marked by struggle, as is common in Madeira. It was an incessant battle to shape a destiny with the odds stacked against her from birth.

Her own mother, Matilde, passed away when Dolores was five after suffering a heart attack at the age of thirty-seven. She left four children behind. There was little money for food or clothing. Motherly affection was missing, and so Dolores, the eldest sibling, took on from an early age the role that Matilde had left vacant.

Her father, José Viveiro, ended up sending the four siblings away to two different religious orphanages. Maria Dolores cried every day. The nuns ruled by corporal punishment and Dolores was frequently chastised for minor infringements like making spelling mistakes. She escaped from the orphanage on several occasions. Punishment, when she was caught, was severe. Her father did not visit her. Her principal motivation and driving force was to ensure her siblings were OK and reunited quickly.

One day José turned up with his new wife, Ángela. The stepmother had five children of her own and was already pregnant with a sixth.

When Maria Dolores turned nine, the nuns decided to give José an ultimatum regarding his bruise-covered daughter: he had to take her away. And so he did.

Her stepmother beat her many times and so she ran away. They tied her to the table legs so that she would not do it again. Domestic violence towards Dolores extended to her siblings. Her father decided to admit her to a mental hospital, but the psychiatrist told him that there was nothing wrong with his daughter. It was not his daughter who had a problem.

Dolores thought about taking her own life.

There was no water or electricity in José and Ángela's house, which was inhabited by twelve people. Five children slept in one room. Her father took her out of school at thirteen. School was for boys. She had to work and started making wicker baskets for the harvest. Work began at 5.30 in the morning, six days a week.

When she was eighteen, Dolores met one of the good guys.

■ ■ ■

She became friendly with a local boy, José Dinis Aveiro, two years older, who worked for a fishmonger. They would bump into each other when she went to the market or on their way home. He made her laugh. He was full of life, made her feel attractive and respected. She fell in love. When her father found out, he gave them a three-month window in which to get married – one less mouth to feed, he thought.

They married and moved in together at Dinis's parents' house, where all four of them slept in the same room, with a curtain separating them.

Time seemed to stand still and Dolores experienced a tranquillity that would provide her first taste of contentment. They did not have big plans. Nor did they use contraception. Elma, their first child, arrived a year after the wedding. Dolores fell pregnant once again soon after, while still recovering from the birth of her first child.

Their happiness would not last long, as Dinis was called up to the army.

Angola, Guinea-Bissau and Mozambique, all Portuguese colonies at the time, were fighting for independence, while Portugal was trying to retain her empire and economic interests.

Hugo, the second child, was born while Dinis was in Africa.

But something in Dinis seemd to die on the front line.

He returned to his parents' home in Santo Antonio ten months later, but was a greyer version. His demeanour portrayed a loss of joy. His smile had evaporated. He had aged ten years rather than ten months. He left his innocence and brightness behind on African soil, his head filled with images of war, as was the case with countless others. Dinis was mutilated by war, although his body remained unharmed. He was simply counting down the days until the end and lost his enthusiasm for everything and everyone, his wife included. Nothing could be done about it. He stopped working.

From that point onwards, you could always find him in the same place from early morning onwards: in the bar.

■ ■ ■

Now Dolores suddenly had to take on the role of father as well as mother. She went to France to work, emigrating alone, as many Madeiran men often did. If she could provide for all of them with her job as a house-maid in Paris, she would pay for them all to move to France.

But what occurred was a new isolation. This time from her children and husband, who were being taken care of by her in-laws.

In a rare moment of clarity, Dinis said to her on the telephone: 'If we were born to be poor, we will be . . . But be close to your children at the very least.'

She returned home five months later and soon after became pregnant with Katia. Dolores was twenty-two at the time.

After the Carnation Revolution and the end of Salazar's dictatorship in 1974, she occupied an abandoned house as many others had done. Dinis watched her run towards the new and half-abandoned property, with a child in her arms and the other two running behind. Everything seemed very distant to him, as if he were on the outside looking in. His anxiety was almost turning him into another child who needed to be looked after. He was still unemployed. He was just another man on the island lacking direction.

At thirty, Dolores fell pregnant once again. This time it was very much unplanned. It was a nuisance. There was not enough food for everyone. And her husband was still 'absent'.

She thought about having an abortion.

In fact, she did try to have one: a neighbour told her to drink boiled black beer and then run until being on the verge of fainting.

It did not work.

The doctor did not want to help her, seeing no reason for a termination. 'It'll be the joy of the house,' he told her.

When the baby was born, he said: 'Weighing that much, he could become a footballer!'

Dolores named him after the then president of the United States, Ronald Reagan.

Cristiano Ronaldo dos Santos Aveiro was born on 5 February 1985.

■ ■ ■

Ronaldo was nearly born in Australia.

José Viveiro, Dolores's dad, had seen many friends leave Madeira and had eventually decided to abandon the island himself and head to Perth with Ángela and her children. Dolores tried to convince him to take the whole family. José replied that there was no room.

As though Australia is small . . .

José and Ángela, who has since passed away, lived in Yangebup, a suburb of Australia's fourth most populous city. Ronaldo paid for their accommodation and travel to see him play in various matches during the 2006 World Cup in Germany, in which Portugal finished fourth.

Dolores was their guide.

■ ■ ■

Before we continue, there is one curious piece of biographical information worth recording: Ronaldo has African roots. Cristiano's paternal great-grandmother was Isabel Rosa Piedade, who was born in Praia, the capital of Cape Verde. At sixteen, she emigrated to Funchal, where she married José Aveiro. Isabel and José had a son called Humberto, José Dinis's father and Cristiano's grandfather.

That African heritage may explain part of his innate ability as a footballer. In short, the muscle fibre prevalent in black sprinters (white, type II, for fast contractions, that produces energy quickly and explosively without requiring oxygen) is the very type that Ronaldo was born with.

■ ■ ■

Back in the new, 'borrowed' Aveiro household, everybody had to lend a hand.

Elma and Hugo left school early to start working. She waitressed in a hotel restaurant while he worked for an aluminium company.

They were not yet seventeen. Dolores also experienced a change as she replaced wicker baskets with a spoon: she now worked in the kitchen of a Funchal hotel. But they still had to count every penny.

There was always bread on the table, and they had cold cuts every two weeks and meat on Sundays. The mid-week menu consisted of a soup that Dolores prepared in the few hours she spent at home, between work shifts. With bread and butter. Chicken was reserved for family celebrations. Nobody went hungry, though.

They never bought clothes; rather, they humbly accepted hand-me-downs from other families. When they outgrew them, cousins shared shirts, trousers and even underwear with the Aveiro children.

The family eventually moved to Quinta do Falcao, a village near the San António cemetery and where social housing had been built for poor residents who had previously lived in shacks. Well away from the area frequented by tourists.

It was certainly an improvement, although the roofs were made of asbestos. They were not rainproof which meant that Dolores had to ask the council for materials to strengthen them. The walls were unpainted brick and wooden slabs.

'We had three rooms, one for me and my sister, one for Hugo and Cristiano and one for my mother and father,' Katia explained in a television interview. 'It was a very humble home, but I remember it being very comfortable and we were happy there.'

In this typical, poor village, where alcohol and drugs are omnipresent, children lived and played in the street, which was the playground for every house. Nobody, though, considered it a limitation – it never is when everyone is in the same situation.

'The house no longer exists,' Katia said. 'When I go around that district, I always get goose bumps and would like to return [to live] one day. I know it isn't possible, but when I remember everything we went through there . . . Words don't do it justice.'

The house was demolished in 2008, despite Ronaldo's rise to fame. No effort was made by anybody to retain it for posterity. It is now an esplanade covered in weeds.

There are still high-rise buildings in Quinta do Falcao where Ronaldo still has aunts and uncles, and whose children once played in the street with him. And in one of them lived Filomena Aveiro, Cristiano's paternal grandmother, until her final days.

People walk in and out of houses without knocking; nobody locks their doors. Ronaldo was born and grew up constantly surrounded by people and that is how he has always lived; his houses in Manchester and Madrid have been guest houses for friends and family.

The door is always open.

■ ■ ■

There is a marvellous photograph of a sixteen-year-old Ronaldo wearing a Sporting Lisbon shirt taken during a visit to Madeira. He went to Quinta do Falcao and asked for it to be taken outside his old house. He was frowning and beaming with pride at the same time. Another emigrant making a name for himself in the capital city, with the spectre of what he had left behind.

It is the only snap from his first home. Nobody had thought about taking one there before.

■ ■ ■

There is no decent place to kick a ball around in Quinta do Falcao without bothering someone. No park. Not even a suitable piece of waste ground. Marítimo, one of the most important clubs on the island, is just a ten-minute walk away, but in that district the youngsters, unless they go a couple of miles away to the beach, have no choice but to play on the steep and uneven streets.

■ ■ ■

Ronaldo's father arrived half an hour late for his own son's baptism. Dinis, who had played football as a child and had become the kitman at the modest local club Andorinha, decided that the team captain, Fernando Barros Sousa, should be the godfather. He thought of him as a good role model for Cristiano, a natural leader, and, thanks to his business success, he seemed to have all the money he needed.

The ceremony was at six o'clock but Andorinha had a match at four, meaning it was obvious that they would not make it. Yet Dinis did not change the plan; he went to the match and could not be there in time for the baptism. The priest had to be calmed down. He had already christened the rest of the children. Only Cristiano remained. And no father present!

If people around you are involved in football, if your role models are footballers and if your father has the cheek to arrive late at your baptism because of a match, it is almost logical for you to end up becoming a footballer.

■ ■ ■

A scene from the documentary *CR9 vive aquí* about Cristiano Ronaldo:

After hearing the voice of Cristiano say, 'I reached the top of the world. Now, I want to be eternal,' you see him put on a child's voice, lean towards the computer screen displaying a mosaic of passport photos of him as a baby, while saying something like 'titititi, Cristiano Ronaldo'. He motions as if to caress the boy in the photo. He moves away and laughs. Ronaldo laughs a lot.

CR: 'It's me! Three months old! Look, look at that boy! How cute! With a gold bracelet on my wrist.'

He then adopts a funny pose, in which it is clear that he is laughing at himself, but he is not self-conscious about seeing himself. Meanwhile, his sister Katia holds her son. Ronaldo asks her: 'Does he look like me?' The shot once again focuses on the photo of baby Cristiano, with big, alert eyes. He is not looking into the camera, but at somebody who presumably is saying something to him.

CR: 'He'll be a footballer like his uncle.'

The baby starts crying and Cristiano reassures his sister.

CR: 'I was like that, too, don't worry.'[4]

∎ ∎ ∎

Katia used to take Cristiano to school and then wait for him so that they could go home together. She used to help him do his homework. As Maria Dolores could not be on top of everything, Katia quickly learnt how to control her younger brother. 'But he didn't pay much attention to me [laughter], no,' she recalled. 'I used to get annoyed with him all the time. My mother would say: "Katia, when you're home, don't let Cristiano go out to play football till he finishes his homework." We had a front and back door. I'd say to Ronaldo (at home we always called him "Ronaldo", not "Cristiano"): "Ronaldo, please do your homework." "OK," he would answer. When I called him, he was no longer there. Then my mother would be angry with me when she got home from work.'[5]

'He was a rebellious boy, but he also knew how to listen. If you grabbed his attention, he would take notice of what you said, he was well-behaved,' says his mother now.[6]

'He was actively involved whenever we did recreational activities at the end of each term such as theatre, dance, singing,' recalled Sister Graça, a primary school teacher at the São João school in Funchal. Cristiano used to ask for starring roles. 'But he was quite lazy, he would forget about the household chores.'

'I remember she would sometimes grab me by the ear and slap me on the hand,' jokes Cristiano.[7]

'I was a good boy because I was controlled by my mum, dad and older siblings. I think I was very hard-working, well, I think so anyway . . . [laughter].'[6]

DINIS, THE FATHER

Dinis Aveiro had received no more than the obligatory education and after his service in the army had to try to earn a living by doing manual labour. After being employed as a fishmonger, he was a stone cutter and a council gardener, but spent more time unemployed than in work. So when the opportunity to do odd jobs at fifth-division outfit Andorinha came up, he gratefully accepted.

The club received grants from the council and today has a floodlit artificial pitch, but in the early days they had to play in rented pitches or at sports centres. Eventually they got given a dirt field, and a small bar and a storeroom were built. Dinis had to collect the equipment, look after the balls, get things ready for the coaches, prepare the kits, clean the toilets and cut the grass . . .

Football's importance was gradually growing in the family, as attending Andorinha matches became a regular activity, especially the ones played by the youth team of which Hugo Aveiro was a member.

Everyone says that José Dinis was a good bloke. He was popular, calm and had a deep, husky voice. And he spent what little money he had on drink.

Many others, several war veterans among them, did the same, drowned in poverty, depressed, trapped by the sea and bored.

People start drinking in the morning in Madeira and they do not stop. They say it is a cultural thing, like in Great Britain or the Nordic countries. The local beverage is a type of spirit mixed with honey and lemon, passion fruit or any other fruit and is consumed hot. It was used by fishermen as a pick-me-up. It packs a punch.

Two glasses and you are well on your way. That is what people drink and it is cheap, of course.

Arnaldo, my guide on one of my trips to Madeira, told me that his father first gave him alcohol when he was four. There was no juice in the bars, but there was a punch that he was given to keep him quiet while the men chatted and drank among themselves. He didn't say no to it, and drank it every time he was given it.

Dinis was not one of those drunkards who demanded attention or believed he was always right. He was polite and quiet as he whiled the hours away.

Ronaldo, at eight, or nine, enjoyed being in his dad's company. Many evenings the clock would strike eleven and Cristiano wanted to go to bed, but without his father home he couldn't relax. He would go to the bar with his sister or a friend to pick him up, although Dinis was often reluctant to return home. He preferred to stay in his spot at the corner of the bar. Quiet, drinking. Without causing trouble. Absorbed in his thoughts.

When he was ready to go back home, he would walk with his arm around Cristiano's young shoulders.

At such a young age, Ronaldo gradually took on the father-figure role that his own father was neglecting.

'I just want my son to be happy and successful,' he was heard saying in the bar. 'I, personally, want to live in my world. His world belongs to him.' In fact, he did not like going to Manchester once Cristiano moved there, and only went a few times.

My friend Moisés would say that he was one of those men who was happy with a plate of green beans. In other words, he asked for little from life.

Dinis initially refused his son's help when his health deteriorated. Ronaldo offered to pay for treatment at the most expensive clinics in England, but it was only towards the end that, to appease his son, Dinis relented. It was already too late. He passed away in a London clinic.

His absence, lack of authority, bonhomie and his faith in Ronaldo as a footballer have earned him a special place in his children's memories.

In a way, he is almost worshipped. At Cristiano's house in Manchester, there were several photos of José Dinis Aveiro, and Katia's little boy is called Zé, the diminutive form of José, as a tribute to his grandfather.

■ ■ ■

We discussed all this with Martinho Fernandes, a Madeiran journalist who was a friend of José Dinis. 'If Cristiano had stayed in Madeira, he would never have achieved what he has,' he explained. He thinks that Ronaldo, like all of us, is the product of his upbringing. He came from a poverty-ridden, broken home, but maybe all that, or some of it, is necessary for an individual to become a success. His ability to overcome hurdles remains with him and helps him grow. Martinho added something else: 'If your parents aren't too much on top of you, that freedom allows you to reach your potential.'

An interesting idea, the one about parents' influence, that came up in a number of conversations.

■ ■ ■

Fernando Sousa, Ronaldo's godfather, never forgot his duties when it came to Christmas presents. One year, he bought his godson a toy car and the boy threw a tantrum because he desperately wanted a football. But why? Especially as his father carried a huge bag of balls around every day and little Cristiano often helped him collect them at the end of training. He, of course, wanted his own ball. Fernando took note and accordingly gave him one the following year. It cost a whopping five euros.

Young Cristiano took it with him everywhere.

His neighbour Adelino Andrade remembered him as a fairly short and skinny boy with curly, dark hair who spent all day in the street with his ball: 'The kid would do all sorts of astonishing tricks with it. It seemed to be stuck to his feet.'[8]

I've seen Ronaldo do numerous kick-ups with a plastic bottle lid, and then the bottle itself, without either touching the floor.

The conversation with the ball started there and then: 'When I was young,' Ronaldo remembers, 'I used to enjoy watching the older guys showing off with the ball and I would do the same.'[4]

It soon became a regular hobby – playing with a football, doing new tricks, in the street, in the warm-up, in training. He says that's the real Cristiano Ronaldo. He does not do it to show off, though, not always anyway. It is part of his relationship with his constant travel buddy.

He used to go to class with a ball under his arm, too, even though one teacher in particular reminded him that a ball was not going to feed him, a ball wouldn't get him anywhere in life. School was where you laid the foundations that would one day allow you to reach your potential. She felt it was her obligation to remind the students the relevance of what they were learning, to emphasise the importance of education and put it into context, a perspective many of them didn't necessarily get from elsewhere. Nothing wrong with that. The teacher was, in fact, right to say it, but Ronaldo happens to be one of the notable exceptions that proves the rule. Yet she has been left with no choice but to apologise repeatedly, as she has done to Cristiano's auntie and mother on various occasions. She said that she would not speak in such a way again.

Twelve-year-old Ronaldo would think about those words when sitting on the plane to Lisbon for the first time.

They had become a motivational weapon.

THE STREET MATCH

Madeira, the island of eternal spring, is blessed with a constant temperature. It hardly ever goes above 33 degrees.

Perfect conditions for playing in the street.

The island was formed by volcanic eruptions, causing the ground to be uneven and the formation of cliffs and caves. Its mountainous terrain leaves room for very few plains.

Far from the ideal scenario for a daily football match.

Cristiano would return home from school, dump his rucksack anywhere, promise to do his homework, grab a yoghurt, make a hole in the bottom of the pot and drink it while heading out of the back door and hearing his sister yell something about schoolwork.

Two rocks served as goalposts on the steep and narrow street next to his house. A plastic bottle or a ball made from bags and paper were used. That is the magic of football: everyone can play and no technology is needed. The rules are crystal clear, too.

When Ronaldo began receiving footballs as gifts, he always brought his own with him and they would play as long as he wanted, and the game that he wanted. The owner of the ball sets the rules.

Those games started after school and it was dark before they finished. Cristiano was the most competitive of the lot. The best. Buses and cars would go down there so frequently the kids had to move the rocks/goalposts to allow traffic to pass. There was time for two minutes of uninterrupted play at most. It was impossible to play the ball long in such a small space, so it was short passes all the way, or, in Cristiano's case, dribbling past everyone. His technique allowed him to do that and more. The unevenly paved street full of obstacles and the many hours of street football helped him develop it.

If nobody turned up, Ronaldo would take the ball to a small field and shoot against a wall. Again and again. For hours and hours.

Or he would go down to the beaches in search of new challenges.

Regulars included his friend Ricardo Santos, whose father was the Andorinha president and who now oversees the day-to-day running of the club as sporting director. 'The competitive spirit found in street football gives you that swagger and confidence.' Or, as Nuno Luz, journalist and friend of Ronaldo, says about anyone growing up on the street, 'In a poor village, you have no choice but to have character. If you don't, they eat you up. Either you step on them or they step on you.'

No one ever stepped on Ronaldo.

■ ■ ■

'When I joined Andorinha at nine years old, he was already there,' recalled Ricardo. 'And when we started playing for the club, we didn't play in the street as much.' What psychologists call 'deliberated game', the football played in the streets, without many rules or timetables, was replaced at Andorinha between the ages of eight and ten by 'deliberated training' – football with kits, cones on the ground, stretching and coaches.

Cristiano was surrounded by familiar faces. His dad, seeing the hours he spent playing in the street with the ball, suggested he should join him at the club where he worked as a kitman, and when he did Ronaldo would bring his ball with him. His cousin Nuno, who played for the club, had invited him to one training session after which he was asked to return. His brother Hugo was still playing in a higher age group.

Ricardo Santos, initially reserved and even dismissive of that time, gradually opened up as we walked around the club's modest facilities. 'He was here for two seasons, but he was mainly playing with kids, two or three years older. We kept an early registration form for him, it's from '94–'95. We used to play on dirt pitches and he was clearly the best. He was a striker and was everywhere. He liked driving forward, dribbling and doing stepovers. He hasn't changed much!'

In the first few weeks, Ronaldo kept to himself. He, in fact, was afraid to get the ball; everybody seemed twice his size. But he didn't need much time to develop relationships with the other kids, to show his playful side.

They used to call him 'the noodle', because he was not particularly tall and very thin. Fear soon gave way to confidence. 'We didn't think he was weak,' Ricardo remembered. 'He didn't need any protection against the older boys, for example. He could look after himself.'

Mid-week training involved three-on-three matches, it was seven-a-side on Saturdays and Ronaldo would ask to play in eleven-a-side games on Sundays. You could see that he was fantastic in small spaces, very fast and had enviable technique with both feet, rare for someone his age. 'He didn't need to come to Andorinha to learn ball-control techniques, how to dribble or do tricks,' said Francisco Alonso, a teacher at his school and one of his first coaches. 'Maybe it's innate.'

Many legendary matches live long in the memory. One day, Andorinha were winning 3–0 when Cristiano went down and had to be taken off after a clash of heads. The team caved in and lost 4–3. He was already that important to his side.

Another day he went into the dressing room in tears because his side was losing. A 2–0 half-time deficit was transformed into a 3–2 victory when Ronaldo began to dominate the ball and single-handedly turned the game on its head.

His team-mates called him 'cry-baby'.

He cried and cried, not just in the dressing room, but also on the pitch if the team was losing. He would cry very easily. Also when he passed to his team-mates and they failed to score – that made him cry, too. And angry. 'Yes, at eight he already showed his frustration if they didn't pass to him. And the other boys answered him back,' recalled Ricardo Santos.

'As a kid, I got so annoyed when we lost . . .' Cristiano says.[6] Every defeat is like a small loss of life for boys like him. Failure has no place, nor has doubt. Only goals and victories are acceptable. The rest is inconceivable. Inadmissible.

His team-mates also called him 'the little bee', for his insect-like speed.

The first trophy that eight-year-old Ronaldo won as player of the tournament in a local competition sits proudly in his museum in Funchal.

While we were speaking, a pot-bellied man took the rubbish out and prepared to take it to a skip, the same job Dinis used to do. He chatted to everybody and finally sat down with customers at the bar to have a small beer. Ricardo asked him to take a ball out so that I could take a staged photo and also so he could show me something they fondly keep: the photo of Ronaldo with his team, his father on one side, tall and proud.

Years later, Ronaldo invited Ricardo and his father to Manchester to visit him at his house and watch a Manchester United game. It was the penultimate time that Cristiano saw his former team-mate. The last one was during the inauguration of the Ronaldo museum in Funchal, although then they exchanged nothing but a simple 'How's everything going?'

'I'd feel embarrassed to speak to him now beyond polite pleasantries,' admits Ricardo.

Andorinha wanted Cristiano to be the patron of their academy, but the star demurred. A club director had, at some stage, given an interview to the local paper *A Bola* in which he had made less than complimentary remarks about Ronaldo's mother. Since then Ronaldo has distanced himself from his first club.

■ ■ ■

'Physical education was his favourite. It was clear to see. He was always picked for activities that required maximum coordination,' remembered Irmá Graça, one of his teachers.[7] That coordination made him good at everything: tennis, pool, table tennis. It also gave him the excuse to be away from books.

'I dreamed about having a son who played football, because I love the sport,' revealed Dolores, a fan of both Luis Figo and Sporting Lisbon. 'Sometimes Ronaldo missed class to play. His teacher told me that I should tell him off for that, but I didn't punish him. He had to practise a lot to become a great player.'[9]

Ronaldo, the youngest sibling, has always had a strong bond with his mother. When he started creating two different paths in his life ('Mum, either I go to school or to football'), she knew how she had to respond: 'If football is what you like, son . . . go ahead.'[9]

Cristiano was laying waste to everyone in his path at Andorinha and word soon reached the Nacional youth-team coach. What happened next was a moment of farce. Having been informed of the fledgling talent, the coach went to see him play. 'I was hugely surprised to discover that he was my godson. I knew he played football, but I didn't know how good he was. He was streets ahead of the rest,' declared his godfather Fernando Barroso Sousa, a crucial figure in Cristiano's early, big decisions.

Ten-year-old Cristiano moved to CD Nacional a few months later, in the summer of 1995.

But why join Nacional when Marítimo, the other big club on the island, had a better reputation for bringing youngsters through and were one of the five or six biggest clubs in the country? In 1994–95, they had become the in-team after surprisingly reaching the cup final, and furthermore it was next door to Andorinha.

Marítimo appealed more to Ronaldo. And to Dinis. The ground was nearby, and it seemed to be the logical next step for the boy.

Andorinha's financial demands made the Marítimo president, who did not appreciate the player's value at the time, break off negotiations. Cristiano's godfather had begun talks with Nacional and when they found out that Marítimo were out of the bidding they took the necessary steps to seal the deal: two sets of kits and twenty footballs was the price that his new club had to pay.

Or so the story has been told, many times over.

But there is something missing from this story about the boy who proudly wore the Marítimo colours and yet was lost to their greatest rivals, Nacional.

The fact is that, but for a quirk of fate, Bernardino Rosa, the poorly paid head of recruitment at the Marítimo academy, could have changed Ronaldo's destiny and perhaps even football history.

But Bernardino was late for a meeting.

Marítimo had a close relationship with their neighbour Andorinha, lending them balls, bibs, kit. As the modest team that they were, Bernardino knew that it would be in Ronaldo's best interests to move to the Marítimo academy with its better facilities and better prospects. It seemed like a natural progression.

In the latter part of the twentieth century, falling birth rates were beginning to affect the talent pool of young players. In the 1970s the annual birth rate on the island was 9,000. By the 1980s it had fallen to 5,400 (today it stands at 1,700). Clubs were becoming increasingly aware of the need to move fast in identifying and attracting emerging stars.

So to make sure the best talent ended up at the bigger club, 'Marítimo always matched any offer from Nacional,' as Bernardino told Andorinha. It had almost become the club mantra.

Talks regarding Ronaldo had begun between Andorinha and Marítimo and were progressing well, despite the then president of

Marítimo being luke-warm. Bernardino was convinced that Ronaldo had great potential and had said as much to the board. Also, he understood that they had first option on him but needed to move swiftly.

Then things stalled.

An Andorinha director had called Bernardino on a Friday to arrange a decisive meeting on the following Monday. Bernardino worked in a bank and couldn't suddenly take time off to attend meetings, certainly not without making prior arrangements. In any case he had to be in Lisbon that particular Monday. 'But if you want to, we can meet today, Saturday or any other day next week,' he told the Andorinha director. Nothing was scheduled and no one called back to rearrange the meeting.

On his return to Funchal, Bernardino called Andorinha to ask when they could meet and put the matter to bed.

'It's all signed, sealed and delivered between Cristiano and Nacional, Bernardino. You didn't show up at the meeting on Monday and now it's all sorted with them.'

Bernardino could not believe his ears. He spoke to Ronaldo again. 'My mother wants me to go to Nacional, my godfather, too. It was my mother who signed, not my father,' Ronaldo told the Marítimo scout. 'I never believed that he'd become the player he is today. You win some, you lose some,' said a resigned Bernardino Rosa. 'That's why I always say things went well for Ronaldo, which is the important part. The truth is I was annoyed at the time, because we could've won trophies with him in the team. Maybe he'd have stayed here longer than he did at Nacional. But that wasn't the case, what can you do?'

Remember what he said about Ronaldo's short stay at Nacional. I'll tell you why later.

■ ■ ■

'When I started playing . . . I felt . . . I felt that I was different.'
'Why?'

'I don't know, maybe I was more ambitious.'

Conversation with Cristiano Ronaldo, 2010

Ronaldo's time at Andorinha taught him about team values, although training sessions were not particularly demanding. They almost never are when you're young. So his first direct contact with high-level academy football was at Nacional, where he spent two seasons.

Although he was brave and had learnt how to avoid physical contact with boys older than him, the Nacional coaches were worried that his undernourishment would slow down his development. They asked his mother to supplement his diet with fish and meat, instead of so much yoghurt. If she could.

In any case, his talent was unquestionable.

This is what ten-year-old Cristiano Ronaldo was like.

António Mendonça, a coach from his spell at Nacional: 'He executed things quickly, he was good at dribbling and had a powerful shot. In one match, he ran the whole pitch, from one end to the other, with the ball under control and without letting it touch the ground.'

Pedro Talhinhas, one of his coaches at Nacional: 'He is a player from the street with exceptional technique in both feet. But it's not just about the fact that he played football in the street. He's a product of running all over the place, climbing trees, jumping over obstacles, walking to school and the beach. He's the typical player who's had a self-sufficient childhood. He spent long periods without any family contact and didn't go to school much. That's how he started finding answers to problems himself. How does that translate into football? Well, it gives you mental weapons to improvise in one-on-ones, for example. It helps you resolve problems the game throws at you. Another player with a more solid family set-up probably wouldn't be the same type of player.'

Carlos Bruno: 'The reduction in creative players is precisely due to the change in children's habits, mainly in more developed, western countries. Football cannot be developed as a creative and free sport in a rigid atmosphere. Boys join clubs or football schools and have stereotypical coaches who sap them of the little creativity they still have. That means they lose the rarest attribute that exists these days: the one-on-one. Players who excel in this department and can improvise in the heat of the moment are the ones that are worth millions, but they're in short supply.'[7]

Pedro Talhinhas: 'Our first battle was making him understand that football is a team sport. He'd do it all himself, there was barely a connection between him and his team-mates or the opposition. He'd pick the ball up and drive towards goal. He felt superior to the rest of the team and hardly passed the ball – he didn't understand their mistakes and would argue with them. His team-mates put up with him because we'd win games by nine or ten goals, mostly thanks to him. We'd start to say to him: "Look, this is your position, this is how your movement should be."'

David Gomes: 'The club gave him his first tactical lessons.'

Pedro Talhinhas: 'He'd train with boys two years older than himself and wouldn't accept the word "defeat" entering his head, be it in a match, training session or a game. He'd cry, too, on the pitch, during the game, leaving the field, in the dressing room. When he got into that state, he had to be left alone. Also, he didn't like being told off in public, he didn't want to portray any weakness. He had to be told things alone.'

David Gomes: 'A normal boy from a stable family who spends lots of time at home and doesn't miss school has an hour and a half or two hours of training. Ronaldo spent ten to twelve hours with the ball every day.'

Pedro Talhinhas: 'We'd train three times a week and on Saturdays we'd play on small pitches on tarmac or concrete. It was seven against seven in the first three months, and then eleven-a-side. We'd train on a five-a-side pitch. There was no gym, the club didn't have many facilities. In fact, no football club in Madeira had a gym.'

Did he say to you that he'd be the best?

Pedro Talhinhas: 'Not to me. He'd say that he wanted to be a footballer, but not the best, no.'

Did anyone think that he could be the best in the world?

Pedro Talhinhas: 'Some coaches say so. I say to them that they should tell me who'll be the best player in ten years so I can go and look for him.'

Did you often see him with his father?

Pedro Talhinhas: 'Ronaldo would come to training alone. His dad would always come to matches, though. He didn't interfere in anything, he wouldn't say anything to his son or the coaches. What the coaches did was good enough for him.'

■ ■ ■

Ronaldo came down with flu before a regional Under-13 championship decider. 'Mum, I want to play,' he begged Dolores, who wanted him to stay in bed. 'If I feel ill, I'll ask to be taken off, really I will.'

'It was impossible to stop him,' says Dolores today. He played.

'I wasn't in any pain,' recalled Cristiano. 'All I remember is that I scored a goal and we were champions. It was worth it.'[10]

It was, in fact, his first team success.

The new president, Rui Alves, presented him with the trophy at the Estádio dos Barreiros, the home of Nacional. Sporting Lisbon took note of what was being whispered at the time: there is this ten-year-old boy at Nacional who is the best player in Madeira in his age group.

■ ■ ■

Ronaldo was becoming too big for such a small and isolated island, despite being only twelve years old, so what happened next was inevitable.

João Marques de Freitas, assistant attorney general and president of the Sporting fan club in Madeira, had never seen him play football but Fernando Sousa, Cristiano's godfather, had told him about his precocious talent. 'Can I pop into the office with the kid?' Sousa asked João. It was carnival season, meaning the timing was not ideal, but it was going to be a quick meeting.

His godfather was about to be involved once again in a key career step for Cristiano.

'This kid is going to be very good,' he told him. 'Why don't we take him to Sporting?'

Marques de Freitas is not a coach, nor does he claim to know everything, as so often happens in football. So he called Aurélio Pereira, the man in charge of transfers at Sporting, who brought talents such as Futre, Figo, Simão, Quaresma, Nani and Moutinho to the club.

'Aurélio, I have a problem. I've met a boy, his godfather says he's really good. I don't know much about football. So what should I do?'

João Marques de Freitas was not just anybody, nor did he generally offer players. But Aurélio was not sure it was necessary to make such a mammoth effort for a boy who had turned twelve in February 1997 and who came from so far away. Today the club set-up ensures they know who the best six-year-old in Funchal is and that they bring him to the mainland, but that did not exist at that time.

Aurélio would do João a favour. He suggested sending the boy over for a week. They could evaluate him and let them know.

As it happened, Nacional owed Sporting €25,000 for a player, Franco, who had been signed by the Madeiran outfit but ended up falling short of expectations. They were struggling to pay the debt and a transfer of the young Ronaldo to Sporting was an obvious solution. But was Ronaldo worth €25,000? That was a considerable amount of money at the time; in fact, such a sum had never been paid for such a young kid. Aurelio had to be convinced the investment would pay off to recommend it to the board.

Having received the all-clear from Sporting and Nacional, João organised the trip. Ronaldo's first venture outside Madeira took place at Easter. He had a reduced-rate ticket; children under twelve do not pay full price. His godfather took him to the airport.

He flew alone.

When Cristiano tells the story now, he says that he went with his mother. Aurélio seems to remember his godfather travelling with him, but the truth is that nobody went with the young Ronaldo.

For the average twelve year old, it is difficult to comprehend the full ramifications of any decision at a time when responsibilities are scarce, but Cristiano admitted to his godfather that he was nervous and had not slept a wink the night before the flight, his first ever. It was as if he knew that something was going to change for ever as soon as he stepped on that plane.

He travelled with a name tag hanging around his neck and a bag containing some clothes.

Aurélio and Mário Lino, another Sporting director, picked him up.

Cristiano sat quietly in the back of Aurélio's car and gazed out of the window at a world heaving with cars and people. 'I thought I was in another country,' he recalled.[6] He surely meant on another planet.

Ronaldo was utterly convinced that he would overcome every obstacle, no matter the nature of the trial and who he was playing against: 'I was confident and relaxed. I knew they'd like me and want to keep me.'[11]

Ronaldo spent the night at the residence adjacent to the old José Alvalade stadium, where boys over the age of fourteen stayed, some of whom he would face in the coming days. The morning training session which he had planned to attend was cancelled and he went with Aurélio to watch a Sporting v. Manchester United Under-19 match.

Cristiano saw the players stretching and, without asking Aurélio's permission, trotted off in his tracksuit bottoms to join in. There is a photo to prove it.

The moment finally arrived.

The trial took place on the now defunct Sporting da Torre pitch, where the youth teams would train. Aurélio, who had a previous engagement, was unable to witness Ronaldo's first point of contact with his team-mates.

He warmed up in his Sporting kit. He performed some jumps, sprints and stretches. The ball then came towards him for the first time.

'I was going to control it . . . and the ball went under my foot!'[6] Yet he remained calm or he appeared to, at least. 'He told me he was very nervous,' his godfather later acknowledged.

'I said to myself: I'm going to do it.'[6]

Interestingly, Paulo Cardoso, who was one of the coaches tasked with submitting a report to Aurélio, did not remember that blip: 'He did something mesmerising when he first touched the ball . . . Wow! I looked at my colleague Osvaldo Silva, the coach of the team that the Madeiran was training with, and we both had a look of "What is this?" on our faces.'

He got on the ball again and again and again. That is when 'the coaches saw I was a different player,' admitted Cristiano.[6]

'Yes, he was different,' said Paulo Cardoso. 'He had that special something that is so hard to find: a huge personality.'

His team-mates also took note. 'After training, all the players were thinking "If he can already do that at twelve . . ."' said a smiling Ronaldo.[6] The thirteen- and fourteen-year-old boys went up to him after training to accord him the respect that he had just earned.

Cardoso and Silva wrote in their report: 'A player with exceptional talent and very developed technique. His ability on the ball in motion and from a standing position is outstanding. He was fast over long and short distances and had a huge range of dribbling skills. Two-footed, fearless and daring.'

On day two, Aurélio went to see for himself if the boy was as described. It was decided that he would play in an Under-14 match on a bigger pitch, the one next to the old Alvalade stadium.

It was easy to see what everyone was talking about. But Aurélio wanted to see beyond that, needed to find out what was inside his little head.

'Today, at the age of sixty-six, with forty-six years' experience in evaluating players, I still have doubts over players,' the head of the Sporting academy says. 'The only certainty I have today is that I am full of doubts. If you don't manage to understand him on the inside, you're unable to evaluate him, even if sometimes there is no way of finding out all those things you need to know: the player's mental strength, ability to overcome obstacles, or how he would cope with being so far away from his family and surroundings.

'On the second day, he was already becoming a leader. He was playing with and against good players from the academy. They were older than him, but they were all behind him and happy to follow him. The other kids would come to tell us how good he was. Whenever a new player comes here to train, I always speak to the captain of the team afterwards. Players can tell me things that no coach can.'

There was one episode that let him see just what Ronaldo was like, rather than how good his dribbling was. The defining moment.

'He's about to receive the ball from a throw-in, he's being very tightly marked. As Di Stéfano would say: "He could feel his opponent breathing down his neck." Just picture it. Ronaldo was a few years younger than the defender. He turned around and said: "Hey, kid, calm down." He called him kid. I jumped out of my seat and went to submit the report. He had to sign for us.'

He spent two more days in training, but the decision had already been taken. Aurélio called Marques de Freitas. 'This Ronaldo is brilliant,' he told him.

There were still steps to be taken, however.

Sporting's financial heads still needed a little push and so Aurélio wrote a second report: 'It'll be a great future investment.' Former club administrator Simões de Almeida finally gave it the go-ahead in summer 1997, four months after the trial.

In the meantime, Aurélio went to Madeira to speak to the player's parents. With his mother, in particular. 'They're coming from the "other side" to speak to us' is how Dinis told Dolores the news. The 'other side' being mainland Portugal.

Cristiano, Dinis, Dolores, Elma, Cristiano's godfather, and Aurélio met at a Funchal hotel.

Dolores's protective motherly instincts came through and she was initially cold to Aurélio. She had never had to make such a decision since starting a family. Her own childhood, devoid of parents, was an experience she didn't want to repeat with her own children. Her brief absence in France had been painful enough.

'Let me go, Mum,' Ronaldo was begging.[10]

Sporting, the club that his mother supported, offered a clear methodology and, more importantly, a family structure: they would be guardians to the boy. Dolores would be in constant communication with them and they would ask her for advice before making any decisions, including any disciplinary issues. Aurélio, who admitted just how exceptional the situation was, would be on top of things. Ronaldo would live in the residence with the other boys. He would continue his studies and he would not be allowed to play if he did not behave in class.

Aurélio was a calm and wise man who spoke softly, but also clearly and persuasively. His sense of conviction masked the fact that he had was plagued with doubts as well.

'We then had to balance the youngster's freedom on and off the pitch with the need to integrate him. But I had my misgivings about it all. If you can't integrate somebody, even a seasoned professional, if he doesn't feel part of his new city, club and team, you'll never see the real player. You'll be unable to discover his true ability. That is why it's so crucial for us to perform this part of the job. Our thoughts have to be perfectly in tune with his.'

As part of the contract, Dolores could travel to Lisbon three times a year and the boy's salary would be paid directly into a family account. His first annual wage was €10,000.

Everything was going to be fine, or so Cristiano said in an effort to stem his mother's tears on the way home. His older sister, Elma, was also in pieces.

■ ■ ■

After only two seasons, Ronaldo was ready to leave Nacional.

'We think his spell at the club has been commemorated appropriately,' the club president Rui Alves says. 'We selected him in the all-time Nacional eleven, there are photos of his time with us in his museum and he gave us permission to use his name for the academy stadium. He's definitely a source of motivation, a model professional.'

The Madeiran's success has had consequences. Today, on any given day, at eight in the evening, 200 boys don a Nacional shirt and dream of being Ronaldo. Many are not aware that they are being pushed by their parents' expectations, forgetting that what distinguished Cristiano from the rest was an extraordinary desire to improve and an abnormally competitive spirit. Ronaldo is unique.

Carlos Pereira, Marítimo president and a friend of Cristiano, calls it 'Ronaldomania': 'It's a serious problem because most parents don't realise they aren't helping their children. In any case, what they can learn from Ronaldo is that the best option the boys have is to leave the island. It's very small, not many dreams come true here. Ronaldo's big success was moving to Lisbon', enabling him to escape poverty, family struggles and alcohol abuse.

'At thirteen, fourteen, he could've become another Dinis,' Pereira thinks.

His brother Hugo stayed put. He could have been a player, but lost his way. Drugs got in the way, just as with so many more youngsters in Quinta do Falcão.

■ ■ ■

In a parallel universe, Bernardo Rosa, the Marítimo scout, decides not to go to Lisbon that Monday and has a meeting with Andorinha. Cristiano ends up signing for his club. Marítimo have no outstanding debt with Sporting, meaning they are not forced to sell him.

Let us imagine that he makes it into the first team five years later and wins silverware at Marítimo. Porto, Sporting and Benfica all battle it out for him and he enjoys success with one of the big three in Portugal.

Europe's biggest clubs declare an interest and he signs for Barcelona, which is not that far-fetched, as we shall see later.

It could easily have happened.

Alternatively, staying in Madeira for longer could have trapped him and he could have become just another precocious talent, stuck on the island and going unnoticed by the outside world.

Pedro Pinto: 'When you look at this photo of your mother, what springs to mind?'

CR: 'She's definitely the most important person in my life. The one who's given me everything, my education and all the opportunities I've had in life. She's always by my side, in the good and the bad times . . . she's never shut any doors. She's always given me the chance to follow my dream.'

Interview on CNN with Pedro Pinto, 2012

On Cristiano's twenty-ninth birthday in February 2014, Dolores responded to a question about her son on Real Madrid TV: 'How do you see him as a man, as a person?'

At first she was unable to speak as tears poured down her face. She took a deep breath. 'As a man, he's a great man, a friend of the family, everyone's friend. He likes to help. Ronaldo has a good heart. That boy was made by God', and she had to stop once again, another sob building up. 'Ronaldo has given me everything in life. What matters to me is having a good son who never abandons his mother, that's everything to me in life.'

There are two versions of the reasons why Dolores felt driven to let Ronaldo go. 'Sometimes when you have very well-educated parents, they might try to control your path more and the result isn't necessarily better,' states Nacional president Rui Alves. 'When they are less educated, there is more acceptance of the children's right to dream. I think this is what happened with Ronaldo's parents: "We didn't achieve it, but our son can dream."'

There is a more cynical interpretation, however. The twelve-year-old boy on his way to Lisbon was not the best in the world, just a kid with a dream. It was a far from safe investment. The Aveiro family struggled to put food on the table at home and, without Cristiano, there was one less mouth to feed.

In either case, Dolores convinced herself that Sporting were capable of looking after her son.

'I went to live in Lisbon at the age of twelve. I remember going into the airport and, although my sisters were wearing sunglasses, I could still see their tears. The whole family was crying.

'But my mum has always said to me: "Son, I'm not going to allow a situation in which one day you look me in the face and say that you weren't a footballer because of me. Or because of your dad. Fight for your dream."'[6]

'Tears started to pour from my eyes when the plane began to take off.

'That's life . . . I wouldn't say they abandoned me, rather they left me on my own for a while.

'It was the most difficult period of my life.'[12]

'What do I regret? Maybe not enjoying more of my childhood.'[4]

Cristiano Ronaldo

TWO

LISBON

SHAPING DESTINY

Erik Erikson, the renowned German psychoanalyst famous for coining the phrase 'identity crisis', suggests that our emerging characteristics can be broadly defined within particular age bands, as expressed in his studies on the stages of psychosocial development.

From five to twelve, children discover things that interest them and begin to identify their particular talent. They also start to reveal their individuality.

From thirteen to nineteen, teenagers go through the transition to adulthood. They seek answers to questions such as 'Who am I?' and 'What can I be?' They develop their own identity, but at the same time struggle to find their place in the world. They want to be independent and self-sufficient and yearn to be treated like adults.

This desire for recognition and acceptance is the seedbed of personality development. Feeling at ease in a group environment (be it at school or in a football team) or simply with their own identity is a very satisfying feeling – they start to be aware of how others perceive them.

Ronaldo was the star player who won matches from day one. He was a natural leader and has maintained that relationship with his team-mates ever since. He now demands that level of deference from them in exchange for his effort and leadership. But such precocity began at Sporting when he was fourteen.

To return to Erikson, adolescent development continues from this point on with attempts to choose a profession and a 'place in the adult world'. Often these reflections lead to career choices that lack insight and, as a result, are of short-term duration. Failure and seemingly insurmountable obstacles can lead to feelings of worthlessness and depression.

In the midst of so many conflicting emotions and doubts, Erikson writes that it is essential to have a reprieve, allowing for exploration and experimentation. An individual can come out of such a dark tunnel with a better idea of who he or she really is.

Ronaldo went to Lisbon at the age of twelve because he did not want to do anything else. He had already made his career choice and entered the adult world much earlier than most. And he missed out on that carefree period of time for experimenting and making mistakes.

From that age of twelve, Erikson explains, we begin to discover that everything has a price and financial reality becomes part of our identity, especially if we have experienced any level of poverty.

Footballing families differ from the norm in that they tend to focus attention on the one talented son in the hope that his future success will provide for their needs. In a sense he becomes the potential breadwinner for the family and usurps the role normally associated with the father. The family therefore becomes subservient to the son upon whom all their hopes and aspirations rest.

This, gradually and inexorably, will become Cristiano Ronaldo's fate.

■ ■ ■

The Ronaldos of this world have complete focus on their targets and use their competitive intelligence above all else. School is an irritation.

Cristiano's education comes from the street and the dressing room. Sporting Lisbon taught him so much through football: discipline, the need to respect authority, hard work as the means to success, results as a measuring rod. It is in that microcosm where new sources of motivation arise, characters evolve and team spirit as well as perseverance are developed.

But studying is an essential part of human development. Not only does it strengthen our personalities, but it facilitates reflection and the ability to make connections. In a word, it helps us think 'better'. We learn to defend our opinions, discover more about our world and the people around us. It is the beginning of self-assurance and critical analysis.

Far too often, footballers are taken away from that essential part of their development, placed in a world of their own, where there is no need to think, where they can remain as children. How convenient for everybody around the player that he should focus all his attention to his talent.

Even for some parents.

Parents usually fall into three distinct categories: the authoritative and distant; those who have an 'authoritative discipline', that is, they are interested in their children but within rules and order; and the permissive disciplinary approach in which rules and control are a rarity.

For this last group, prizes are commonplace, while punishments and demands are few and far between. Errors are forgiven, problems are avoided and communication is one-directional and barely effective. In my opinion, such was the parenting model adopted by Dolores and Dinis.

Rui Alves, the Nacional president, the coach Pedro Talhinhas and Martinho Fernandes, journalist and friend of Dinis, spoke about such concepts when suggesting that an overly interventionist family would not have allowed Ronaldo to grow up with the freedom necessary to become the player that he is.

Maybe such freedom allows a child to become 'streetwise', but with little or no parental control there is a risk of negative character traits developing: selfishness, intolerance, arrogance and, perhaps most damaging, insecurity.

If a youngster grows up in an environment without rules, without any obvious role models and with an absent father, that can only create insecurities on the path to adult life. It does not help to define the journey or decisions. It only creates confusion in the long term.

Insecurity? Is Ronaldo insecure?

Have you ever considered the possibility that his effort to maintain the perfect body could stem from insecurity? Do those who accept themselves and are satisfied with what they have always need to be perfect?

Think about it.

Without the social norms provided by a stable home, the male adult is often an immature boy who lets out a 'boooo' (remember the Balon d'Or 2014?) in the wrong place and even when he knows he is being observed; some might call it a lack of class. In reality, it is a lack of behavioural awareness.

So, without rules there is insecurity, and the accompanying defence mechanism is arrogance. It is just a cover-up.

There are those who defend Ronaldo saying that he is, above all else, honest. That what you see is what you get with him. That he doesn't hide what he feels.

What I see is a little boy lost.

If we accept that Cristiano's arrogance and behaviour are the consequences of his upbringing, should we try to justify some of his actions? Such as when he kicked out at Córdoba defender Edimar, receiving his fifth red card in the Spanish league in the process? Or his subsequent gesture when he ostentatiously brushed the dust from his FIFA World Champion shirt badge?

It is not easy to empathise with his actions, but they all stem from the same issue.

José Ángel Sánchez, the Real Madrid general manager, offered his assessment in Mario Torrejón's biography: 'When we don't understand behaviour or a public gesture by these boys and criticise them, we're judging them using criteria from a normal life that they don't have.'[13]

■ ■ ■

Cristiano Ronaldo admitted that he believed in Santa Claus until he was ten or eleven.

He emigrated the following year.

By the age of thirteen, he had already travelled all over Lisbon by underground, often alone.

■ ■ ■

In September 2014, I set off on another trip to Funchal and Lisbon with renewed energy. This time my researcher and right-hand woman, Maribel, was part of the crew. Manoj, from Mozambique, was our knowledgeable guide who navigated his way down the trickiest roads. Accompanying us on this trip were a Sky Sports producer and a cameraman (the talented Dan and the patient Christian, who, after sixteen interviews, came down with flu-like symptoms. I really burn the candle at both ends; I will have to look into that!).

After convincing the channel's documentary department (project presentation for the head of department, Paul King, took place on Monday, we flew out on Thursday; that is the beauty of the company: 'Should we do it?' 'We're doing it.' 'Let's get going.'), we grabbed the opportunity to record a documentary about Ronaldo's childhood up until the moment when he first set foot on the Old Trafford pitch. We called it *The Making of Ronaldo* and today it is shown at football schools and academies all over the world because his journey is an extraordinary, inspiring one.

■ ■ ■

'I had to get by on my own so often, almost all the time. I'd wake up, iron my own clothes, do the washing, make the bed, for example . . . I did things that a normal kid wouldn't do at that age, they wouldn't worry about such things. They'd always have someone else to do it for them. I wasn't used to that. I learnt so much, I grew to be a man.'[4]

Cristiano Ronaldo, who perfected the art of folding his own clothes at
the age of twelve

Cristiano had touched down in Lisbon in August 1997 and remained in the capital until August 2003. The city reminds me of a grand old lady, still beautiful but her days of youth and glory long gone. The people are much more open than in Madeira and seem genuinely pleased, when I explain my assignment, to be part of Ronaldo's triumphant story.

Three people were fundamental to Ronaldo's development during his time in the Portuguese capital. Aurélio Pereira, of course, was a mixture of father, godfather and adviser. Leonel Pontes, a fellow Madeiran, was his coach and mentor in his first few years. Nuno Naré was Ronaldo's youth-team coach who kept an eye out for him for four years.

At the time, Sporting did not have a structured academy, nor were there boys so young in the ranks. There were about twenty in all, most of whom were at least fourteen. Ronaldo was the first twelve-year-old, which posed additional problems.

Mobile phones were not as common as they are now, and the world seemed a much larger place. 'If boys from Porto, which is three hundred and fifteen kilometres away, find it hard, imagine what it's like for someone from Madeira,' said Aurélio Pereira.

The evenings were the toughest part for the youngsters.

'The players have to feel we're not replacing their families, but, rather, we're helping to solve their problems,' added Aurélio Pereira. 'It's hard for those who come from miles away during the first few months when there's no school and making new friends isn't easy. Their families are far away and they spend evenings alone. It gives them too much time to think.'

Those first few months are definitive; many go straight back home. 'All of us, managers, coaches, doctors included, had to adapt to the boy and look after him. Every step we took was something new. We had to integrate him into the group; he soon became the older boys' pet in the academy.'

The pet.

Not for long.

■ ■ ■

During my stay in Lisbon I spoke to Hugo Pina, one of Ronaldo's team-mates in the academy. He is thin and good-looking, shy at first and with a soft voice. Slumped on the sofa in the hotel where we met, he gradually sat forward as the conversation progressed. He, in fact, ended up sitting on the edge of his seat, interrupting my questions, putting theories forward and telling stories.

This is what he told me:

Hello. I am Hugo Pina.

You've probably never heard of me. Definitely not.

I shall tell you briefly. I started out at Belenenses, a first-division team from Belem, a Lisbon neighbourhood, and spent seven years there. Sporting signed me when I was fifteen.

Wait, one more thing. Before signing for Sporting, I nearly joined Barcelona, but they wanted me to have a two-week trial which happened to clash with a tournament for my Lisbon team. I was the captain and my mother and I decided not to go. I do not think about it now. It did not happen and that is it.

Sporting paid €300,000 to sign me. I joined at fifteen and everyone knew the figure. My team-mates were asking one another: 'Who's this guy and why have we paid so much for him?'

That amount was a constant topic of discussion in the dressing room, even on the pitch. Other players took the mickey out of me and that fee. But you gradually meet more people, everybody gets to know you and the famous figure gets forgotten.

When you arrive, you find yourself with all sorts of boys; that is another small challenge: making friends. You seem to become friends with some of them instantly and there are others that, even after four months, you are thinking: 'And who is this guy?'

Our adolescence is not at all normal. It can feel like a prison sometimes, everything is controlled, things that have to be done at a certain time – wake up, train, eat, talks, school, sleep. But in any case at Sporting many people looked after us. At fifteen, we were at the best club in Portugal (well, that is my opinion) and, of course, the coach is god.

Cristiano was a fourteen-year-old Sporting trainee when I joined the club.

I joined the Under-17s and Cristiano was still in a lower-ranking team, but as he was much better than the others they moved him up to our group. That is how we met.

He did not speak Portuguese like we do in Lisbon because the accent is different in Madeira and he was quite embarrassed. He always says that his first day at school was terrible. On that day, he had to go alone from the training ground to the Telherias district to find his school. He got lost, was late and the teacher was already calling the register. He was number five or six on the list. He raised his hand when his name was called and, as soon as he said a word, a group of boys started laughing at his accent. He began sweating, he wanted to leave. They say he threatened to hit the teacher with a chair, but I am not sure about that.

Cristiano thought it was very strange that people did not understand what he was saying! He cried a lot, he told his mother that he wanted to go home.

His mother told him not to pay any attention to the children. That was the first crisis.

Football would later put everyone in their place. The jokes dried up. The ones in bad taste, at least. Respect started to grow. That is what being good at football does for you.

We clicked early, the odd joke here, the odd joke there; childish stuff.

Cristiano is quite the joker. For example, he looks at me, he says hi, he laughs and says: 'Take a look at those legs?!' I have long legs. And he laughs some more.

I am convinced that many people do not know Cristiano Ronaldo at all. The Cristiano on television is not the one I know, honestly. His way of celebrating goals or even speaking often does not correspond with what Cristiano is actually about. Cristiano is very caring and loving with his friends.

We used to have dinner in our club residence rooms, his or mine; we also used to have breakfast together all the time.

Each bedroom had to choose its own leader and he became one pretty quickly. His was the popular room, there was always something going on.

And the first training session . . . this will not surprise you. Or maybe it will.

He was the same as he is today, he wanted to do the lot, irrespective of his age: he wanted to take free-kicks, corners, penalties . . . he was a year younger than us and we thought: 'What the hell do you want?' And we got angry with his reactions and his demands, but at the end of the day we could see that he was better than us. Eventually we gave him the ball and looked on in awe. It was much easier to win games with him.

He was a phenomenon.

Cristiano wants to make history, that is his aim and the rest is secondary. Yes, he wants to improve, help his team and break records . . . But, above all, he wants to make history.

He wants to be the best.

Ronaldo would train alone so that he could be as fast as [Thierry] Henry, the quickest player in the world at the time. We would say to him: 'What are you doing?' He would reply: 'Give me two weeks and I will be as fast as him.' We had a Brazilian player at Sporting called Andrés Cruz whose muscle mass was immense. Cristiano saw him lift 90 or 95 kilos and said: 'I'm definitely going to manage to lift 90.' He started practising and did not stop until he managed it. He must have been thinking: 'If he can do it so can I.' That is what he is like.

He would do sit-ups and press-ups in his room every day.

He would wake up during the night and go to the gym without making a sound. Two or three times a week. He would go on his own or take a couple of friends. They would jump the fence where the gym was, go up on to the roof and get inside it through a window. As he thought he was far too skinny, he would then do weightlifts and run around forty minutes on the treadmill.

He would often get caught because he was not allowed to be there and yet he would go back. He was fourteen! Crazy! He was already playing for a team in the year above, he did not need to do more!

They had to install locks to stop him getting into the gym.

I went to Madeira on holiday with him a few times. Cristiano would wake up early and put some music on the radio. Then we would go out to eat, maybe he would do some training or we would go for a walk, then a bit of partying in the evenings. Ronaldo has never drunk alcohol; he does not drink. That is what our holidays were like. Football was always involved, always, always, always.

I would wake up in the mornings and he would already be playing with a ball. Hitting it with his right foot, then left, then right, then left . . . He would also go to the gym and say: 'When I have a house, the first thing I'll do is get a gym built.' Nobody in the world thinks like that, buying a house and getting gym equipment straight away [laughs].

He would run with weights on his ankles on the very steep streets. Sometimes it was more than 35 degrees, the heat . . . Or he would put them on and move as if he were playing with an invisible ball to build up strength in his legs.

I didn't do any of that. Too hot.

We would play football, though. There was a pitch next to his house. He used to like playing there with his people. They spoke like him, they had known him since he was a boy, they were his people.

Messi has definitely not worked as hard as Cristiano to come as far as he has. Cristiano has two things: so much quality and above all a huge desire to be the best. They are closely related.

It is the one who puts in the most hours, perseverance and hard work who ends up achieving his goals in the end.

Do you know what? Ronaldo is never satisfied with what he does. He even said so yesterday on a television programme: his aim for the current year is to beat what he achieved in the previous one. Many footballers win many things and then relax; not him. He wants more and more and more. He wants to break his own Champions League goalscoring record and win another Champions League medal. He wants to win La Liga again with Real Madrid, he is incredible. And he already has everything, in football and in life.

He is not one of those players who plays at eleven in the morning and watches another game at three. He likes his job and he loves playing football, he loves training, he loves improving . . . but not watching matches.

Oh, and if he had decided to play table tennis, he would be the best in the world. Or pool. He is so good. Very competitive.

The boys in the Under-15s would go to watch him when he was part of the youth team. It was quite a spectacle.

Ronaldo gradually turned into the captain. He did not wear the armband, but he was the captain. The pitch was his home and his life. And he knew that he was better than the rest. So he started ordering the others around.

Did he run the team to improve it or so that they would pass to him? I am sure some of you are asking yourselves that. The answer is both [laughs]. And to have more goalscoring opportunities. He always wanted more. We could be 4–0 up, but if the centre-back passed the ball back, there would be shouts of: 'Oi, what are you doing? Let's go forward to grab more goals!'

Not everyone enjoyed the fact that he was so very competitive.

I have a friend who had countless problems with Cristiano Ronaldo. Ricardo Quaresma, who was also at the academy, used to get angry with him. And they competed all the time. If Ronaldo did something, Quaresma wanted to do the same thing, but they did not pass to each other. Both were forwards, one down the left and the other down the right. But they passed to each other very rarely. They spoke to each other very little. Today they do not speak at all.

I am a centre-midfielder, I would give the ball to the man in the best position; that was my job. If I passed to Cristiano, Quaresma would moan, and if I passed to Quaresma, it was Cristiano doing the complaining. Ronaldo is very impulsive, he would criticise you on the pitch. That happened a lot, very often. [Laughs.] 'But, what do you want? There's only one ball,' I would say to him.

But Ronaldo was not a bad boy. Ten minutes later, he would say to me: 'Come on, let's go out for a meal.'

One time, we had to go to play Marítimo in Funchal. Cristiano was so excited about seeing his family and his childhood friends after so long. He did not train well that week, however. His head was not in the right place and it affected him in training. He was playing alone, didn't pass the ball; he would pick it up and take shots on goal, and would fight with anyone who did not pass him the ball . . . He trained really badly.

So the coach left him out of the squad.

Cristiano could not believe it. He looked over the list four times, to no avail. He started crying and crying and crying because he was not going to be able to see his own people. He wanted to speak to someone about it, he was fuming. The lesson was that you had to train well; irrespective of your quality or the next game, you always have to give it your all in training. Imagine! His opportunity to show off his skills to his family and he never got the chance!

A moment is etched on my memory from when he was fifteen or sixteen. Those boys who had been punished for whatever reason were made to clean the dining rooms and take the rubbish out to the street using those wheelie bins. One day, it was him: 'Hahaha Ronaldo, you have a Ferrari, eh?' He replied: 'You'll see. One day I'll be the best in the world and I'll have loads of Ferraris.' Well, it did happen!

I'm not sure why he suffers more criticism than anyone else. And his defence mechanism is to be a bit arrogant.

I think he thinks: 'Bloody hell, fifty goals a year and two Champions League winner's medals, I have everything, and people still doubt my worth? People say I only score against small teams and don't score in finals?'

I don't know, it is all rather strange.

I spent a total of five years at Sporting. I then joined a Segunda B team in Portugal and second-division team Córdoba signed me after that on a five-year deal. I was only there for two. I then spent a year and a half at Guadalajara before returning to Portugal and here I am at CD Mafra in the second division.

These days I speak to him two or three times a month, because he has his own life, he is a public figure and it is not easy to have time with him. My mother went to Manchester when he was there, I did the same in Madrid . . . When he joins up with the national team, we meet up and have dinner together if possible. As I play in the second division, if I ask him for boots or some kit he gives it to me straight away. When we see each other, it's as though we've never been apart. As if he has never changed; he hasn't.

He still jokes about my legs.

. . .

Hugo Pina left one story half finished. The one about Ronaldo not being picked to go to Madeira.

It happened in 2000–01. As Luis Miguel Pereira and Juan Ignacio Gallardo discovered in *CR7: los secretos de la máquina*, complaints about the Madeiran had piled up just a month earlier. This is a report from that period: 'The player Cristiano Ronaldo stole a can of iced tea from a colleague at the training ground and two yoghurts from Mrs Emília. He also deprived player Rui Lopes (who is ill) of his lunch without permission.'[7]

Cristiano had exceeded half the number of offences permissible by club regulations. The reason he had given for his misbehaviour was 'the player is scared of coming to school due to a fight with a group of black children', the report said. 'However, he was seen at school many times playing football without attending class.'

His coach at the time, Luís Martins, had already written an anxious note along the same lines: 'This young boy has evident problems of emotional stability; he frequently loses control.' Martins added that there was still time to address the issue: 'We're convinced that the player is one of the cases that deserves psychological guidance because he still has an immature personality and is therefore not yet fully formed.'

Ronaldo, feeling devastated and in search of an ally, cried down the phone to his mother when he saw his name had been left off the squad list to go to Madeira. Dolores went in search of the coaches as soon as the team landed in the island. They explained what had happened, and she understood and sided with the club.

Dinis, on the other hand, spent the match next to the dugout giving Luís Martins a piece of his mind.

. . .

A different angle on the problems that Ronaldo experienced regarding his accent.

Some context first of all.

Napoleon was born on 15 August 1769 in Ajaccio, the capital of what is now Corsica, an island ceded to France in 1768. He was the fourth of eight siblings of a minor noble family with scarce resources. His father, though, managed to get him a scholarship to study at the Brienne military school, where he went at the age of ten.

He always spoke French with a strong Corsican accent, his native language, and never stopped making spelling mistakes in French. He proudly defended his 'foreign' descent but the other students, mostly of aristocrat families, would continuously laugh at him.

He wrote this letter to his father as a fourteen year old:

Brienne, 6 April 1783.

Oh, Father, if you or my protectors do not give me greater means by which to sustain myself more honourably, please take me back near you. I am tired of showing myself to be destitute and to see insolent students smiling, whose only prevailing feature over me is their fortune, given there is not a single one of them that is not miles below the noble feelings that run through me!

No, my father, no, if I am not able to improve my luck, take me away from Brienne. Take me, if necessary, to a factory.

Despite the doubts expressed in his letter, the young cadet persevered by deciding to put all his efforts into his studies and also the demanding physical tests. He was compelled by a desire to show his superiority over his peers. His intellectual achievements, principally in mathematics, provided him with a scholarship to attend the Paris military school, which he joined the year after writing the missive.

Some years later, Napoleon changed the world.

■ ■ ■

'I always had a gift. I was shown the skills and I am a fantastic footballer but I do believe God gave me the gift.'[14]

Cristiano Ronaldo

Maybe it was divine intervention. Maybe it was the thousands of hours that he spent playing football as a boy. The debate about the concept of 'natural talent' took up a large chunk of my biography of Lionel Messi, so here I would like to focus on the training Ronaldo received and the philosophy imbued at Sporting Lisbon, a club in the shadow of Porto and Benfica. Not the richest, nor the most successful, nor does it have the biggest fan base, but it does have the best academy.

As head of the youth teams, Aurélio Pereira was a constant presence. He never coached Ronaldo directly, but was integral to the 'spiritual training' philosophy at the academy. 'I'm from a coaching era where we were all self-taught. There was no training available for coaches in Portugal. That is why our influence on the players was more spiritual than tactics-related. We have always had that internal strength that allows us to have plenty of patience when educating youngsters, ensuring that football becomes part of their soul. We make them understand that making mistakes is part of the learning process. We needed to plant the seeds that would bear fruit later on. That's the football education that Cristiano Ronaldo received.'

People in charge of the boys were both teachers and coaches. The ideal profile for a football academy, I would add. Still is today.

■ ■ ■

We are now in August 1997. Ronaldo's mother signed his first training contract for three years with the promise that the deal would be extended by a further two when he turned professional. He first earned €50 a month which Dolores was in charge of managing: everything went into her account, and she would then send him half to buy clothes (after Ronaldo complained that his team-mates wore branded clothing) and toiletries.

He was on €250 a month just two years later, and the club arranged for six round trips to Funchal for him to visit his family or them to visit him. His mother saved the lot, barring the €50 she gave her son.

Meanwhile, reports on Ronaldo kept highlighting his talent, but also 'a certain sporting arrogance and a determined character', as Aurélio Pereira recalls.

His first residence was in the Centro de Estágio situated next to the Alvalade stadium: seven bedrooms with four boys in each, a television room and showers. Ronaldo lived with other boys from other far-flung parts such as Mozambique and Nigeria. Leonel Pontes, the man at the club who kept in contact with his family, offered up his own house whenever necessary, especially in the first few months, when life in Lisbon was very tough for young Cristiano.

'When he was only twelve, a young African player attended training, but there was nowhere for him to stay at the residence. Ronaldo said to him, "You sleep in my bed, I'll sleep on the floor,"' Aurelio remembers. In reality, according to Cristiano himself, what he did was put two beds together, his and his room-mate's. But you get the idea: he soon had a strong sense of camaraderie.

His routine from the start comprised: breakfast with the others in a local café; a one-kilometre walk to school; back to the stadium to eat in a restaurant linked to the club. A break. An afternoon snack at the same café. Go to training on a coach to whichever dirt pitch was available. Dinner in the restaurant once again.

For three seasons he earned €5 per game as a ballboy in Sporting matches (Gabriel Heinze, former Sporting full-back who played with Ronaldo at Manchester United, remembers him) and after the game he would run out of the Alvalade with his team-mates to a restaurant that offered two-for-one pizzas.

At the end of many days he struggled to get to sleep, kept awake by homesickness.

And the next morning he would start all over again.

He would get a phone card two or three times a week, go to the phone box and speak to his siblings and parents with an eye on the minutes counting down.

Ronaldo would cry during every conversation, but he would always return to the residence dry-eyed. Standing up straight.

'Life isn't easy sometimes,' Pontes would tell him when he was upset, although he rarely saw him cry after speaking to his family. 'I believe he thought he couldn't show any sign of weakness.'

In any case, the young Madeiran was not going unnoticed.

'When he left for Lisbon, the talk of the island was "Cristiano Ronaldo is a phenomenal player, he plays like the very best . . ." I think that was when our family realised he was not just another boy,' his sister Katia explains. 'Suddenly everyone wanted to work with him, he started signing contracts with businessmen . . . Something extraordinary was happening.'[5]

■ ■ ■

During a training session with the Lisbon Under-14s, Ronaldo felt a strange sensation in his chest: at times his heartbeat would accelerate and he would get abnormally tired. It had happened to him previously, to the point where he was substituted in a Sporting match just six minutes into the game.

After examinations at the club and the local hospital, doctors concluded that the young boy had a racing heart and needed surgery.

It was a simple procedure involving a laser. Dolores feared the condition could mean the end of her son's career, so she immediately signed the authorisation form. He was operated on in June 2000 at Hospital do Coração, not far from Lisbon. Aurélio Pereira and Nuno Naré, who had already replaced Pontes in the Madeiran's upbringing, stayed with him.

He was back at the residence the following day. Sporting waited three months before letting him play again after making sure everything was fine.

■ ■ ■

How did Cristiano play at that point? How did he adapt to Sporting's characteristic 4-3-3? Why was that formation adopted throughout the club?

The Sky Sports team and I headed to the outskirts of Lisbon in search of new 'talking heads', as they say in production slang – new faces, new statements, new angles. We crossed a never-ending bridge over the Tagus and, after getting somewhat lost, we reached a green oasis amidst the sprawling city suburbs: we had arrived at the Sporting academy which was inaugurated at the start of the 2001–02 season.

We went straight into Aurélio Pereira's office, a small room with a picture window allowing the bright Atlantic light to filter through. It was full of memorabilia: three signed shirts behind the office table, two of which were Ronaldo's, and two boards covered in photos of notable footballers who came up through the academy, including several of Cristiano: one of him as a boy looking anxious while stretching in his tracksuit bottoms and another, more recent one, of him hugging Aurélio.

'4-3-3?' Pereira asked himself. 'It's the easiest system for the players to understand and it can be easily adapted into other systems: 4-4-2, 3-5-2. Sometimes people say that we only produce wide players, wingers; it is not true. We like speed down the wing but we want the good players to play down the middle from the age of fifteen or sixteen. They can improve their speed of reaction, get more touches of the ball and learn to create space in an area where it is limited. You have to give the good players the ball as much as you can.'

When it came to Ronaldo, coaches had to instil in him the idea that the ball was *not* his. Aurélio Pereira became overwhelmed with new concerns: 'How do we educate someone like that? By telling him that he's the same as the others?'

He was not. You could see as much from his overconfidence. 'How is he not going to be [confident] if he's been considered the best ever since he was a boy?' continued Aurélio. 'Confidence has been a constant companion on the path that he's taken. His reactions on the pitch are the result of the rebellious streak that has made him the player that he is, and of the passion that he has had since he was kid.'

The head of the academy allowed him to be arrogant. In truth, he was forgiven for many things on the pitch that others would not get away with. Just like at home. Aurélio saw the positive effects that his attitude had on the pitch to both the player and team morale. He just needed to improve Ronaldo's discipline off the pitch. But, at that point, the coach was not sure if his assurance as a player was linked with the difficulties he had with rules and authority that he showed as a student – if they were two sides of the same coin.

Regardless of all this, Ronaldo, the artist, had to be converted into an effective player – that was the progression. While that happened, he did not win a single title in the lower ranks – it was not the priority either.

As the years passed, Aurélio celebrated the fact that Cristiano seemed to be settled in Lisbon and at the club. And that was a club success: the head of the academy was very aware not all Madeirans are suited to leaving the island. 'I've seen fifteen- and sixteen-year-old boys who already had their bags packed to go home on day two.' The distance kills just as much as it can strengthen.

At fifteen, he moved into a residence in central Lisbon. As someone who knew every nook and cranny of the city, he would use his free time to walk around, go for runs in nearby parks and challenge himself to race cars stopped at traffic lights. He would only set foot in the residence when it was time for bed.

One night, on the way back from a shopping centre after curfew (knowing full well that he would be reprimanded), Cristiano and three other fifteen-year-olds were confronted on the metro by a gang wielding knives. Two of the footballers ran off, two stayed. Guess which group Ronaldo was in?

He was, of course, one of the two boys who stood up to the muggers. Nobody was robbed in the end.

'He suffered, but we looked after him. He felt our human warmth,' analysed Pereira. 'It prepared him for what came later. It isn't a friendship that joins us, but more of an eternal connection. That's what we offered to him.'

■ ■ ■

As Hugo Pina said, Cristiano does not drink (barring rare exceptions), he does not smoke and hates drugs. He saw what happened to his father and brother Hugo.

His older brother started taking drugs when Ronaldo had been in Lisbon for two years. Dolores had to ask for a loan so that he could be admitted into a specialist clinic, but he relapsed two years later. And occasionally thereafter.

Ronaldo was already earning good enough money at Sporting and had begun to fulfil the role that his father had never been able to make his own. He took care of the bills and more. He went to see his brother when he refused treatment and insisted on him being admitted to a rehabilitation clinic.

Today he has made a full recovery.

■ ■ ■

Allow me two thoughts and one image.

Cristiano used more and more of his money to help his siblings achieve their goals. Katia recorded a CD. Hugo, after managing a painting company with fifteen employees, took charge of matters relating to the museum in Madeira. Ronaldo bought houses for his mother. Another example of a footballer's family in which the traditional roles seem to have been reversed.

Dinis was an alcoholic. Hugo a drug addict. Ronaldo has an addictive relationship with physical exercise. There is no doubt that psychological and social factors contribute to addiction, but there are studies proving that genetic factors have their influence, at least in the propensity for addiction and its subsequent development. Genes are estimated to constitute 40–60 per cent of the risk in alcoholism.

And the image: in Lisbon after clinching *La Décima*, Cristiano and Hugo locked in a firm embrace.

It was the end of a very long journey for both.

■ ■ ■

Sixteen-year-old Ronaldo became the first player in Sporting's history to play for the Under-16s, Under-17s, Under-18s, reserves and first team in the same season (2001–02). That year he moved to a new residence in plaza Marqués de Pombal in central Lisbon. That is where Sport TV headed to carry out the first report on the young star. Perhaps you have seen it: Ronaldo on the metro as well as sitting in a modest bedroom with two beds and a television. Note his insistence on one matter: he told the journalists that he had a marvellous job that allowed him to meet many players and earn a good salary.

In the report you can hear him speaking to a friend about a PlayStation: 'Eh? How much was it? Did you buy it? I have one of them at home.'

Later on in the interview, Cristiano said, 'I earn around three hundred euros . . . Plus a bonus of three hundred.'

Money used as a barometer of status and personal value, perhaps typical comments by a boy who rose out of poverty.

When Ronaldo received his professional contract, his agent was José Vega, the best-known in the country. The amount on his release clause included seven zeros.

He was two years away from becoming a Manchester United player.

■ ■ ■

A couple of years after that TV report, an eighteen-year-old Ronaldo often told his friends that he was scared women wanted him for his money. They would poke fun at him in response: 'Yes, because you're so ugly. They definitely only want you for your money!' They would add, 'But you're going to earn a lot! You'd better start getting used to the idea that some will want a slice of what you earn!'

Ronaldo admitted that having Irina, the millionaire model who became his first steady partner, by his side made him feel calm – it was a relationship of equals. Sadly, it was not to be, as she admits today, a relationship that would last a lifetime. More on that later.

Many stories have been told about his summer romances in Madeira and I have heard dozens of versions of the alleged incident in a Lisbon nightclub involving a rival suitor being thrown into the river by Ronaldo's bodyguards.

Ronaldo has spoken before about a dream he had in his early twenties. It involved his own wedding. All he could remember about it was that his bride was very beautiful, and that his mother was present and very happy. At the point of Cristiano recognising himself not as a young man any more but as a man, he woke up relieved. I imagine that feeling came perhaps from his fear of commitment.

He also mentioned in interviews that he wanted a son who loved football as much as he did and who perhaps would develop the same skills, that they might share the same 'football genes'. He has admitted that he would be happy if his son looked like him.

Shall we just say that many fathers have fantasies like this? Or maybe it reflects something deeper.

■ ■ ■

Luis Boa Morte, the former Arsenal and West Ham winger, also came through the ranks at Sporting Lisbon and is a coach in their academy today. He has experienced some of the good and the bad things that Ronaldo and many of his team-mates faced as teenagers.

'Many players get . . . carried away with the sudden success. It seems like they'll make it and then they don't, because of a bad investment or bad advice. When things aren't going well, all those new friends disappear. You end up alone, and that goes from being a small problem to becoming a big one if it doesn't get corrected. It can be so big that it even causes suicide.'

He saw Cristiano increase his circle with the first sign of success, but gradually reduce it to its minimal form, trusting in fewer and fewer people over time. It is the story of many youngsters. 'Cristiano came to Sporting when he was really young and had to prove his potential. Then agents come along and you have to protect yourself. You need to ask your parents for advice, but sometimes they aren't by your side. Then the agents start to put pressure on your parents. As you're underage, your parents have to be the ones to sign. It starts a rollercoaster, really quick, really young. Sometimes you get lost along the way.'

José Veiga began representing Ronaldo in April 2001. Sixteen-year-old Cristiano signed a two-year contract which was later shown in court to be damaging to the player's interests. The first chances to move abroad started appearing.

Jorge Manuel Mendes, another Portuguese agent, recommended the player to Inter Milan, one of the leading powers in the transfer market at the time. Luis Suárez, club president Massimo Moratti's adviser, travelled to Lisbon to watch a Belenenses–Sporting match. Ronaldo did not play particularly well, but Luis Suárez was impressed with his physical presence, his ability to change pace, his speed and shot. His ambition also stood out; throughout the game he did not stop demanding the ball.

Luis Suárez had a meeting with Cristiano before returning to Italy to report back to Moratti a few days later.

'We have to sign him, he'll be one of the best players in the world,' Suárez told his president. 'How old is he?' 'Sixteen.' 'Pah, we sign the ready-made article.' 'He costs only two million dollars!! I'll put in a million from my own pocket,' Luis Suárez told him.

But Moratti was not convinced and the bid did not materialise.

Gérard Houllier, Liverpool manager at that time, knew about Ronaldo and sent scouts to watch the European Under-17 Championship, but also thought he was too young at the time.

Strangely, José Veiga, the biggest Portuguese agent back then, did not seem to realise what he had on his hands – his colleagues admit today that he probably rested on his laurels, happy waiting for clubs to come to him, instead of proactively looking after the careers of his own players.

Jorge Mendes knew that a unique opportunity was in the offing. He asked Jorge Manuel if they could work together. 'Let's go for Quaresma, Ronaldo and Hugo Viana,' proposed Jorge, three stars at the Sporting academy and on Veiga's books. 'I don't know,' replied Jorge Manuel, who was reluctant to mount such an attack on the big agent's interests.

Jorge Mendes spoke to all three players, who were still under the age of nineteen, and promised that he would find them big clubs and they would all earn at least a million euros, and fast.

He convinced them. Hugo Viana ended up going to Newcastle United. Quaresma signed for Barça.

'Jorge helped me so much in the first few months when I joined Porto,' admitted former footballer Jorge Andrade. 'He made Deco, who he also represented, my mentor. I ate with Mendes, Deco or my brother every day. It had a relaxed family feel to it. They started to call us up to the international squad. Mendes was important in that process, too.'

That is where you find one of the keys to Jorge Mendes's success. He works hard on the details.

He is always by the footballer's side, he keeps his promises, he opens up the international market at the highest level, his contacts are limitless. He gets close to the families as part of his approach. He buys things for the parents, brothers and sisters, and the player, too: a television, a car, a flat . . .

There is no doubt that Mendes (another Ronaldo in his own field, an obsessive and hard-working perfectionist) is the best agent in the world. Look at some of his clients past and present: Ronaldo, José Mourinho, Nani, Quaresma, Paulo Ferreira, Carvalho, Diego Costa, David de Gea, Ángel di María, Falcao . . .

In 2001, Jorge Mendes, aware of Ronaldo's value, drew up a strategy to entice the player.

THE 2001–02 SEASON: RONALDO'S BREAKTHROUGH

Cristiano told his mother that when he started to earn money she would no longer have to work and he would give her a house because she'd never had a proper one.

His first pay cheque as a professional did not provide for much, but it was enough for him to ask Dolores to quit her job at the hotel and move to Lisbon to live in a flat that the club paid for. Elma would look after the rest of the family in Funchal. Soon after, mother and son moved into a high-spec flat in the Expo neighbourhood.

Meanwhile, the distance separating Ronaldo from the first team was becoming smaller by the day. Sporting's new first-team coach, the Romanian László Bölöni, would sometimes call up the younger players – Cristiano received his at the age of sixteen.

When that day came, he had spent the morning at school, and, on returning to the club's recently inaugurated training ground facilities on the outskirts of Lisbon, the Sporting B team coach, Jean Paul, called him into his office.

'Get ready, you're going to train with the first team this afternoon.'

A wide-eyed Ronaldo asked to use the telephone to call his mother. It was a quick conversation, but he had to share it with her. He ran to the dressing room to put on his football boots.

His ecstasy, however, was gradually turning into apprehension.

There were two and a half hours to go until training started at 4.30.

An hour and a half.

An hour.

He was ready before anyone else. Mário Jardel, João Vieira Pinto and André Cruz were getting ready . . .

Half an hour.

He was taking everything in. How they got changed and put on their boots, who was speaking to whom.

He sat quietly in the corner. Nerves were fusing with fear (he couldn't stop wondering what he was doing there, next to those great players) and a sense of responsibility. He would have to show his worth in this first training session. He did not want anyone to forget him.

They went to the training pitch.

His heart was racing.

It was important that he recognise that he was nervous but also that he had what it took to be there. Nobody was given that kind of opportunity without there being a good reason.

He didn't excel, but nor did he make a fool of himself.

It was the same scenario on the following occasion when he joined the senior team.

Nothing to write home about.

The very worst script was being played out: he was going unnoticed. Ronaldo was unable to implement his game.

He was growing impatient. The door to success had been opened for him, but he was unable to get through it.

He never knew at the time that Bölöni wrote a report on him:

'Technique (negatives): Aerial game poor; technique insufficiently worked on; poor defensive game – Physical (negatives): Not much strength – Tactics (negatives): No tactical awareness as an individual or team player; Individualist – Mental (negatives): Selfish; lacking mental strength; concentration.'

But then, three or four months down the line, in the same way as an emigrant gets to grips with a new language, everything suddenly clicked into place. The calm set in overnight. He felt integrated. His heartbeat returned to normal.

His fear of the ball evaporated.

He dared to nutmeg a veteran player. A *sombrero* flick over another. Dribbling aplenty.

According to a snippet in Pereira and Gallardo's detailed biography, in a first-team training session, after a strong tackle on an older player, he received the classic treatment: 'Calm it, kid . . .' Ronaldo turned around and answered, 'We'll see if you call me that when I'm the best player in the world.'[7]

The Ronaldo from Madeira, the one who had impressed in the youth system, was back.

But he did not play in matches.

The academy's two other stars, Ricardo Quaresma, a year and a half older than Cristiano, and Hugo Viana, two years older, did feature from the halfway point in the season onwards and were crucial elements in the club's excellent campaign.

Ronaldo would continually ask members of Bölöni's coaching staff if he would be training with the first team the following day.

Cristiano might have been in a hurry, but Bölöni was not.

'He didn't stop complaining that he wasn't playing as much as he wanted to,' recalled his team-mate Toñito, a Spaniard who played for Sporting and drove him to the training ground every day. 'He was a nonconformist and was convinced he'd be the best in the world. He'd say it with a surprising amount of certainty.'

Under-17 coach João Couto and Bölöni prepared a specific training regime for Ronaldo, including two weekly muscle-building sessions with either the Under-17s or the first team. When it is well managed, such a regime prevents injuries and prepares the body for competing with the elite, but resistance, flexibility and coordination must be developed in parallel. Ronaldo would trick the two coaches: he would tell Couto that he had not done muscle work with the first team, and vice-versa so that he could double up.

The coaches were trying to avoid a training overload, but Ronaldo was determined to make his dreams come true.

'One night I saw him alone on the pitch with a bag of balls,' recalled goalkeeper Tiago Ferreira. 'He started shooting and shooting at goal. I asked him why he didn't ask a goalkeeper to stay behind. "I train for myself," he told me. He always did the same movement; he would strike the ball with the same part of his foot. He would also train using oranges.'

'Every day I'd have to wait until nightfall to take him home,' jokes Toñito today.

But if Cristiano had had at his disposal the information and technology available today he could have improved some of his attributes further. It sounds strange, doesn't it? Bölöni, for example, realised his running style was powerful yet unconventional and demanded that he persist with the coordination work.

In a match against Celta in season 2012–13, Ronaldo ran eighty metres in 9.05 seconds at 31.8 kilometres per hour . . . in the 87th minute! With such a speed he would have reached the 100-metres final at the London Olympics. But he could have been faster.

Usain Bolt realised Ronaldo's running technique still needed improving when they met in 2009, but they concluded it was already too late. 'When he is running and reaches top speed he starts to tip over,' Bolt explained. 'If he brought his foot down on the centre of gravity, or even in front of him, it will be much easier. He will be much better and he will go faster for longer.'

Certain things needed correcting, but without suppressing others. The balance was not easy: Ronaldo, who had already shown his explosive dribbling, too often resorted to exaggeration or excessive use of trickery. Bölöni was very strict and took him to task several times (even threatening not to pick him if he did not change) for what he called 'unnecessary exhibitionism', especially the stepovers that he used to perform after receiving the ball. Sometimes up to three or four.

The Romanian coach won the treble during his first season at the club: the league, cup and super cup. The blend of experience and youth worked well, in spite of Ronaldo's desire for greater involvement.

■ ■ ■

A moment from an Under-17 match between Portugal and England played that season lives on in the memory. Not for the result or Ronaldo's performance, but for a conversation that took place after it in the tunnel between Juan Carlos Freitas, the national team's press officer, and Aurélio Pereira.

'I saw Quaresma in training the other day, he'll be phenomenal,' said Freitas.

'Remember what I'm about to tell you. The one who'll succeed is the boy from Madeira who played up front for Portugal today, Cristiano.'

'Why?'

'Because he's a professional. At sixteen he's more professional than the professionals, because he came here alone. He spent a few months crying at the start because he wanted to go home and I asked him: "What do you want to do with your life? Play football or go crying to your mother?" His answer: "Play football."'

■ ■ ■

Ronaldo had arrived in Lisbon with considerable gaps in his schooling. In Funchal he had had to repeat two courses. And his first year in the capital had been complicated, so much so that his adaptation seemed impossible. On three occasions Sporting thought of getting rid of him. It was not only his difficult behaviour, but also his attention to schoolwork was minimal. Even Ronaldo himself thought of giving it up, but a truce was agreed: the club sent him home for a month between December 1997 and January 1998, but that meant that he'd fail yet another missed course.

He returned to school, but from the following season he would sit with kids two or three years younger. When he reached the age of seventeen, Ronaldo's commitments to his club (he trained with and played for the Under-17s and soon with the first team) and country (in his age group) limited his school attendance even more. In Year 9 (2000–01), he failed seven subjects. His Year 10 report was not completed because he only appeared in class in the first three months of the academic year.

His father, meanwhile, was proudly reading cuttings about his son that he collected from newspapers and would take them with him to the bar in San António to show his friends.

■ ■ ■

Ronaldo signed his first professional contract that season. It was a four-year deal worth €2,000 a month and included a €20 million release clause. José Veiga was still his agent.

Around that time, Jorge Mendes organised a dinner with one of his business partners, Ronaldo and his mother. There was empathy between the agent and the player, nineteen years his junior, from the first minute. Jorge's charm pervaded the evening. His partner managed to keep the player occupied while Jorge went to speak to Dolores. When he returned, Mendes told his colleague, 'Cristiano is going to be with us.'[15] His mother had been persuaded.

At the start of the following season, in September 2002, José Veiga's agency received a fax signed by the player and his mother in which it was stated that he did not want to renew his agreement with the agent, because he had shown 'a systematic lack of interest in improving the conditions' of the contract between them.

Mendes took charge of everything soon after that fax.

Ronaldo spoke about his new agent soon after relations with José Veiga were cut off: 'I could see in Jorge's face that he was someone who really cared about me . . . He's like a father to me.'[15]

'He never says "no", he's always willing to help,' says Dolores today. 'I consider him a friend, or more than that: he's become part of my family.'[15]

Mendes: father, brother, agent. According to journalist Luis Miguel Pereira, he managed to buy Ronaldo a flat before he was of legal age. He is in almost all the photos from Ronaldo's individual awards. He behaves like a friend, he tells him off like an older brother, he cries, he gets excited for him and his successes, he defends him in public and in private.

Many of his other players are envious of that tight relationship. They say Jorge only cares about Ronaldo.

SEASON 2002–03: COMING OF AGE

Bölöni, who knew that Jardel, the first-choice striker, wanted to leave Sporting soon, was looking for another attacking player down the middle or on the wing for the new season. The director of football, Carlos Freitas, asked the board how much the budget was. 'Zero', he was told. He proposed a solution: 'Cristiano Ronaldo.'

'*Ça ce n'est pas le présent, c'est l'avenir,*' answered László in French. He isn't the present, he's the future.

'Maybe, yes. He's seventeen,' replied Freitas. 'But would you say the same if he were from Romania or Bulgaria?'

Bölöni thought about it for a few seconds, 'You're right, let's bank on him.'

Cristiano played in many summer friendlies, including one against PSG for an hour. After shining at the academy as a striker or second striker, where he admitted to feeling more comfortable, his first-team role was as a tricky winger. And he was shining there.

Bölöni could contain the beast no longer, nor did he want to. He felt that Ronaldo had made two years' progress in one, having improved in several aspects over the previous season. It had been impossible to do so in others, but he finally sent Cristiano into the ring. And did so, too, in the press conference: 'He'll be better than Eusébio and Figo,' stated the coach in front of sniggering Portuguese journalists.

Ronaldo became a fully-fledged member of the first-team squad, and the player felt he belonged there. He would boast about jumping further than Jardel, the first-choice striker. Story has it that his sister Jordana was the first girl that the newly confident Cristiano fell in love with.

'People still haven't seen anything from the real Ronaldo, this is just the start,' said the player himself after a match against Lyon.

He did not wait long before climbing another rung of the ladder: 3 August, friendly against Real Betis. The score was at 2–2 when he came off the bench with fifteen minutes to go.

His adrenalin was pumping.

The last minute of the game.

He used a heel kick to put the ball in front of him. The Betis goalkeeper came off of his line.

Cristiano dribbled around him, but ended up at a tight angle. A defender, Rivas, was running back towards goal to cover.

On the touchline, Ronaldo lobbed the ball towards the far post. It went over two defenders, with Rivas already standing on the goal line.

His first goal for Sporting Lisbon.

His eyes were coming out of their sockets. He had felt nothing like it before. That rush felt like the best moment of his life.

'Custodio Ronaldo' was the scorer, according to the graphic used by the TV channel that broadcast the game live.

With that goal, 'a work of art' according to the headlines in the Portuguese press the following day, the fear disappeared, too.

■ ■ ■

Important matches were coming along in quick succession. He made his debut against Inter Milan in a Champions League qualifier which ended 0–0; the Italians would eventually go through to the next round. His league debut came against Braga. His first two goals were scored against Moreirense in the cup in October, the first one after picking the ball up fifty metres from goal, getting away from defenders using his pace, a stepover on the edge of the penalty area and a dinked finish over the onrushing goalkeeper. In the stands his mother fainted.

He appeared in the final ten minutes against Boavista, Portuguese champions two years earlier, and unlocked a tight 1–1 with a winning goal.

He was in and out of the starting eleven. Jorge Mendes, who was aware of interest coming in from many European sides, set the alarm bells ringing at the club, convinced that a move elsewhere to a bigger club as soon as the following season was the best step for him. Unless he was a definite starter. It was up to Sporting, Mendes would tell the Portuguese club. The agent was in regular contact with Real Madrid, Barcelona, Parma, Juventus, Arsenal, Manchester United, Liverpool, Inter . . . They all showed interest in the winger.

By the end of that season, he had played in twenty-five matches and racked up five goals. The team's inconsistency saw them end it without any silverware and, as a consequence, László Bölöni was sacked. Porto, coached by José Mourinho, won the league that year. The winning manager enjoyed what he had seen from the scrawny young man and declared that summer: 'The first time I saw him I thought: "That's Van Basten's son." He was a striker, but above all a very elegant player, with great technical quality and movement. He astonished all of us, he really stood out from the rest.'

■ ■ ■

June 2003. Ronaldo said the following in an interview during the Under-20 tournament in Toulon where the eighteen-year-old became one of the sensations of the competition won by his country (Javier Mascherano was voted player of the tournament): 'I'm very pleased to hear many important clubs are interested in me.' He was asked if there was any truth in Manchester United's interest or a possible verbal agreement with Valencia: 'No, nobody has spoken to me . . . My dream is to play in Spain or England, they're the best leagues in Europe.'

Paco Roig, a candidate for the Valencia presidency in 2003, had 'signed' Ronaldo that same year. He was not the only one. The agreement with Jorge Mendes was firmed up in Madrid around January and February and included Ricardo Quaresma. Both would have signed for *Los Che* if Roig had been elected president in the club elections that summer. The fee: €9 million for both. The deal included a clause: whoever was elected had the possibility of activating a preferential option until 30 May to buy Ronaldo, with two years remaining on his contract, for €5 million.

The Spanish club's financial difficulties made them reluctant to pay so much for a teenager before the deadline. During the summer, having seen Ronaldo's progress in Toulon, they changed their minds and offered €6 million plus striker Diego Alonso for the teenager. Too late.

If the clause had been applied, he would have featured in the year that Valencia won the double (La Liga and UEFA Cup) under Rafa Benítez.

Despite the agreement with Valencia, Jorge Mendes had other meetings with all of Europe's top clubs in early 2003. The priority was not money, it was about the right destination.

Liverpool decided to offer €8 million. In the wake of their interest, Ronaldo publicly stated, 'They're one of the best clubs in Europe and it'd be a dream to be able to play for a club that represents so much tradition.' Negotiations with Juventus took place and an agreement was also reached, but their Chilean striker Marcelo Salas did not fancy joining Sporting in a swap deal. Mendes had an €8 million offer on the table from Parma, but the Italians wanted Ronaldo to spend another year in Lisbon. Ramón Martínez, head of the Real Madrid academy, had also had a meeting with the Lisbon club after hearing of the possible availability of Cristiano.

At the start of the summer of 2003, Mendes met representatives of Barcelona to talk about Ricardo Quaresma, Tiago, Deco and also Ronaldo. The Catalan club already had a very positive report: 'Quick, powerful, can play on both wings and is a goalscorer. Let's sign him.' Finally, Barcelona went for Quaresma but agreed a preferential precontract for Ronaldo, which eventually counted for nothing.

The sporting vice-president, Sandro Rosell, knew other clubs wanted to get him but could not find enough backing or even finances to bring in a second emerging star. Rosell did send the technical secretary, Txiki Beguiristain, to follow Cristiano in the friendly against Manchester United, but by then the dynamics of the transfer had changed considerably.

The club making the greatest headway in that 2003 was Arsenal. Chief scout Steve Rowley met Mendes and Ronaldo in Lisbon early in the year to plant the seed. 'There was a time when I really thought he was going to Arsenal,' admitted Jorge Mendes.[15]

Cristiano travelled to London with his mother in January to see the club's training ground, and to meet Arsène Wenger and one of his idols, Thierry Henry. 'We were in a car and Jorge kept calling me to reiterate I had to make sure nobody saw me,' recalled Ronaldo. 'We stopped at a service station and I had to have my face covered. Jorge was calling me every five minutes: "Be careful, be careful around people!"'[15]

Cristiano fell in love with the club, what it offered, the philosophy and the care with which young players are treated. Arsenal, who wanted to confirm that he had the personality required to change his own lifestyle, country, language, had no doubts after his visit: he was ready.

The player wanted to sign for the London club. Mendes, too. As did Arsène, who kept the number nine shirt for him.

The club's vice-chairman, David Dein, travelled to the Portuguese capital to seal the deal, but the initial offer was too low for Sporting. 'Arsenal, with the construction of the new stadium, were short on funds and it wasn't possible to make the move happen,' stated Mendes.[15]

The mistake by Arsenal was that, despite the very advanced negotiations, nothing was signed, nothing tied the player to them.

'My biggest regret? I was so close to signing Cristiano Ronaldo,' revealed Wenger in 2014.

Meanwhile, Manchester United agreed to play Sporting Lisbon in a friendly that very summer.

SEASON 2003–04: MANCHESTER UNITED CAME CALLING

Carlos Queiroz, Alex Ferguson's assistant in 2002–03: 'I knew about him when he was sixteen. During my first year at United, I didn't take on any responsibility in terms of recruiting young players, but I informed Alex about Cristiano. We couldn't let him get away. As the club was struggling to make up its mind, I forced the signing of a cooperation agreement with Sporting over coach and player training. They asked us to play them in a friendly in August as part of the collaboration, because they thought Manchester United were the club with the greatest impact for the inauguration of their new stadium.'

The match, the first one at the new José Alvalade ground, would be played on 6 August 2003.

Phil Neville: 'We were in the States for around twenty days or so in pre-season. I think we'd played AC Milan, Juventus, Bayern Munich and Inter Milan' [author's note: in fact, they played Celtic, Club América, Juventus and Barcelona and beat them all].

Rio Ferdinand: 'The tour had been very long, we'd just won the league and people wanted to see us in many places.'

Phil Neville: 'The game in Lisbon was just a pain in the backside because we just wanted to go home.'

Quinton Fortune: 'The rumour about players having a drink [on the plane]? No chance! No no no no no. I don't think the manager would ever have allowed that, and obviously our captain Roy Keane wouldn't either.'

Rio Ferdinand: 'We'd arrived very late the previous night, there was little time to relax.'

Phil Neville: 'We were all jet-lagged. I remember seeing four or five players at four in the morning walking around.

'It was a long day, we weren't allowed to sunbathe because of the game at night.'

Rio Ferdinand: 'We arrived at the ground knackered.'

Luis Lourenço, a former Sporting player: 'It was a great day. 50,000 fans. A packed stadium. We were playing against a top side.'

Phil Neville: 'The pitch was terrible, it was the stadium opening; it was unplayable. Grass was coming off, it was one of those new pitches and none of us wanted to play.'

Ryan Giggs: 'I've never ever been so tired before a game. I was sub for that game, thank God. I remember sitting on the bench and thinking, "I'm so glad I'm not playing today."'

Rio Ferdinand: 'Nobody warned us about Cristiano, there was no talk about him before the match. The boss picked a strong team:

Paul Scholes, Barthez, Nicky Butt, Mikael Silvestre, Solskjær, John O'Shea, me too. Eric Djemba-Djemba made his debut that day.'

Phil Neville: 'I remember his name because you see the team sheet come in and you see "Ronaldo". That was it. You think he's got to be some player. With a name like that he's got to produce.'

Rio Ferdinand: 'He had these long limbs and funny hair, he was quite tall.'

Phil Neville: 'And then he came out and I just remember his boots. His boots were colourful. He was like a scrawny little kid, but he had these blond streaks in his hair, wavy, almost permed-like hair, and I think he had a brace as well, a big metal brace in his mouth as well, so he was obviously someone who liked himself.'

Hugo Pina: 'We used to pick on him for his dress sense and hair. He'd get quite annoyed. I remember we went to the hairdresser's together a few days before the game against Manchester United, we got blond highlights and let them grow longer.'

Ryan Giggs: 'He looked more like a tall, gangly player . . .

'All of a sudden he started passing players on the outside, then on the inside . . . I suddenly sat up. A few of us started giggling, mostly at John O'Shea, who was defending him.'

Quinton Fortune: 'Fortunately enough for me I was playing left-back! John O'Shea was playing right-back and throughout the game he was just, like, "What's happening to me?"'

Ryan Giggs: 'We were just thinking, "He's not bad this lad, is he? Who is he?"'

Rio Ferdinand: 'The crowd were loving him and you could hear them screaming every time the ball went to him.'

Quinton Fortune: 'He was doing stepovers, tricks, the whole thing and the confidence he had was just unbelievable.'

Due to injury, Gary Neville watched the game from the comfort of his sofa at home on Manchester United TV: 'He made a run that

I think only world-class players make. It was like a double movement, then a run in between centre-back and full-back. He spun in behind John O'Shea, and I was like, "Whoa". It wasn't the skill, the dribbling, the lollipops, the fancy stuff that he used to do; it was actually a run off the ball that caught my eye.'

Carlos Freitas: 'The English were looking at me in the directors' box and saying, "Who is this guy?"'

Luis Lourenço: 'There had been rumours in the papers about several clubs being interested in him. Everything came off for him that day, because he was especially motivated.'

He actually made a slow start to the match. After a quarter of an hour, Ronaldo started to grab the spotlight, with a shot that Barthez smothered. Filipe opened the scoring for the home side before the break.

Phil Neville: 'I think even Sheasey came into the changing rooms and said something like, "Who the fuck's that little thing?"'

Rio Ferdinand: 'John O'Shea was sitting there like he needed some oxygen.'

Phil Neville: 'He needed more than "some"!'

Roy Keane: 'Sheasy ended up seeing the club doctor at half-time because he was having dizzy spells.'[16]

John O'Shea: 'It's true that Ronaldo killed me in that match, but not that I was dizzy.'

Ryan Giggs: 'Ferguson told us they'd been following him for a while. I had no idea who he was.'

Rio Ferdinand: 'Scholesy, Butty and I were saying, "We have got to sign this guy", because, remember, we'd just missed out on Ronaldinho, so we needed to sign a top player.'

Ryan Giggs: 'Ferguson looked at us with a smile that said: "Yes, I know."'

Rio Ferdinand: 'We said, "Boss, are you going to sign him or what?"'

Ronaldo continued his exhibition in the second half. Pinto scored Sporting's second goal. Sir Alex played his trump card, bringing on Dutch hitman Ruud Van Nistelrooy, who replaced Quinton Fortune, but it was not enough to save United.

Phil Neville: 'I came on in the second half in midfield, but ended up going to left-back for the last five minutes to plug some gaps.'

Sporting, who had lost all their other pre-season friendlies, had just destroyed the English giants, who did manage a consolation goal (a Hugo own goal).

Quinton Fortune: 'We had just got absolutely taken apart by the kid. I mean our excuse was that we'd had a long trip . . . but it wouldn't have made any difference!'

Phil Neville: 'After the game I think it was Roy Keane that said, "We've got to sign this player." And I think Fergie actually came out and said to Peter Kenyon, "We aren't leaving this country until we get Cristiano Ronaldo."'

The deal did not go quite like that.

Rio Ferdinand: 'And so we finished the game and we were on the coach waiting for about an hour and a half. I remember we were sitting there thinking, "What's going on?"'

Phil Neville: 'We'd heard that Real Madrid were in for him at the time, we heard that Chelsea were in for him, too, and they were at that period where they were beginning to [buy everyone] . . . Abramovich had outbid us for Robben and for Duff at the time, so they were flexing their muscles. Trying to get him was a no-brainer because he was sensational.'

Rio Ferdinand: 'They got word down to us on the coach that the manager and the chief executive were trying to broker a deal for Cristiano Ronaldo. So we weren't too pissed off about being late.'

Gary Neville: 'I think I texted my brother after the game. I think Ferguson is quoted as saying that I said we needed to sign him up, on a text to my brother, and Ferguson texted me saying, "Don't worry, it's already done."'

Roy Keane: 'We always joked with Sheasy that he'd sealed the deal by playing like a f— clown.'[16]

Phil Neville: 'I think the agreement before the game was that we were going to sign him in a year's time, but then after the match it was like, "We need this kid now."'

Ryan Giggs: 'I was at the back of the coach, and someone told me that we'd signed him.'

Phil Neville: 'In the charter flight to the UK, Ronaldo was the talk really – we were bringing home this kid.'

Aurélio Pereira: 'We'd have liked him to stay for another year. But Sporting don't have the resources to compete in a market filled with sharks.'

Carlos Freitas: 'The Sporting coach, Fernando Santos, spent pre-season preparing the team to play 4-3-3 with Ronaldo which had to go back to a 4-4-2 without him.'

Luis Lourenço: 'It was a sad and happy day for us. We lost a great player, we could've won things with him.'

Carlos Freitas: 'Cristiano was ready to leave, to take up a new challenge.'

The following morning, the front page of the Portuguese sports paper *Record* read: 'Wonderkid Ronaldo'.

In Britain, the *Guardian* branded the match a 'meaningless friendly'.

■ ■ ■

Ronaldo was one in a thousand, or even ten thousand: he left home and hit the big time. He owes Sporting so much. They stood by him and kept him at the club when sending him back to Madeira would have been an easy option. The story did not begin with a friendly against Manchester United.

But United, unlike Arsenal, had done everything necessary to prevent him slipping through their fingers.

THREE

JOINING MANCHESTER UNITED

NO LONGER CHILD'S PLAY

'He went to Manchester United for one reason.'
  'His performance against them in that friendly?'
  'That's what everyone thinks.'

Interview with Jorge Mendes in Luso Football, *2006*

Jorge Mendes took advantage of his increasingly important and trusted position within the Aveiro clan to offer personal advice. 'Your only business should be your assets,' he would repeat to the player. 'You can't trust anyone in this world, don't get involved with investments. Just think about football.'[13] His guidance soon went beyond a commercial relationship. Mendes had a soft spot for Cristiano, a youngster with emotional needs that he did not hide. He was also aware that he had a rough diamond in his charge.

From the outset he made his opinions known, usually face to face, even if they were difficult for the teenager to hear. He sought to instil a level of self-criticism that is often lacking in footballers who, together with their families, are more inclined to blame others for mistakes or defeats.

Mendes has always valued Ronaldo's intelligence and instinct. He wanted the player to attend meetings that would advance his career from the start, including those with Manchester United. 'That's why Cristiano is a complete professional at all levels,' said Mendes.[13]

But in order for a transfer to go through, somebody on one side must say, 'Let's go and see this kid.'

Everything started for Manchester United one year before that friendly. Carlos Queiroz, Sporting coach from 1994 until 1996, had received reports on Ronaldo and knew that he had to act swiftly. He suggested a special relationship with the Lisbon club using an exchange of methodology and ideas as an excuse which would subsequently make certain deals easier.

Ferguson sent Jim Ryan, former reserve-team coach and his assistant at the time, to watch Sporting in training. Just a day later, he called Sir Alex:

'I've seen a player . . . I think he's a winger, but he's playing as a central striker in the youth team. I wouldn't wait long to declare our interest. He's seventeen years old and there'll be other clubs after him.'

Jim went beyond that. Following Ferguson's advice, he subtly mentioned the Madeiran's name during a conversation with Sporting directors. Sir Alex asked him to suggest a transfer including a one-year loan deal to keep the player in Lisbon. He was not the only one with such an idea. Sporting were determined to hold out.

'We want to keep him for a few more years' was the answer Jim Ryan received.

'When Jorge spoke to me about Manchester United's interest, I was overwhelmed and couldn't believe it,' recalled Ronaldo. 'I used to watch Man Utd on television, I followed them in the days of

Cole, Yorke, Rio Ferdinand, Van Nistelrooy. The club was a dream to me. And at seventeen, I said, "Let's go!"'[15]

Yet, at the same time, the deal with Arsenal was practically sealed. But only verbally.

The evening before the Sporting v. United friendly at the Alvalade, two Sporting directors (José Bettencourt and Miguel Ribeiro Telles) had dinner with a shattered Ferguson, who had just touched down from the United States, at the Quinta da Marinha hotel in Cascais, half an hour from Lisbon. Jorge Mendes and Luis Correia, his nephew and right-hand man, later joined the dinner. It was the first meeting between the agent and the Scot.

The restaurant was half empty on that Tuesday. The diners sat at a round table with a view of the golf course. Such meals are common in the luxurious restaurant. In fact, so much so that nobody remembers that particular one today.

Manchester United were at that point desperate to sign Ronaldo and Mendes told the Sporting directors as much before the meeting: David Beckham had signed for Real Madrid in June, Juan Sebastián Verón went to Chelsea and Ronaldinho turned the club down. The discussed figure hovered around the €8 million mark, which would break the transfer record for a teenager, the €6 million Barcelona had just paid for Ricardo Quaresma. Mendes insisted that they could ask United for even more.

Mendes insisted that United had to go hell for leather if they were interested. Aside from Arsenal, Inter, Barcelona and other European giants were lying in wait. Real Madrid were, too, given that Queiroz, by now their new coach, had mentioned Ronaldo to the Spanish club board. 'At that point, everyone wanted Ronaldo to spend a year at Sporting on loan,' added Mendes.[15]

At that evening meal, it did not take long for the conversation between Sir Alex and the Sporting directors to veer towards Ronaldo's future.

'We understand young players. Look at Manchester United's history, it's made up of lots of young talent,' pointed out Ferguson.

The Sporting directors, who knew that Ronaldo had no intention of renewing his contract, rejected one of Mendes's theories: the one stating that the player was not going to be an automatic first choice in the Lisbon side the following season. In reality, Fernando Santos was preparing for the upcoming campaign with Cristiano in the team, but the doubts boosted the agent's narrative: his talent was not appreciated at Sporting; it was therefore time to seek pastures new.

Mendes knew, but did not tell Ferguson, that the directors had been instructed to negotiate and try to reach €15 million.

So, Sporting were happy to sell, United needed new blood and the agent knew all too well that such a deal would accelerate him to the forefront of football deals.

Those were the cards dealt.

After dinner, Mendes had a two-hour meeting with Ferguson in the manager's room. Alex launched the bait that the agent would use to convince his client – the decisive sentence. 'We will look after him.'

Although Mendes had to speak to Cristiano first, a gentleman's agreement was reached that evening – the agent felt the English club was perfect for the next step in Ronaldo's career. Only the figure had to be agreed. Ferguson, an expert in appearing to be in complete control of any deal, was aware that his club had the financial power to outbid anyone else, but left the final step to chief executive Peter Kenyon.

A deal was in the offing, one that would become the first of many between Mendes and Kenyon. The Englishman, who joined Chelsea one month later, would open doors to some of Mendes's other clients: Paulo Ferreira, Tiago, Maniche, Ricardo Carvalho and

José Mourinho. Kenyon and Mendes collaborate today on several footballing matters, such as advising five Jersey-based funds.

Ronaldo slept soundly and played it very cool in front of his teammates, even though he knew that Sporting had reached an agreement with the English club the night before the match. Inside, it was a different story – his future was in Manchester and that excited him.

The following day, Ferguson decided that John O'Shea would play at right-back because Gary Neville was at home nursing an injury.

Ronaldo received his first pass. He controlled the ball and looked to go on his first dribble and succeeded.

'For Christ's sake, John! Get tight to him!' shouted Ferguson from the dugout.

O'Shea shrugged his shoulders. The winger was roasting him over and over again. The defender's face reflected the pressure he was under.

It was Sir Alex's first glimpse of the Portuguese youngster live. Even today he gets emotional when remembering the moment that coaches who enjoy discovering new talents aspire to. 'A revelation. The biggest surge of excitement and anticipation I experienced in football management. The next best was from Paul Gascoigne.' Although he had been unable to sign Gazza, that was something he always regretted and told himself he would never miss such an opportunity again.

'Bloody hell, boss! He's some player, him!' said the other players in the dugout.

'It's all right, I've got him sorted.'

'As if the deal had been done ten years ago,' recalls Ferguson today.

According to kitman Alec Wylie, John O'Shea asked to be substituted: 'I'm fucked. This guy is incredible, I can't keep up with him . . .'

The manager went up to kitman Albert Morgan: 'Get up to that directors' box and get Kenyon down at half-time. We're not leaving this ground until we've got that boy signed.'

Peter Kenyon wanted to make sure and asked Ferguson, 'Is he that good?' The Scot offered medical proof: 'John O'Shea's ended up with a migraine. Get him signed!'

Kenyon warned Ferguson that Real Madrid had offered £8 million for him.

'Offer them nine, then.'

Sir Alex continued to dish out instructions during the match. He asked one of his other assistants, Mike Phelan, to keep everyone occupied after the match and to make them wait in the dressing room for an hour, or on the coach. 'We have to speak to the club. Mike, keep everyone happy.' The assistant coach gave out food and drink slightly more slowly than usual. 'Come on, Mike, we want to go home,' piped up a player. 'What's happening? Maybe they're signing the kid!' said another.

'May we speak to the boy directly?' Kenyon asked the Sporting directors. He was granted permission.

While Ferguson was having a shower after the friendly, the small coaches' dressing room filled up. Peter Kenyon, Cristiano and Jorge Mendes were there. The kitmen left the room half tidied and disappeared from the scene.

'Jorge, translate for me,' announced Ferguson, once he had reappeared, now repeating the promise that had convinced Mendes the night before. 'You won't play every week, I'm telling you that now, but you'll become a first-team player. There's no doubt in my mind about that. You're seventeen years of age [he was actually eighteen]. It'll take time for you to adjust. We'll look after you.'

A brief digression here. Carlos Freitas, who was the Lisbon-based club's sporting director, offers an alternative story. 'The first agreement was for the transfer fee to be settled with Ronaldo staying in Lisbon for another year. After the match, their priorities changed and they said, "We'll pay more, but he's coming immediately."'

Back to Ferguson:

'Next year you'll play in half the games,' repeated the United manager, a message that Mendes had already passed on to Ronaldo.

His development would be controlled, but without delay.

The transfer fee was agreed quickly. Manchester United paid well above typical market value, preventing any sort of auction in the process: £12.24 million (around €18 million) on a five-year deal which would see his salary go from €24,000 to €2 million per year.

Sporting included just one condition: if the Red Devils decided to sell the player years later, they would have a buy-back clause.

'A couple of days before we sold him to Real Madrid, we had to tell Sporting that they could have him back, but it would cost them £80 million. Not surprisingly, no cheque was forthcoming,' explained an amused Ferguson.

Another dream was coming true for the boy from Madeira. Ronaldo suggested celebrating the moment. 'Come on, Jorge. Let's celebrate!' But Mendes was tied up. 'Jorge was already on to the next thing, he couldn't, he had to go somewhere,' recalled Cristiano. 'I celebrated alone [laughter] . . . So it was a very simple celebration. I was there with a sports bag and Jorge was on the phone. I went to bed and that was it.'[15]

Just a few days later, Manchester United hired a private jet to take the player, his lawyer, mother and sister Katia to England. During the trip, Cristiano revealed to his mother that she could start looking for a house in the best neighbourhood in Madeira.

Ronaldo thought that he was going to visit the club's facilities and finalise the details of the agreement. He turned up without a suitcase, signed his contract and asked when he could go back to Lisbon. Despite what Ferguson said in the dressing room at the Alvelade, Ronaldo was convinced he was returning to Sporting, convinced that he was going to stay in Portugal for the duration of the campaign.

Ronaldo expected something like this from Sir Alex: 'So, now you go back to Lisbon, you are going to learn English and when you return to stay, everything will be stabilised and it will be great.'

Instead, as Ronaldo confirmed in the press conference that presented him to the world as a Manchester United player, he heard: 'We want you for this season.'

Cristiano did not believe it. He suddenly felt as if he had doubled in weight. The rest of the story was explained by Ferguson in the same press conference.

'But I no bring anything, no clothes!'

'Don't worry, you'll train with us tomorrow and then you'll go to Portugal to get your things.'

On that day, he also visited the training ground at Carrington, where Ronaldo bumped into John O'Shea. The full-back asked him for commission for the transfer. He deserved something after what the players considered a decisive participation. The message was translated for Cristiano and he laughed.

He was wearing a Versace sweater that made an impact, and not a good one. Black sleeves, a colourful front with red, yellow, blue and green horizontal stripes, and other fine black lines running down it; it was far from discreet. And it did not go down well in the dressing room. In fact, it was never forgotten. It reflected, in many people's eyes, the fact that there was work to do in order for Ronaldo to be considered a fully-fledged Manchester United player: appearances were crucial.

'Who is this guy?' kitman Ian Buckingham asked himself before concluding, 'This one really likes himself.'

He was not the only one with such thoughts. In fact, Paul Scholes, Rio Ferdinand and others decided that his two blond streaks in his hair, still present, had to be *executed* because they did not fit in at United.

Ferguson knew that he had to give the fans, and even the team, a prospect, and a new star after Beckham's departure. An idea came to mind.

Ferguson asked him on their way to Old Trafford which number he wanted to wear. Ronaldo told him he was happy with twenty-eight, a vacant number. Ferguson had a surprise for him: he was going to be Manchester United's new number seven.

The legendary number seven shirt sported by George Best, Steve Coppell, Bryan Robson, Eric Cantona and David Beckham. The aura around that number was all Ferguson's idea. It was a way of creating legends at the club and increasing the demands on the player wearing it. Now it was Ronaldo's turn.

On 12 August 2003, six days after the friendly at the Alvalade, United unveiled Brazilian midfielder Kleberson (who played twenty matches in two seasons) and the Portuguese teenager, who was wearing a discreet white T-shirt this time. And the blond strands.

'I wasn't at all surprised,' recalled Hugo Pina, 'when I was watching his official presentation on television and saw him with those two strands.'

Ronaldo's arrival provided new momentum at the club, which needed to be refreshed, after all the juice had been extracted from a squad that had not stopped winning trophies since the historic treble in 1999. Three league titles had been clinched since then, including the most recent one, against an Arsenal side including Patrick Vieira, Robert Pirès, Thierry Henry, Ashley Cole and Dennis Bergkamp. That was how Ferguson did his business: he made changes when he was at the very top.

The Cristiano effect could go even further and relaunch the Premier League if it came off. Everyone agreed that his potential could turn him into one of the most important players of the century and that he was on the ideal platform from which to flourish.

That is how they all tell the story of Ronaldo's transfer from Sporting to Manchester United. Yet there was a second part. There were other obstacles to be navigated and other protagonists, some of whom would find themselves in a courtroom in Portugal some years later.

■ ■ ■

The following are extracts from David Conn's article published in the *Guardian* on 19 January 2011. Formation, a football agency, filed a lawsuit against Jorge Mendes's company, GestiFute, because they thought that they had not received the commission they were due.

Conn, who had access to confidential documents, sets out several unanswered questions linked to the transfer.

Why did United pay £12.24m when it was rumoured Sporting Lisbon had been discussing a fee of €6m with other English clubs, including Arsenal?

Formation's court case against Mendes's company, GestiFute, with piles of the original documents filed in the Porto district court, reveals more details about the deal.

According to Formation's claim, Mendes told them at the time that he had received €400,000 from United for the Ronaldo deal. Then United reported in their 2004 accounts that they had paid £1.129 million (€1.5 million) to agents for the transfer. The Football Association, through which clubs must pay all agents' fees, is understood to have stated, following court orders that disclosed the detail, that United did indeed pay 'another agent' – not Mendes – £1 million.

That other agent was Giovanni Branchini, who had not been involved in the negotiations.

What role Branchini performed to merit being paid remains unanswered . . .

The court claim alleges that Mendes did not pay Formation 50 per cent of that €400,000 fee, as it had been agreed between them and as they had equally shared the fees of previous deals. Instead he offered £80,000 to the agency.

The agency says it accepted that figure, substantially less than it was entitled to, to preserve the relationship with Mendes, who had signed up most of the Portuguese internationals playing their way to prominence . . . The relationship between the two agencies broke down terminally after the arrival of José Mourinho at Chelsea and the signing of several Portuguese players through Mendes, for which Formation received no fees . . .

The issue became even more complicated when the Football Association revealed that, according to the figures, Mendes had not received €400,000 as he had said, but €150,000 instead.

Nobody from GestiFute called David Conn to contradict a single one of his statements.

In the end, both companies reached an out-of-court agreement. GestiFute paid Formation a substantial sum.

■ ■ ■

Only four days had passed since Ronaldo's unveiling and ten since the friendly against Sporting when Manchester United opened their Premier League campaign against Bolton Wanderers in front of 67,000 supporters at Old Trafford.

Ronaldo thought he was going to finally be able to return to Lisbon to pick up his belongings on that weekend. But Ferguson informed him on the Friday, to his surprise, that he was going to be in the squad for the Bolton game.

The starting line-up was: Tim Howard; Phil Neville, Rio Ferdinand, Mikael Silvestre, Quinton Fortune; Nicky Butt, Roy Keane, Ryan Giggs; Ole Gunnar Solskjær and Ruud Van Nistelrooy.

It was the Bolton side with Iván Campo, Jay-Jay Okocha and Kevin Nolan.

Sixty-one minutes had gone by with the home side enjoying a slender 1–0 lead. Sam Allardyce's troops had not given up the ghost.

'Warm up.'

Ferguson's order set Cristiano's heart racing. The fans applauded the new arrival with greater expectation than usual for someone so young. The Manchester United TV subscribers who had watched the friendly against Sporting had already been waxing lyrical over the Portuguese star.

Fans, and the club, wanted to believe the new arrival could relegate Beckham's departure to the back of everyone's minds.

A tall, thin boy got ready to come on; his ankles were strapped up and he still had those two blond strands.

'I had no idea who he was,' recalled Allardyce.

He was going to play in attack, down the right, and replaced Nicky Butt.

His first touch was decent. It gave him confidence.

The Ronaldo who took to the pitch was the continuation of the one in the friendly against United. Direct, different, attacking, brave, confident. He only looked for goal. He targeted full-back Nicky Hunt and centre-back Ricardo Gardner, who were gradually dropping deeper and deeper.

The noise of the crowd rocketed in expectation whenever he received the ball.

Heads were turning in the press box with journalists on the edges of their seats, knowing that their match reports were about to take on a new perspective.

United notched three goals in the final half-hour with Ronaldo involved in the build-up and winning his side a penalty that Van Nistelrooy failed to convert.

Nobody talked about the departed David Beckham, nor Ryan Giggs's goals. Ronaldo scooped the man of the match award, of course.

The game ended, but Ronaldo could have played another full one from the start.

'Marvellous,' said Ferguson after the match. 'He's a level above the rest,' added Allardyce.

Ronaldo made his first-team debut for Sporting at seventeen and for Manchester United at eighteen. Four days later he would take his international bow at senior level under Luiz Felipe Scolari in a friendly against Kazakhstan.

Everything was going very fast.

The matches against Manchester United in Lisbon and Bolton created false expectations, however.

In fact, his team-mates were not yet convinced that his style fitted in with that of the Premier League.

And in a sense they were right – the next steps for him were all downhill.

■ ■ ■

If Ronaldo could do that in half an hour, what would he not be able to do over an entire match? And every week. We will win the league again. And the Champions League. The standard supporter's logic was applied to the Portuguese.

Two matches later, Ferguson played him from the start in a home clash against Wolves. Former United full-back Denis Irwin did not give him an inch, putting pressure on the youngster when he received the ball and preventing him from turning. He was withdrawn after sixty-seven minutes. He had played badly. The travelling supporters sang 'He's not the real Ronaldo' and 'What a waste of money!'

Cristiano's footballing education had just begun.

Leicester City striker James Scowcroft told how his coach Micky Adams instructed him to 'let Ronaldo know what English football is all about'. A 'Welcome to the Premier League' tackle, or something along those lines.

In England, with that strange mindset that could partly explain why English football seems to languish when compared with that of other more progressive footballing nations, crunching tackles are accepted as a sign of manliness.

'I tried to do what the gaffer asked,' admitted Scowcroft, 'but I looked over my shoulder and Ronaldo was twenty yards ahead of me.'

Maybe Leicester City did not manage to give Ronaldo the welcome they so desired, but the rest of the Premier League defences went to great lengths to do so. 'Atlas would've gone down under the challenges he received at Charlton,' moaned Ferguson after a visit to south London. It was rough treatment of the highest calibre.

And Ronaldo reacted badly.

His complaints, exaggerated falls and dives painted the picture of a frustrated player. Emotional. Foreign. He earned the type of reputation that destroys careers.

His challenge was enormous if he wanted to survive in the Premier League. Not only did he have to avoid violent tackles, but he had to do even more.

He had to change his physique and football style.

That's all.

■ ■ ■

Inside every dressing room roles are clearly defined. The manager's assistants, for instance, are there to make life easier for the players.

Ferguson had one at Carrington who, instead of going to the players and finding out what they needed, waited for them at the gym. Quiet. Sitting on his chair. Patient.

When Ronaldo came across him, he looked him in the eye and said, 'I want to be the best player in the world and you're going to help me.'

■ ■ ■

Ronaldo, with his funny broken English, hung around with the group of Spanish-speaking players (Quinton Fortune, Diego Forlán and Ruud Van Nistelrooy with whom he enjoyed a positive initial relationship; and later goalkeeper Ricardo, fitness coach Valter di Salvo, Gerard Piqué and Gabriel Heinze), but he did not need to say much.

They all 'got' him straight away.

'He walked with his chest out. He was so confident. His eyes looking straight into yours,' recalled Phil Neville. Many youngsters had passed through that dressing room without daring so much as to look up at Roy Keane, Gary Neville or Ryan Giggs. 'Bloody hell, this lad,' thought Neville when he saw how Ronaldo looked him straight in the eye. 'I likened him to Cantona. Cristiano arrived here saying, "This isn't big, this is just where I belong."'

Of course, such behaviour comes at a cost. You cannot emerge from it unharmed.

The new boys usually dress discreetly, for example. Not Ronaldo. His dress sense, with very visible branding, did not seem to fit in.

'He'd come into training dressed as if he was going on a night out.'

'He dressed as though in the next ten minutes, he might either meet the prime minister or meet his future wife.'

The jokes were flooding in from day one. Incessantly.

'He would just wear the tightest clothes. Armani or whatever, and the jeans were just the tightest ever. It was probably the style in Portugal. The style he had! We'd say to him, "Any room down there in that area?"' explained Fortune.

'Ronnie, you need to look at yourself.'

They would take the mickey out of his hair and shoes. His almost see-through T-shirts. His sunglasses. His teeth and skin. He quickly decided to have some extensive orthodontic work done on his teeth and use skin-care products.

'He surely overdressed for training,' revealed Gary Neville. 'But then . . . I look back now and think: "Those were high standards." As a young boy, I always remember the youth coach Eric Harrison saying that we represented Manchester United whatever we did, and that we should always be smart, always wash our hair, always look clean-shaven. I never really carried it through to that extent, but Cristiano always looked immaculate, always wanted to have very clean boots, perfect training kit, perfect hair, the best clothes even into training.'

Then there was the mirror episode . . . Ah, yes, the mirror. More on that later.

Ronaldo would get vexed. The worst thing you can do in such a situation. 'We got a reaction from him, so we kept doing it,' recalled Fortune. 'If he'd just ignored us, I think we would've stopped.'

'Ronnie – someone would say – we have heard you're just keeping that shirt warm for David Beckham. And you can use his locker till he comes back. He's not going to be happy when he comes back.'

And if he attempted a comeback, Fortune, Rio or whoever would come out with, 'Speak to me when you've played in the World Cup', to which the rest of the players would respond with an 'Ahhh, Ronnie, he's killed you, he's killed you!'

Typical dressing-room banter.

'Looking back, I think it was a very unforgiving changing room; you had to be tough to get through it,' admitted Gary Neville. 'I honestly think it was the making of him.'

Magical as his play may have been, that was certainly not reflected in how he was treated in the dressing room.

. . .

A little observation.

When it came to his kit, he never demanded anything different.

'Whatever kit was out was fine. He would put on his cotton socks for training and off he went,' recalled kitman Ian Buckingham.

'Is this my training kit? This is what I will wear then.'

Once on the pitch, the magic could not be found in what was worn.

. . .

Ah. And the blond strands, a source of ribbing from day one, remained in place for two more weeks, which can be considered a little triumph for the Portuguese considering the flak he endured. Scholes and Ferdinand lost that battle.

. . .

'Every match he runs through the same routine,' revealed Wayne Rooney. 'The kit goes on, the boots go on. Not long after, Ronnie turns to his reflection and stares, psyching himself up for the game. If there's one person with a bigger self-belief than Ronaldo, I haven't met him yet.'

Good time to tell the mirror story.

When he arrived, Cristiano just so happened to choose the locker that was opposite a mirror, a choice that has been discussed since that day.

Or, according to some, it was he who put it there. 'He put up a two-metre mirror,' recalled Phil Neville. 'He was the first one to do something like that at Manchester United.'

Was that really what happened?

Quinton Fortune tells it differently: 'We even put a mirror in his locker so he could have a look at himself.'

Really? Was it down to the players?

'All I know,' said Gary Neville, 'is one, he had a locker; two, there just happened to be a mirror there on the column around the corner opposite where he got changed; and three, he liked it.'

Kitman Alec Wylie, one of those masters of small details, has the last word.

'The old dressing room was very small and we had it rejigged at one point. There was only one mirror in the bathroom, so Stu, the maintenance lad, put a full-length mirror in there. Cristiano, when the players returned to the refurbished changing room, had to have that locker. Since then he couldn't walk past it without checking himself out.'

Roy Keane described Ronaldo in his book as 'good-looking and he knew it. He was vain in that sense – at the mirror. He was a big lad, a big unit. I'd think, "Good on yeh." Looking at some of the other lads in front of the mirror, I'd think, "Yeh f****** nugget." But Ronaldo had an innocence to him, and a niceness. I don't think he ever slackened off, or that he was ever more worried about the mirror than his game. I always felt that football was his love.'[16]

There was definitely vanity involved in the decision to choose that locker.

The most fascinating interpretation of his relationship with the mirror will be provided later on by someone who delves much deeper.

■ ■ ■

He was not fazed if it was Roy Keane, Giggsy or Scholesy.

He would try his tricks on all of them.

At the same time, however, his obsession with impressing would take him down dead ends. He wanted to do more stepovers than his opponents, more nutmegs, and dribble past as many opposing players as possible. Playing with the team and scoring goals took on secondary importance at times.

He wanted to, first of all, most of all, earn his place and the admiration of his team-mates.

'At the beginning he would say "I pass you" which is probably like him saying, "I'm the best,"' revealed Quinton Fortune. 'He'd say it with the face you see when he scores and points at himself like he's saying, "I'm Ronaldo." That one.'

If somebody balanced the ball on the back of his neck, Cristiano would repeat it the following day with some variation, as if to say, 'Look, I've done it!' 'He'd have practised for days,' recalled Fortune. 'What's wrong with this guy, he's obsessed' was the reaction at Carrington.

Ronaldo is, taking one of Pep Guardiola's phrases, an 'ideas thief'. He likes to copy a trick that he sees in the dressing room, on television or on YouTube. He devotes hours to it and ends up perfecting it, if not improving it.

'Players, like, so confident, are tested in the first three months,' stated Phil Neville. One day Scholesy went in for a criminal tackle. The following day it was Keane. That was the way to teach him how to choose his one-on-ones carefully and when it was time to dribble. Above all, they had to put paid to that arrogant attitude.

'I put him to the test,' continued Phil Neville. 'He did have that little bit of "You know I can take the mickey out of you, so I'm going to do it once, I'm going to do it twice, I'm going to do it three times." Bang. Gary would go for him, so would Gabriel Heinze . . .

I think he got kicked so many times, but never once did he come in after training sulking.'

Some believe that those unwritten rules are the way in which average players can survive at Manchester United – by slaughtering any ounce of talent. In fact, it can certainly be interpreted as a defence mechanism against a more talented player, but it is also a way of understanding football. If it is 0–0, you cannot do these gratuitous tricks. If it is 1–0, you cannot do these gratuitous tricks. If it is 3–0 or 5–0, you cannot do these gratuitous tricks. At United, you always have to think about the most efficient way to kill off the opposition.

'We were winning 4–0, and I remember chasing after him at Old Trafford and screaming at him, "You don't do that." He'll remember it. He tried to flick it or dink it for a goal, rather than just finishing it in the corner and winning 5–0,' said Gary Neville. Previously, that is what Bryan Robson, Steve Bruce, Roy Keane, Gary Pallister and Peter Schmeichel taught the former right-back.

'The club has a working-class philosophy and the city has that feel to it,' stated Ferguson's assistant Mike Phelan. 'Get up and get at them, working hard. Skills? Yeah, now and again, but it's more brute force.'

As Ronaldo was still learning how to release the ball at the right time, those suffering the most at United were the forwards. Especially one in particular, none other than the team's top scorer.

■ ■ ■

There is no need to dwell further on the club's particular culture, but I would like to make the following observation.

In Portugal, British influence is widespread, but its inhabitants are mainly Catholic. This divergence of the two cultures accentuates fundamental differences between the British psyche and that of Catholic Europe, which, if you allow me, will eventually take us to football, where similar divergences exist.

The difference in moral psychology between Catholics and Protestants is too complex to enter into here. But it can be generally said that there is a more laissez-faire attitude to morality among European Catholics than the more rigorous British Protestant ethos allows. There are reasons for that.

The English Protestant Reformation differed from its European counterpart in that it was essentially political rather than theological. The newly formed Anglican Church embraced the rigorous theology of German Lutherism with its focus on hard work, strong ethics and a rigid moral psychology based on Holy Scripture.

By the end of the sixteenth century, Britain was an island at war with Catholic Europe. The Catholic Church would ultimately lose the battle for spiritual and papal hegemony and England forged ahead with the creation of a very distinct church of her own, the Anglican Church.

What followed in England and later the United Kingdom was four centuries of deepening hostility and suspicion of all things Roman, i.e. Catholic Europe.

The rigorous doctrine of hard work, loyalty to the Crown, family values and national superiority would reach its zenith during the Victorian age when, at the apex of its imperial might, the Queen Empress and Head of the Church of England stood as a living symbol that God was clearly an Englishman and the English, by extension, were His chosen people. How else to explain such global power? British superiority and a fondness for seeing British values as the only ones that mattered had become well and truly entrenched in the British character.

One more thing before we bring this to football. The Protestant ethic is rigorously legalistic. Rules are there to be obeyed. Two millennia of Catholic moral exactitude led to a mentality that sought to bend the rules while staying within the parameters of salvation. There was always confession to wipe the slate clean. Natives of Catholic countries don't generally care too much about rules. What they care about is how to circumvent them without being caught. Which is why corruption in those countries, mine included, is part of their culture.

I have the impression that plenty of this, as general and even a touch simplistic as it might be, also applies to football.

That sense of British values being superior to those of other nations is never more apparent than when lack of fair play, by British standards, i.e feigning injury, diving, etc., is held up as an example of the perfidy of an entire nation.

Yes, such tactics as diving, etc., are used by English players but they are usually explained as being a result of either 'too much foreign influence' or, the best one, bad sportsmanship!

On the other hand, a very different attitude to rules explains why in Catholic countries players too often try to con the referee and celebrate if they get away with it. When a player dives in the box, the defenders run to the referee to tell him not to be deceived by that. In England, they first direct their anger towards the offender as if to say, how could you do that? Why bend the rules that way?

This is only the tip of a huge cultural iceberg that may go part of the way to explaining why Spanish or Portuguese people on the one hand and English on the other will not always agree on what makes a good game, or which players deserve the most praise. Let's talk it over with a pint next time we meet in a pub or at one of the events that will follow the publication of this book.

■ ■ ■

We were saying that instead of dribbling and crossing, Ronaldo would fool around. The man making a run into the area, that precise exercise of deception, geometry and speed, was starting to get pissed off.

'I can't play with this guy. He doesn't even cross the ball,' Ruud Van Nistelrooy would often shout in training. 'I can't make my runs because he's not going to cross the ball.'

On a few occasions Rio Ferdinand heard the Dutch striker say that he did not want to play with Ronaldo again.

'I think Ruud was used to David [Beckham] crossing the ball every time he had it,' explained Edwin van der Sar. 'David didn't have pace to dribble and beat opponents, so he had to do something else. Ronnie had the pace and the tricks.'

Cristiano was a winger with a striker's soul. Or a striker exiled to the wing.

There was something else in that conflict, a more human element. Van Nistelrooy, who scored 150 goals in five seasons at the club, was United's big star when Cristiano arrived. All of a sudden, a thin, adolescent Portuguese trickster was winning over supporters.

The situation would only get worse. 'They had a couple of arguments,' revealed Ferdinand. 'Ruud Van Nistelrooy kicked him one time and after that I kicked Ruud just to protect Ronnie a little bit and Ruud swung a punch at me and he missed.'

That incident took place just before the final match of the 2005–06 campaign against Charlton. Cristiano started while Van Nistelrooy did not make the squad. The Dutchman would never play for the club again.

■ ■ ■

Rio Ferdinand spent eighteen months giving Cristiano the same message before every match: 'Goals and assists!'

Other players reminded him that he had to stay on his feet as his dives were costing the team points. It is true that all sorts of tackles were flying in on him, but his theatrics were going against the Portuguese. Ferguson had to speak to him frankly: 'Look, we didn't get a penalty and we didn't get any fouls at Leeds because every time you went down, you weren't getting the fouls because referees thought you dived and went down too easily. In the next game at Charlton, every time you touched the ball, the crowd would boo and that can have an effect on the away team. You're going down too easily!'

'He had major difficulties because he wasn't strong enough; he used to go down a lot. I don't think he had at that point the strength to perform for ninety minutes,' suggested Phil Neville. 'I'm not so sure that he had the understanding of how to play in a team, to get back into shape and sacrifice himself. His specialness meant that the team had to evolve around him, more than him around the team, but firstly he had to earn that.'

Although he could play on both wings, Ferguson always played him in front of Gary Neville so that the veteran could talk, cajole and manage him. 'When we used to play against Arsenal,' Phil Neville reminisced, 'it was imperative that Ronaldo got back into shape. They had Pirès on one side, Ljungberg on the other, we weren't allowed to have any gaps and in training leading up to the game, the focus was probably on him, particularly in the early years, to keep his shape.'

But he would often forget his responsibilities. During his inaugural season at the club, his manager was hard on him.

In Ronaldo's first match back on home soil since signing for Manchester United, a Champions League game against Benfica, Ferguson could not contain himself any longer. Things had not gone to plan as the Portuguese team ran out 1–0 winners in Lisbon. The winger, who spent the game trying to prove why he was a Premier League player, had a bad day at the office.

Ferguson showed no pity.

'Who do you think you are? Trying to play by yourself? You'll never be a player if you do this!'

Ronaldo began to cry.

The other players left him be. 'He needed to learn,' said Ferdinand. 'That was a message from the team, not just from Ferguson: everyone thought he needed to learn.'

After the telling-off and a few tears, the Portuguese's reaction was the same as always: keep working in training to improve.

Predictably, the group responded by winding him up. Quinton Fortune and Rio Ferdinand reminded him of the incident a few weeks later.

'He's crying in the changing room again!'

'Fuck off! What are you talking about?'

'Cry-baby, cry-baby!'

Ferguson knew that after the stick, he had to apply the carrot – it was the best treatment for the special talent of the boy. 'Every now and again, the manager would ask him in front of the squad, "Why did you dribble rather than cross?"' recalled Alec Wylie. 'He'd even shout at him sometimes, but nothing too heavy. But then when he'd finished his rant, he'd go and sit next to him to explain why he'd had a go at him. "Don't take it badly, but you need to know that English football is different."'

Ferguson had never treated any other player with the same respect and affection as he did Ronaldo.

■ ■ ■

Cristiano stayed in a hotel after touching down in Manchester, but soon rented a house where his mother and siblings would stay for extended periods of time.

'But he never stopped moaning about the weather,' Alec Wylie remembered fondly. 'Every day he would say, "The sun never shines here. It's rubbish. Shit weather. Shit weather. Shit weather," and that went on for six years. Then we were playing Porto one year in the Champions League, and we flew into Portugal and it rained non-stop, so that's all he got: "Shit weather. Shit weather. Shit weather." He just said: "Ah, no, it's not Lisbon.'"

'One wintertime we took a flight from Manchester to Newcastle at something like two o'clock in the afternoon,' recalled Mike Phelan. 'It was light in Manchester. We landed in Newcastle and it was dark. Straight away, I remember Cristiano saying: "Where's all the light gone? Who turned off the lights?"'

'I liked the lad straight away,' Keane said in his book. 'He had a nice presence about him, and a good attitude . . . After the first few days, watching him train, my reaction was, "This lad is going to be one of the world's greatest players." I didn't say it publicly, because I'd always be wary of building up a player too early – or knocking him down . . . The shape, the body language – they were there. A bit of arrogance, too . . . He was immediately one of the hardest working players at United.'[16]

There was even growing tolerance for his perfectionist approach to fashion. 'David Beckham was like that,' Gary Neville recalled. 'But even David Beckham would have dress-down days. Andy Cole was an immaculate dresser, Ryan Giggs was very sharp, but Cristiano, every day was like perfection. He had to have everything in line, everything had to match.'

Next in the conversation, Gary touched on a fascinating element: 'You could see earlier on that Ronaldo was like Beckham – they both wanted to go beyond football. They were big players, but they need to reach beyond that as well. As if football was not enough for them.'

Ronaldo gradually found new allies over time such as Carlos Queiroz who returned to be Ferguson's assistant during the player's second season at the club. 'Carlos used to go crazy at some of the tackles on him,' revealed Phil Neville. 'But I think Sir Alex was pulling Carlos back a bit because he thought this might be good for the boy.'

Cristiano spent three years getting down to the nitty-gritty with Italian fitness coach Valter di Salvo, who saw a kind of 'perfect storm' effect in the player's development: 'We're all conditioned by our surroundings, by the people we live with and the people that help us down our paths. Many things have to coincide in order to bring out the best in us, details that may not appear significant individually.'

Di Salvo referred to how 'Manchester United is the ideal place for someone like Ronaldo, and Ferguson is the ideal manager, because of his experience and the human relationships he develops with his players: he gets the best out of the boys and creates a perfect structure around them, a type of bubble so that the player can develop without fear and excessive pressure'.

'Ferguson has two different sides and both have helped me become what I am today,' Cristiano admitted. 'I learnt from him every day and knew that no matter how much I improved, he could always teach me new things. Every piece of advice that he's given me has made me a better person. He was like a second father to me from the day when I arrived in Manchester. I don't just respect him, I feel the same affection towards him that a son feels towards his father.'[17]

Sir Alex came across countless rough diamonds during his managerial career, but never demonstrated as much patience with the others as he did with Ronaldo. Although 'everything comes down to business' for the Scot, it will never be known if his efforts to win Ronaldo over were due to his huge potential or simply a genuine connection that certainly exists between the two.

'Sir Alex talks to players a lot,' Phil Neville explained. 'If you look at video footage of Ferguson talking to Ronaldo, he's always got his arm around him.' In return, Cristiano gave him his 'heart and soul' (just like the player once stated himself), total daily commitment.

Ferguson discovered that players who are used to a sunny climate suffer hugely when it is taken away from them. He was also aware of the difficulties foreigners can experience when living in the United Kingdom, and how tough the competition is, which is why he decided to give Ronaldo an occasional week off to return home. The pair of them would make up stories about his fitness or take advantage of suspensions to give Ronaldo time to recharge his batteries.

As Pep Guardiola said, every player wants to feel special and wants the coach to love them. Even more than the others, if possible. That is what Sir Alex offered.

'Everyone was looking around and asking, "Why has he got a break?" "Easy, tiger, you'll get a break later on,"' Mike Phelan revealed.

'Whatever Ronnie wanted, Ronnie got,' stated Quinton Fortune. 'The manager would slow things down just to protect Ronnie, not to fly too much into tackles, and just to give him that freedom and confidence that he already had.'

'Ronnie was eventually the only player who the coach told, "You don't need to go back to your position, stay up front and see what the opposition does,"' revealed Ole Gunnar Solskjær, who spent eleven years at the club and was close to Ferguson.

The other players had to accept that Ronaldo was different. 'What's the point of having a go at them if they're that good?' Ryan Giggs asked himself. 'It could be frustrating for the rest of us, if you do have a bad game or if you don't lay it off if you were in the same situation, you would get the hairdryer off Sir Alex.'

The squad would make jokes about the special relationship with a mixture of laughter and envy: 'He's your dad; he's your dad!'

Given the absence of a father figure, Ronaldo has lacked a role model. As a result, he has devoted his life to finding one. Authority figures such as Ferguson and Jorge Mendes have filled the gap.

That lack of paternal love was also a magnet that attracted coaches to him. 'He had that boyishness where you wanted to love him, help him and bring him through,' Mike Phelan observed.

Meanwhile, Dinis preferred not to be part of that world and hardly travelled to Manchester. Whenever he did go to the United Kingdom, he was always delighted to get home to Madeira.

■ ■ ■

Ferguson had left Ronaldo on the bench for a meaningless match against West Ham. The player, half smiling, asked the manager if he had heard the new chant the fans had for him. Fergie knew the usual one: 'He plays on the left, he plays on the right, the boy Ronaldo . . . lalala.' The new one was a variation of it: 'He plays on the bench, he plays on the bench . . .' Sir Alex burst out laughing.

Nobody spoke to Ferguson that way. Especially a recent arrival.

'He caught the manager out brilliantly one day,' John O'Shea revealed. 'This is before the game. I think he was hiding under a treatment table, and he'd do a thing with the ball where he'd roll it towards you, so you'd go to stop it with your foot or your hand, but then he'd stop it himself before you got to it. He got a bit of sticky tape, so he was able to roll it a certain way towards the manager, and obviously the manager's gone to pick it up. But next thing, he pops out from under the treatment table to take the ball back, just as the manager's nearly falling over. The whole place erupted, and that was just one of many. That one stood out particularly, because of how angry the manager got for a few minutes, even though he soon realised it was a bit of banter.'

■ ■ ■

In any case, his progress was barely noticeable during his first season. Doubts remained.

'There was a doubt in my mind,' admitted Ryan Giggs. 'I would ask myself, "Is he going to be the real deal?" It was because of the inconsistency, his wrong decisions and his insistence on trying to do too much.'

■ ■ ■

Ronaldo kept working hard in the meantime.

'He has his parents to thank,' Valter di Salvo said. 'They've given him fast-twitch muscle fibres. You can't get that from training alone. He's developed his physique as an athlete, rather than a normal footballer.'

'He has outstanding physical, technical and tactical ability, combined with his mental strength. They are the four conditions that make him unique,' concluded Di Salvo. Ronaldo is powerful when it comes to acceleration thanks in part to the strength in his lower body. He is very precise, combining technical moves at high speed, another product of both hours on the training ground and his genes.

There are thousands of examples of his efforts to shape his own body and destiny. It is not true that he does 3,000 sit-ups every day, but what follows is.

Ronaldo would ask Alec Wylie for ten balls. John Campbell, another kitman who did not like people diverging from the script, would shout at him, 'Where the fuck are you going now?'

'To practise free-kicks,' Ronaldo would answer.

'Fuck it,' was John's reply; he wanted to take all the kits to the laundry room. 'Fucking hell, Ronnie!'

'I won't be long. John, I'm going to be the best player in the world. I need to do this.'

'At the end of training he'd pull me to one side so he could take free-kicks,' explained Edwin van der Sar. '"No, take Tomasz [Kuszczak] or something," and he'd just say, "No, I'm taking you; I want to score against the best." "But Ronnie, you never score against me!" "You wait, I'll score, I'll score!"'

'Of course, he scored a few against me, with his famous free-kicks swerving around,' added Van der Sar. 'After I'd ask, "Ronnie, can you give me a couple for crosses, or something?" Then he was less energetic, that bored him!'

'I was accused of not training hard and being injured all the time,' French striker Louis Saha recalled. 'So I started working really hard, the hardest I've ever worked to make sure nobody complained. Then I tried to do stuff that Ronaldo did, but I couldn't follow him. He would set up his own training exercises so he would run side to side on the pitch, or a hundred metres separated by cones and he would just dribble, accelerate and dribble cone by cone, and then he would rest for a few seconds and do it again. Acceleration is the thing that kills you in football, you do it once and that's it, but he did it one way and then the other way three or four times – it's impossible for anyone else to do that.'

But Ronaldo was not born knowing it all, he needed guidance to reach his objectives.

■ ■ ■

'I'm going to be the best in the world and you're going to help me.'

That is what Cristiano Ronaldo told Mike Clegg.

The Portuguese arrived, quickly grasped where he was (or at least where the people that could help him develop were) and came across an obsessed fitness coach. Another eager beaver.

Mike is not a football man and never will be. He prefers be considered a scholar of the human body and its limitations.

Two of his sons, coached by him, have embarked on weightlifting careers. In 2000 he joined the club where his two other sons were coming through. They were not especially talented, but stood out because of their physical condition, which they had developed by working with their father at a gym in Ashton-under-Lyne, a market town near Manchester. One of them (Michael) even broke into the first-team after impressing Ferguson with his imposing physical presence.

Mike Clegg ended up becoming the power development coach, a title that did not actually say much. He was given carte blanche to improve player output. And he did manage to do it: he prolonged Roy Keane's career and prepared Ryan Giggs to continue playing until the age of forty.

Any attempt to try to explain what Mike thinks and his work with Ronaldo in the form of a report would not do him justice. So take a seat in that chair in the middle of the office Mike has in his gym. Dozens of photos of athletes adorn the walls of the room. There is also a table covered in papers and technical books on fitness training. Mike makes himself comfortable on the other side of it. And talks in a relaxed manner as he looks you straight in the eye.

I was the power development coach at Manchester United when Cristiano arrived. Briefly speaking, I had to improve players' speed and power.

When a new player comes in, he gets introduced to the group, to the assistants, and off to training. Football is the centre point, of course. But then, there are the peripheral things going around it. This is where Ronaldo was very clever; he wanted to understand everything – not just the main course, also the starters, the salads and the condiments.

Everybody at clubs wants to have an office, including sports scientists; I don't have one, I have a gym, I have a chair. That is where you will find me.

When he arrived, he looked around and one day he came to the gym when I was on my own. We sat and chatted. He told me a little bit about his history, and that he was a very determined individual. His English was just OK.

I always remember he had a go at some of the lads. They used to say, 'You should speak English when you're in England,' and he used to reply, 'You English pigs, you can only speak in one language.'

They would also take the mickey out of his clothing and he would say, 'I don't care, I'm going to be the best player in the world, laugh all you want.'

There was a spark to him that you rarely find.

So anyway, he came in to see me.

He looked me in the eye and said, 'I'm going to be the best. Now I need you to help me.'

A lot of people say that, but . . .

He wanted to know what I did, he wanted to tell me what he wanted to do. Many people do that and then don't carry it through. I could tell he was different.

Cristiano, only eighteen, had looked at what everybody else was doing and then said, 'I've got to do more, I've got to do it better and I've got to do it more often', and that was his philosophy.

That's what makes him so magical.

I rubbed my hands. 'Let's do it,' I said.

I realised that I was going to be working with a perfect physical specimen. His muscle structure, body fat, size, resistance, flexibility, power, strength . . . He had the perfect balance.

I used to arrive at nine o'clock every morning. He would probably get in at that time or just before and prepare for his training, whether it be a massage or rub. Then he'd come to the gym.

Next, we would spend about twenty to twenty-five minutes with the latest thing we were trying.

After he would join the team to do some bike or stretching for another twenty to twenty-five minutes.

They would all then go outside and play boxes, which is very, very important. People don't realise how important that bit was. And obviously the football training session would start with the coaches, where they might dribble around cones or whatever. At the end, he would often stay for some shooting practice. Then everybody goes in.

Not him.

Have you been to Carrington? There is a hill at the back of where the training is, so he'd go there and practise his skills. He wanted to be on his own because you don't want people looking at you when you're practising them. An audience interferes when you are learning new abilities.

A few days later, he would start bringing that skill into the training session, and the development of that skill continues, now in front of damn good players. Ultimately he'll play it in a game. Which one? Not in a big match against a Chelsea or an Arsenal, he used it in a lower game against, say, Derby County or Bolton. He knew that if he made a mistake as he was trying it, the crowd would get at him. And he certainly got absolutely taunted at times by fans, and probably managers and coaches too. A stadium is a dangerous place to make mistakes, but that didn't worry him because he was developing his skills for the future.

So he'd come and see me regularly in the gym and we'd work on whatever it was, speed or power or boxing or whatever it needed to be.

It started with Roy Keane who did boxing training and with Ryan Giggs who did everything. Prior to Cristiano, Giggs was the man. Cristiano really didn't want to do boxing, but it was part of what we did and he thought, 'Other people are using it like Ryan Giggs so I'm going to try it.' And he did. I think I upset Ryan because I said Cristiano was the one that wanted it more than anyone else, and was willing to try more than anybody else, and that he even actually put more time in than Ryan.

He liked individual sessions, but sometimes asked someone else to train with him. For the challenge of beating him.

We would experiment. We would make a note of what he needed, what worked and ditch what was not needed.

Then he'd finally go home.

He was one of the first to have a cook in his house. In the main he'd go there to have his food and then he'd go to bed to have his siesta. Then he would get up and go in his pool. After the swimming, some more stretching, then he'd have another meal, and in the evening he would go out for a few meals with friends, he didn't drink.

He gave out a lot to a lot of people, always surrounded by people close to him. Usually friends and family from Madeira. He was never like, 'It's all me, me, me.' He had Nani and Anderson living with him at one time. He created his own world around him to have fun and release the tension and efforts of the day-to-day.

And then he would go to bed. No television in the bedroom to avoid distractions.

Then the next morning he got up again. And it all unfolds, day after day, week after week, month after month.

It's all about the brain, that is the thing that controls everything – the mentality, the cognitive and visual learning, the emotion.

That, the emotion, is so, so important in top-line sport. I don't think people realise that.

Cristiano is obsessive. Very, very obsessive. Me, too. We had that in common. As well as our desire to construct a body that would improve his performance on the pitch.

I don't think he won all the time. He lost many battles. It wasn't a constant, linear path to the top. And losing them is good.

What is important is that he has it all planned in his mind. What he needs to do and how he needs to do it. That's why he's a genius. I have never met a player like him.

Does he love football? He loves the battle. He loves that journey. I mean everyone wants to be at the top, but they forget the real fun is the journey to get there.

It's like an artist. If they paint a beautiful picture, it starts off very bland but you've got to keep at it, keep on at it, and eventually you would paint a perfect picture.

Of course, he wants to be a great player and, yes, of course he wants to be very successful. But he wants to have fun along the way. He might seem like he isn't having as much fun as other people because of the pressure he puts himself under, but everything is worthwhile when you can say at the end, 'Yeah! I did it!'

That's why he celebrates as he does. People don't realise what's gone into that achievement. It's as if he's chiselled out of a piece of marble. I can understand him feeling so proud of himself because, as he would say, 'I worked damned hard for that.'

The vain bit is part of the plan. He has to see himself. If you think about practising, it's hard to see what you're doing, but the more you introduce yourself to yourself, the better your image of yourself becomes, as well as the thing you're actually creating. You need a mirror.

Vision is actually the thing that leads the brain more than anything else. Every time he looked at himself in the mirror, I don't think he said, 'Look what a beautiful guy I am.' He's probably saying, 'Look at that bloody pimple there' or 'I'm getting fat, what's my diet like?' Or, 'I'm not sure I trained hard enough yesterday.' He'll be thinking what he has to do next.

Maybe at first he put too much emphasis in the skills, but soon it became clear that scoring goals was the most important thing for him. Yes, he wanted to play football, do well for the team, but he was about scoring goals. Everything was about losing that player, getting into space, and getting the ball in that net. That is what he really wanted.

Of course, he had dark days. He only told me what he wanted to tell me. I never asked questions. You could see that in himself when he was a bit worried. Sometimes it felt like you were building Lego and a piece in there was disrupting everything.

There were times when he became very, very frustrated, when things weren't going his way and people were getting on his back because we weren't winning or he would fall over and people would criticise him. I'm sure the manager was one of them. And that's really depressing because he knew how hard he was working, but people didn't understand the plan. He understood the plan, I understood the plan, but nobody else did.

I was fortunate to be there during the early days, the eighteen to twenty-three period is massive and I was there with him every day, sharing little conversations, the things that upset him or annoy him, things that make him feel great. You could see his progression coming. Nobody could stop him.

One day he left the club.

I was left with a heap of information about his staggering progress. I had been collaborating on a daily basis with the best player in the world, helping him develop. There had been a new aim every day, a new challenge accomplished.

Others came along who said they wanted to be the best, but I didn't believe them. They didn't even look me in the eye for starters.

They didn't last long, as expected.

What should I do with that encyclopaedia? Who should I give it to?

Cristiano left a gap that I was unable to fill.

So I quit football.

So two fitness-fixated friends reconvened at the Carrington gym on an adventure to create a new body. As Jorge Valdano said, 'He went from a slim build like Johan Cruyff to a gladiator.' The former Real Madrid general manager believes that Cristiano represents the type of player that we will see more frequently on football pitches in a decade's time. He is currently unique, but repeatable in terms of his physical power.

Valdano, though, considers that more a problem than a reason for optimism: 'In football there are powerhouses like Cristiano, who can knock down doors. But the art of playing has nothing to do with player size. I'd say it's more of an inverse process.'

Valdano champions the idea that a small footballer has to develop the brain and overcome his physical deficiencies with intelligence which, in theory, makes him better suited to play the game.

■ ■ ■

Ronaldo understands it differently. His motivation is a continuous need to improve, and he relates that with working hard to take his body to the limit.

But why that urge? What lies behind that constant need to get better, to be the best?

Earning money is not stimulus enough. Or it might be at the beginning, when players go from poverty to affluence. No matter how much they want to be rich, that is not the engine driving them to Ronaldo's competitive level.

There is a school of thought that suggests such success-driven individuals are motivated by nothing less than the desire to be loved. There is an inherent deficiency (not being loved elsewhere) that can only be compensated for by the adulation of others. That desire is child-like and yet a powerful driving force that is carried over into adolescence and adulthood. Sometimes in an almost exhibitionist way.

That obsession to improve is the means by which they can achieve their goal: widespread appreciation.

So, really, it all starts for them with a gap that needs to be filled.

■ ■ ■

One more thing.

Mike Clegg admitted to being obsessive in his work method, a perfectionist.

His parents, meanwhile, were alcoholics.

Some addictions are clearly healthier than others.

Surely the similarities with Ronaldo and his family situation are pure coincidence. Or not. Maybe that addictive gene they share (if it exists: it is murky territory because scientists are not in agreement) allowed them to connect sooner. And to understand each other.

Or maybe it was just that their past helped them create that powerful emotional connection.

■ ■ ■

At first, you wouldn't say he was THAT player who could win you a game there and then.

Wes Brown, former Manchester United defender

Ronaldo would often enjoy glorious moments in training, but then he would stop enjoying it so much when it came to a structured drill.

'Right, we're going to play possession football,' Mike Phelan would shout.

'Two-touch? This is shit.'

'Cristiano, believe in us and in what we are doing. If you can pass the ball earlier and more often, you will grow. We cannot add more ability, it is all there, but if you can involve your team-mates more often in the game, you're going to be better for it.'

'This is shit . . . Two-touch! Crap!' he insisted.

'He became English,' recalled Ferguson's assistant with a smile. 'He moaned a lot!'

And so, day after day, training session after training session, Ronaldo was gradually, subtly, adding more weaponry to his repertoire. He was adapting.

The strange thing is that while that transformation was taking place, little by little his attitude was, in turn, changing the culture of a historic club that thought it had everything worked out.

Cristiano single-handedly made the gigantic institution that is Manchester United change course.

And he did so from the small space that is created in a box.

■ ■ ■

'On the training ground you would be tested to the maximum and players have been broken in United training,' revealed Phil Neville, reflecting on his ten-year spell in the Manchester United first-team squad.

'Especially in the boxes, or "*rondos*" as you call them in Spanish.'

People think it is a simple game to warm up before training. A bit of fun.

How wrong they are.

It is where relationships are created, hierarchies are established. It confirms the player's ability in small spaces and his reaction speed. It helps build the football style the coach wants to implement. It also challenges the new arrivals.

Can you overcome the test?

When he made it into the first team, Phil Neville had to control devilish, difficult passes that were fired at him by Ryan Giggs. Phil looked at him as if to say, 'Mate, there's no need . . .' The response was the silent treatment with a penetrative stare into Phil's eyes. On another day he would be on the receiving end of a crunching tackle by Roy Keane when the Irishman was in the middle and a Paul Scholes pass was given while looking the other way. Phil had to react quickly to be accepted. And positively.

'If you come with a price tag, as soon as you miscontrol it, it's like, "How much did you cost?" – we paid too much, we signed the wrong player,' revealed Ryan Giggs.

There was, and still is, a Champions League box (also known as the *millionaires'* box) and a foreign one (the *cheap* box) at United; sometimes there was one for the younger players. On his arrival, Cristiano joined the one that the veterans named 'Championship', the second division, which was full of foreign players, but not the crème de la crème: David Bellion, Louis Saha, Kleberson, Djemba-Djemba, Diego Forlán, Quinton Fortune . . . Van Nistelrooy was in the other one.

Those 'secondary' players enjoyed themselves in the Championship box. It was not overly intense, they could try out new things and have a laugh.

The veterans looked at them askance from their box.

Eventually Cristiano had to move boxes. Not as an invitation, but as a natural progression: it was a sign that his hierarchical position was gradually changing.

'As a young player you want to stay with your friends for life,' Phil Neville explained. 'But then you look around and think, "Ooh, I'm the oldest in here" or "I no longer belong in this group".'

When Ronaldo joined the Champions League box, he spent long periods in the middle chasing the ball.

'He didn't like defending,' added Phil Neville. 'So we tried to make him run after the ball for as long as we could.'

When he was in the circle, passes would be fired at him that he could not control and he would have to return to the middle. Or if he nutmegged somebody, he would receive an x-rated tackle that he would have to dodge for his troubles.

One day he started receiving good passes: he had earned the veterans' respect.

'I'd say it probably took eighteen months,' stated Phil Neville.

Imperceptibly a chink of light had appeared.

'When David Beckham went to Real Madrid, they played little *rondos* and he used to fire balls through the middle. The foreign players used to laugh at him, "Ah, an English pass!" because they're all tippy-tappy around the circle. I think Ronaldo was the start of a change in mentality. He introduced a new way of doing the *rondo*,' explained Neville.

Instead of practising his passing, he would practise his technique.

He would roll his foot over the ball, faking it one way and dragging it another. Or he would play it through his own legs. Or he would do a back heel.

It would rile the British players. 'You'd think, "He's taking the mickey out of me here,"' recalled Neville. '"What's he doing?"'

On some occasions, players would applaud. On others, he would be told to cut it out.

And then, one day, Ryan Giggs tried a back heel. On another, Scholes rolled his foot over the ball. Even Gary Neville started trying something different – but without going too far.

Those new tricks were gradually incorporated into training.

And then into matches.

It was transmitted to the bench and the stands.

Something that started in a box changed the style of the club.

'Five years later, we had Tévez, Evra, Vidić . . .' explained Phil Neville. 'At that point both boxes were doing more continental type *rondos*. No more straight passes through the middle or firing balls at each other.'

■ ■ ■

Other things were happening almost invisibly. Let us go behind the scenes at the Carrington training ground.

Phil Neville: 'The training was intense, ferocious. He got pummelled. "Get up, get on with it," we would tell him. Do you know what used to get me about Ronaldo? It's a small thing: he used to wear studs every day. The forwards and ball players wear moulds, the defenders wear studs, but he used to wear studs and I was like, "Why are you wearing studs?" He'd say, "I do so in games, no?" But then, I asked why studs. "It makes me faster. I need to perfect it." When a forward wears studs, that worries the defender. If we tackle someone, we know it hurts them. But if he is actually wearing studs, I have to be careful, tackle differently, perhaps less aggressively, because he could hurt me back.'

Gary Neville: 'Cristiano was having a sort of "Cantona effect". "If he can do it, we can, too."'

Ian Buckingham (kitman): 'I'd clean his boots after training and he'd come in with a ball and say, "Bucks, can you do this? I'll give you a hundred quid if you do." But it was that fast, I never even saw what he did! Every day he'd have a new trick. "Can you do this one?"'

Rio Ferdinand: 'He'd be doing tricks an hour before the match. He'd get dressed and mess around as if he were a freestyler.'

Phil Neville: 'Does he love football? Let's put it this way. If you said to him, "We're playing 11 v. 11 today in training," I think he'd go, "Oh no!" But if you said we're doing 2 v. 2 and 1 v. 1, or if it was a head tennis game, or a 2 v. 2, or 3 v. 3, where he can show his ability, he'd go and join in.'

Ian Buckingham: 'He used to wear gloves, which nobody did. Nobody felt the cold. Then the boys started copying him in that, too.'

■ ■ ■

The 2003–04 season was the one in which Alex Ferguson discovered his limits as a consequence of his clash with John Magnier and JP McManus, owners of 25 per cent of the club. He challenged them but, in the end, he must have realised they were bigger and stronger.

Ronaldo's first goal in a Manchester United shirt came along in November during a 3–0 victory against Portsmouth, just four minutes after entering the fray, a free-kick from the left-hand side that was put into the box as a cross but, badly defended, went in.

The game against Everton on Boxing Day was the first time Wayne Rooney (a Blue then) and Cristiano crossed paths. An aggressive tackle reacting to some excessive showboating won Rooney a yellow card. After that match, Ronaldo disappeared from the team until 17 January. He spent the rest of the festive period in Funchal with his family, having played in nineteen of the first thirty-one games of the season, although only eleven were from the start.

In February, Manchester United took on José Mourinho's Porto in the Champions League round of sixteen. The first leg at the Estádio do Dragão ended 2–1 to the home side. Ronaldo was not involved. Ferguson's side took the lead in the second leg. Cristiano came on in the seventy-fifth minute, but picked up an injury and was stretchered off just eight minutes later. Costinha sealed a dramatic equaliser for Porto in stoppage time, knocking United out in the process.

The United team failed to find the consistency required in the Premier League (they finished third behind Arsenal and Chelsea) and their only chance of silverware was the FA Cup after defeating the Gunners in the semi-final. The final was against second division Millwall.

Phil Neville had been a regular, but Ferguson told him that he would not play in the cup final, as Darren Fletcher and Ronaldo got the nod. 'Why?' the defender enquired. The manager wanted them to experience what it was like to win a trophy. Ronaldo had never previously lifted one with either Sporting or United.

The final piece of the puzzle seemed to fit into place during that match. More so for Ronaldo than for the team as a whole. Everything seemed to make sense: all the advice, the battles in the *rondo*, the hard tackles, the two-on-twos in training . . . It was the most important match of his career to date. And he did not disappoint.

He was the outstanding performer in Cardiff that day and he capped it with a header from a Gary Neville cross on the brink of half-time to open the scoring. He took off his shirt and celebrated by beating his chest.

Robbie Ryan, his marker that day, was substituted with fifteen minutes to go. He admitted that it was the first time in his life that he was happy to be withdrawn. Today he works for London Underground.

Final score: 3–0 in Ronaldo's first big match and his first photo with a trophy.

'The team was in transition from 2003 through to 2006,' recalled Gary Neville. 'Winning that trophy and the Carling Cup two years later kept the winning spirit alive. It was a good way for young players like Ronaldo and later Rooney to learn how to win. I remember my first season in the team, you feel weighed down, but you get over the line and it gives you belief and confidence. And you say to yourself, "I like this feeling."'

'Also,' Gary continued, 'to be the best player in the world, you need to win. People need to see you in the biggest matches and you need to have, as he had done in the FA Cup final, a big impact on them.'

In his debut season, Ronaldo had won his first collective club trophy after playing forty games in all competitions, twenty-four of which were starts. He netted six goals, too.

The Portuguese influx would land at Chelsea the following campaign as José Mourinho took over and reinforced the squad with Paulo Ferreria, Tiago, Ricardo Carvalho, as well as Petr Cech, Drogba and Robben. Manchester United brought in Wayne Rooney, Alan Smith and Gabi Heinze.

■ ■ ■

Ronaldo, as he had promised, bought his mother a house in Madeira with his first salary as a Manchester United player and took his family out of the property that they rented from the Funchal Town Hall. They grabbed their belongings and moved to São Gonçalo on the other side of the town. It was a discreet and pretty house on two floors with white walls and a teak-wood terrace overlooking the Atlantic.

For the first time everyone had their own bedroom. Dolores hung photos of her son wearing a Nacional kit in the lounge, as well as a giant screen in order to watch his Manchester United matches. Dinis also lived there until their separation. And today it is where the Aveiros spend Christmas and the occasional birthday.

On one occasion, Cristiano discovered a convertible Mercedes SLK on sale in Alentejo. It was Dolores's birthday, so he put it on a ship, hid it in a garage and gave it to her at the end of that day.

He would later buy other houses for his mother. He also opened a CR7-branded clothes shop that Elma managed.

What would they be today if their brother hadn't been a superstar?

■ ■ ■

When he started to earn big money at Manchester United, a good friend asked him, 'Are you still keeping track of your bank account?' And he responded, 'There are so many zeros that I don't really know what I have.' Ronaldo is a giving person. He enjoys giving presents. He does it with his team-mates, physios, boys in the academy. He gives out iPads, watches and replicas of his individual trophies. It is not something at all common in the football world.

Rio Ferdinand believes that when he celebrates his goals and goes around the training ground tensing his pectoral muscles, it is his way of saying, 'I'm the strongest. I'm so strong that I can carry all of you on my back.'

But he also cries after the odd defeat. He jokes around like a boy. He is a constant giggler.

Let me introduce to you another child adult.

■ ■ ■

I asked Bill Beswick, one of the top sports psychologists in the world, to read through some extracts of the book to direct me and suggest avenues to explore. This is one he put to me: 'Footballers are ordinary people, it is just that they have an extra-ordinary talent', Bill wrote in an email. 'Those with the greatest talent, and therefore of the greatest value to their coaches, the media and the agent/family/support group, have the challenge of trying to remain an ordinary person.'

The trial is huge. The distractions, potentially destructive. They walk a thin line.

'Those from a strong, balanced family background have a chance, but for those young players from dysfunctional families, there is less of a chance,' Beswick added. 'Their whole world revolves around and is dependent upon their talent, so is it any wonder that Ronaldo displays the characteristics of immaturity, selfishness, insecurity, narcissism and fear of commitment to anything outside his football. Perhaps there is a price to be paid for that level of devotion to talent and football greatness.'

One of the prices is that they are allowed (forced?) to remain in a bubble, overprotected, in an eternal state of childhood.

'It is convenient for football,' Beswick concluded, 'to limit players to a child-adult relationship, as it ensures compliance – the agent, the coach, the club remain in control.'

Football – a parallel world where children dream while their hands are tied.

■ ■ ■

After speaking to her son, Dolores decided to leave her new house to the rest of the family and move to Manchester to look after Ronaldo, who had rented a converted farmhouse in Alderley Edge, overlooking green fields grazed by cows and sheep.

Alderley Edge is an interesting neighbourhood. The suburb is about a twenty-five-minute drive from central Manchester and a similar distance from the training ground. It is a small village, like any other, until you take a closer look. On the corner, instead of a newsagent there is a Louis Vuitton shop. Rather than cafés serving a full English breakfast, there are restaurants with white and/or black walls, fashionable places (fashion from the 1990s, anyway) with names more befitting London such as Gusto, The Grill on the Edge and The Alderley Bar and Grill.

I recently went for lunch with David de Gea there. Bryan Robson was sitting at an adjacent table. While we said our goodbyes at the restaurant entrance, Michael Owen went in and he was soon followed by Steve McManaman. It is a mini Hollywood for footballers. As soon as you leave the only high street, mansions with extensive gardens begin to materialise. They look more like small hotels than private homes. Neo-classical architecture is mixed with modern styles, all in good taste. Money is clearly aplenty, but it is not a paradise for the ostentatious. Wilmslow and Hale are nearby, two other villages with similar characteristics inhabited by Manchester City and United stars.

It is the ideal place to live like a normal person, provided that is what you want. There are stories that, when Robinho signed for Manchester City, he got angry when nobody recognised him. The odd photo or autograph, but nothing else. It suited Cristiano down to the ground.

There is little to do there. Even less for a woman like Dolores who preferred to stay home waiting for her son. The language barrier was a burden for her. And the weather. There is a microclimate in Manchester. It must be true because everyone says so. It certainly rains a lot, more than most places. Plus, the city of Manchester was a huge unknown. She would spend the day alone cooking and missing the rest of her family.

Ronaldo found a solution. He brought his cousin Nuno over to Manchester and, after spending some time in New Jersey, also Katia and her husband Zé, who both spoke reasonable English. Hugo remained in Funchal with his wife, while Elma was living with her father in the new house overlooking the sea that Cristiano had purchased.

It was like being on a permanent summer camp: they would spend all day on the PlayStation, they would all go out shopping, they had daily sporting competitions and spent the evenings out on the town when the schedule allowed it.

'There were always ten or twelve of his friends and family with him in Manchester. Always people around the dining table,' explained journalist and friend Nuno Luz. 'We'd drink wine or beer . . . He wouldn't. He didn't drink at all until he was much older. He started having the odd tipple of champagne or wine in Madrid, but barely anything. When it's time for bed, he hit the sack even if there were people in his house.'

Ronaldo hardly went out with his team-mates. '"You're my work friends" seemed to be his message without explicitly saying it,' stated Phil Neville. 'He didn't really mix apart from football things. The atmosphere gradually changed when Rooney, Evra and Anderson joined. He became more relaxed and felt more comfortable.'

Yet he kept his cards close to his chest. 'He didn't mention his family or what he had gone through,' confirmed Quinton Fortune. Gerard Piqué added, 'These things from the past are not normally shared in the dressing room. Players speak mainly about the present.'

The hours that were not devoted to training or relaxing were filled with tennis, table tennis and card games with his visitors and family members. Nuno and Zé, as well as Rogério, a Portuguese friend who lived in England, dealt with the heaps of fan mail that came in from all over the world.

Home life was similar to that in Quinta do Falcão. The door was always open with people coming and going. The spoken language was Portuguese with that strange Maderian accent. 'He needs to feel at home,' explained Carlos Pereira, Ronaldo's friend and the president of Marítimo, who visited him in Manchester on more than one occasion. 'He never had many friends. The core nucleus of people around him were Madeirans and family members. He's always pined for a normal life and felt nostalgic about the carefree nature of childhood. That period of his life flew by.'

Ronaldo gradually imprinted his style on the decor. His trophies and kits were on display in a bulletproof glass cabinet. He bought three sunbeds: a vertical one was placed by a television, there was a horizontal one and the third was cross-shaped. His towels bore the CR7 brand, as did the sheets, chairs and sofas (in his Madrid house he added the logo to his glasses, furniture, dining-room table and even plates). There were mirrors everywhere. He hung a photo of Jean-Claude Van Damme, his favourite actor at the time, alongside others of himself. The rooms were always impeccable, and cleaned every day.

Dolores, however, never adapted fully. She spent three years there until she finally decided to return to Madeira. Zé took on her role, even in the kitchen. From then on Ronaldo's mother would only return for short periods of time.

■ ■ ■

The end of Ronaldo's first season at Manchester United was followed by Euro 2004 in Portugal.

Ronaldo had stood out during the Under-20 Toulon tournament, which Portugal won and he received his first call-up to the senior squad just a few days after joining United. On 20 August 2003, Scolari, who had been the Portugal coach for nine months, gave Cristiano his debut in that friendly against Kazakhstan when he replaced Luis Figo. 'Stay calm,' Figo told his replacement. 'Play as if you were at your club.' Cristiano was voted man of the match by the Portuguese press.

But it was far from plain sailing with the national team.

The highly regarded journalist Enrique Ortego tells a story in his biography of Ronaldo about his early days with the national team. 'They are doing some running drills in a training session. Cristiano is at the head of the group and starts to set a fast pace. The veteran players, Figo and Rui Costa, his minders, tell him to calm it and lower the rhythm. Cristiano obeys them.'[17]

It is the same old story. The new kid must learn that there are limits always imposed by the veterans.

Ortego's story contains a second part that will be of little surprise if you have read this far: '. . . everyone in the dressing room was astonished at the end of training to see he was wearing ankle weights to train and therefore feel lighter in matches without them.'[17]

Scolari knew that he had to manage the situation delicately. That is the big challenge for all coaches: to balance out the environment. It was a tight-knit group, made up of the so-called 'golden generation' that retained the 1991 FIFA World Youth Championship won two years earlier: João Pinto, Figo, Rui Costa, Abel Xavier, Rui Bento, Jorge Costa . . . Scolari had to mix the 'rough diamond' that he had discovered during the friendlies ahead of Euro 2004 with that group.

Big Phil was planning to subtly build bridges with the player. The odd conversation here, the odd joke there, while always trying to make it seem like this extraordinary athlete was just one more member of the squad.

Yet that connection seemed impossible when Scolari saw him join up with the squad for the first time. Eighteen-year-old Cristiano was wearing a baseball cap the wrong way round and never took it off, not even at meal times. His enormous sunglasses and headphones blaring out music that could be heard a mile away painted the picture of another teenager who thought he was the bee's knees.

He did not feel an overwhelming need to listen, or so Scolari sensed. Immature, selfish on the pitch and a circus performer, but blessed with outstanding technique. That is how Scolari viewed him but saw no reason not to follow Ferguson's formula: be patient and polish him.

But was not proving to be an easy task.

'I don't think he understands what I say,' Scolari moaned to his press officer, José Carlos Freitas, according to one of my sources, a few days before a pre-match press conference ahead of Portugal–Sweden in which he tried to bring Ronaldo back down to earth.[18]

Scolari had decided to tell him off via the press: 'He's a good kid, but someone must've told him he's the best in the world. And if he thinks he is, it'll be very hard to work with him.'

Ronaldo got the hump but took note. Scolari told him in a private conversation after the press conference that he was preparing him not only to be an international, but to be a crucial big-game player. The national coach added that if he corrected his attitude, he would end up captaining the national side one day.

Cristiano's evolution in the national team's social order was also supported by Luis Figo, even though, in spite of the initial advice, it was more unspoken than explicit. He was not going to pave the way for the youngster, but the contest for space at the group would be a fair one. For now and for a while, though, the right wing belonged to the then Real Madrid star, as did the number seven shirt.

Cristiano, who asked for number seventeen, showed Figo respect, but was also willing to fight to replace him.

That transition was going to last two years when Scolari bid farewell to Luis Figo, his 'special son', in 2006 and offered Cristiano centre stage by building the team around him.

But preparations for Euro 2004 came first.

His first start with the national team came in October 2003 in a friendly against Albania in Lisbon when he was withdrawn at the break for Simão. But he was not yet a regular.

The final squad for the Euros came through. Eighteen-year-old Ronaldo made the cut and became the sixth youngest player in the competition's history.

. . .

Let's go off on a brief tangent. You will not be surprised to hear that the Portuguese press baptises the national side and players as the country's real ambassadors, whose mission it is to put the nation on the map. It is the typical nationalistic stance that, paradoxically, goes hand in hand with the maxim that football must not be mixed with politics.

As sociologist João Nuno Coelho explains in 'Entre a esperança e a tormenta: futebol, identidade nacional e o Euro-2004' (Between Hope and Torment: Football, National Identity and Euro 2004), the bigger the event, the more widespread and universal is the projected image of the national team, Portuguese players and their peculiarities.

What is that image like?

According to the general media consensus, the Portuguese see themselves as 'unique, defining and distinctive', Coelho wrote. 'Capable, creative and fantastic improvisers. But, on the other hand, disorganised, irresponsible, incoherent, lazy and unpredictable. Easily identified with our "geo-cultural" Latin roots. Capable of the best (especially in the hardest situations, such as the Euro 2000 group stage) and the worst.'

Portugal had not won anything up until that point. Who was to blame? Unlike the British press who usually blame the national coach, the Portuguese media targeted other areas: a lack of unity, not taking responsibility and leadership failure. There is another very Portuguese version to explain footballing fiascos: the *system* does nothing but remind them they are from a small country, which is not allowed to put its head above water, while the larger countries receive all kind of favours.

On home soil, at the Euros, players would enjoy the support

of a nation that believed in the dream of putting an end to their invisibility.

■ ■ ■

Cristiano Ronaldo did not start the opening game against Greece. Portugal were losing 1–0 against the ultra-defensive Greeks. He came off the bench and was overzealous in his approach, giving away a penalty for a challenge on Seitaridis that even today he believes should never have been.

'Collina, it wasn't a penalty!'

'It was, and you know it.'

That was the exchange between Pierluigi Collina and Ronaldo in a public conversation during the Christmas holidays in Dubai in 2013.

Cristiano scored a header, his first goal for his country. But it came in stoppage time and was too little too late. Portugal lost 2–1.

After the 2–0 victory over Russia, Portugal had to beat Spain in order to qualify for the next round. It was the first official start for Ronaldo, who, as the press reported, 'was a breath of fresh air on a warm summer's night'. It was a memorable victory, and he was man of the match.

England were up next.

'I had the silly feeling that I had done my duty.' That is how his mother Dolores said she felt in the stands when she saw him come out on to the pitch with the rest of the team.

It was a very tense match and Ronaldo's mother was overcome with emotion: she fainted while her son was busy qualifying for the semi-finals of the Euros on penalties.

He shone once again against the Netherlands in the next round and, just as against Greece, scored a header from a pinpoint Luis Figo corner; it was the side's first goal in a historic 2–1 win to secure a place in the final.

Ronaldo retained his place for the final against Greece, making him the youngest player ever to do so.

The match was similar in many ways to the tournament opener. Portugal were unable to defend a Greece corner which saw Charisteas score a header in the fifty-seventh minute. Ronaldo had the dubious honour of missing his side's best chance of the match: the Madeiran controlled a Rui Costa pass perfectly, but his shot was smothered by an inspired Nikopolidis. There were to be no more goals in that final of surprises.

Luiz Felipe Scolari was the first person to console a devastated Ronaldo.

■ ■ ■

It had been a very intense summer. On his return to Manchester, something had changed for ever in his young life.

FOUR

FLOURISHING IN MANCHESTER

BUT NOT THE FINISHING LINE

Gary Neville: 'He'll have thought I was just this strange northern English guy . . . "What's he doing? He always shouts at me. I play football, while this guy kicks the ball away and takes throw-ins. You throw it to me and you shut up." I played right-back, and I had my right-sided player in front of me. We defended as a two and worked together. But he never understood that . . .'

Mike Phelan: 'He was courageous and brave, but structurally he wasn't quite there.'

Phil Neville: 'The frightening thing is that every time he's had a little setback, his game has gone up again. "How do I become better than them?"'

Carlos Queiroz: 'When I came back to Old Trafford after my year at Real Madrid, I started working with him morning, afternoon and evening . . . I realised I was dealing with a superhuman.'

Gary Neville: 'He never would understand [his defensive duties], and in the end it got to the point whereby, if you're going to do that, you've got to be very special. That was the tipping point. Do you live with him for another twelve months, where this player is doing OK but not scoring twenty-five goals, where he can turn off and not do the defending?'

Mike Phelan: 'In one pre-season, he came back a totally different animal. It was after the Euros. He must have done something. He came back a man. His body shape was different, his facial features were different and we just thought, "Wow, there's a physique now. That's an athletic physique for the British game." He was tough, and then his speed and aerial ability developed . . . I don't know whether puberty kicked in or whatever. His personality came through then: "I've arrived. I'm the man."'

■ ■ ■

Just a quick note.

It was common practice to analyse matches on the computer. Cristiano would review what he had done well and not so well, analysing each decision, calculating if he should have released the ball or gone on to dribble, shoot or cross.

Ronaldo would play each match twice.

■ ■ ■

Bill Beswick has dedicated his professional life to scrutinising that strange space inhabited by those who go from good to brilliant, and showing them the path that they need to follow to reach that even more unique land – greatness.

If we put greatness at ten out of ten, Beswick explained that in order to get from zero to seven all you need is talent, or, as he calls it, 'hardware': 'If you're physically, tactically and technically good, you get to seven easily.'

It is very tough to get past seven. That is where most stay put and pitch their tent.

In order to reach eight, nine or the final step, you need but one thing: the mind.

That is what Beswick calls the 'software'.

If you reach that level, you land on a new stage. The stage of the chosen ones.

The *greats* feel comfortable in uncomfortable environments. You see them smiling out on the pitch and exchanging pleasantries with defenders when the whole world is looking on.

'I watched Maradona warming up before a game, he was dancing to music,' recalled Beswick. 'He owned the field.'

The dog's bollocks.

Great players are not halted by fear and are spurred on by challenges. Instead of fearing possible disappointment by not achieving a goal, they dare to climb the highest mountains.

They believe they can do the lot.

'The mental and emotional strength of Ronaldo is what is driving his talent,' Beswick added.

I have always considered that constant search for overcoming obstacles as a small tragedy. That pilgrimage towards uncomfortable territory is usually never-ending. It is a continuous exploration that prevents players from enjoying what they achieve.

Beating or overcoming the last obstacle entails a level of gratification, but is instantly followed by the setting of the next target, just like an artificial hare in greyhound racing.

I put those thoughts to Beswick.

'I don't get many top players telling me that the contest is enjoyable. What they get is a certain satisfaction from doing it one more time.'

Never complete fulfilment.

'Certainly the need to be the best and to be appreciated is a desire that must be satisfied regularly – the fear of being second best never goes away'.

It all sounds like an addiction. And, like all of them, deeply unsatisfying.

'It's an adrenalin kick,' said Beswick, who added, 'it's sort of being who you can be, but never quite knowing.'

Here is perhaps another small tragedy: being continuously on the move means you can never truly settle anywhere.

■ ■ ■

In late 2004, nineteen-year-old Ronaldo travelled to Dili, the capital of East Timor, and discovered that his position in the world had changed. Thousands of people filled the streets. They wanted a piece of Ronaldo, an autograph, a photo, a hug even. The intensity of the emotions on display (his and his fans') made it one of the most powerful moments he had ever experiences. It also reminded him that his gestures would be watched and repeated by those kids, by his fans. With fame came a huge amount of responsibility.

Days later he followed reports of the tsunami that affected several countries in the Indian Ocean – six-metre-high waves moving at 700 kilometres per hour. Almost 280,000 were killed and 510,000 injured. Six months later, he travelled to Indonesia, the country that was most deeply afflictcd by the tragedy.

Among many stories that emerged from that catastrophe is that of Martunis, a seven-year-old boy who survived despite spending nineteen days completely alone. When he was rescued by the Sky News team, the kid was wearing a Portugal shirt (with the number ten and the name Rui Costa on the back) and was invited to meet the national team along with his father just a few months later. Martunis declared that he was a Manchester United fan and admirer of Ronaldo, whom he met. Cristiano promised to see him again and did so six months after the tsunami in Banda Aceh. Nothing prepared Ronaldo for what the boy had to say, and he was astonished by the extraordinary survival instincts that had helped him get through those nineteen days. It was a relationship that would last beyond that first meeting.

■ ■ ■

Cristiano intervened so that Martunis was later signed up at the Real Madrid Foundation's football school in his local town and, eleven years later, became a Sporting Lisbon Under-19 player.

■ ■ ■

It was a period of transformation. Some were visible and physical, while others were deep and internal.

■ ■ ■

During a match at Highbury against Arsenal, who United would face again in the FA Cup final that same season, Ronaldo scored half of his side's goals in a memorable 4–2 victory.

After scoring the first of his brace, he put his finger to his lips. He wanted to silence the home fans.

■ ■ ■

'The performance that really stood out for me was when we lost the FA Cup final on penalties to Arsenal in 2005. I was a substitute that day, but when you look back at his performance, that probably gave him the self-belief that he could really push on and be as good as he wanted to be, he was outstanding. Little things like that – his performance against Ashley Cole – give you that bit of belief.'

Alan Smith, former Manchester United forward

Cristiano played forty-one times in the Premier League and Champions League that 2004–05 season, thirty-two of which were starts. He notched five goals as Jose Mourinho's Chelsea won the league. United finished a long way behind in third and were eliminated from Europe in the last sixteen.

Ronaldo's second season had been inconsistent. He was voted FIFPRO Special Young Player of the Year by supporters but could not yet claim his position as one of the team's most important players. And things would take a turn for the worse in 2005–06.

■ ■ ■

Alan Smith reflected with a smile on how he only received one assist from Ronaldo in seventy or so matches. 'For a winger, he very rarely crossed the ball, but you also understand what he could give the team,' he recalled. 'He could draw two, three or four players towards him and then pop the ball off to someone else.' When he did pop it.

Cristiano's first passion was the ball. His second was dribbling. 'When you're young, you always want to shine, do the most spectacular move or dribble, something that makes you stand out from the rest. It's my style. It's my life,' stated the player.[17]

At a height of almost 1.90 metres, he enjoyed exploiting his speed with a long running stride. At the time Cristiano played on both wings, although he was often given the chance to shine as a second striker or centre-forward in training, just like at the Sporting academy. He was a winger with a striker's soul.

He would later prepare himself for a love affair with goals, although Ferguson did not initially think that he would be a prolific scorer. On the other hand, Carlos Queiroz always believed that the penalty area would end up being his stamping ground. 'It'd be a waste for him to do twenty eighty-metre sprints in a match,' he used to say. 'Over time, when he's twenty-eight or twenty-nine, I'm sure he'll become a pure striker.' He also highlighted a difficulty that Queiroz himself would have to fight against not long after: 'He doesn't like being the main striker.'

How did teams prepare to halt that erratic winger who had enormous potential and caused rival defences huge problems whenever he found space? 'The closer you got, the less you allowed him to think; and the less time he had on the ball, the easier it was to stop him. Relatively,' was Xabi Alonso's analysis, having faced the Portuguese both as a Liverpool and Spain player. 'When he faces you one-on-one he has two profiles: he can go down the right and he can go down the left, so you have to give him as little space as possible. The procedure was to help the full-back when he played on the wing. But he would kill you with his physical resistance. His constant sprints would tire out both your brain and your legs.'

■ ■ ■

Ronaldo's father Dinis died at the start of the 2005–06 season, on 6 September.

He was fifty-two years old.

Ronaldo was twenty.

■ ■ ■

I had just received a message from Norway. A television channel (TV2) had footage of Dinis Aveiro. They interviewed him for inclusion in a report about his son just a few months before his death.

I spent some time imagining his body language and voice, which I hoped to hear soon. I imagined a man with a calm demeanour, the type that inspired confidence simply by the way he looked at you. And his voice? Definitely scratchy, as with most persistent drinkers.

The message read: 'The cameraman, Toby, says that he has the tape with that recording of the whole interview with Dinis in the attic at his old flat. He'll try to find it this weekend.'

■ ■ ■

Journalist Enrique Ortego asked Cristiano, who had just joined
Real Madrid at the time, to choose the best eleven people in his
life. This is what he said:

Mãe, my mother Maria Dolores, the pillar of the family. Elma,
my older sister, for the education she gave me alongside my
other siblings. She lives in Madeira where she has a CR7-branded
clothes shop. Hugo, my brother, for the help he gave me in
football and always offering good advice about what I should
and shouldn't do and how I shouldn't complain. He was a player,
too, but not a professional. He has a painting business in
Madeira. Katia, the little one, although she's older than me. For
the affection she gave me when I was a baby and for changing
my nappies. She was a singer, but no longer sings. She has a
CR7-branded shop in Lisbon. Zé, my brother-in-law. He's lived
with me since I went to Manchester and has been at my side
since Funchal. He's Katia's husband. An unconditional, true
friend. Jorge. He's much more than my agent. He's influenced
every aspect of my life. He's my friend and other older brother,
like Hugo.[17]

And the final player, a special name on the list . . .
'*Pai* [Dad], because of his generosity and friendship with all his
children. An extraordinary person whom I'll always miss.'[17]
Cristiano had a routine with his dad: Dinis would come along to
training, quietly watching and suggesting something here and there
at the end of the session, then they would share some food together.
Especially during his time at Andorinha. Ronaldo recalled how
the modest, local club used to play stronger sides such as Marítimo
and Câmara de Lobos who would inflict damaging, demoralising
defeats on the minnows. One day, Ronaldo said that he did not

want to play as he knew they would lose. He did not even turn up for the next match. His father hunted him down on the route from the pitch to their home and told his son that only weak people gave up. Both of them went back to the pitch.

Andorinha were thrashed, of course.

But Ronaldo remembers that day as a victory.

■ ■ ■

'Dinis drank himself to death and that destroyed Cristiano.'[9] Those are Dolores's words.

Ronaldo discovered that money does not open all doors. He offered to pay for various forms of treatment for his dad, but José Dinis did not want to budge an inch from where he was.

According to someone close to the family who prefers to remain anonymous, Dinis went so far as to sell the shirt that his son wore on his Manchester United debut to make sure he had enough to drink for a while. Hugo had done something similar a few years earlier. Addicts do not follow protocol.

His kidney and liver problems, which had seen him hospitalised two months earlier at Centro Hospitalar in Funchal, eventually took his life, although he died in a London clinic organised by Ronaldo, with his son Hugo by his side.

Cristiano was in Moscow with the Portugal national team ahead of a World Cup 2006 qualifier against Russia. When the news reached them, Luiz Felipe Scolari and skipper Luis Figo went to his room, where Scolari told him his father had died.

Ronaldo stared blankly at the wall. He later admitted that he felt nothing. No words, no emotion. He was empty. In shock.

Scolari suggested he could go home.

Part of Ronaldo did react. While Cristiano the child had gone silent, still and empty, Ronaldo the footballer, the one that lives in a constant dynamic between training, rest and matches, spoke, telling his team-mates that he wanted to stay and play.

He wanted to show the world that he could separate his private life from his professional one. He was convinced that playing for his father and scoring would be the best tribute. He told his coach that he could count on him. That he was ready.

Once Figo had departed, Big Phil spoke to him about how important his own father had been to him and the need to remember Dinis's good points in order to apply them to his own children further down the line.

At that moment, his connection with Scolari grew. Ronaldo had found another father figure who understood him. They both cried as Big Phil told Cristiano about the death of his own father.

Big Phil also told him that his family was the absolute priority and football should take a back seat at that time.

Yet that was not what Ronaldo needed.

'This boy surprises us every day,' the Portugal coach told the other members of the management team in Moscow. He had not imagined that the player's reaction would be to want to play.

'He started calling me "father" that day,' recalled an emotional Scolari.

The match was a strange one. The mood in the Portugal camp was reflected in the build-up. Everyone shared Ronaldo's mourning, but it was difficult to show him the emotional support that they wanted to in the pumped-up atmosphere of the dressing room.

'Act normally, be yourselves, don't change what you always do,' Ronaldo told the group, according to one of my sources: he knew what the medicine was for the other footballers at such a time. Cristiano started doing what he always did before a match: playing with a ball in the dressing room. Passing to a team-mate, doing a trick or two and enjoying some technical maneuver to relieve the tension and pain. Football always took his mind off things.

He did his best to score, but maybe the 0–0 draw mirrored how it felt to be on the pitch better than anything else.

Ferguson also offered him a break, but Cristiano only missed one game to go to his dad's funeral in Madeira.

Scolari decided to give him the captain's armband for the following game, against Brazil in London. 'This boy is going to be the number one in the history of Portugal, although he's only twenty years old,' he announced in the pre-match press conference.

He said it to encourage him, but also because he believed it.

■ ■ ■

Ronaldo does not like speaking about death. As if it is something that does not exist. An unnecessary worry.

Maria Dolores once told him that she would die one day and would not always be around to protect her children. The typical sort of comment a mother makes to remind her children that she is indispensable.

Cristiano cried like a child and changed the subject.

He does believe in life after death, though. As if he could not conceive that we are so weak, so ephemeral, that we will eventually just disappear.

■ ■ ■

Another message from Norway: 'Toby hasn't been able to find anything. His last hope is that the tape is at his parents' house. He won't be able to check until April. Can you wait?'

Yes, of course. I had to hear Dinis. To know how he spoke about his son.

■ ■ ■

Cristiano has seen the damage that alcohol and drugs can do close-up. 'That is part of what has contributed to him being who he is today,' Dolores explained in an interview in *l'Equipe* in 2008.

> My four children have seen the dangers of drug addiction first-hand. But Cristiano's only addiction was football. If he hadn't become a professional footballer, he'd have got lost. He probably would've resorted to drugs or something else equally terrible. Many of his friends from the village have succumbed to drugs and alcohol. One of them recently died from an overdose. Despite all my efforts, it would've been difficult for him to have a stable life . . . Fortunately, he had a gift.[9]

Katia admitted that at home they had a rather innocent outlook: 'As Cristiano has money, my father will go to a private clinic and definitely be cured. He'll get over it.'

They suddenly discovered that neither fame nor money could halt the tide of fate.

Hugo explained that, after Dinis's death, Ronaldo told the family: 'My money hasn't managed to save our father, so we're all going to enjoy it.'

Cristiano wanted to keep the image of the father who took him to training and gave him advice. He filled his Manchester home with photos, oil paintings and portraits of Dinis Aveiro.

His father didn't live to see him achieve success and global stardom.

Ronaldo thinks that fate determined it that way. Like all of us he prefers answers to mysteries.

■ ■ ■

Someone who knows Ronaldo very well, and whom I cannot mention (so once again I can only tell half the story), someone who never understood why he cried so much even late into adolescence, asked me a question: 'Did Ronaldo stop crying when his father died?'

This person did not tell me what was hidden behind the question. Maybe he was suggesting the tears were the product of his broken home. Following that line, Ronaldo was suffering deep sadness because his father had relinquished his role very early on, which made him fragile and uncertain at decisive moments in his life. Dinis Aveiro's disappearance could help him sever links with a past he was not comfortable with, setting him free without being indebted to anyone.

Obscure theory, I know. And I am not sure that is what that friend of his was trying to tell me. But the question intrigued me.

I had to find out if he had cried since September 2005.

■ ■ ■

In the end, Toby did not find the tape in his parents' house. I had to make do with watching the small clip in the report in which you see Dinis talking to the journalist about his son's childhood. Behind the voice dubbing him, you can hear a deeper, slower one talking about his son's desire to become a footballer. Dinis, who appeared confident, leaning against a wall, was filmed side-on. The modest surroundings (run-down houses, lots of weeds, clothes drying at windows) said just as much as those few seconds of Dinis, who in my eyes instantly took on a new dimension.

He was no longer simply a distant character in a biography.

■ ■ ■

Cristiano's third season at United (2005–06) was becoming a new challenge for his emotional stability.

In October, he was questioned by police after two women made allegations of rape against him. Ronaldo reported voluntarily to a London police station, an act that was described in the British press as 'arrest'. A few weeks later, his cousin Nuno Aveiro was also interrogated. Ronaldo was not charged with rape, as there was insufficient evidence against him. One of the young girls, a Frenchwoman, eventually withdrew her allegation. It had been invented, an exaggerated version of a night out, or a trap by a prostitute with a knack for hunting out celebrities, according to the *News of the World*. If the visit to Dili and Indonesia had shown Ronaldo the power of his global influence, the incident in London showed him the darker side of international fame.

He could trust no one.

That confusing campaign was a mix of the absurd (a red card against Manchester City, his third for the club, for responding to tough tackles with a wild lunge on Andy Cole; giving the Benfica crowd the finger after being substituted in a Champions League match) and the brilliant, especially in late 2005 and early 2006.

An example of the latter would be his brace on New Year's Eve against a Bolton side that had no answer to his irresistible performance. He scored his first trademark free-kick against Fulham in February, a powerful strike with an unpredictable trajectory which he would soon become known for, a fitting reward for the hundreds of hours on the training ground with and without a goalkeeper.

Those defining moments were a source of both satisfaction and frustration: why did he not always play like that? While that elusive consistency was sought, Ferguson took him out of the team for several weeks.

Meanwhile, cracks were appearing in his relationship with Ruud Van Nistelrooy. The Dutchman needed to score; it was his fuel and the only way he could keep his position in the team and among supporters. He had gone from relying on David Beckham's pinpoint assists to having to depend on an erratic young talent.

His goalscoring percentage was waning, too – from thirty goals in 2003–04 to sixteen in the following season, although injuries also played a part as he made just twenty-seven appearances. The return of Carlos Queiroz further fuelled the idea that there was some level of favouritism towards the Portuguese player.

The clash with the striker had reached such magnitude – long silences, tellings-off in training and the odd physical skirmish – that some members of the coaching staff and even veteran players thought that Ronaldo (whose goalscoring was inconsistent, whose assists were not prolific, who made too much of fouls, overdid it with tricks and did not track back after losing the ball) would bite the bullet.

In many people's eyes, his settling-in period was lasting too long.

For the time being, his performances were not justifying Queiroz's insistence on changing a 4-4-2 system into a 4-3-3 one that would benefit the Portuguese and also Wayne Rooney.

■ ■ ■

Small changes were taking place in the club culture, like seeds germinating – slowly but inexorably.

Gary Neville: 'Before coming out for training, he and Rio would warm up with a two-touch game in the dressing room. They were so good, even if they were wearing sandals. It could last a lifetime. Paul Scholes also played with them.'

The Portuguese displayed a great knowledge of his body.

Phil Neville: 'Ronaldo used to say, "Too much water kills the plant." In training, he would be doing runs with us. We would all go at maximum pace for all eight of them. That is what you are supposed to do. But he would blast six, then he'd calm down for the last two and finish at the back. He knew exactly what he wanted to do to be playing on the Saturday.'

Yet doubts remained.

Gary Neville: 'Sir Alex Ferguson made all the decisions, but I questioned Ronaldo's performance in his mid-third year. I was getting to the point where I wondered whether he would actually be a top player.'

■ ■ ■

In 2005–06, Ronaldo scored nine times in thirty-three appearances, twenty-four of which were in games he started. One of the goals was his first European strike in the Champions League, but Manchester United were unable to progress from the group stage. After losing to Liverpool in the FA Cup fifth round, a League Cup final against Wigan in February provided the club's only chance of silverware in an otherwise below-par campaign.

Ronaldo was in the starting line-up for his third final in three years. Van Nistelrooy was benched. Saha scored one, Rooney two and Cristiano put the cherry on the cake in a 4–0 demolition of the Latics. Another trophy, another step forward. In Ferguson's opinion, and developing Ronaldo's simile, it was just the right kind of water for the plants.

Supporters were not so sure, however. There was a lingering feeling that United were light years away from a mega-rich Chelsea, who had just won a second league title after a fifty-year drought. The Red Devils finished eight points behind them, in second place.

That summer, while José Mourinho signed Andriy Shevchenko (AC Milan), Salomon Kalou (Feyenoord), Michael Ballack (Bayern Munich) and Ashley Cole (Arsenal), Manchester United sold Ruud Van Nistelrooy to Real Madrid after the Dutchman lost the war. He was not replaced by a striker. The only squad addition was midfielder Michael Carrick.

Hardly enough to generate excitement.

Roy Keane had also left the club after playing for Alex Ferguson for twelve years. The Irish midfielder's departure was shrouded in controversy that still separates him from his former manager today.

Ferguson was, against public opinion, working his magic once again.

Ferguson did not attach excessive importance to three years without a league title. To use the analogy of an expert gardener, he had sown the seeds and planted bulbs in the field and was now nurturing those plants and preparing to put them on display, while removing the weeds, the ones that prevented others from growing.

In botany, incidentally, the concept of weeds does not exist. It is only used in the context of plant growing. Football is the same. There are no bad footballers, just those who do not fit in, for which Ferguson had an incredible eye.

Before the new season began, Cristiano Ronaldo had the small matter of his first World Cup.

■ ■ ■

Portugal had fallen at the final hurdle at home in the Euro 2004 final against Greece and were therefore considered contenders for the tournament in Germany. Luiz Felipe Scolari had managed to bring together a core group of quality players (Figo, Nuno Gomes, Valente, Pauleta) and the spine of the Porto side that won the 2004 Champions League (Deco, Maniche, Carvalho, Costinha). Others added consistency (such as Petit) while Ronaldo brought to the table a youthful ability to open up defences, after scoring seven goals in a straightforward qualifying campaign.

Big Phil had also created that team spirit that is so crucial in, and often missing from, the Portugal national team.

Ronaldo scored in his second game, against Iran, as Portugal progressed as group winners ahead of Mexico and Angola to set up a last-sixteen clash with Netherlands. It was a very physical contest including four sendings-off and sixteen yellow cards. Ronaldo picked up an injury, but Portugal progressed with Maniche scoring the only goal.

An England side with Beckham, Lampard, Gerrard and Rooney was up next in the quarter-finals. Sven-Göran Eriksson's team, who had dispatched Ecuador in the previous round, were favourites.

With an hour gone and the tie goalless, Rooney got tangled up with Petit and Carvalho in front of the referee. He appeared to stamp on the latter in the nether regions. It was an accident in the English striker's eyes who later on admitted that 'it looked worse than it was.'

While Rooney apologised and protested his innocence, Ronaldo, after sprinting to the scene of the crime, asked Argentinian official Horacio Elizondo for an explanation. And a red card.

Heresy in English fair play.

Rooney gave his club team-mate a shove out of anger. At that moment Ronaldo was a Portugal player, not a Manchester United one. And nothing is bigger than the World Cup.

Elizondo asked Rooney to move away from the fallen Carvalho and put his hand in his pocket.

Rooney kept asking for the official's understanding.

Red card.

Soon after, Ronaldo was shown on camera swiftly walking away. What he did next lasted less than a second, but inflamed an entire nation.

He looked at someone who was dishing out instructions.

And winked.

There was an hour to go, including a tense extra-time period. The tie would eventually be decided on penalties. Ricardo saved three for the first time in World Cup history. Ronaldo scored the decisive spot-kick.

There might have been talk of Eriksson's troops' heroic performance with ten men. Or the fact that in the first half Rooney, as he himself admitted, had 'tried to get Ronaldo a yellow card after telling the referee that he was diving . . . What I did was just as bad as what he did.'

Yet the British press already had the perfect scapegoat for everything. Absolutely everything.

■ ■ ■

The message behind the wink was crystal clear according to the English press: 'I got involved, I got him sent off, now we'll win.'

Cristiano said, though: 'They told me to push further forward to make the most of the numerical advantage and that's how I responded [to the instruction].'

■ ■ ■

Alex Ferguson: 'The ref was going to send Rooney off anyway, but Ronaldo's intervention didn't help.'

Horacio Elizondo: 'It was violent conduct and that's why he received a straight red card. People can say whatever they want, but Ronaldo's protests had no influence.'

Alex Ferguson: 'Ronaldo regretted what he did.'

I am not so sure . . .

Ronaldo did what anyone would have done. He has said so himself.

■ ■ ■

The following day, the Sun reported that Rooney had said in the dressing room that he wanted to 'split Ronaldo in two'. It fitted the narrative that had been established in the press box in Gelsenkirchen: it was the end of Ronaldo at Manchester United, he would not be able to go back to the United Kingdom and Rooney would never forgive him. Their professional relationship had become untenable.

The story did not quite go like that, however.

Let's go back to the match.

. . .

After scoring the decisive penalty against England to send Portugal into the World Cup semi-finals, Ronaldo looked up to the sky and raised his hand in tribute to his father.

Gary Neville knows the rules of the game: 'You win some, you lose some.' After the shootout, he did what he deemed most suitable considering the historic moment he had just experienced: he headed to the Portugal dressing room to swap shirts with Cristiano and wish him luck.

. . .

Once in the changing rooms, Ronaldo looked for Rio Ferdinand.

'Rio, I didn't mean it, I didn't wink like that.'

'Let me go and get Wazza,' Rio said.

Then the three of them chatted and discussed the matter just after the match, despite blood still boiling.

'The fans will be going mad over this one,' Rooney warned Cristiano. 'They'll be trying to make a big deal of it, so we'll just have to get on with things as normal because there will be talk about it all summer.'

On the coach back to the hotel after the game, Rooney asked Steven Gerrard what he made of it all.

'Honestly, Wazza, if we were playing Spain and [Liverpool teammates] Xabi Alonso or Luis García winked at the referee or gave a signal for me to be sent off, I'd never speak to them again.'

. . .

Portugal were knocked out by France 1–0 in a tight semi-final, while Ronaldo was named the third best young player of the tournament (behind Lukas Podolski and Luis Antonio Valencia) at a time when, back in England, shirts with the slogan 'I hate Ronaldo' and dartboards bearing his face were booming in popularity.

Then came the threatening letters.

Cristiano seriously considered not returning to Manchester.

■ ■ ■

Rooney and Ronaldo exchanged messages over the summer. In fact, Ferguson believes the English striker's attitude was what saved their relationship.

Sir Alex spoke to Rooney to encourage him to phone his team-mate from time to time and the player suggested a joint interview as the best way to silence the hysteria. Ferguson did not think it was a bad idea, but Mike Phelan feared it would appear both prompted and artificial.

Thinking about it carefully, it was also a marvellous opportunity for Sir Alex, was it not? It just had to be managed carefully.

Cristiano Ronaldo expressed his thoughts at the start of the summer. 'If the situation doesn't change, I could not return to Manchester United. I've had no support from the club's sporting director or manager on this matter. They should've come out in my defence, but they haven't.'[11]

Two clubs were waiting in the wings if the situation went past the point of no return. He said so himself: 'Real Madrid or Barcelona?' It would be one of the two.

Cristiano went on holiday with Jorge Mendes and there was talk of little else. The player was wondering if he had to leave, if it was the best option. His agent insisted that he should stay at United. Mendes was sure it was the right thing to do.

Sir Alex knew that he had to choose the right moment to sit down with the player and his agent. He felt capable of finding a solution.

The weeks went by. Ronaldo still had not heard from Ferguson. Sir Alex complained that Cristiano was not replying to his messages. The manager then found out that he was sending them to an old number.

He got the new one. They spoke and decided to meet for lunch in the Algarve. Ferguson hired a private jet and flew out to Vale do Lobo with chief executive David Gill.

It was a very delicately balanced situation. Ferguson had to present sufficient arguments in the meeting, not only for Cristiano to stay at Old Trafford, but to do so with the right attitude for his continued progression.

'You're one of the bravest players to come to Manchester United, but walking away isn't courage.'[18]

Ferguson told him how Beckham had gone through the same after his sending off against Argentina in 1998 when England were knocked out. 'They were hanging effigies of him outside pubs in London. He was the devil incarnate. But he had the balls to fight it.'[18] The English, he told him, are all bark but no bite.

'They won't do anything to you,' Ferguson insisted.[18]

Ronaldo spoke to the press a few days later. 'There's no reason for me to leave a club that has always supported me. Everything will be decided in the next week.'

On the first day of pre-season, Ferguson decided to speak to Gary Neville, the club captain. 'Gary, he's staying. But we have to work hard so that he doesn't escape from our grasp,' Ferguson told him.[18] He later asked Rooney and Ronaldo into his office. Both Sir Alex and Neville knew that there were no barriers to knock down. Nothing had come between them.

The jokes in the dressing room were varied and revolved around the same topic; the supposed dislike between the club's two young stars. Somebody brought boxing gloves in case there was a fight before training. Many laughs were had.

Before training, Ronaldo confided in fitness coach Valter di Salvo and Gabriel Heinze, who both said: 'Don't listen to people, do your talking on the pitch. You'll have to show great heart.'

And they went out on to the pitch.

Ronaldo appeared a different man. He had grown. His shoulders upright, his chest puffed out, arms and legs stronger than before. If he went from boy to man in 2004, he had transcended that barrier in 2006. He was a fine physical specimen. Enormous. Ready for battle.

Defenders bounced off him when they tried to stop him. He continued to enjoy an excellent relationship with the ball.

Rooney had a hunch after that first training session: 'It's going to be a bloody good season.'

Ferguson had what he wanted, a unified dressing room.

And almost equally important for him: he created the feeling that the entire world was against Manchester United.

■ ■ ■

Going back to the World Cup briefly . . .

The Netherlands decided in the last sixteen that the best way to neutralise the Portuguese talent was to take the law into their own hands. Mark van Bommel stood on Ronaldo's foot and was cautioned. Seven minutes into the game, Khalid Boulahrouz put in a violent challenge on the forward with his boot connecting with Ronaldo's calf, triggering an injury that would see him withdrawn half an hour later.

Ronaldo bit his lip on the walk to the dugout, believing that his World Cup campaign was over. Once he had taken a seat, he decided not to hold back his tears.

No, his father's death had not dried up every tear.

■ ■ ■

It was the first match of the 2006–07 season at home to Fulham, the standout fixture of the opening weekend for obvious reasons. So, accordingly, it received the greatest media attention, and every step, gesture and reaction by Wayne Rooney and Ronaldo was scrutinised.

The transfer window was still open until the end of August, meaning that in spite of Ronaldo's insistence that he was staying put, nobody was ruling anything out. A bad start to the campaign could heap the pressure on the Portuguese. Defeats would allow the media to interpret every action in line with their agenda: Ronaldo and Rooney do not get on.

Manchester United clicked straight into gear and dished out their most comprehensive opening day league win (5–1) since the Second World War. Rooney scored twice and Ronaldo netted the fourth from a Rooney assist. The back pages were filled with photos of the pair celebrating the goal.

But when it came to away matches, nobody forgave Ronaldo for the wink that inevitably had become the reason for England's defeat. Insults were pouring in, he was booed during the warm-ups, during the matches themselves and whenever he left the pitch. He was being provoked.

The club's first visit to the capital, where Ronaldo was expected to receive the worst treatment of all because of London fans' connection with the national team, was against Charlton on a Wednesday evening. Ferguson decided to sit in the directors' box during the first half. One home fan spent the first forty-five minutes hurling abuse, 'You Portuguese bastard' being one of the politer epithets. Five minutes before half-time, Ronaldo received the ball, danced round about four players and hit the underside of the bar with a shot. Ferguson remembered perfectly how 'that guy did not rise from his seat again'.[18]

It deflated him. 'Perhaps he thought that his screaming had motivated him,' wrote Ferguson in his book.[18]

By this point, the press had turned its attention towards Manchester United's attempt to wrest the title away from Chelsea, forgetting the World Cup incident before supporters did.

Ferguson's squad, particularly Cristiano, were hungry for success and played with an extraordinary level of ambition, speed and precision. Gary Neville went so far as to say, 'The start of that season was the most enjoyable six months that I've seen at United.'

'I always remember a game away at Bolton that was just out of this world for thirty minutes. Giggs, Saha, Rooney and Cristiano in the first six months of that season really had everything. We were so difficult to play against,' explained Neville.

The heated atmosphere was gradually diminishing as people grew tired of provoking Ronaldo, who seemed to thrive on the hostility, while the Old Trafford faithful made him one of their own. Ferguson's patience was being rewarded as he readied his new side to make history.

The fans were witnessing the very public and prominent birth of a legend.

■ ■ ■

Cristiano's stronger incarnation in 2004 was superseded by his muscle development in 2006, a consequence of his daily efforts, which was accompanied by an almost absolute comprehension of exactly what was needed to be a success in English football.

Just when many at Carrington thought he was a lost cause.

It was as if the penny had suddenly dropped. The pieces to the puzzle had been assembled over three years and were now ready to be slotted into place.

'I just thought he was never going to get decision-making, the understanding and appreciation of his team-mates, in possession and out of possession,' admitted Gary Neville.

For Gary, there was a moment in a match that made him change his conception of football for ever. And it was in a game that is no more than a fleeting memory for so many.

Away to Fulham in February 2007.

The right-back was unable to play that day due to injury. Manchester United were about to throw away two crucial points at Craven Cottage, but Ronaldo suddenly popped up with a vital winner.

'He scores that goal that wins you the title. The special players over the years are the ones who will produce it when you most need it. That game was a massive moment for him.'

At the end of the season, it is the type of match that is only remembered in the champions' dressing room. 'It does, it wins you the league. You shiver when you're talking about that goal because . . . you're finished otherwise . . . That was the game when I finally felt, "This guy is proper, this is real."'

'He changed my way of thinking,' Neville continued. 'He taught me it's possible to accommodate the individual ambition that he had with the team's aims and make them work together.'

Ronaldo was becoming less artistic, but far more effective. He was eradicating the superfluous elements of his game. But was still in search of glorious individual moments.

'He could do whatever he wanted and the rest of us would just fit in wherever. We'd make alterations for him. Did Manchester United ever do that for any other player in the time that I was at the club? No, not even Cantona. It finally dawned on me what he meant by his "Too much water kills the plant" comment and I thought, "Yes, that's quite clever."'

Ronaldo was a chance-making machine. He was hungry, had technique, explosiveness, resistance, speed, he could score goals with his power and quality, and started to win matches single-handed. His team-mates sought him out. Opponents learnt that physical intimidation was not enough because he could give any defender a good run for his money in terms of strength and aggression.

Gary Neville himself was on the receiving end of it in every training session. And every morning the full-back would end up repeating between gritted teeth, 'I'm going to retire soon. Nobody can cope with this.'

■ ■ ■

'After what happened at Manchester United with Rooney, I'm used to everything. People speak to me at hotels and airports and seem to really love me. Then comes a match and I'm a devil. They call me all sorts of things . . . I'm used to it, but sometimes it leaves me a bit, I don't know . . . They are trying to make me lose focus, but they only do that with good players, right?'[6]

Cristiano Ronaldo

He sees the hostile relationship from opposition fans 'as part of the challenge and part of the recognition of who he is. He feeds off it.' That is how my conversation with sports psychologist Bill Beswick began.

You against 40,000. Imagine.

I tell Beswick that it is something that many would not be able to understand or overcome. When Ronaldo is on the pitch, he is wrapped in a layer of confidence and emotional stability that enables him to cope with anything. That strength emanates from off-the-field stability: the club was helping him, his family was helping him, his efforts were turning into results, it was clear to see. Everything was in order.

He had made the pitch his kingdom.

'Such players love being in a stadium in front of thousands of pairs of eyes. It's more home than being off a football field,' explained

Beswick. 'It's what they do. It's where they can be themselves, when they are at their best, where they're recognised, where they get self-esteem and their identity is complete. It's off the field when they have a difficult time. Waiting to get back on to the field.'

In order to make that part more bearable, they spend hours at the training ground, they buy gym equipment and get swimming pools built at their properties, and recreate states of emotional wellbeing that assure them of happiness: what they live on the pitch is extended beyond it.

In this regard, I proposed the following theory to Bill Beswick. As has already been mentioned, Ronaldo likes to give presents to his family, friends, players, the coaching staff, physios. He had a room built in his house in Manchester that could easily become a small nightclub. He would invite friends and would often give them a gift. I do not think that he is buying their appreciation, but is tacitly asking them to have walk-on parts in that other part of his life. The one in which he must live comfortably, without challenges, doubts and conflicts.

'That's a good way of putting it,' Beswick answered. 'In the sense that if you're acting, you're unreal. You're unreal, in my opinion, because you're not able to deal with this extraordinary dichotomy. Extraordinary athlete, ordinary guy. I used to say to David Beckham, "Listen, mate. When you leave the training ground, stop at the red light. You may be extraordinary and deliver the best cross I've ever seen in my life, but if you don't stop at the red light, you're dead or somebody else is." And that's really what sports psychologists should tell these athletes when they are twelve-, thirteen- and fourteen-year-olds.'

But so many cannot stop. It is what Beswick labels 'the treadmill personality'. If such an athlete is on the treadmill, nothing can damage or stop them. They do what they know best. It makes people happy and they applaud. They stay busy by working and learning so that they do not have to think about anything else. They are constantly on the move to overcome any possible anxiety and not to have to think beyond their profession.

They prefer to take their mind and body to the limit before stopping.

It must be exhausting.

And, of course, they must pay a heavy price when they retire. When the treadmill stops. Because they collapse.

But I digress . . .

■ ■ ■

Hundreds of sports pages were devoted to the war of words between Ronaldo and Mourinho who accused referees of favouring Manchester United. 'He never recognises when he's wrong,' was Cristiano's response.[11] José called his compatriot a liar ('If he says that it is false that Manchester United have conceded penalties that were not given, it's lies') and decided to go even further. 'Maybe it's a consequence of his difficult childhood and not having an education.'

Elements of the English football press prefer to focus on controversy and big personalities. Ronaldo (and Mourinho, of course) offered them the best of both worlds. 'Maybe because I'm very good,' was Ronaldo's answer when asked why he was involved in so much polemic that season.

Tabloid journalists had lapped up the juicy content, although they already had surplus football material in the shape of the Portuguese's exceptional season.

After annihilating Roma 7–1, including a Ronaldo brace, AC Milan awaited in the Champions League semi-finals. Cristiano was rewarded with a new bumper contract until 2012 in light of his outstanding performances, making him the best-paid player in the club's history. Ferguson celebrated the fact that one of the best players he had signed and developed was extending his Old Trafford adventure.

There were dreams of another treble to replicate 1999. The league was possible and the club reached the FA Cup final. Chelsea stood in their way in both competitions.

The first leg of the Champions League semi-final was played at Old Trafford. Ronaldo opened the scoring with a header, but a sublime Kaká turned the match on its head with two goals. It would not end there. Wayne Rooney, on perhaps one of his greatest European nights, scored twice, including a last-minute winner, to leave Manchester United in pole position to reach the Athens final. Ronaldo's impact that night was limited to his goal and a strike from distance that Dida parried.

The return leg at the San Siro, however, did not go to plan. The home side played spectacular football with goals by Kaká, Seedorf and Gilardino – no less than they deserved. Ronaldo played down the left, but was ineffectual.

He did win the Premier League, however, his first in four years at the club. He was at home on the sofa with his brother-in-law Zé when it was all confirmed, as Chelsea failed to beat Arsenal at the Emirates. United finished six points ahead of Mourinho's side.

The domestic season came to a close two weeks later against the Blues in the inaugural FA Cup final at the new Wembley. Based on how the campaign had gone, Chelsea's 1–0 victory with an extra-time Drogba goal was considered a bit of a shock. Ronaldo was once again on the left wing, but once again ineffectual.

■ ■ ■

Ronaldo's 2006–07 Premier League campaign was stunning. He had never scored so many goals (twenty-three in all competitions) or provided so many assists (thirteen, the same as Arsenal's Fàbregas).

Plaudits (large and small) flooded in for the twenty-two-year-old who discovered the inherent happiness that top-level consistency can provide.

Among the small ones was one from a linesman who said to Ronaldo when the player passed him on the pitch, 'Play with a smile on your face, we like to see you smile.'

Among the big ones was being named Player of the Year and Young Player of the Year by the Professional Footballers' Association (nobody had won both awards in the same season since Andy Gray in 1977). He also scooped the Football Writers' Association Footballer of the Year and Professional Footballers' Association Fans' Player of the Year awards.

Ferguson waited for the opportune moment to make his own tribute.

He signed Anderson and Nani in summer 2007, and Ronaldo turned his growing dressing-room presence into something more: he was the leader of the group of new arrivals, facilitated by a common language and style of play. He was happy to protect and guide them.

On top of that, the manager wanted to acknowledge his work on and off the field by offering him the emblematic captain's armband for a home clash against Bolton. He had reached such a level of maturity that nobody grumbled when he was asked to represent the club in such a way. Ronaldo responded as usual when he feels appreciated and is offered responsibility: with a sterling performance and both goals in a comfortable victory.

He had won everyone over. Opposition fans, the press. No doubts remained. The Manchester United platform had allowed him to reach such a level that not even the sky was the limit. The rest of the team was fully behind him and willingly followed his lead.

In many people's eyes, Ronaldo had become a small god.

■ ■ ■

The twenty-two-year-old from Funchal was bending the will of his team-mates and supporters from all over the country.

He felt tremendously comfortable in that space, something like being in the eye of a hurricane only inhabited by the chosen ones. Ronaldo was delighted to take to the field every week in front of crowds that had travelled the country from far and wide to get a glimpse of their gods in action. And when they made it on to the field, Ronaldo and the other players would dance for them.

Let me explain the analogy.

We are speaking about the same territory that William Dalrymple narrates so brilliantly in his book *Nine Lives*. In the chapter entitled 'The Dancer of Kannur', he takes us to the Indian city in the state of Kerala. In the midnight shadows of a forest, illuminated only by a bonfire and camphor lights, six Dalit drummers have been gradually raising their tempo surrounded by devotees from all over India.

A god is about to incarnate itself into the dancer's body, while he raves in the middle of the circle. 'He is frenetically pirouetting around the clearing, strutting and jabbing, unsheathed sword in one hand,' Dalrymple writes.

Hari Das, the man who ends up being possessed, has been turning for twenty-six years into the god Vishnu in front of hundreds of believers. Following a conversation with him, the author describes how he felt before, during and after the process.

In the build-up, he cannot avoid nerves in case the god refuses to come. The level of devotion determines the intensity of the possession. 'If you lose your feeling of devotion, if it even once becomes routine or unthinking, the gods may stop coming,' explains Hari Das.

When the dance starts and he is possessed by Vishnu, he is not aware of what is happening to him. A blinding light hits him. He becomes the deity. He is just the vehicle, the medium. He loses all fear and even his voice changes. 'The dancer is an ordinary man – but this being is divine,' explains Das who is a manual labourer during the week and, at weekends, a prison warder.

The trance does not, nor can it, last a lifetime. When coming out of it, the dancer feels 'the incision of a surgeon. Suddenly it's all over, it's gone.'

Does this not sound like the perfect description of a footballer in a big match? Or, to a greater or lesser extent, maybe in every single game.

And when they turn the corner away from the pitch, life often reminds them, as it does Das, that footballers are not gods.

■ ■ ■

Ronaldo's mother discovered that she had breast cancer.

While Cristiano was battling for his first Premier League title, Dolores was operated on at Cruz Carvalho hospital in Funchal and began her recovery, which, after six weeks of radiotherapy, would be pronounced complete.

Look at the photos that were taken months later during the 2006–07 title celebrations at Old Trafford, especially the one with Zé, Hugo, Nuno, Rogério and Dolores alongside Ronaldo on the pitch.

He had come, he had seen and he had conquered. Another chapter was closing.

■ ■ ■

In 2007–08, Ronaldo reached a level that would dwarf his previous season in comparison. Nani and Anderson were joined by Owen

Hargreaves and Carlos Tévez, while Chelsea reached an agreement to terminate José Mourinho's contract by mutual consent early into the campaign.

Ferguson knew all too well that the team had to get the ball to Ronaldo.

'We stopped getting frustrated about him sometimes switching wings without saying anything to anyone when we understood that his versatility was our strength,' explained Gary Neville. 'He had become the star of the team. When you score thirty or thirty-five goals, you can do what you want.'

'He got subbed one game,' recalled Phil Neville, 'and it was as if someone had shot his mum. Ferguson told him, "We want you to rest." "No, I need a goal." He wanted to play in every game. Sir Alex dreaded telling him he was going to rest him. He couldn't take him off in the end.'

Ronaldo was crystal clear on where he was and where he was heading. He was happy with his duties and the responsibility of winning matches for his team-mates, as the leader of the team. A specific type of leader: one who does things as he wishes and forces the rest to do what he wants. If he cannot convince them, he does it all the same.

Ronaldo had to achieve his goal no matter what.

■ ■ ■

'Over a period of time, realising how good he was, he started to get this idea that everything should revolve around him,' explained Mike Phelan. 'All good players do that, "If I don't get the ball then nothing can happen." He got so irritated with his team-mates when they didn't release him on the ball all the time.'

Normally the team accepted they all had to recover possession to get the ball back to him, yet Scholes, Giggs and Nani were all capable of unlocking defences themselves. So they sometimes hit their great passes elsewhere to show their value. '"Don't need to use you today," was their message. You could tell how that frustrated Ronaldo,' added Phelan.

'Sometimes his bad temper would come out,' confirmed Gerard Piqué. 'He didn't like losing and I saw him say a few things in the dressing room at half-time on more than one occasion. He could get us into gear.'

'You had to stay strong with him sometimes,' said Phelan. Ferguson's assistant admitted in private that the worst spell of his career as a coach was the years when he shared the dressing room with Ronaldo. The worst and best, at the same time.

'Even on days when all the lads would say, "Enjoyed that today," he would say, "I didn't get anything out of it."'

So Cristiano began knocking on Phelan's door every morning.

'What can you give me that's different?'

'This, do this,' Phelan would say.

On the first morning he asked, Ronaldo returned to the office after the session.

'This thing you gave me, what the hell was it? This is shit.'

'So what do you want?' Phelan asked him.

'I want to be the best in the world and you have to give me things every day to achieve that.'

Phelan started spending hours and hours in front of his computer, asking colleagues, reading manuals, assembling an encyclopaedia of exercises and targets for him. 'I've never gone so long without sleeping,' he admitted to his circle of friends. 'It was very tough,' he says today.

Ronaldo would ask the same question the following day: 'So what do you have for me today?'

'Back then, if you asked anyone at Carrington who was going to be the best in the world between him and Messi, everyone would've said Ronaldo. Nobody could match his drive,' revealed Phil Neville.

He scored the first hat-trick of his professional career against Newcastle at Old Trafford in January 2008. 'He was no longer a winger, but a formidable and powerful striker,' recalled Gary Neville. 'He could beat centre-backs in the air. In fact, his best United goal for me was a header.'

It was a goal that emerged from the challenge that Ronaldo had set himself.

'This isn't enough for me, I need more.' Those words had become his mantra at Carrington. He demanded that everybody, coaches and players alike, be one step ahead and improve. The coaches explored new avenues, tried to take him out of his comfort zone to please and help him and also to add new ammunition to the team.

They started asking him to play down the middle rather than on the wing. As a number ten. Or as a number nine. He had done so at the Sporting academy and had the attributes for both positions.

Ronaldo enjoyed it when the team had plenty of possession and the play would always go through him. He would get more touches of the ball and chances to get involved, and that way he could decide games from a central position.

But in big games, when the team had less possession, he soon realised ('He worked things out really quickly: what was good for him and what wasn't good for him,' said Mike Phelan) that the Manchester United number nine often needed, as well as scoring goals, to be able to receive the ball to feet, turn, run in behind, wait for the pass. It did not suit his game and also that meant others carried the ball. He was not so pleased about that either.

'In big matches, he didn't see a lot of the ball, it didn't always go straight into him and I think he realised that maybe he was better off in a different area where he could influence more,' continued Phelan.

Despite Carlos Queiroz insisting he could become the most complete centre-forward in the world, 'he didn't want the role all the time probably because he was getting the ball in areas where he wasn't comfortable,' observed Phil Neville. 'This was new. Maybe he thought that he wasn't going to score as many goals.'

So he was half-heartedly learning to be a number nine, forced to play in that position in key games, but not convinced that was where he could get his best stats. And yet, he was scoring classic striker goals. Just like the one that Gary Neville mentioned.

It was against Roma.

Goalless with six minutes to go to half-time in the Champions League quarter-finals at the Stadio Olimpico (1 April 2008), Paul Scholes put in a cross from the right towards the penalty spot where Ronaldo should have been (Rooney played down the left).

The ball, now in the air, did not seem to belong to anyone in particular.

And then . . .

'He jumps up, all the muscles in his neck were straining,' Wayne Rooney wrote in his autobiography.[19]

'He jumped like Michael Jordan and finished like Joe Jordan,' said Gary Neville. 'He was like a fast-speed train.'

'I've never seen anyone travel in the air like that,' recalled Phelan. 'He's not even in the picture, but suddenly this body flies through the air, wallop, it's on his head and it's in.'

'I'm a striker and I know that that isn't my ball,' stated Louis Saha. 'I'll never get to that ball, but he managed to jump, you see him in front of the mirror putting gel in his hair and then all of a sudden, you see this giant jumping up and heading the ball.'

Ronaldo's lower body strength and height help him lift off with five times more power than his body weight, reaching seventy-eight centimetres. That is seven centimetres higher than the average for NBA players (Michael Jordan could reach 1.20 metres). With his gym work, he went from winning 40 to 66 per cent of balls in the air that season. Thanks to his improved timing on the back of hundreds of hours of training, he could head a ball at a height of 2.63 metres.

'He connected very far out, almost on the penalty spot, but the ball flew in like a bullet,' recalled Gary Neville.

And it beat Doni.

'And he's still in the air as the ball hits the net. You don't coach that; you're just glad to be there to see it,' Phelan reminisced.

It was his thirty-sixth goal of the season and Ronaldo also considers it one of the best of his career.

'One of the best headers I've ever seen . . . Alan Shearer could've scored it,' stated Rooney, who converted the second and final goal of the game.[19] After beating Roma again at Old Trafford, Barcelona awaited in the semi-finals.

Along with the power of his jump and the velocity with which the ball flew off his head, there is another aspect that everyone remembers with bemusement. Ronaldo hung in the air.

Is that possible?

■ ■ ■

It takes exactly the same amount of time to reach a height as it does to come down. When we are at the highest point, our vertical speed is very low, while our climb and descent rate is very fast. While we are up there, we barely move and that is partly where the feeling of hanging in the air comes from.

Greater strength and a lower weight do not mean a longer ascent, but a faster take-off speed resulting in more time in the air. Gravity makes us all equal when we leave the ground, but athletes start their ascent at a greater speed, meaning their rise and fall will be bigger than ours.

There is something that amplifies that virtual fantasy of hanging in the air: bending your legs in the first phase and stretching them in the second. When gravity is at work for the fall, legs fall first and body stays at the same height.

And that helps give the visual illusion of almost floating.

■ ■ ■

Ronaldo is a powerhouse.

In the 2007–08 season, he scored a staggering forty-two goals (thirty in the league, including nine headers), despite not opening his account until late September and carrying an ankle injury in the last two months of the campaign. He kept playing with a prodigious physical and mental effort, thanks to the anti-inflammatories, specific treatment and barely training at all.

He did not want to miss a single part of a season that had all the ingredients for becoming a historic one.

United travelled to Barcelona for the first leg of the Champions League semi-final to take on Frank Rijkaard's declining side, with Ronaldinho and Deco approaching the end of their spells at the Camp Nou.

Carlos Queiroz convinced Ferguson to play Cristiano as the team's striker once again. First of all for defensive reasons. He would not be capable of tracking the Barcelona full-back or winger, while Park Ji-sung would be better suited to such a task. On the other hand, they felt that Ronaldo could expose Gabriel Milito's supposed physical frailties and lack of pace.

Yet Ronaldo did not like the idea (and even told me so in the mixed zone after both games, first off the record and then into the microphone). His facial expression reflected as much on the pitch.

He missed a penalty early on at the Camp Nou and had barely been influential, while a twenty-one-year-old Leo Messi's attacking play at Barcelona was making the world take note. United had to wait for a Paul Scholes screamer in the second leg to decide the tie.

It was the club's first Champions League final in nine years. It would take place in Moscow against Avram Grant's Chelsea, who had dispatched Liverpool in the semi-finals, and who were level on points with United in the league with two matches remaining.

The final day saw United take on Wigan whose defender Emerson Boyce felled Wayne Rooney in the box after thirty-three minutes. Ronaldo asked for the ball. His miss against Barcelona was not weighing him down. He scored. Ferguson's side won 2–0, while Chelsea could only muster a 1–1 draw at home to Bolton.

Manchester United had won the Premier League once again.

'I felt that I owed Ronaldo my championship medal in a way that I had only previously felt with Schmeichel and Cantona in 1995–96,' Gary Neville wrote in his book.[20]

The Champions League final remained.

■ ■ ■

When the ball that was to be used in the final at the Luzhniki stadium arrived at Carrington, Cristiano asked to stay behind after training. He noticed that it was very different from the one that had been used in the rest of the competition. Carlos Queiroz kept him company and they analysed its surface and weight. Ronaldo took shots from different distances using a range of techniques, with his instep to hit it over a fictitious wall or the inside of his foot to go around it. He looked to generate maximum impact by kicking the valve of the ball. It did not respond. Queiroz suggested a change of technique, varying his run-up and his body position, but nothing worked.

He tried the same the following day.

'He suddenly hit one and it flew into the top corner,' the Portuguese coach recalled. '"That's it, I've got it." From that point on, they all went in.'

It was a small detail: he had to take an extra step back in his run-up.

Ronaldo had a free role in Moscow. Ferguson wanted him to make daring, aggressive runs at the centre-backs and right-back (Avram Grant surprisingly picked midfielder Michael Essien to play as a full-back). They knew that he could frighten John Terry and Ricardo Carvalho and that if the Portuguese defender decided to come out of his position, as he frequently did, Cristiano would take advantage of the space if his team-mates could find him. If Carvalho man-marked him, or if Terry did it himself, it would open up the possibility of getting in behind them using his pace.

Other players (Rooney, Tévez and Scholes) had to be alert to take advantage of each of Ronaldo's victories in that titanic battle with the centre-backs.

Ferguson wanted opposition defenders to have to make decisions based on Cristiano's potential and his possible threat.

'I thought he could go past Essien whenever he wanted,' recalled Ryan Giggs. 'But it was such a tight affair against a tough, experienced Chelsea.'

Ronaldo endured some uncomfortable moments and disappeared for periods.

'Very few players play well in a Champions League final,' explained Gary Neville. 'When the other team has had ten days or two weeks to prepare just for you, they've sorted every little detail to stop you.'

There was no fluidity to his game, yet he managed to open the scoring with a header from a Wes Brown cross from the right. Essien did not even try to jump to battle for the ball: he must have thought that it was too high. Not for Cristiano.

Frank Lampard's equaliser before the break was the last goal of the game as a goalless extra-time period meant a penalty shootout was required.

Cristiano stepped up to take the third penalty. He picked up the ball with determination. He kissed it. He placed it on the spot. He stepped back, hands on hips. He did a dummy on his run-up that would go against the rule book nowadays. He stopped mid-run-up. Maybe he had doubts. His shot was at a comfortable height to the goalkeeper's right.

Petr Cech stopped it.

He scrunched up his face and briefly covered it with both hands.

He was the only Manchester United player to miss. John Terry could have won Chelsea their first Champions League, but slipped at the vital moment and failed to convert. Edwin van der Sar denied Nicolas Anelka and it was all over.

Ronaldo was overcome by a childish sob combining tears of relief and happiness.

Such a reaction did not compute with the team spirit.

Instead of running towards his team-mates, he stayed on the ground in the centre circle, stretched out, face down. Pure Ronaldo. We will never know if he wanted to be the centre of attention, but some players took his gesture in that way.

Gary Neville went up to him to demand he celebrate with the team, but Ronaldo was enjoying the success in his own little world.

He later thanked Edwin van der Sar for his cup-winning save.

An extraordinary season came to a close with a double in which the Portuguese had shown he was the best player in the world.

Without any doubt.

But that night had a bittersweet end for the Manchester United supporters.

Ronaldo's behaviour in the mixed zone seemed to suggest that he had just played his final game for the Red Devils.

FIVE

THE REAL MADRID TRANSFER MAZE

A TORTUOUS AGREEMENT

'Science is built on facts the way a house is built of bricks: but an accumulation of facts is no more science than a pile of bricks is a house.'

Henri Poincaré, French philosopher and mathematician

The construction that Cristiano Ronaldo had assembled was made up of myriad pieces forged over the years. He was not born like that. Look at the front and back cover of this book. Layers of hard work and learning had coalesced for the scary look of the kid to become the assured gaze of the man.

At least five coatings are necessary if we take a well-known comment by pedagogue Jesús Beltrán Llera, in which he answered the question of how we learn.

Simple. By choosing (or stealing), organising, elaborating, applying and evaluating.

Stealing? Beltrán Llera explains it with a story by Rabindranath Tagore, the eminent Bengali writer and poet. His family received a visit from a great musician who offered them classes to thank them for their hospitality. The mother accepted, but Rabindranath did not learn anything from those lessons. Daily the guest performed a marvellous concert. 'That's where I learnt,' told Tagore. 'I stole everything from that beautiful, artistic and harmonic musical display.'

Learning also involves organising, arranging furniture. Once you have chosen and arranged it, the information is transformed into knowledge, but you have to personalise it and make it your own in the same way that a new colour can be generated by the fusion of two or more hues.

And then you have to try and apply that acquired knowledge. Beltrán Llera compared it to riding a bicycle: somebody helps you maintain your balance until you have enough experience to do it for yourself. From that point, you can pedal and use the bicycle however you want.

Evaluation, a crucial component, entails knowing whether goals have been reached, noticing mistakes made and learning how to learn to keep learning.

Cristiano Ronaldo had several guides for this final phase; experienced people who had studied the path and who were seasoned teachers. During the Premier League and Champions League double season, that job was meticulously performed by René Meulensteen, Alex Ferguson's Dutch assistant.

Although they would see each other on a daily basis at the training ground, René took advantage of Ronaldo's three-match ban after seeing red against Portsmouth to look back over the path trodden by the player up to that point and see where he found himself. And to offer new ideas, too.

A big chunk of the effort focused on understanding the impact of his body language.

Meulensteen recorded footage of Ronaldo and showed it to him. 'Look at yourself,' he told him. They watched a clip in which Cristiano was visibly relieved and happy after scoring an important penalty against Everton. He turned around, smiled and acknowledged his team-mates. Another showed him being fouled against Wigan and calmly getting to his feet as if nothing had happened.

However, after another foul, he was disgusted and demonstrated his anger, having clearly been affected by the incident. There was also the stunning free-kick that he scored against Portsmouth, after which he turned around and celebrated as if to say, 'Only I could've done that, I'm the man.' There was a similar incident against Sporting Lisbon when a spectacular Ronaldo rocket flew into the corner. Ronaldo faced the crowd, shrugged his shoulders, arched his lips down and held his hands out.

'What were you trying to say? "Sorry, I scored again?"' René asked him. 'Or "Only I could've scored that?"'

Meulensteen saw it as a gesture of self-fulfilment. 'That's what millions of people think. That's why they think you're arrogant,' he told him. 'You often do the same thing when you get a kick. "You can't kick me, I'm Cristiano Ronaldo." Wrong reaction!'

Perception of the opposition is crucial. Roger Federer plays as if he is never exhausted and nothing gets to him. That is how he wins many matches before he even starts them.

Ronaldo had to accept that it was better for opponents to kick and foul him than the other way round. 'The moment they stop doing that, they've found a way to break you,' René told him. All he had to do is see it coming and react diligently and intelligently. As if the opposition did not exist. As if everything they did to try to stop him did not affect him.

Ferguson's assistant also tried something to increase Cristiano's goal-scoring ability by advising him to steal the essence of other strikers.

'Set a target for the new season,' René suggested. 'I can score thirty or thirty-five goals,' stated the forward. 'Well, I think you can get to forty,' the coach answered, before trying to educate him on the tactics that would help him improve.

To start with, he made him see that he was not a finisher. Not yet. He had scored twenty-three goals the previous season, a beatable figure if the player abandoned the idea of scoring the perfect goal. 'Look at me, I've put it in the top corner,' seemed to be his message with every shot. 'The top players are the ones that lift the team, not themselves,' maintained René.

'I took him upstairs after training and let him watch clips of Denis Law, George Best, Ruud Van Nistelrooy and Solskjær.'

'Just tell me what you see,' René asked him.

'Basically, George Best was the most like him, scored the most exciting goals, whereas the others were all clinical finishers. Their range of finishing: tap-ins, volleys, headers, one-touch, two-touch . . . I said, "You're like Best, but we need to add this (the others) to your game, and that's what we're going to work on."'

Individual sessions were organised to focus on Ronaldo's visualisation of goals, his body movement, identifying the best parts of the penalty area for scoring, technical details and runs.

In late January of that 2007–08 season, Ronaldo had scored twenty-seven goals and Meulensteen asked him to adjust his target.

An insatiable, mentally strong Ronaldo ended up with forty-two goals over the campaign, although René believes there was a key moment when the player lapsed back into his old habits.

The penalty that he missed in the Champions League final against Chelsea: 'Key moment, everbody looking, he is the centre of the universe. His focus again totally on himself, rather than the team. So what happens? He missed it. Because he didn't want to score for the team, he wanted to score for himself.'

. . .

In the mixed zone in Moscow after the Champions League final, Ronaldo's answers posed more questions than they clarified, following on from some statements made to the Spanish press a few days earlier: 'I've said a thousand times that my dream is to play in Spain. Sometimes your dreams don't come true, but I'm still dreaming. I'm happy at Manchester United. As for my future, nobody knows what's going to happen.'

Real Madrid were evidently in the hunt. Had the first conversations between the Spanish giants and Jorge Mendes taken place? Or did Cristiano's words simply reflect his longing for a transfer? The answer is simple: when players send out such a message, something has already been said between the seducer and the seduced. Why bring it up otherwise?

Ronaldo was the best player in the world in 2008. The type of player they like in Madrid. There was talk that the Euros in Austria and Switzerland could be the perfect shop window.

'I had him round the neck saying, "Come on, man, stay, we're going to make history at this club together. We'll be the best team to ever play for Man United", recalled Rio Ferdinand. 'He said, "Yeah, I'd love to but . . ." I was also holding Jorge Mendes round the neck saying, "Come on, man! Make him stay!"'

From the day of his arrival at Old Trafford, Sir Alex and Carlos Queiroz often asked themselves how long they could hold on to him. The Portuguese coach had it clear in his mind: 'If you get five years out of him, you've struck gold. There's no precedent for a Portuguese player going to another country at seventeen years old and staying five years.' Ferguson knew that, as Ronaldo was now a global idol and that five-year period was up, it would be difficult to manage him as he had so far been able to.

In addition to the daily warmth shown to him at Carrington, the club made it its mission to ensure there were no contract-related problems. Only once did a small conflict occur when Mendes sent out a message through the Portuguese press in February 2005 that the latest contract offer was not enough. Manchester United reacted accordingly and, although negotiations progressed at a snail's pace, a new deal was penned in November: a two-year extension (until 2010) worth £50,000 a week.

In April 2007, both Mendes and the club agreed that Ronaldo's spectacular season deserved a reward in the shape of a new deal: until 2012 on £119,000 a week.

The season of the double league and Champions win was Cristiano's fifth at United and the one that Queiroz believed could be his last.

'We knew that he wanted to leave since summer 2008,' explained Gary Neville. 'He used to discuss it openly in the dressing room. He wanted to play in a hot climate and the prestige of Real Madrid was a magnet for him.'

The Portuguese became the main favourite to win the Ballon d'Or. Although Ferguson historically preferred to ditch those whose commitment to the team could be adversely affected by such individual recognition, he was willing to make an exception for Cristiano.

'The best we could do was get him to stay for another twelve months,' stated Gary Neville.

■ ■ ■

The first time I spoke to Cristiano was at the heart of Old Trafford. It is strange, but if you are on television, and I had been on Sky Sports for ten years by then, introductions are often unnecessary. A nod of recognition is sufficient to start a chat. Back then there was talk of Real Madrid's interest and Cristiano knew that I had been mentioning it regularly on our weekly Spanish football show, *Revista de la Liga*.

Ronaldo would later make use of that platform.

I noticed how he played with the Spanish press in the days leading up to the Champions League final and how he dispersed his doubts that night in Moscow. When he took leave of the press room at the Luzhniki stadium, he looked at me with a mischievous smile.

We saw each other again at Euro 2008. He gave me an exclusive interview. A little beauty.

■ ■ ■

Entrusted with managing a transitional period in the Portugal squad, Scolari had to resolve the small matter of captaincy before getting to Austria and Switzerland. Ronaldo was, without doubt, the star man, but the rest of the group did not see him as a captain. Furthermore, Big Phil knew that appointing him could increase the envy that was starting to filter through his players towards the Madeiran.

The previous captain had been Nuno Gomes, one of the heroes of the 'golden generation' and the perfect man to bridge the gap between the veterans and the ambitious youngsters who were impatiently waiting their turn. Scolari eventually decided on joint captaincy: Nuno, Cristiano (as second captain having already sported the armband in a friendly against Brazil at the Emirates in London), Petit, Ricardo Carvalho and Simão Sabrosa.

The Brazilian, though, did not make allowances for something that would end up being pivotal. Ronaldo had opened Pandora's Box with his enigmatic statements about his future and his life was to become a media circus that would affect his performances. Scolari, in hindsight, admitted as much himself.

Football-wise, the national team coach had relieved most of the old guard of their duties and began to surround Ronaldo with facilitators as well as talented midfielders. It was no longer Rui Costa and Figo pulling the strings in midfield, but Deco, who put in dominant, spectacular performances that summer. Ricardo Carvalho had replaced Fernando Couto.

In the group stage of the Euros, Portugal finished top after wins over Turkey and the Czech Republic. Defeat in the final game against Switzerland was of no significance. Germany surprisingly finished second in their group, meaning they would face Scolari's side in the quarter-finals.

The Germans, led by an imperious Michael Ballack, made light work of a subdued Portugal side whose short-lived dreams of grabbing a late equaliser after Hélder Postiga halved the deficit in the eighty-seventh minute were quickly dashed as they were deservedly dumped out of the competition.

Ballack was Germany's talisman. Ronaldo was not Portugal's just yet. The striker did not link up well with Deco and disappeared from the game.

Another important match in which Ronaldo found it hard to take the bull by the horns.

■ ■ ■

That was the day I felt closest to Cristiano.

After elimination from the European Championships, the player walked past the group of journalists who were waiting for him in the mixed zone without stopping. He was the man of the moment and this was the last chance to hear from him that summer.

On that very same day, Real Madrid had admitted that they were waiting for Ronaldo to make a move that would allow them to open negotiations with Manchester United. Had he played his last game for United? Why did he speak so openly about his desire to go to Spain?

He looked at the floor while holding a washbag and avoiding questions. He limped slightly.

I usually stand at the end of the mixed zone in order to have small private conversations with the players whom I get on with best.

I looked at him. He smiled at me and slowed down, which I took as a signal. I took out my voice recorder and we had a chat.

'I have a dream.'

'Not all dreams come true, but I want this one to.'

'Everyone knows what I want.'

'I hope that things can be resolved over the summer.'

'I'll always be grateful to Manchester United.'

I immediately wrote an article for my recently launched website and called Sky Sports News. I explained what Ronaldo had just told me, I announced that his full statement was on my website.

But the site crashed and barely anyone was able to view them.

In any case, Cristiano's message had been clearly sent out.

What had made him declare his intentions?

What followed was a tumultuous and fascinating story of intrigue and disagreements.

■ ■ ■

For Ronaldo and Real Madrid, the romance began in 2003.

Although Jorge Mendes spoke to the Spanish club about a talented seventeen-year-old that half of Europe was fighting over, Real never seriously tried to sign him from Sporting.

Los Blancos received reports on Cristiano after his impressive Toulon Under-21 tournament and sent a scout to watch the friendly against Manchester United. Queiroz, who had just been appointed Real Madrid coach that summer, made his new employers aware of his countryman's potential, without overly insisting because he knew that Ferguson was after him.

The Real Madrid board began showing real interest in a phone conversation two years later in the summer of 2005. Almost innocently. Almost.

José Ángel Sánchez, the chief executive and the man in charge of the day-to-day running of the club at the time, was in the car when he received a call from Jorge Mendes. He soon asked, 'When are we going to bring Cristiano here?'

'That's impossible!' replied the agent. Ronaldo had only been at Manchester United for two years and was still striving to fulfil his potential.

'That's fine, but we have to bring him to Real Madrid one day,' Sánchez told him.

Such conversations take place by the dozen and are implicitly small commitments. José Ángel, a man with a constant welcoming smile on his face and the charm of one who never seems to be doing business, had just opened up a line of communication. From that moment onwards, Cristiano almost always came up in conversations with Mendes.

That 'he has to come here' line was the ticket to future negotiations.

Ronaldo clearly fitted the Real Madrid '*galáctico*' phase. José Ángel also knew that Cristiano (just like his mother) had a soft spot for Real Madrid. What the chief executive was not aware of was that a sixteen-year-old Ronaldo had told his friends while watching Real in action on television, 'I'll play for that team one day.'

The president that summer 2005 was Florentino Pérez, a man who seems to have hundreds of the same coloured suits and who carries his authority lightly, with the ease of a seasoned politician.

He surprisingly abandoned the club presidency just a few months later in February 2006, disillusioned with the behaviour of the stars that he had spoilt by constantly giving in to their demands.

Or so we think. He never clearly explained his exit, which seemed to be a hot-headed reaction rather than a premeditated decision. In fact, he started to plan his return no sooner than he had left the presidential seat.

That puzzling behaviour by Florentino was the root cause of an institutional civil war that turned the Ronaldo deal into a political saga.

Pérez decided to leave his presidency to the incumbent director Fernando Martín. Not everybody accepted the decision, however. Ramón Calderón, a lawyer and one of Pérez's former executives, understood that an electoral process was required. Ramón is a traditional man of an advanced age who belongs to another era, exemplified by the way he speaks, his classic style and tailor-made suits. He sounds and looks like someone who has been to the end of the world and back.

He had never considered being president; he actually felt comfortable watching the bulls from behind the barrier, as a good second or third man in charge. After discussions with his family, though, he decided to enter the battle and Fernando Martín agreed to call elections for 2 July 2006.

The whole process was tarnished from day one. The exchange of personal accusations was besmirching the candidates' prestige and the postal vote, which was under suspicion, was cancelled in court after Calderón filed a complaint.

The lawyer won the elections and decided to accept the mandate without calling a repeat vote, despite not having great support among the public or the media. He had convinced club members by having the legendary Pedja Mijatovic in his ranks, but his presidency had a constant air of crisis: Florentino seemed to enjoy feeding the idea that he was considering his return. And he casts a long shadow.

Calderón used the bait of a generous salary increase to convince José Ángel Sánchez to stay and perform the same role that he had done so brilliantly with Pérez. Leaving the executor behind the *galáctico* philosophy within the club was a strange strategic move by Calderón. Unless, as some sources claim, Calderón was initially Florentino's successor entrusted with the job of keeping the hot seat warm until Pérez organised his comeback.

A month after Calderón took over, head coach Fabio Capello asked the club to cancel a tour of Chile that ex-president Florentino had committed to. The Italian believed that the flight from the United States, the previous destination, and the temperature change would affect the team unnecessarily. Calderón agreed with his coach and Pérez never forgave him. According to some sources, that is where the relationship between the two broke down.

If Calderón really was chosen by Pérez, he did not wait long to demonstrate his independence and he certainly believed himself capable of weathering any storm. Yet Florentino's activity behind the scenes, which was backed by greater media support than Calderón's, gradually ate away at the new president's tenure.

There was always one solution to win everyone over. As has always been the case.

Sign a star.

■ ■ ■

In January 2007, six months after the presidential change, Jorge Mendes and José Ángel Sánchez touched base once again. Soon after, Ramón Calderón was told the good news: the agent confirmed that the player wanted to leave United. He had only won one FA Cup and one League Cup with the English club, and he was on track to win his first Premier League title. Yet he was willing to bring his English adventure to an end.

'I know Real Madrid are interested, but I can't speak about it. Alex Ferguson and Carlos Queiroz know too and have banned me from speaking about Real Madrid,' revealed Ronaldo with a certain level of ambiguity that everyone was able to see through. Ferguson immediately responded: 'We sell the players we want to sell and there's no way Cristiano Ronaldo is going to leave.' First round.

Ramón Calderón knew that he had made the right call after enjoying the Champions League semi-final between Manchester United and AC Milan in spring 2007. Cristino Ronaldo and Kaká (an electoral promise made by Calderón that Pedja Mijatovic did not follow up after discovering that the Brazilian had hip problems and a dodgy knee) were a level above the rest. At least one of them had to wear the famous white of Real Madrid, the president thought.

In March 2007, Ronaldo insisted on implementing the strategy that would dominate the following twelve months: 'Everyone knows that I love Spain. I'd like to play there one day. However, I'm happy at Manchester United. If I don't leave now, if I leave in two, three, four or five years, I'd be happy.'

One month later, he extended his Manchester United contract until 2012. It included something rather unusual for Premier League players: a €75 million release clause in case Real Madrid or another big club decided to splash out on him. There was one condition: confidentiality was essential; nobody could make public that Ronaldo had a price.

'I don't like English clubs . . . I want to see my son play for Real Madrid before I die,' Dolores told *AS* in January 2008, and she was also photographed with an image of her son's face superimposed on to a Real Madrid player. 'In the future . . .' she added.[21] Although uttered in all innocence by a mother who was simply convinced her son's destiny was marked in the stars, such comments were not well received at Manchester United.

Cristiano was the fourth, unexpected, child.

One of the few pictures of Ronaldo at CD Nacional. Is he challenging the photographer?

Look at the physique. The transformation was beginning.

A historic game. Ronaldo played for Sporting knowing his transfer had all been agreed with Manchester United the night before.

Ronaldo signs for United. That jumper . . .

Sir Alex Ferguson was the ultimate father figure, essential to Ronaldo's development. But would they have been so close if Ronaldo had been less vulnerable? Or a lesser player?

(left) He was man of the match on his Manchester United debut. But he could not always maintain that level of expectation.

Ronaldo on his debut for Portugal. He had to wait a few years before he was given the space and influence he deserved in the national team. Figo stopped his progression.

The 2008 Champions League final versus Chelsea. Can he hover in mid-air?

I presented a couple of events with Ronaldo. He was always courteous and very professio
about it all.

Signing for Madrid, he had never been so nervous. But the day was a triumph and the fulfilment of a real dream.

José Mourinho was more foe than friend over the years.

So close, so far apart. The same path, the same goal, but such different relationships with the world around them.

Exaggerated alpha-male celebration at the end of the 2014 Champions League final. Or was it? Do you know why he did it?

With Irina Shayk. If you take her out of the photo, is there anyone missing?

Jorge Mendes has been another father figure, brother, confidant, guardian. Other Mendes players are very jealous of Ronaldo's relationship with him.

Ronaldo's third Ballon d'Or, at which his son stole the show. The family, always close.

Most of Cristiano's sending offs, including this one for kicking Edimar in January 2015, stem from petulant behaviour. Further proof of immaturity, perhaps?

The relationship with Gareth Bale will define Cristiano and the club's immediate future.

Dolores's wish was combined with constant public statements from Calderón about signing Ronaldo. The Madrid press published reports that *Los Blancos* were willing to pay €120 million for the player, but the club knew that €75 million would do the trick. While José Ángel Sánchez stayed in touch with Mendes, Calderón was in direct contact with United's chief executive, David Gill. Whenever the Real Madrid president asked about the Portuguese's situation, he would receive a polite rebuttal. Their relationship gradually deteriorated.

David Gill finally responded to the pressure that was being applied from Madrid: 'There's no way we're going to sell him. The money doesn't matter.' Manchester United decided to send Ramón Calderón a letter imploring him to stop the talk about Ronaldo as they had no intention of getting rid of him – the player would continue to wear the red of Manchester.

Real Madrid still had a very powerful weapon in their armoury: Ronaldo was willing to tighten the screw.

In summer 2008, after beating Chelsea in the Champions League final and clinching the championship, Cristiano believed that he had reached the summit in England. He had spent half of his career there and, at the age of twenty-three, was ready for the next step: to conquer the world.

Nothing was happening by chance, not least his impromptu interview with me in Moscow or the one his mother gave to *AS*. The strategy devised by Jorge Mendes and Cristiano, which was also suggested in the upper echelons of the Santiago Bernabéu, involved publicly acknowledging the player's desire to sign for Real Madrid. Safe in the knowledge that the release clause was present in his latest contract, the club understood that the best route was for both Real Madrid and Cristiano to keep the pressure on.

Alex Ferguson raised the tone of the debate two days after the Champions League final in Moscow. 'Calderón's talking, [the coach

Bernd] Schuster's talking, they use *Marca* as their vehicle to unsettle players,' he declared. 'Ronaldo has got another four years left on his contract and Calderón makes the great statement, "slavery was abolished many, many years ago". Did they tell Franco that?'

In summer 2008, *AS* published news that Real Madrid would meet Ronaldo's release clause. But Ferguson was ready for battle: he could not accept what he considered a public attack. He told Jorge Mendes to forget about the contract as the confidentiality surrounding the release clause had been broken. He had proof. It had been leaked to *Marca*, *AS*, the Bayern Munich board and Michel Platini. Ferguson told Ronaldo's agent more: the player's contract would be renewed under improved terms, making his departure more expensive.

A few days later, just after the Euros had kicked off, Manchester United took a further step: they reported Real Madrid to FIFA.

Alex Ferguson organised a trip to Portugal to put a definitive end to the Spanish club's efforts and, more importantly, to try to convince Ronaldo that he could achieve even more at Old Trafford. Carlos Queiroz offered up his house in Lisbon for the meeting. Cristiano, Ferguson, Carlos and Jorge Mendes sat down for discussion in the living room.

It was clear from the outset that Ronaldo's pressure strategy and Ferguson's military stance had damaged their relationship and they had to mend fences. The Scot was convinced that he could not budge an inch. Real Madrid's media campaign had made up his mind for him: he simply could not let the player leave. It was much more than a sale, it was about maintaining his position of authority on the global stage. Fergie was the one who decided if and when his stars jumped ship.

The other element of the equation was Jorge Mendes who wanted to be the mediator and keep everyone happy. Ferguson suspected that Mendes feared losing the player if he went to Real Madrid, and he said as much in his autobiography. It is what sometimes happens at the most renowned clubs when new agents and new strategies are suddenly on offer.

Ferguson had developed a Machiavellian strategy in the previous weeks. He prepared for a possible outcome in the event that he would be unable to convince the Portuguese to stay, by contacting Barcelona to ensure that would be his next destination. Anything but Real Madrid. But Ronaldo was crystal clear about where he wanted to go. In the midst of the tense calm, the Manchester United manager listened to the player's wish: he was determined to leave, nothing would make him change his mind. It was time and Real Madrid awaited.

Sir Alex eventually reached a gentleman's agreement with the player, having already confirmed it with Mendes. This is how he explained it in his book:

> You can't go this year, not after the way Calderón has approached this issue. I know you want to go to Real Madrid. But I'd rather shoot you than sell you to that guy now. If I do that, all my honour has gone, everything's gone for me, and I don't care if you have to sit in the stands. I know it won't come to that, but I just have to tell you I won't let you leave this year.[18]

In return, if Ronaldo behaved professionally in the following twelve months, if he gave his all for the club and Real Madrid came back with a world-record offer, Sir Alex promised to let him go.

Cristiano accepted.

■ ■ ■

Real Madrid, Manchester United and all other top clubs know that when verbal agreements are reached it is not even necessary to sign anything. What was arranged at Carlos Queiroz's house was law. Both sides would respect it, although it had to be documented, of course.

Ferguson explained the agreement to David Gill, who passed the details on to the club owners, the Glazer family. 'At that point we were petrified that the details of the agreement might creep out,' wrote a speculative Ferguson. 'We warned Cristiano about it. I don't think he told Real Madrid.'[15] He was wrong.

While Ramón Calderón was in Bogotá on 7 or 8 August ahead of a friendly against Santa Fe, the Real Madrid president received a call from Jorge Mendes.

'President, I'm going to put the boy on, he wants to tell you something.'

'President, you have to forgive me,' Ronaldo told Calderón. 'I know we'd said that I'd come to Real Madrid this year, but I can't. Ferguson has asked me to stay, the club has asked me to stay. I have many things to thank Manchester United, the fans and Ferguson himself for. He's like a father to me. So I can't join this year, but we're going to arrange everything for next season.'

Cristiano spoke honestly on the English club's website and in the Portuguese daily *Público*. Only he was responsible for his words, he said, Real Madrid had nothing to do with it. His intention for 'some time' was for Manchester United to sell him to the Spanish giants. 'Saying the opposite would be deceiving the people and my own conscience.'[22]

Now it was just a matter of preparing his arrival for the following summer.

■ ■ ■

According to my sources, a pre-contract was subsequently written in 2008 linking Real Madrid with Cristiano Ronaldo.

It was not very long, but contained the necessary signatures. It promised that the Spanish club would sign the Portuguese and, if it were not to happen because one of the two parties decided to break the agreement, they would be obliged to pay €30 million in compensation.

That contract was the result of several meetings in Porto involving José Ángel Sánchez and Carlos Bucero, assistant to the sporting director Pedja Mijatovic. Club lawyer Javier Calderón also attended one of them.

Bucero worked through the night until he came up with an idea of how to arrange a pre-contract with Cristiano without putting both parties in danger. He eventually managed it. Mendes gave his seal of approval and then it had to be made legal: finally on 12 December 2008, the document was read out in the presence of a notary, signed by Ramón Calderón and on Ronaldo's behalf by Jorge Mendes, who had the player's authority.

The agreement was deposited with notary Pablo Durán de la Colina in Madrid. If anybody had wanted to consult it and take it away before 30 June 2009, they would have needed signatures by both Mendes and Real Madrid. After that date, if either party contravened it by making it public, the notary would have to give a copy to both of them.

Logically, there was a pact between Real Madrid and the player, under contract at Manchester United, not to make the agreement public.

■ ■ ■

I have seen a copy of a document which seemed to be the pre-contract, kept in a drawer in a majestic bottle-green-leather-top walnut desk. The person who showed me it took a key out of his trouser pocket while speaking to me. I was sitting on a sofa facing the only window in the office.

He passed me the document. Neither of us spoke for a while so that I could examine the contents of the document with a fine-tooth comb. He is not the only one who has a copy, but he does not want to make it public. Nor will the others, so he says. Or maybe they will. He told me that there is someone who may be interested in the document coming to light and people discussing it. He told me how to approach him and how to convince him.

Questions were flooding into my head. Was it legal? Could a player under contract sign such a document? Was it necessary? Who was the first party to leak the agreement? Because it *was* leaked. It was leaked to me: I shall explain more later.

Two additional documents were allegedly drafted at the same time as the main one: one in November 2008, which was a private and confidential agreement between the player and Manchester United, to establish the £80 million transfer fee. Real Madrid were not involved in that one.

The second was a letter signed by Cristiano Ronaldo detailing the contract terms: the player accepted the agreed £80 million release clause to leave Manchester United at the end of the 2008–09 season, and if he decided to stay at the English club he would have to pay Real Madrid €30 million. The Spanish club would have to pay the same figure to the player if they reneged on the agreement.

■ ■ ■

Ramon Calderón had been tempted to arrange a meeting with Ronaldo, but the matter had been resolved and his intervention was not needed. They spoke on the phone on 12 December after the main contract was signed by Mendes and the president. 'I'm very excited,' the player told Calderón. 'We'll welcome you with open arms,' he replied. It was the last time they spoke.

Real Madrid only had to ensure that they could stump up the money. They arranged a €70 million loan from Banco de Santander and took out a €1 million currency forward contract in case either the pound or the euro fluctuated considerably (which eventually saw Real Madrid save €4 million as the pound increased in value).

All that remained was to respect the pact of silence.

When everything was confirmed, Real Madrid celebrated the signing in secret and Mijatovic even discreetly sent Cristiano a kit.

On 12 January 2009, a month after the signing of the agreement, I announced on Sky Sports and wrote in an article for *AS* that everything was done and dusted between Ronaldo and Real Madrid.

The person who reveals such an exclusive finds himself in a strange place. My sources were reliable, I knew the ins and outs of the story and decided that it could be announced, but declaring that a star is leaving a top side is an invitation for public outcry and a flurry of insults. You are suddenly in a lonely place: nobody is going to confirm it, nobody is going to get their hands dirty for you. You have to put your head down and live with it until the day the deal is officially announced.

Meanwhile, Manchester United denied it vehemently.

Confirmation of the deal was the worst-case scenario for Florentino Pérez who believed, and wanted people to believe, that his return was necessary. And so, according to numerous media reports, movements behind the scenes were put in motion to pile the pressure on Calderón in order to force early elections and be able to be the man who unveiled Cristiano to the world in the white kit of Real Madrid.

■ ■ ■

Ramón Calderón knew that he had a battle on his hands from his very first day in office: Florentino Pérez was there and was not there. He would not confirm if he planned to be back in the near future, but everyone behind the scenes believed his return was imminent. Interestingly, on 30 October 2008, several qualified people resigned from various football-related companies, all of whom later ended up at Real Madrid. Florentino had discreetly begun his inexorable drive to return to the Santiago Bernabéu.

Calderón reached the end of his second year in office expending just as much energy in defending himself from continuous attacks on his reputation as in celebrating the consecutive league titles clinched under Fabio Capello and Bernd Schuster. He spoke about covert activities behind his back calculated to undermine his authority and his presidency was tarnished with suspicion, insinuation and accusations of all kinds.

The media pressure during that chaotic period at the club finally reached breaking point on 16 January 2009, the day Ramón Calderón announced his resignation as Real Madrid president. He left with his head held high. In the coming months, five lawsuits were filed against him concerning his tenure at the club (he was alleged to have been implicated in a fraudulent vote by post, falsifying accounts, fraudulent commission, manipulating ticket sales).

He was never convicted on any charge. He denied all the charges and none of them even made it to court.

Just before his resignation there occurred one of the two crises that could have seen Ronaldo end up at FC Barcelona or Manchester City. Radio programme *El Larguero* confirmed that Cristiano had an agreement with Manchester United allowing him to leave at the end of the season 'for a reasonable amount'.

The programme's host, José Ramón de la Morena, revealed that the Portuguese had a pre-contract including a confidentiality clause that could invalidate the agreement if broken. Clearly, somebody had ignored it by telling the journalist the details. Jorge Mendes, Ramón Calderón and José Ángel Sánchez had to make urgent phone calls to calm Ferguson's rage. Meanwhile the Scot once again insisted to the English press that Ronaldo was going nowhere.

The second crisis would be much more serious. It took place while powerful businessman Vicente Boluda was president, in charge since the departure of Calderón to steady the ship and ensure the elections took place by 14 June at the latest.

On 18 March, Eduardo Fernández de Blas, president of the lobbying group Ética Madridista, spoke at the Ferrándiz–*AS* Forum. His analysis of the Real Madrid situation centred upon Ronaldo and the lack of players from the Spain squad at the club. 'There are more Spaniards at Liverpool than at Real Madrid,' he said.

And added, 'Cristiano is one of the best players in the world, but Manchester United are asking a lot for him and with that money we can sign two players from the Spain national team. We'll have to see how advanced the deal is and what the coach wants. We also need to evaluate how responsible such an investment is, as it could put the club's solvency at risk. Maybe it would be wiser to invest €100 million in several players rather than just one. And Spaniards, if possible.'

Fernández de Blas was supposedly independent, but his statements among groups of journalists and club members suited, or even chimed with, Florentino's electoral campaign. Fernández de Blas ended up as vice-president on Pérez's board a few months later.

De Blas giving a kick-start to the campaign meant Pérez (whose actions also hinged on his wife's poor health) could find out who his possible rivals would be and how they stood on delicate issues such as the cost of Ronaldo.

Vicente Boluda was startled to hear the accusation: he could not allow such a stain on his reputation or be accused of wasting the club's resources. It was a very serious matter to hear De Blas say that he was putting the club's finances in danger when in fact there was €140 million in the club coffers and the operation had been arranged with minimal risk attached.

Fernández de Blas had painted a very distorted image of the club with such strategically timed populism, just before the chosen members' assembly in which Boluda had to be ratified in order to be able to call elections further down the line.

'So this is how far we've come,' thought Vicente Boluda and he decided to take a change of direction that would free him from accusations.

As has been established, terminating the agreement would cost €30 million, so he called Jorge Mendes personally and offered to break the contract between Ronaldo and the club, and to pay the penalty.

There was another, cheaper possibility. If the termination was agreed by both parties, no money would need to change hands. Real Madrid would free themselves from 'throwing €94 million down the drain' and, as Ronaldo still had his agreement with Ferguson, he would then be able to sign for any other club in the world.

The step taken by Boluda was extremely bold and incurred unpredictable consequences. Would Mendes accept? And would Ronaldo, after taking so many steps towards touching down at the Bernabéu? What would the candidates to the presidential elections say if they found out? Could they halt Boluda's tenure? And what would stand him in better stead? Paying the controversial €94 million, knowing that fans have short memories, or cancelling the agreement that would allow a wonderful player to sign for a rival?

Jorge Mendes's reaction was surprising. He said it was fine to break the agreement with no cost to Real Madrid. He would send his lawyer Osario de Castro to Madrid the following morning. When Boluda told José Ángel Sánchez what had happened and how Mendes reacted, the chief executive could not believe it.

And so began one of those crazy days.

What was Mendes's reaction down to? Ronaldo's agent had two other offers for the player, both for a larger amount than Real Madrid's and superior to what Ronaldo and Manchester United had agreed. One from Manchester City that some sources suggested could have reached €150 million and another one from FC Barcelona for €105 million.

A twenty-one-year-old Leo Messi who was enjoying his second season under Pep Guardiola might have shared the dressing room with Cristiano Ronaldo.

José Ángel Sánchez and other important Real Madrid directors feared that missing out on the Portuguese could result in a long period of struggling. 'If Barça sign him, we won't win a trophy for ten years,' said a senior board member.

Ronaldo had to join Real Madrid.

José Ángel Sánchez asked people close to Boluda to help make him change his mind. 'It would be a crazy step backwards,' the president was told.

But Boluda insisted that he would not be the 'dickhead' who would put the economy of the club in danger with such a brutal expenditure.

Tensions reached boiling point.

In the end the crisis was resolved in a most unusual fashion.

Sánchez convinced Boluda to call Florentino Pérez. The suggestion could sound strange because the former president had not yet confirmed his candidacy, nor was he part of the club, nor did he have any type of influence, in theory at least. But nobody doubted that he had some role in Fernández de Blas's statement.

The businessman from Valencia decided to follow his advice.

It was eleven at night, after a pressure-filled day of phone calls.

Boluda, who was with his trusted associates including José Ángel Sánchez, put the phone on speaker.

It was a swift conversation. Boluda explained that he was fed up with Fernández de Blas's messages about Cristiano, the inconvenience of the signing, how expensive he was and the false statement that it would put the club's finances in danger.

Florentino answered quickly: 'De Blas won't say another word on this matter.'

Despite being a signing 'by the enemy', Pérez could not conceive returning to the club to take on a Barcelona with Leo and Cristiano in its ranks. Florentino therefore asked for the contract with Ronaldo not to be broken and for the signing to go ahead.

Mendes received a call that very same night and his lawyer Osorio did not fly to Madrid after all.

Crisis averted.

A few days later, Florentino Pérez finally announced that, as expected, he was running. With this news, the rest of the candidates knew they would struggle to gain the required number of signatures just to enable them to stand.

The newspapers were filled with questions about the agreement with the Portuguese star and Florentino's position in that regard. Would he break the contract signed by Calderón? Would he accept the arrival of a *galáctico* that he had not brought in himself? How was he going to elaborate on his message to make it appear that his intervention in the signing was, or seemed to be, decisive?

■ ■ ■

The season 2008–09 was a tough one for Ronaldo. He had just won the double and spent the summer trying to force his exit. He had one more year at United, but, with his mind elsewhere and disruptive injuries, it would end up being the worst of his final three.

He had a niggling injury to his right foot that had been causing constant inflammation since March 2008 and the problem worsened during the Champions League final. He was at 70 per cent during the Euros and on anti-inflammatories, but a stamp by German Arne Friedrich left him writhing in pain and he decided to go under the knife. Dutch doctor Cornelis Nicolaas van Dijk performed surgery on two pieces of cartilage that had come away from his ankle, keeping him out of action for six weeks.

'He was very professional that whole season,' recalled Gary Neville. 'But he was counting down the months until he could leave.' There are those who believe that Ronaldo gradually distanced himself from the rest of the group as the campaign progressed. He found it harder and harder to join in with club affairs and even abandoned his role as Nani and Anderson's 'babysitter'.

Despite moments of brilliance, a combination of his complaints to referees, insistence on not wanting to run without the ball, desire to be the centre of attention, angry and ill-disciplined reactions that brought him red cards (in the Manchester derby, for example) and reluctance to celebrate with his team-mates tested the patience of a section of the Manchester United fan base once too often. Their reaction was forceful and one that Cristiano prefers to forget or ignore today.

Interestingly, such an attitude was present to a greater or lesser degree in the two previous seasons, but supporters forgave him because of his spectacular performances.

There was less and less tolerance for his perceived arrogant attitude on his last season which explains why, in a crucial victory over Aston Villa thanks to a last-minute Federico Macheda goal, Ronaldo, who scored a brace, was booed by his own supporters for gesticulating and going down too easily just before scoring his second goal of the match.

After a Champions League and two consecutive league titles with a third approaching fast, there was enough quality and confidence in a squad that had been strengthened by Dimitar Berbatov to allay fears for the club about Ronaldo leaving if a generous transfer fee was involved. There was talk on radio programmes as well as in and around Old Trafford that he should be shipped off if he did not want to stay.

In any case, he was a worthy winner of the 2008 FIFA World Player of the Year and his first Ballon d'Or, almost doubling Messi's points. 'People who know me and live with me know that this is a dream that has finally come true for me. This trophy is so important that I want to win it again. I'll wake up every day and say to myself, "I have to keep improving."' Ronaldo's words confirmed the value that he attached to an individual award that, incidentally, no Manchester United player had won in forty years since George Best in 1968.

There was nobody to overshadow Cristiano Ronaldo at the summit of world football. Absolutely nobody above him. Only his own demanding nature.

'There was a time when he forgot his roots or, better said, how he managed to score forty goals one season: the running without the ball, the teamwork . . .' admitted Gary Neville. 'Messi arrived at just the right time to give him a little push and remind him that he was just behind him.'

Cristiano seemed side-tracked by football paraphernalia for the first time. He enjoyed showing off his Ferraris. He crashed a red 599 GTB Fiorano that he had brought over from Portugal against a barrier in a tunnel near Wilmslow. The front of the vehicle was completely demolished, but the player emerged unscathed. It could have been so much worse.

Meanwhile, the Ronaldo who had hypnotised the Premier League did show up occasionally. In the Champions League quarter-finals away to Porto, the score was 0–0 when Ronaldo lined up a shot from a seemingly impossible distance. He was forty metres from goal. 'Ronaldo! What are you doing?' Rio Ferdinand shouted at him. The next words the centre-back uttered were 'What a goal!'

His behaviour in the derby against City at Old Trafford fittingly summed up the end of his career at Manchester United. He scored from a free-kick, his last for the Red Devils, and Ferguson substituted him in the second half. It was not to his pleasing. He began showing his disgust: he appeared not to want to leave the pitch and when Alec Wylie handed him his top, he swiped it out of his hand on to the floor. The action spoke for itself and he shook his head while jeering tumbled down from the terraces. It was interpreted as his way of saying that he no longer wanted to be there.

Manchester United won the league, the Carling Cup and reached the Champions League for a second straight year, but Ronaldo's goalscoring figures went down from forty-two to twenty-six.

He had one final match in the red of United to say goodbye in the most fitting way.

In Rome, against Pep Guardiola's Barcelona spearheaded by Leo Messi.

■ ■ ■

In Great Britain, Manchester United were considered clear favourites in that final. The first ten minutes of the contest seemed to justify such a belief when Ronaldo made life difficult for Víctor Valdés with a rasping free-kick and an effort that clipped the post. Pep Guardiola then made a tactical change that transformed the match – moving Samuel Eto'o to the right wing and making Messi a false number nine.

Mike Phelan and Ryan Giggs remember it clearly.

Mike Phelan: 'We were thinking, "How are we going to impose ourselves on Barcelona?" It was all about the space in behind. Ronaldo could exploit it. But Puyol, and especially Piqué, knew all about Cristiano and weren't going to allow him into those spaces.'

Ryan Giggs: 'We were favourites, but we didn't turn up and they did.'

Mike Phelan: 'And then Piqué took Ronaldo out. He knew exactly what he was doing.'

Ryan Giggs: 'If we had gone 1–0 up . . .'

Mike Phelan: 'Ronaldo was clean through, Piqué took the booking for it. I'm not saying it would've changed the result, but it would have given us that belief to have another chance at it. But Piqué was cute.'

Ryan Giggs: 'It was a frustrating night for everyone; I was the most disappointed I've ever been.'

Mike Phelan: 'It was very tough not having much possession.'

Ryan Giggs: 'Ronnie played up front, I played just behind him and we just didn't get any flow to our game whatsoever. I played too close to him, I should've played deeper in midfield and tried to control the game, but we just didn't have the ball.'

Mike Phelan: 'We had a "philosophical" issue with those two finals against the Catalans. Barcelona played football and were a top team, United played football and were a top team. Tradition, history, everything came into it. We thought about all sorts of things, discussed it, and in the end it came down to the fact that we were Man United and we could only play our way. We couldn't get people behind the ball because even if we'd have won the game that way, we'd have got hammered for it – we wouldn't have been true to ourselves. I remember playing Barcelona in the semi-final the year before the Rome final, and we drew over in Barcelona, nil-nil. We never crossed the halfway line. That is the first and only time of being part of Man United that I've ever seen that much of a defensive approach. And I hated it.'

Ryan Giggs: 'When Ronnie got the ball it was as if he had to do something and was under that much pressure because nothing was happening. No one played well in our team that night. They were by far the better team.'

Barcelona won 2–0 with Lionel Messi scoring the second goal with a header.

Cristiano spoke after the final: 'We didn't play well, our tactics weren't good . . . Everything went wrong.'

27 May 2009 was the last time Ronaldo wore the red of Manchester United.

■ ■ ■

Two months earlier, Ryan Giggs asked him, 'Are you sure you want to go? It's tough in Spain.' Yet the Welshman knew that Ronaldo was determined and set on his next target.

During the title celebration party, Rio Ferdinand broached the topic again. 'Come on, man. Just stay!' Cristiano called him just a few days later. 'Rio, I'm going to go.' Ferdinand responded with a concise, 'OK, man. Go. We'll see you again soon and good luck.'

The squad and coaching staff had dinner in Rome together after the Champions League final. Ronaldo said his goodbyes to everyone.

'You don't know how good you've got it here,' Gary Neville told him, half jokingly, half seriously. 'You'll miss us more than you know.' Ronaldo answered him, 'Why should I listen to you? You'd never leave Manchester, even on holiday.' And they laughed.[20]

'It was a mix of excitement about a new project in his life and sadness,' recalled Ryan Giggs. 'He knew that we'd looked after him. But he always looks ahead, just like me.'

On 11 June, Manchester United announced that they had reached an agreement with Real Madrid which would make Ronaldo the most expensive footballer in history. £80 million (€94 million) changed hands.

Ronaldo was packing his bags after six years, nine trophies, 292 matches and 118 goals. His season-by-season tally was: 6, 9, 12, 23, 42, 26.

'The pressure from 2003 through to 2009 was enormous but we helped him handle it,' explained Gary Neville. 'Maybe if he'd been at Madrid at that time, he wouldn't be where he is now. He learnt how to win with us and to be a league player, not a cup player. Anyone can be a cup player.'

'The fact that we had him for six years was a bonus,' said Ferguson. 'In that period we won a European Cup and three league titles with him. I consider that a pretty good return.'[18]

'I felt saddened by it,' admitted Mike Phelan.

Because the club helped him make the jump from a good footballer to a great footballer and eventually to a world-class footballer. And Mike did his bit.

Because Ronaldo was the perfect example of everything that a coach could dream of: he wanted to learn, he listened, he challenged himself and accepted challenges. Every day.

Because he refined his intelligence and ability in front of everyone.

Because he accepted everyone's help and made demands of everyone.

Because he had a warm personality.

Because he never hid his ambition.

Because everyone knew that they were close to and helping someone very special.

Mike, the other coaches and the players knew that they would not come across anyone else quite like him ever again.

But he had decided to take flight.

And they had to open the door and let him go.

■ ■ ■

Cristiano Ronaldo still dreams of returning to Manchester United. But would it really be sensible at this point for the English club to spend a huge amount on a 31-year-old with no subsequent sell-on value? The Red Devils board consider the €60 million fee it would take to prise him from Real Madrid, coupled with the €50-million-a-year wages he would demand, to be excessive.

In any event, for several years United let it be known to Jorge Mendes that they had the financial clout to secure the star's return. Indeed, in summer 2013, the club's new manager, David Moyes, believed that they were about to convince Ronaldo to come back. That was the message that the club's board transmitted to him. Having played both sides so effectively, what ensued instead was a contract renewal for Cristiano at Real Madrid that turned him into the best-paid player on the planet in September 2013.

In summer 2014 he told a Real Madrid player who was about to leave Los Blancos that he saw himself at United in two years' time.

'I think his admiration for Manchester United is growing over time,' stated Gary Neville. 'The club offered him stability and security, which do not seem to be part of his relationship with Real Madrid, where everything seems to be a rollercoaster.'

The feeling that Carrington was the ideal place to pave his path, Old Trafford to play his football and the Premier League to feel loved, gradually developed in Ronaldo's head. At Manchester United, he was completely focused on his target. In Madrid, other things are demanded and the sporting rewards may be superior (although that is open to debate) and the commercial side more profitable (ditto). But the level of universal appreciation from his own fans is far inferior at Madrid.

Despite the boos in his first and final seasons, at Manchester United he felt loved as he has never felt since.

Alex Ferguson reminds him whenever he can that the door is still open. However, since stepping down as coach, the Scot's influence on the club's decision-making has waned.

Anyway, in my opinion, it does not make sense for him to return to Old Trafford. Neither for the club nor for him. They are in parallel universes. Ronaldo would go back to the city that he wanted to leave behind for so many years. He would have to fight against his own shadow. Manchester United have a big enough global following and sufficient financial firepower to be one of the strongest clubs, on and off the pitch, without him.

They no longer seem to need Cristiano Ronaldo.

He will remain a Manchester United legend. A memory that both club and player still feed off today.

SIX

FIRST YEARS AT REAL MADRID

LIVING THE DREAM?

The deadline for candidates to stand for election as Real Madrid president passed and in the end only a single pretender met the criteria: Florentino Pérez. Although he was not voted in, the general feeling was that the former chief was the only solution in the eyes of supporters to restore stability after a tumultuous period that Pérez had helped create.

He was sworn in as Real Madrid president on 1 June 2009, and so began his second spell at the club.

What happened in the period between his investiture ceremony and the confirmation of the Cristiano deal ten days later? Did Florentino change his mind and try to stop it, as some have suggested? Is it true that without the new president's input and his financial background the Portuguese would not have worn the white of Real Madrid?

Has Florentino ever treasured Ronaldo as if he were his own signing?

Ferguson wrote: 'Madrid paid £80 million in cash for him, and do you know why? It was a way for Florentino Pérez, their president, to say to the world, "We are Real Madrid, we are the biggest of the lot." It was a clever move by them and a declaration of their intent.'[18]

Even the Scot, who actually sold Ronaldo to Ramón Calderón's Real Madrid, seemed hypnotised by what Florentino represented.

Pérez is a well-known businessman, an engineer, former politician and president of ACS, one of the leading construction companies in the world. He introduced a model at Real Madrid that allowed it to become the global sporting institution with the highest revenue: it went from €366 million in 2004 to €604 million today. There is not even a sporting establishment of such calibre in the United States and *Forbes* made the club the most valuable in the world in 2014. And it is still growing year on year.

Real Madrid are no longer just a sports club, but a global entertainment company that has outlined its business model in the same way that the Walt Disney Company did: it has its own communication methods, audiovisual content, consumer products and even the equivalents of Pluto, Donald, Goofy and Mickey Mouse, *galácticos* that have their own personal brand and boost the Real Madrid image by being linked to the club. Even a theme park called Real Madrid Resort Island has been designed on the artificial island of Al Marjan in Ras al-Khaimah in northern UAE, but that project is currently on hold.

The club has become an industry that leans on football in order to bring in the revenue that allows for continued prosperity. Players are not signed for tactical reasons, but according to what the global project requires. Members, no matter how often it is said, are no longer the club owners. Real Madrid's main source of revenue is marketing (35 per cent) while fans only constitute 25 per cent if we include gate receipts.

But, of course, when there is passion there is no place for reason. Bad results on the pitch have little bearing on the business concept, but they do affect the club's image and the board's endeavours, and so it is vital to rekindle excitement regularly.

Five of the ten most lucrative transfers in football history (Ronaldo, Bale, James Rodríguez, Zidane and Kaká) involved players joining Real Madrid when Florentino Pérez was president. Names are no guarantee of success, but Figo and Zidane, for example, triggered winning cycles that included a Champions League victory.

Cristiano Ronaldo's name cropped up from minute one in conversations between Pérez and Jorge Valdano, who was Florentino's sporting director at Real Madrid during his previous tenure and was going to be upgraded to general manager this time round. The Portuguese was the new *galáctico* and paramount to Florentino's strategy on his return.

Ramón Calderón had got in ahead of him for the transfer, but if Florentino managed to reduce the fee, he could put a spin on the saga and claim the goal himself. To paraphrase Winston Churchill, history would be kind to him because, among other things, he would write it himself with the help of some loyal press.

There was talk that Ramón Calderón had left the club without sufficient funds to finance the transfer and that it was essential to renegotiate the fee for Cristiano. But as we know, there was €140 million in the coffers, and there was a currency forward contract in place, too.

Despite everything being agreed, it took Real Madrid ten days to inform Manchester United of the decision to sign the Portuguese star. Florentino says today, 'I had and have a very good relationship with Sir Alex Ferguson and we could've signed him for less money.' Yet there was no time nor were Manchester United interested in reopening negotiations. 'That week we signed Cristiano, Kaká and Benzema,' explained the president.

Mentioning Cristiano in the same sentence as Kaká (one of Florentino's dreams as Calderón was unable to sign him) and

Benzema (a Pérez whim) perhaps reveals the prevalent position afforded to the Brazilian and Frenchman and some would say Pérez's (unconscious?) limited enthusiasm for Ronaldo, a signing that was not entirely his.

'Ninety-four million euros was an exorbitant amount, but it has become a reasonable one over time,' said Jorge Valdano. He added, 'When a signing is strategic, there is no possible alternative. In that situation money is stripped of its importance.'

Ronaldo was on holiday in California and received confirmation of the transfer at two in the morning via a Mendes phone call. He had just become a Real Madrid player and one of the best-paid footballers in the world with the highest release clause, €1 billion.

■ ■ ■

The day of his unveiling, 6 July 2010, was a hectic one. 'I remember I was very tired when I arrived in the afternoon and it was scorching hot,' recalled Ronaldo. 'I was doing bits and bobs all day. Getting to the hotel, changing quickly, going to the unveiling, interviews, photos . . .'[4] What a day it was.

He landed just before one o'clock at the Torrejón Air Base.

The car that picked Ronaldo up from the airport, which also carried Jorge Mendes, was followed all day long by journalists and intrigued onlookers. On the way to town, Ronaldo asked the driver to go round the same roundabout several times until they ended up behind all the followers. How they laughed in the car.

He was peering out of the window wide-eyed for the rest of the journey. He felt like a child of five and a twenty-four-year-old at the same time.

The Real Madrid TV camera that immortalised those moments was with him every step of the way, including the hospital visit for a couple of tests, despite having undergone his medical in Lisbon ten days earlier.

Next stop after the clinic was the Puerta 57 restaurant inside the Bernabéu. From the table where he was sitting with Jorge Valdano, he could see the pitch at his new stamping ground and the structure that had been erected for his unveiling. It seemed more befitting a rock star.

Valdano explained the details of the event to him. During the presentation, he would be surrounded by photos of Alfredo Di Stéfano, Juanito, Raúl and Zidane behind him. Juanito? Valdano waxed lyrical about that legendary number seven from the 1980s. The general manager told him that 40,000 people had turned up to greet Kaká a few days earlier. Benzema's unveiling would take place a couple of days later.

Eusébio, the 1965 Ballon d'Or winner, honorary president Alfredo Di Stéfano ('Let's see if you wear the number nine shirt well,' the Argentinian told him), and other club legends such as Zoco, Santamaría, Pachín and Amancio were all sitting at a nearby table.

Excitement surrounding Ronaldo's presentation had reached fever pitch. Expectations were huge.

After a light lunch, Cristiano went to the Mirasierra Suites hotel where he spoke to some journalist friends and planned his personal touch for the unveiling. 'Should I kiss the badge? OK, I will do it, but what else? That's it. Or maybe I should get some crowd participation going? *"Hala Madrid!"'* And so he started rehearsing in the hotel.

AS journalist Tomás Roncero was with him two hours before the much-anticipated unveiling: 'He asked me, "Do you really think the Bernabéu will be full to capacity just to see me in white?" I answered, "It's going to be too small. You can't imagine how much happiness your arrival has generated among supporters."'

While in the car en route to the stadium, he asked in an astonished tone, 'Is there a game on?' on seeing the queues surrounding the entire Bernabéu as fans impatiently waited for the gates to open.[4] He could not believe his eyes.

He put pen to paper on his six-year deal, met the new president and got changed in a packed dressing room: a television cameraman, club employees, board members and former players. He put on several different number nine shirts (Raúl was the number seven) with his name in Japanese, Chinese, Arabic and more . . . He finally grabbed a football, kissed it and performed some tricks.

And he waited.

'You wait and wait, getting more and more nervous,' recalled Cristiano. 'On the one hand I was excited to be with the fans, but on the other I wanted it all to be over because . . . I don't know. I wasn't used to that type of thing.'[4]

He did some stretches, went down the steps, stopped in the tunnel and took a deep breath. The sound of the club's centenary anthem was booming out.

He peered up to get a glimpse of the ground and was flabbergasted. His heart was racing.

An 80,000-strong crowd. An absolute record for a player unveiling. Nothing of the sort had ever been seen before.

He was a bundle of nerves and was scared of forgetting the two or three lines that he had prepared.

'Mr President, say it.'[4]

'From that moment, he understood that this is a very special club, he was starting a new phase in his life. Nothing was going to be the same again,' stated Jorge Valdano.[6]

'Announce me, Mr President, so we can wrap this up.'[4]

'I'll be honest,' Ronaldo said years later in a television interview with TVI of Portugal. 'I had some notes and I'd rehearsed the words I wanted to say. But when the president said my name and I entered the stadium and heard the roar from the terraces . . . I knew it wasn't going to be easy. I went up to the stage and when I was on the microphone, I didn't know what to say. I said whatever came into my head . . .'

A nervy Cristiano, who was kitted out in Real Madrid colours, looked slightly out of place alongside the suited and booted trio of Florentino, Eusébio and Di Stéfano. He said the following after a few minutes of euphoric 'Ronaldo, Ronaldo' chants reverberated around the stadium: 'My childhood dream of playing for Real Madrid has come true. I didn't expect this. It's amazing. Thank you very much. Now I ask you all to say with me, I'm going to count to three and we'll all say "*Hala Madrid!*" OK? One, two, three . . . *Hala Madrid!*'

'I think it went down well,' said Ronaldo in an interview he gave to the Spanish TV channel Intereconomía. 'People were happy, it went well.'

The messiah had arrived.

■ ■ ■

Florentino Pérez announced that he had to be extremely active in the transfer market and do three summers' worth of business in one. Pérez considered the catastrophic season that Real Madrid had just endured (two coaches, three presidents and only a single Spanish Super Cup to show, as well as memories of a painful 6–2 defeat by Barcelona at the Bernabéu) an enormous step backwards that could only be resolved with determination and big-name signings.

Despite winning two league titles in three years, it was hardly a Real Madrid side brimming with excellence. The greatest representative of *Madridismo* of them all, Raúl, was still surviving thanks to his commitment and battling qualities. Contrary to what many feel, *Los Blancos* have not distinguished themselves solely because of their exquisite style of play; it is also their persistent endeavour, a relentless, terrier-like tenacity and full-blooded commitment. Raúl was the epitome of this ethos but reaching the end of his career at the club.

So €254 million was ploughed into squad improvements in summer 2009. Raúl Albiol, Garay, Negredo, Granero, Arbeloa and Xabi Alonso were brought in as well as the three big stars already mentioned.

Beyond that essential core, and after rebuttals by Arsène Wenger and Carlo Ancelotti, Manuel Pellegrini was brought in as coach, entrusted with transmitting his personality and passion for aesthetically pleasing football, as seen at Villarreal.

The main rivals would be FC Barcelona which, in the season that had just ended, had been successful after moving forward from within (Pep Guardiola, Busquets and Pedro). They were planning to continue the evolution of their style and to hand over more power to Leo Messi, both the style and the player responsible for the historical treble they had just won (La Liga, Copa del Rey and the Champions League).

Pellegrini and especially Ronaldo were considered the antidote.

Cristiano had not only to compete against himself. He had landed in a league inhabited by his nemesis – a small, quiet guy who pointed to the sky when celebrating his goals rather than to the ground as Ronaldo did.

In 2009–10, Real Madrid's new striker scored four goals in his first four games, his best return at the start of a campaign. The Portuguese believed that he could improve on his goal tally in Spain, given that he was playing for a team that would allow him more touches of the ball and would create more chances. His aims seemed to bear fruit during his first month: maybe he did not quite reach the very high level of excellence that he normally aspires to, but he did rack up six goals.

Until that point, Pellegrini had opted for a starting eleven including Raúl and the three big signings, with Ronaldo playing down the left, Kaká on the right and Benzema in a central position.

The Chilean coach admitted in private that he would have liked to give the Portuguese a roaming role as a modern number nine, a similar role to the one he performs now, in fact. This would have given him freedom to start out on the wing and cut in, take players on, look to get in behind and develop his potential, but the squad that he had inherited did not fit into that system.

Goals were flooding in, but at both ends.

Ronaldo accepted the dressing-room hierarchy without question. Although it was Raúl's final season at the club, the Spaniard was still the leader which Cristiano respected completely, as seen by the shirt-number scenario. He would be reunited with his beloved number seven after the legendary forward left for Germany.

Unfortunately, the Madeiran suffered an injury early on in the campaign on 30 September.

He took a kick to his right ankle against Olympique de Marseille. The bone bruising was not given the recovery period that it needed and, eleven days later, he suffered a recurrence of the problem when Portugal took on Hungary. He was sidelined for a month and a half, one of the longest injuries of his career.

The timing could not have been worse.

■ ■ ■

In terms of the hierarchy, it would be more accurate to say that he respected Raúl, but found it easier to challenge other team-mates for territory. A disagreement over a penalty in February is a suitable example.

Real Madrid were beating Villarreal 5–2, Cristiano had scored one of the goals and was later brought down for a penalty.

'I said to him, "Cris, leave it for me,"' recalled Xabi Alonso. 'And he wanted to take it. I had to insist more than usual for him to let me take it, because he wanted to add to his tally whenever possible. In theory he should have taken it, but I thought, "I haven't scored yet this season."'

Cristiano had a sulk and said 'Leave me alone!' before Xabi took the ball off him. It was Real Madrid's sixth goal and Ronaldo distanced himself from the celebrations.

'He got irked because he always wants more, but it went no further. In the end I scored and he ended the season with thirty-three goals.'

His irate reaction did not go unnoticed, however.

■ ■ ■

In spite of a very promising start to the season, the Portuguese was unable to meet his own exacting standards after returning from injury, which created a damaging level of anxiety. He wanted everything to fall into place straight away. As René Meulensteen warned him, that was the easiest way for others to discover his weakness. Opponents could smell it. They provoked him, sought him out and opposition fans riled him. Even his own condemned him on occasions as they struggled to understand what was behind those gestures of disapproval towards his team-mates.

Ronaldo's first Real Madrid red card came soon after recovery from injury in a match against Almería at the Bernabéu: an initial booking for taking off his shirt after scoring the final goal in an enthralling 4–2 victory and a second resulting in a sending-off just minutes later for kicking an opposition defender off the ball after a scuffle. He received his marching orders for the second time a month and a half later against Málaga at the Bernabéu. Ronaldo turned away from Patrick Mtiliga, but a flailing elbow connected with the defender, fracturing his nose in the process. The offence was not deemed violent conduct and the Portuguese accordingly received a two-match ban.

In Europe Real flattered to deceive. Ronaldo, who had played in the previous season's Champions League final, could not hide his disappointment after elimination in the last sixteen at the hands of Lyon when speaking after the game: 'It hurts to get knocked out. I've gone very far in the Champions League in recent years. Being eliminated in the last sixteen is painful.'

Jerzy Dudek told in his autobiography how during an open training session for the public the following day the players were able to invite family and friends. Dudek brought along Polish-German boxer Dariusz Michalczewski. Cristiano was still fuming and ignored the children who were waiting for him after the session. 'No photos, no photos,' he repeated. Dariusz could not believe it: 'I'm going to give him a good punch . . .'[23]

Dudek, who understood his reaction and disgust, went to speak to him. But Ronaldo was not in a diplomatic mood: 'I'm not here to take fucking photos, I'm here to win games,' he told the goalkeeper. 'Lyon beat us. Let me leave. I'm really pissed off.'[23]

Pellegrini's side remained competitive in La Liga, although a 1–0 loss at the Camp Nou after an Ibrahimović goal in the fifty-sixth minute would eventually prove costly. *Los Blancos* outscored league winners Barcelona by four, but ended up three points behind Pep's record-breaking side. Real Madrid also made history, having never previously won ninety-six points in a thirty-eight-game season. Pellegrini has always believed that, had Cristiano not suffered an injury, Guardiola's second La Liga title would have been his.

Cristiano scored thirty-three times in thirty-five matches (0.95 per game). Injuries and suspensions reduced his impact somewhat, but at the time it was his second-best season in terms of goalscoring, only bettered by his Ballon d'Or-clinching year at Manchester United. The variety of goals scored gave a clear indication of his talent: dribbles in the area and rounding the keeper, free-kicks, long-range shots, sometimes from a seemingly impossible angle. Individual skill was usually involved and, interestingly, he rarely scored headers or tap-ins like a classic number nine. That would come over time.

The summer would bring changes. Pellegrini, backed by Jorge Valdano, was a football man, but not the leader that Florentino Pérez wanted for the team. The leader was, in fact, the president and that combination did not bode well. The coach felt like an outsider from day one when he asked for Robben and Sneijder to stay, only to see them both sold. The Chilean was discredited inside and outside the club and soon knew that he would not stay for a second year.

Florentino and José Ángel Sánchez wanted to follow their global strategy by bringing in someone with undeniable prestige: José Mourinho. His Inter Milan knocked a Barcelona side out of the Champions League semi-finals that had won the lot in the previous twelve months. The night before the final against Bayern (which the Nerazzurri won), Florentino and Mourinho thrashed out the basis of an agreement.

The Mourinho era was about to begin.

■ ■ ■

By the time Ronaldo reached the 2010 World Cup in South Africa, his team-mates and countrymen no longer considered him just a guy from Madeira, but a fully fledged Portuguese. Without Figo, Cristiano was the country's indisputable leader, although talk was growing that the player performed better for club than for country.

The Portugal national team has been revolving around him both on and off the pitch since the final years of Luiz Felipe Scolari's tenure. 'Whenever he goes to Óbidos where Portugal train, he always rests on the first day,' explained Sergio Fernández, a *Marca* journalist who knows the player well. 'They tell you he's in the dressing room. If you look at Cristiano's recent international call-ups, he's never trained on the first day. Cristiano is in charge in Portugal.'

The twenty-five-year-old was participating in his second World Cup, this time under the stewardship of Carlos Queiroz, who tried to instil a more conservative approach. Ronaldo played as a striker, a position in which he was not completely at ease. He had gone sixteen months without scoring for the national team, but did find the net in a 7–0 rout of South Korea. Portugal succumbed to eventual winners Spain in the round of sixteen, in a contest lacking in quality as Vicente del Bosque's side's dominance translated into few clear-cut goalscoring opportunities. A David Villa strike at the second time of asking decided the tie.

Ronaldo was anonymous on the pitch that day. 'Ask Queiroz,' he said in the mixed zone when asked for an explanation. The coach was sacked and has not spoken to Ronaldo since. 'I don't care,' says Carlos today. 'We don't owe each other anything. If Cristiano thinks he has to react to me in that way, I respect that although I didn't expect it. I don't think it was appropriate behaviour from the national team captain.'

Criticism was heaped on the manager. The Portuguese press prefers to show respect towards Cristiano rather than delve into his influence on the national team. He is untouchable for many. 'Criticising Ronaldo requires a very thick skin,' stated sociologist João Nuno Coelho.[24]

The Portuguese make no secret of Cristiano's individualist tendencies, big ego and how his desire to win occasionally places him above the interests of the national team. For example, a captain should never forget to go over to supporters at the end of the match, so they say. But sometimes he did. Furthermore, as he does not look like your typical Portuguese, they find it hard to identify with him.

Yet criticising him equates to removing one of the few positive images in a country enduring economic hardship and an identity crisis. He is perceived as one of the last saviours.

'On a certain social level, people look at his character with irony,' explained Coelho who I hope will forgive my addition: on a 'certain social level' people look at the rest of the world with irony. Haughty people are aplenty out there. 'People sometimes take the mickey out of Ronaldo's family, but I don't think it's a generalised feeling.'[24] Former Porto and Deportivo defender Jorge Andrade believes that '80 per cent of the Portuguese public appreciate him. Some prefer other types of players: Figo, Eusébio, Paulo Futre, Rui Costa . . . But we're proud to have someone like Cristiano. Of course, the player is one thing and the person is another. There will always be people who don't like his lifestyle.'

Supporters, though, hope that his medal collection can become a contagious virus that infects the national team, too.

■ ■ ■

The following may ring a bell. This is what people who shared the dressing room with Ronaldo during his early days at Real Madrid recalled in various interviews and books.

Jorge Valdano:

He works hard no matter the circumstance. If he wins the Ballon d'Or, he trains the following day. If he doesn't win it, he trains.

If he wins a match, he trains the following day. If he doesn't win it, he trains. If he renews his contract, he trains the following day. If he doesn't renew it, he trains. These are all determining factors that affect sportsmen, but in his case, there's never been a day when he's taken it easy and said he's achieved one of those goals.[13]

Jerzy Dudek:

He's the first one in for training. If the session started at eleven, he'd be there at nine-thirty. He'd do some gym work, then have a massage. Training for an hour and a half and then back to the gym.[23]

Xabi Alonso:

He's very methodical in terms of his preparation. He works with people he trusts. He needs to feel in tip-top shape with no muscles showing even an inkling of being tight. He always sees the physio before the match to add his little tweaks, stretch and that's it. He gets changed, he gets ready and then does some ball-work in the dressing room. He wanted to get a feel for the ball. But to be honest, I never saw that trick-obsessed side to him.

Former Real Madrid doctor Juan Carlos Hernández:

There are three basic pillars: suitable training without any strange drills or experiments, a suitable diet and suitable rest time. He kitted his house out with everything that helps him improve. There have been several occasions when we've got back from a Champions League away match at four in the morning and we've gone down to the baths at Valdebebas to put his legs in ice and give him a massage to aid his recovery from the match . . . The others wake up the following morning with swollen legs and Cristiano is almost as good as new and ready to train.[13]

Jerzy Dudek:

He never behaves selfishly, he doesn't act like a star. He likes to take the piss out of his team-mates who wear strange shoes or very tight trousers. Typical dressing-room banter.[23]

Dr Hernández:

On away trips, he never asks for special pillows or sleeping pills, just for compression socks to avoid his legs swelling up too much.[13]

Jorge Valdano:

Maradona played a total of twenty-nine games in the year of Mexico 86. Ronaldo has played nearly seventy games per season.[13]

Ronaldo ensconced himself in a gated community called La Finca in a mansion that he rents for nearly €15,000 per month, near team-mate Raúl. He took his two dogs with him, Abelhinha (he used to be called that as a boy) and Marosca. The property has seven bedrooms, a garage containing several luxury cars that he takes out for a drive, occasionally as far as Lisbon, a spa, a gym, an outdoor swimming pool in a marvellous garden where they often have family barbecues and an indoor one where he likes to swim every afternoon. They may not say so in public, but more than one Real Madrid doctor has been worried that he overdoes his preparation, especially away from the Valdebebas training ground. They do recognise, however, that his zeal for rest and recovering help him. He takes a two-hour nap every day, alternates between cold and hot showers, goes cycling and goes to bed early as he needs ten hours' sleep a night. He also has a special chef, his mother, who ended up moving into a nearby house in the same area.

Valter di Salvo, former Real Madrid fitness coach:

> We've never seen him touch a drop of alcohol, he hates fatty food, he measures the number of calories he consumes and bases every-thing on the Mediterranean diet. He doesn't indulge.

Mario Torrejón, a Ronaldo biographer:

> He was well supported by his friends during those first few days. He knew Pepe from the national team and Marcelo, but quickly got to know and get on well with Kaká . . . In fact, during those first few league games, Marcelo and Ronaldo always looked for each other in games, they took attacks to wherever the other was and celebrated goals with private jokes that only they understood, to the annoyance of more than one of their team-mates.[13]

Hafid Benzema, Karim's father:

> Karim likes Cristiano Ronaldo because he helped him a lot in training and in terms of settling in at the club. They arrived at the same time and they're friends.[13]

Diego Torres, *El País* journalist:

> An amazing side to him is that he's incredibly generous towards the most irrelevant members of the dressing room. He does it because he likes giving presents, but also because he likes to be rewarded in terms of appreciation. He needs to create a

community around himself. A community that gives him security.

Alberto Toril, former Castilla coach:

The relationship that he had with kids coming up through the ranks was positive and he was always a role model. If the youngsters see that a global star is professional and hardworking, the first to arrive and the last to leave, he's a great example for them. I spoke to Jesé [a former Real Madrid B player who is now in the first team] about Ronaldo many times.

∎ ∎ ∎

Cristiano represents modern football in the twenty-first century. He is the superhero with footballing attributes that seem to be straight out of a laboratory. We expected it. From his android-like appearance, with his more mechanical than artistic gesticulation, to the stride, shot and jump that have a supernatural power, everything about Ronaldo takes us to the future.

Jorge Valdano

We have always needed to put our idols on pedestals and Ronaldo is certainly a modern hero with his beauty, narcissism and halo of greatness. He seems close and friendly; we know plenty about him, could even get an autograph, yet he is unreachable. We want him, but he does not need us. He is a hero who never tires and usually achieves his goals, even if they are individual ones in a team sport.

If heroes of old used to be emblematic figures whose actions transformed the world into something better, today's heroes are more fleeting children of our society in which the superfluous and ephemeral are the rule, obsessed as we are by appearances.

We look for them in reality shows, the celebrity world and in football, a social phenomenon that everyone takes part in, from children to the elderly, men and women, intellectuals and labourers. The beautiful game has become a point of reference as well as a social and behavioural model. Close-up camera shots on television and the individualistic nature of society accentuate the idea that the pitch is full of heroes, guys who can save matches and boost a whole country's self-esteem: nowadays a single individual seems to carry more weight and be more influential than a whole team.

In Manchester they all know by heart the story of this Superman who landed at Old Trafford from Krypton. He refined his extraordinary talents in front of their eyes until he became the almost perfect specimen.

A strong, triumphant and apparently indestructible Superman had arrived in Spain. Yet the opposition (fans and players) discovered the kryptonite, his weaknesses, very swiftly. The odd bout of provocation here, a subtle kick there and Ronaldo reacted. 'See? He's not Superman after all,' they said in the stands, because nobody is. Until it can be scientifically proved, nobody believes in the existence of such a figure.

It is not just healthy scepticism. I think it is something much worse.

Let me introduce to you one of Spain's national sins: envy.

'Envy! This is the terrible plague of our society; it is the inner disease of the Spanish soul.' That is how our philosopher Miguel de Unamuno described us a hundred years ago. The Argentinian writer Jorge Luis Borges used to say, 'If the Spanish think something is really good, they say, "It's enviable."' Vocabulary does not deceive, it exposes us.

If Protestantism favours the sort of mentality that can easily be confused with a mistaken sense of superiority fed by narrow-mindedness and former glory linked to the empire, Catholicism has multiplied and fed envy, despite it being one of the original seven deadly sins. That is, in brief, the take of the sociologist Salvador Giner.

The Church has separated our Spain from the rest of Europe for centuries. While the western world progressed, we fell by the wayside. From the Church to governments, we have blamed our misfortune on the rest of the world; the examples they set did not help us improve and self-criticism was simply rejected, like a smear campaign signed and sworn by the homeland's/God's enemies.

So, increasingly, we have allowed envy to become part of our way of thinking.

Closely linked to it, another national trait poisons our judgement: contempt, or more specifically, contempt for excellence. Maybe people do not envy Ronaldo or Messi, but they hope the stars fail in order for them to be able to repudiate them with an 'all that training and hard work, for what?' Or a definitive 'he's finished' that is so often heard from the terraces. Or one of my favourites: 'If I trained like him, I'd also do what he does.' Yes, of course.

Spanish people rarely admire someone who stands out from the herd and, as soon as someone does, they get shot down; there is regular refusal to give merit where it is due and, if necessary, they are punished for their talent. Even worse, those pouring scorn on others are considered intelligent. They think flattery is reserved for morons.

In order to be a success in Spain, your self-esteem has to be at just the right level, you have to be a good communicator and try to be as normal as possible. There is no need to stand out. And if you do, make sure people excuse you for doing so.

In northern European countries, for instance, they have been more intelligent about it: there is greater reward for individual effort and merit. 'Envy has been transformed into emulation which has allowed them to be successful in business,' said Giner. 'In these countries, they've chosen to encourage competitiveness over dying of envy,' which has helped them be better when it comes to matching and overcoming a rival.

Generally, Spanish society attaches greater value to luck or the capriciousness of fate than to effort. And appearances are everything. You can open any doors as long as you look the part.

When Cristiano arrived in Spain he thought that showing his special abilities would be enough to earn him the appreciation that he so badly needs and that he would be forgiven for any slip-ups. Just as had happened in England.

But no.

■ ■ ■

During Ronaldo's first few months in the Spanish capital, dinners were organised in which life at Real Madrid was explained to him. Valdano was the key man in this regard, as he made the Portuguese see things from a different perspective. As the player's wild gesticulations continued, especially at the Bernabéu, Pedja Mijatovic and his right-hand man Carlos Bucero had to meet with him again to tell him that his behaviour did not fit in. 'In the seventy-fifth minute, run for the ball even if you're losing 5–0. Get stuck in, go in for a slide tackle to try to win it back and people will applaud you: that's what the Bernabéu wants,' they told him.

It is fascinating that the team that has hosted and produced some of the biggest stars in the history of football has a set of fans that rewards effort so consistently: good players must run, too, it is non-negotiable. Commitment and fight are worthy of fervent applause. Zidane was booed in his early months at the Bernabéu, as were Figo, Guti, Benzema, the Brazilian Ronaldo and Manolo Velázquez, technically gifted players who were never entirely trusted. Meanwhile, Zamorano and Santillana were fan favourites despite not having that magic. David Beckham's commitment transferred to the popularity polls, while Fabio Capello, who wanted every player to run, was much loved by supporters in spite of persistent criticism from the press.

'I'd dare to say it's a bit of a Castile thing, the whole concept of hard work and battle,' was the analysis of Orfeo Suárez, a Catalan journalist for *El Mundo* based in Madrid. 'Madrid detest prima donnas.' This is crucial. The Bernabéu faithful rarely offers the star that total support that is seen in British stadiums. It is the fans who set the rules, while the team has to get the crowd going, rather than the other way round.

A simile is often used to describe Real Madrid supporters. They are like those who sit in *Tendido 7* at Plaza de las Ventas (the Spanish capital's most prominent bullring), the block hated by great bullfighters: they are the demanding experts who know what bullfights are really about, and, aware of the high prices of their season ticket, have no intention of accepting a bullfight that does not go as they wanted. They know their rights and, as they are more knowledgeable than anyone else, they boo when maybe they should not.

'Real Madrid fans clearly identify with success,' explained former president Ramón Calderón. 'It's not just a football thing. Seventy-five per cent of them were not born in Madrid, which isn't the case for Barcelona, Sevilla or Deportivo, clubs that represent the region. We go to the stadium as if it were the opera. If they don't sing well, we boo, whistle and take out our handkerchiefs. It's something foreign players don't grasp: "Why do they criticise us? They don't support us," they say, gobsmacked.'

'Players who broke through in the Premier League will always prefer it to La Liga,' admitted renowned journalist Paco González. 'Here we go by the principle or suspicion that these guys are rich, spoilt, do sod all . . . And on top of that, they lose! So I'll boo them. Most players that have enjoyed success in the Premier League are never entirely happy here because of that.'

Ronaldo, according to the football equivalent of *Tendido 7*, came with baggage. How could anyone forget his €94 million price tag? As for physique, most Spanish supporters think you don't need to sculpt a body like Ronaldo's in order to win football matches. Most members of the Spain squad that won the World Cup were less than 1.80 metres tall.

Maybe he has the same problem that basketball player LeBron James endured with NBA fans: his powerful physical presence was intimidating and the average fan found himself distanced by the star's unattainability and could not consider him an equal.

Ronaldo is a very Anglo-Saxon player. In England, people partly like him because he runs faster than most, scores more often than most, jumps higher than everyone, all this in a culture where they like to quantify things. He stands out above all others and is methodical in his preparation, another highly appreciated attribute in the United Kingdom.

All and all, many struggled to warm to Cristiano in Madrid because he was not Hispanic enough.

Ronaldo had joined a troubled Real Madrid squad, while Barcelona seemed to have the answers to everything. *Los Blancos* entered a state of emergency and the Portuguese was perceived as the mercenary who had arrived to take down the opposition at just the right time. The general feeling was that he was there to win games; he was not *really* part of the club.

Ronaldo's tendency to score goals without thanking whoever had provided the assist confirmed that thinking but did not go down well. He seemed to be thinking only about himself, his goals, his sparkle. He found it harder to see the pass than the individual route because, it seemed, team play reduced his prominence on the stage.

In away matches, Cristiano could hear deplorable chants of 'that Portuguese son of a bitch'. The Portuguese and Spanish do not get on all that well, although it is not a completely negative relationship either. In general we look east and north, forgetting that we have neighbours next door – for centuries we have exhibited a remarkable level of indifference. The Portuguese often feel like lesser citizens or visitors when they come to Spain. It is harder to accept an arrogant person from Portugal than from anywhere else, except maybe France, our other neighbours, of course.

I do not think that, in his first few months, even years, Cristiano felt he received the deference he was due as the best player in the team. He had been placed on the same level as Benzema and Kaká, and was even told he needed to earn the club's appreciation.

Something else was preventing the connection with the player: envy of the good-looking, rich, famous boy.

Ronaldo built himself and had the perfect physique, but Jorge Mendes had forgotten that in this day and age it was essential to put the same effort into his image. Something had to be done.

It was not the first time that Cristiano had to sway general opinion. He was up for the fight.

■ ■ ■

Jorge Valdano, from his position as general manager, chose his verbs and adjectives carefully to defend the player, with that skill that typifies him, in an interview with *Soho* magazine:

He's selfish? I don't know any goalscorers who aren't. He's vain? Like everyone who performs in front of an audience. He's defiant? He's always defending himself because he's attacked so despicably.

He's ambitious? Of course, with a professionalism that, as we'll see, only conforms with perfection.

Attention often focuses on minor issues: if he gave a friendly smile or a dirty look, whether or not he made a gesture, a word here, a word there . . . What we must do every day is speak about how he trains and lives as a professional as well as his ability to exceed himself year after year. He's truly extraordinary and is one of the best players in football history.

He's disappointed all those who hoped he would be a walking performance act hopping from one nightclub to another. Cristiano hops from training session to training session.[25]

Despite such staunch defence from the club, it would be years after the day of his record-breaking unveiling before the legendary Bernabéu stadium would chant his name again with such fervour.

■ ■ ■

One of the most surprising exercises in my research was analysing the conscious and unconscious gestures that Ronaldo exhibits on the pitch and discussing them with a body language expert. I searched for someone who, knowing little or nothing about football, could analyse Cristiano's behaviour on the pitch from a purely academic standpoint. Dr Peter Collett, psychologist and former Oxford don as well as a world expert on this topic, ticked the boxes.

Collett searched for YouTube videos and photos on and off the pitch before reaching some interesting conclusions.

Before beginning the study, Collett knew that Ronaldo was an extremely competitive player; everything he saw of him confirmed that. He managed to see beyond that straight away. 'He has the most incredible body balance I've ever seen,' he told me on the phone. 'He's like a ballerina, he could spin on a coin.'

We think that he finds it hard to accept other people's talent, but is capable of acknowledging a technical skill from which he can learn. In one video, Collett discovered Ronaldo admiring Anderson while the Brazilian performed some tricky skills without the ball touching the ground. 'It opens up a new window, he isn't just competitive. If he sees someone doing something better than he does, he recognises it and uses it to improve.' Deep down there is respect for the same path that he has trodden, the one of excellence.

Collett was fascinated by the theatrics that accompanied Ronaldo, often unconsciously. The act is performed in front of a very large audience. Cristiano is consciously or otherwise in constant dialogue with supporters, whether in the stadium or watching on television. His exaggerated gestures are aimed at the world, rather than himself or his team-mates – all of it is done for us. And all of it stokes his engine.

During his first few years among the elite, he would celebrate his goals by stretching out his arms as if he were about to fly (or land), angrily shouting in recognition of the hard work behind the goal or looking at the terraces with a fearless expression, as if to say: 'Well, of course . . .' Pure theatre.

When he scores and makes a calming action with his hands, he is replicating many political experts; it is a demagogic gesture. He is looking for control of the masses; cutting the applause is an expression of false modesty. It is not a request; it is an order.

He performed one of his most famous gestures for the first time with Portugal: a jump with hands pointing towards the ground and a shout of 'I'm here'. René Meulensteen was not a fan of the celebration and told the player so. Collett avoided judgement, comparing it to a theatrical rock act by Freddy Mercury. It is a demonstration of strength and an order at the time: for people to accept that he is the best.

Collett gathered together dozens of examples that showed a Cristiano who was aware of being number one and the corresponding tension created between the team and the lone warrior. During Ronaldo's first seasons at Real Madrid, he used to distance himself from the crowd of team-mates that wanted to celebrate with him.

In fact, he has never liked excessive physical contact. He wants to be alone, according to Collett. His hugs tend to be brisk taps on the back rather than prolonged exchanges. He does not need to share that moment or be congratulated by his team-mates.

What he wants is for the whole world to worship him.

Why does he not celebrate his team-mates' success? 'It's another way,' explained Collett, 'of punishing himself and showing his anger that he did not do what his team-mate just did. Self-recrimination.'

The psychologist believes that when Ronaldo loses his temper because the ball does not reach him, for example, it is because he sees it as a lack of recognition of his status as the best.

I added that it must be tiring to be constantly on the hunt for such assurance. Yet Ronaldo does not show any signs of tiring. Collett agreed and noticed how the player's museum in Madeira contains a collection of objects that allows him to send out the unequivocal message that he is the best.

He constantly changes his haircut (he would do so for every match during the 2014 World Cup in Brazil). If individuality requires its space in a team sport, it can only surface in this way. As well as in goal celebrations, of course.

When he takes his shirt off, he sends out multiple messages: intimidation, which sportsmen often use; vanity, given that in reality that much muscle is not needed to play football; as well as another graphic sign that he is above the rest.

In the videos that Collett saw of Gareth Bale's first season at Real Madrid, he discovered enough signals (such as reacting to the

Welshman's goals with vacant stares) to dare to make the following statement: Ronaldo does not think Bale is on his level. As we will see later on, this creates an interesting conflict because the club would like them to be on the same level.

Collett was able to observe Ronaldo off the pitch with his partner Irina and his son. But never the three of them together. It seems as if he never wanted to share his son with any woman, apart from the one who looks after him, his mother Dolores. Collett went beyond that: he had the feeling that his relationship with women was one of mistrust, as if they existed to take advantage of him, as if Cristiano were a giant piece of bait.

The international press speculates obsessively over Ronaldo's love life. He has been linked with dozens of stunning models and glamorous television presenters, many of whom are willing to sell their story with the footballer, be it true or false.

I would add that when a mother is omnipresent, the relationship established between a son and his girlfriends is often not equal, for one simple reason: the mother considers them rivals and the son discovers that nobody else can hold a candle to his mother.

In Collet's opinion, these seem powerful enough reasons to make it hard to find a woman to share the rest of his life with.

When they were together, Collett suggested, Irina and Cristiano always looked like a couple on stage: too artificial to be real. 'Cut Irina out of any photo of them together,' he suggested. 'Does it look like anyone is missing?'

■ ■ ■

The 2010–11 campaign would see the pressure on Cristiano turned up a notch. It was José Mourinho's inaugural season as Real Madrid coach.

Both Portuguese icons had made their peace after various verbal conflicts in the Premier League. Ronaldo admitted that Mourinho made an apology during the pair's last meeting at Stamford Bridge: 'As far as I'm concerned, it's all done and dusted.'[11]

As part of his strategy, the new coach multiplied the tension tenfold with a Barcelona side enjoying the best spell in its history. It was the year of the 5–0 drubbing at the Camp Nou, four *clásicos* in two years, and it felt as if Real Madrid had used all their weaponry in a bid to close the gap. They seemed to have managed it only by the end of that rollercoaster season.

Ángel Di María joined the club alongside two German internationals, Mesut Özil and Sami Khedira, and veteran Portuguese defender Ricardo Carvalho. Raúl left for Schalke 04 and Cristiano at last got his hands on the number seven shirt.

Mourinho believed that the squad at his disposal would be able to take Barcelona on man for man, but that humbling 5–0 defeat in the season's first *clásico* at the Camp Nou set the record straight. The coach also used it intelligently to demand more responsibility and changes at the club, including Jorge Valdano's departure.

Ronaldo was put on the right wing during that pivotal fixture and Mourinho asked the team to play on the break to benefit the Portuguese and Benzema. The mistake was made in the team's pressing: the players thought that they had to press high up the pitch, but the coach wanted them to sit deep and protect the space in behind. It did not go well.

Mourinho looked to use conflict on and off the pitch as a vehicle for the change he felt *Los Blancos* needed. However, an already complicated dressing room quickly split, as *El País* journalist Diego Torres explained in *Prepárense para perder* (Prepare to Lose). There was the Spanish group and Benzema on one side, with the Portuguese's clan on the other (Pepe, Khedira, Marcelo, Özil and Di María) that revolved around Cristiano and Jorge Mendes, who Mourinho was almost using as director of football in parallel with Jorge Valdano.

In accordance with Mourinho's plans, Cristiano's presence forced the team to drop deep in order to create space in attack. The Portuguese, clearly recognised by the new coach as the best player in the team, was freed from all defensive duties and other teammates considered that protection of the striker was excessive – that created a dislike towards Cristiano, who was given the nickname 'the Anxious One'.

'They played a key match away to Racing Santander at the Sardinero,' explained Diego Torres when we had a coffee in a hotel near the Bernabéu. 'Cristiano was injured and most of the others hatched a plan at the hotel, apart from the group close to Mendes: "Now the Anxious One isn't here, we're going to put in an incredible performance and see what his daddy says." Mourinho's pre-match team talk went something like: "I already know you're going to put in a great performance because Cristiano isn't here." José had great intuition. And they did play brilliantly, bloody well in fact, and won 3–1. Yet Mourinho chose to lay into them, saying in his press conference he didn't enjoy the match, it was rubbish and he told the players as much in the dressing room: they did not do x, y and z, did not defend well, didn't create enough . . .'

Once again Jorge Valdano came out in defence of Cristiano. 'I hope people don't say Real Madrid played well because Cristiano isn't there, that would be utter rubbish. With Cristiano Ronaldo, this match would have had a much more flattering scoreline.'

The game confirmed the mistrust towards the new star and the start of an irreparable divide.

The four *clásicos* came along in April.

REAL MADRID 1–1 BARCELONA
(LA LIGA, 16 APRIL 2011)

Neither side really played for the win on a dry Bernabéu pitch with both teams desperate to avoid defeat in the first round of the heavyweight clash. The home side defended very deep while Barça controlled the game in typical fashion. The draw benefited the Catalans in terms of the table. Ronaldo scored a penalty, but had little influence on the game.

BARCELONA 0–1 REAL MADRID
(COPA DEL REY FINAL, 20 APRIL 2011)

The plan was to play it long for Cristiano who played as a number nine. The defensive line was pushed further forward with Sergio Ramos, who had been a full-back up to that point, surprisingly selected at centre-back. The team fought for every ball as if it were the last. A one-two between Di María and Marcelo in extra-time set up Ronaldo to outjump Adriano and head an unstoppable winner past Pinto. Cristiano ran to celebrate by the touchline with a knee slide before reacting coldly to his team-mates' hugs.

A key goal at a key moment, the first of many against a Barcelona side that Real Madrid had finally managed to overcome.

REAL MADRID 0–2 BARCELONA
(CHAMPIONS LEAGUE SEMI-FINAL
FIRST LEG, 27 APRIL 2011)

Mourinho's tactics were to get a draw and decide the tie in the return leg. He tried to attack Barça with long balls up to Cristiano, although the forward had to ask the midfielders behind him to push further up several times during the match. The visitors did not take any big risks either. Pepe received his marching orders for a high tackle on Dani Alves. An irate Mourinho was also shown red. Messi scored a brace in the final quarter of an hour. There were physical skirmishes between both sides' players in the tunnel. Mourinho asked himself in his press conference why Barcelona always received favourable refereeing decisions against his teams.

Jerzy Dudek revealed in his biography that, in the changing room, Ronaldo was enraged and harshly criticised his manager's tactics. He had been isolated by his team-mates, failing to muster a single shot on target, and asked the coach to play a more attacking style.

Yet in the mixed zone Cristiano defended Mourinho's strategy and complained about the supposed refereeing favours that Barcelona benefited from. He was, however, unable to resist a subtle jibe at his coach: 'As a forward, I don't like to play like this but I have to adapt to what the team asks of me.'

Mourinho saw it as a rebellious act, stopped speaking to Cristiano and dropped him for the following league match against Zaragoza.

Ronaldo blew his top when he found out, punching lockers and kicking anything that was in his path. The message made it through to the rest of the group loud and clear: if the best player received such treatment, it would be advisable not to contradict Mourinho.

It was the last time Cristiano was dropped by Mourinho for 'tactical' reasons.

BARCELONA 1–1 REAL MADRID (CHAMPIONS LEAGUE SEMI-FINAL, SECOND LEG, 3 MAY 2011)

According to Diego Torres's book, this is the conversation that José Mourinho had with Cristiano Ronaldo in front of the players ahead of the second leg:

You! Cristiano! Come here, I've got something to tell you. I'll say it to your face: you complain that we play defensively here. But do you know why that is? It's your fault. As you don't want to defend and close down the wings, I have to push the team further back. You got angry because I didn't play you in Bilbao [he was on the bench against Athletic ahead of the Champions League quarter-final second leg at Tottenham], because when you go out there, you do your own thing. You want to achieve your personal goals. Maybe the guilty one is me for allowing you to. You're in your own world. You go to the press and instead of doing what you should, you criticise us because we're defensive. Do you know what you should've done? Criticise the referee, think about me and the team . . . I have to love you because you're my brother's brother and when someone is your brother's brother, he's your brother too. But the other day, you went and criticised my tactics instead of doing as I told you. You criticised me! You don't respect your team-mates. You watch them run. You watch how Pepe and Lass run and you raise your hands complaining if the ball doesn't reach you! You could be a better team-mate and go to the press conference to speak ill of the referee instead of raising your hands! I've invented a formation just for you, so that you're comfortable, don't have to run and can score goals! We play like this because of you! If I put you on Alves, you'll let him get away from you . . . And what? Do you think Di María is a lesser player than you?[26]

Diego Torres related how Ronaldo replied angrily, spouting many expletives including: 'That son of a bitch has taken me to the cleaners!'[26]

And Kaká asked, 'Who's the brother of the brother?'[26]

Real Madrid did not play at all badly at the Camp Nou, but were lacking that cutting edge. Barcelona's ticket for the final was never in doubt.

Los Blancos finished the season as Copa del Rey winners and runners-up in La Liga. Ronaldo, who was starting to feel more comfortable alongside a dynamic striker such as Benzema rather than a predator like Higuaín, had scored four goals in a match for the first time (against Racing on 23 October 2010). He had reached 200 goals in his professional career by November and started to have an average of a goal per game, a record that brought the times of Ferenç Puskás to mind. After his brace on the final day against Almería, his tally stood at forty-one league goals, a record in the competition's history. Or forty if you do not count the goal off Pepe's back that *Marca*, who give out the Pichichi award for top scorer in the league, awarded to Cristiano while referee Mateu Lahoz attributed it to the centre-back. His season total was a staggering fifty-four, twelve more than his previous career best, clinching a second Golden Boot in the process.

The figures said one thing, while his words in private said another. His second season in Madrid had been frustrating. Not only did Barcelona scoop both major trophies (they beat Manchester United in the Champions League final), but they had once again charged into the Bernabéu like a Roman army and crushed all before them. The cup final victory was a step in the right direction, but not a sufficient reward for fans or the Portuguese.

Cristiano was suffering and underwent a period of personal problems that were exacerbated by the tension created with Mourinho and certain team-mates.

His relationship with Iker Casillas, for example, suffered considerably after the goalkeeper's girlfriend, journalist Sara Carbonero, said the following on the television programme *El programa de Ana Rosa*: 'Ronaldo is fine. He isn't depressed, he hasn't gone to see a psychologist to be told to take the pressure off himself as people have claimed recently . . . Ronaldo has always been like that, selfish and individualistic on the pitch and Real Madrid signed him like that.'

Ronaldo, who did not hear the statement first hand, sent Casillas a message questioning Carbonero's words, to which the Spaniard responded by defending his partner. The mistrust between the two made the group even more fractured than before. There was a deep conflict between two leaders. The club president and other players successfully intervened in order for peace to reign or to call a truce at the very least.

Ronaldo was well aware that he did not enjoy the same influence or receive the same affection as at Manchester United. He knew that making the move was a good one as it was the right time, but in summer 2012 he discussed with his inner circle how he maybe would have achieved more in Manchester.

Well, at least he would have been happier.

■ ■ ■

Off the pitch, the marriage of the Real Madrid and CR7 brands was a hit. Ronaldo began starring in an increasing number of commercials, as well as featuring in more and more events, where he conducted himself with the same professionalism he showed in training.

I hosted a couple of these events. The first of them was for Castrol, the motor oil company, at which the player had to beat his own speed record dribbling round obstacles. The organisers had asked me to get him to repeat the exercise three times, but after the second Ronaldo felt he had done his job.

'One more time, Cristiano?' I said into the microphone. The small audience in attendance (around 150 guests) looked on expectantly. His back turned to them, Ronaldo shot me a murderous glance, the sort he flashes at referees from time to time. I raised my eyebrows.

He did it, of course.

On the other occasion, at a memorable Nike function at the iconic Battersea Power Station, south London, with its ruined interior, I had to interview Cristiano in front of a hundred or so international journalists. Cristiano, who had travelled from Madrid, showed up late because his flight had been delayed, but he cut a relaxed figure, smiling. Talking to me in the room where the stars were received, where tidy rows of bottled water and canapés of all shapes and sizes had been laid out, he spoke about that weekend's match and remarked on the unusual venue. Meanwhile, next door, the questions were screened several times before being accepted by Bárbara Vara, a member of Jorge Mendes's inner circle and the person directly responsible for Ronaldo's image management. The event was stripped down to the bare bones, with Ronaldo only having two hours to carry out his commitments.

Eventually he answered everything he was asked in an affable, breezy manner.

That is the essence of the image he sells.

■ ■ ■

Esteve Calzada, the former chief marketing officer at Barcelona, has analysed Ronaldo thoroughly. Along the way, he has identified a number of factors explaining why CR7 has risen to the top of the advertising world. 'Firstly, he maximises his potential,' Calzada said. 'He capitalises on his good looks, the club he's at and an aggressive marketing machine.' Ronaldo's social media posts are among the most effective out there for advertisers, garnering 53 per cent more hits than Messi's, albeit the latter is not on Twitter because of an agreement with Chinese social network Weibo. One of Cristiano's advantages is that he can realistically claim to communicate in both Spanish and English, even if he does not do the posting itself. As a result of all this, a single tweet by him can be worth €50,000.

GestiFute, the Jorge Mendes-run agency that looks after Cristiano's image, has it down to a tee: 'Ronaldo has a price for whatever you need,' Calzada said. 'That's not always the case: with other stars, there's much more improvisation.' His schedule is packed full of publicity commitments throughout the season (from events to advertising shoots and photo sessions) and he fulfils all of them in good spirit, something that is not widespread among big stars.

'Ronaldo is advertising dynamite,' Calzada went on. The world of cosmetics and other high-end sophisticated brands queue up to have him promote their products. It is hard to imagine Messi advertising a 'super-cool' cologne, or an exorbitantly priced car or watch. Leo remains a kid from the block, while Ronaldo is the boy who came up in the world and is drawn to luxury.

Since his arrival at Real Madrid, Cristiano has been picked out as the player with the biggest marketing potential by a number of studies, and he has in GestiFute very active representatives who have always sought to score as many commercial deals as possible for their star. Calzada calculates that he could be pocketing some €30 million a year from advertising.

According to *Forbes* magazine, David Beckham is the only footballer, past or present, to outearn him on this front. And, like the Englishman, Cristiano has outgrown the sporting arena to compete with other celebrities such as Shakira and Justin Timberlake. There is no sign that he has hit his ceiling yet with his profile expected to keep soaring after he sold his image rights to Peter Lim, a shrewd move particularly in terms of growing in the Asian market.

Despite all this, he has made the odd strategic mistake. I do not know if he would see it that way, but having a brand called CR7 (featuring luxury items, jeans and T-shirts for men, and accessories and costume jewellery for women) is for many people a confirmation of his excessive self-absorption. Beckham went about things much more subtly by creating a range for Marks & Spencer. Ronaldo placed his sisters Elma and Katia in charge of the CR7 shops in

Funchal and Lisbon, but they have only seen limited success and it does not look like any more will be opening any time soon.

In July 2014 he announced the launch of CR7 Footwear, with a target market in the 'premium and fashion segment, with a relaxed and casual lifestyle'. Nike, one of his main sponsors, was angered by his failure to discuss his plans with them and in the end he had to withdraw all the products that competed with the North American brand.

Ronaldo is a perfect fit for the image Real Madrid want to convey. Still, let's play a game. Imagine if he had signed for Barcelona, which was a possibility. Would he have had to change his image? Would he have pulled it off? Would the two brands have been in tune? To answer all these questions, let me ask another question: how would he have got on with Carles Puyol?

There you go, then.

■ ■ ■

Money has not been a concern for Ronaldo since his time at Manchester United, but he likes to boast about how much he has in the bank. During a recent international break, he asked a Portugal team-mate, half-jokingly, to guess the size of his fortune. Was it €100 million? No. €150 million? Nope. €250 million was the answer.

An interview he gave the *Daily Mirror* in 2011 landed on my desk. He was not asked about Messi or Mourinho, but, rather, about his wealth and what he liked to spend his money on.

Ronaldo set the British tabloid straight when talking about his appearance on the *Forbes* rich list, which had his fortune down at $160 million (£99 million), telling them that it was actually more like $245 million.

Yet another competition he wants to win.

He also enjoys sharing his riches. Especially with his family, whom he helps to start businesses. 'I bought my mother a £400,000 house in Portugal, she lives there with her partner and my son. I bought my sisters houses as well,' he revealed in the same interview. Did he really need to specify the price?

He splashes the cash to treat his friends and family to meals and he foots the bill at parties. 'I have my circle of friends, my club. People who've been with me a long time. I look after these people. I take them to five-star hotels, I pay for private jets, I pay at the bar. I never drink in public. I drink Red Bull while I buy my friends champagne at £1,000-plus a bottle. It's no problem – I like my friends to be happy.'[14]

■ ■ ■

Cristiano's private life is not simple: such is the price of fame. A couple of years ago he decided to go and see *The Lion King*, the musical, in central Madrid. He tried to go incognito by wearing a cap, but it was not long before he was recognised by several audience members. People started getting up to take photos and he ended up leaving way before the end.

Cristiano has not found a way to enjoy the city without the fear of being mobbed.

When he wants to go out, his Portuguese friends call a number of nightclubs and restaurants, booking tables under other names. Then they eventually go wherever they think he will feel most comfortable and will not be harassed by journalists. But it is easier and more common for him just to hold parties at his house in the gated community of La Finca, like the one he organised for his birthday one year, in which he set up a casino in the basement, using chips that people could exchange for real money . . . Ronaldo's money.

Or he discreetly rents a nearby mansion for the occasion.

'I try to avoid public places. I usually go to quiet spots, to restaurants where there's a secluded table,' he revealed in an interview with

Téléfoot. 'I'll look to enjoy myself more in the future, when another Cristiano will have taken my place.'

■ ■ ■

Jorge Valdano said that there is something fascinating about Cristiano: the difficulty in pinning him down. An elusive hero, he materialises and then vanishes. 'One day, while on holiday, he appears in a photo with Paris Hilton and there's a huge commotion. Then we don't know where he is for the next three months because he hides, he disappears. That mystique helps to give his persona an indecipherable quality, which enthrals public opinion.'[13]

That said, we do know some things about him.

Paris Hilton and Cristiano met in Los Angeles in 2009, shortly after he had signed for Real Madrid, and were spotted together in very public engagements on a couple of occasions. There are lots of photos that confirm as much, because Paris Hilton always had at least one photographer in tow. Speculation about a romantic relationship ensued, but when the pictures were published Cristiano called Florentino Pérez and told him, 'Mr President, I'm not the clubbing type.'[13] Paris Hilton claims that things ended badly and that she broke up with Ronaldo because he was a 'sissy', although I would not consider her the most objective source.

We know that Cristiano always wants the best, and that goes for girlfriends, too. Take Irina Shayk, for example, who has been one of the most in-demand models in the world since she was sixteen. They met at an Armani photo shoot in May 2010 and subsequently holidayed together on Cristiano's yacht in Corsica. While he was with her, he seemed to forget his deep-rooted fear of being taken advantage of.

It would appear, according to what a couple of his friends have said, that for a long time he would ask his mother to approve his girlfriends. She seems to have been a stumbling block for some of the candidates and, if the Portuguese press are to be believed, would prefer her son had a Portuguese girlfriend. As his sister Katia has put it, 'My mum is very protective.' Dolores had to be reminded that her son, as he approached thirty, was old enough to decide for himself.

We also know that he appreciates female beauty. In the words of *Marca* journalist Sergio Fernández, 'He's a bloody normal guy. One day we were having coffee together, along with Ricardo Carvalho, and a beautiful woman walked past, so he nudged us and said, "Check her out" and so on. Carvalho didn't look, so Cristiano remarked, "This guy's like Kaká."' Both players are well known for their religious fervour.

We know that if a woman, or anyone, lets him down once, he cuts her out of his life just like that. I have the impression (and this is my own theory, having discussed the subject with several psychologists) that perhaps he has a lot of sex when what he is actually looking for is genuine affection.

Nevertheless, he is less a sex symbol than an example of self-improvement, at least among women. A few months ago I had a fascinating conversation with the wife of an Argentinian football legend who has been puzzling over the Ronaldo phenomenon for years. 'A lot of us women feel that something is off,' she said. 'Many of my female friends say the same, pointing to the way he grooms his eyebrows, those perfect teeth and how he dresses.'

The image he conveys is too metrosexual, or, to put it another way, not very masculine, although, the ex-player's wife says, maybe he is more so up-close. The impression he gives is that he is only in love with himself, or at least loves himself more than anyone else, and that diminishes his attractiveness in many women's eyes.

Seeing him cry, that he is in touch with his feminine side, attracts the maternal instinct in many, but it does not awaken a desire to bed him.

The fact is – she concluded – Ronaldo does as much sexually for many women as one of Michelangelo's perfect statues.

Perhaps this is the root of the idea that Cristiano is gay, which has been repeated regularly in both Portugal and Spain. Envy almost definitely has a role here, too.

■ ■ ■

Ronaldo, whom many consider arrogant and narcissistic, had a son in June 2010. This is not a contradiction, but it had been hard to imagine Cristiano taking care of someone. As is almost always the case, fatherhood has changed him.

Ronaldo had imagined one day having a son who would be his friend, his companion, who would watch him play – while he was still at the top – and would, ideally, want to become a footballer himself. After announcing this dream to his family, Cristiano talked to them a great deal about it. He had a clear idea as to who would look after the child: his mother, Dolores. So his son would also be his brother, and the mother/grandmother would have to take care of both.

Dolores's authorised biography explains that an American woman discreetly gave birth to Ronaldo's first child, and it was Dolores who travelled to Florida just before Cristiano Jr was delivered on 17 June 2010.[10] The baby weighed nine pounds and seven ounces. The player was in South Africa for the World Cup, which was in full swing. A few days later, after registering the birth at a Portuguese Consulate in the United States, Cristiano's mother flew back to Madrid with her grandson in her arms.

Dinis, Katia and Zé's son, was also born around this time.

The Aveiro family are unwilling to talk about the boy's origins. The most widely known account is that Cristiano had a one-night stand with a mystery woman who ended up pregnant. They signed a contract agreeing to hide her identity, in which she handed over full custody to the player, reportedly in exchange for €11 million.

Cristiano Jr has asked who his mother is on more than one occasion. Ronaldo has an answer prepared and repeats it: 'It's not important who your mum is. She's travelling. All that matters is that daddy loves you.'[27]

His sister Katia once told the boy that his mother was dead. Cristiano asked her not to do so again. In any case, she does not exist in Ronaldo's world, so she may as well be.[27]

Cristiano is the most maternal of fathers, always attentive, always playing with the kid, training at home with him, although Dolores spends long periods with the boy, both in Portugal and at the house she has next to her son's in Madrid.

On one occasion, Cristiano Jr was asked who his dad was. He replied emphatically, 'The best in the world.'

■ ■ ■

In the 2011–12 season, with Zinedine Zidane installed as director of football in place of Jorge Valdano, the Real Madrid captains (Xabi Alonso, Iker Casillas, Álvaro Arbeloa and Sergio Ramos) requested a meeting with the Frenchman. Complaints about Cristiano Ronaldo had been left hanging from the previous season. They could not understand why he failed to track back, why he did not work hard enough. They felt that with him in the team and being used the way he was, they were playing worse: because of him, Mourinho made everyone else drop too deep. Everyone's job was to create space for Cristiano; they all saved Cristiano's energy, every pass had to go to Cristiano, Cristiano scored the goals.

One of the great football minds once told me that a team of Real Madrid's quality would be unbeatable if all eleven players defended. However, if ten players defended, they might win something, but would be dangerously inconsistent. If nine defended, they would win precisely nothing.

The Spaniards, who had been part of the team that had lifted the World Cup a year earlier, asked for Ronaldo to be given defensive duties. While they were at it, they demanded that he be treated the same way as the rest of them. Mourinho's staff interpreted this as jealousy.

'Guys, you have to suck up to Ronaldo,' an experienced club official said to them, 'don't you see that he's the one who wins games for you?'

The club captains did not feel the need to devote themselves to Cristiano quite so unreservedly.

■ ■ ■

Everything that prevented Ronaldo enjoying his football came together during a Champions League game away to Dinamo Zagreb. Chants of 'Messi, Messi' (traditionally performed by opposing fans ever since it was heard in a previous play-offs against Bosnia-Herzegovina to which Ronaldo responded by giving them the finger) rang out endlessly and provocatively from the die-hard crowd, who whistled and hurled insults at him – as had become commonplace in matches away from the Bernabéu. He was also on the receiving end of a vicious, high tackle which left his ankle bleeding.

He was seething at the end of the game, which ended 1–0 to Real Madrid thanks to a Di María goal.

Jorge Mendes had told the club and Oscar Ribot, the press officer for the first team at the time, not to allow Ronaldo to talk to the media when he was in that sort of mood.

But that day he wanted to get some things off his chest.

Mendes, imagining as much, called the general manager José Ángel Sánchez to urge him to stop Ronaldo from speaking.

No one could.

He got into the mixed zone and exploded.

'The referee? He was awful. This is a disgrace.'

He felt like he was not being protected by referees, or anyone for that matter.

And he was being targeted by the opposition supporters. He thought he knew why and so he said something that will haunt him for the rest of his life.

'Because I'm rich, handsome and a great player, people are jealous of me. There is no other explanation.'

You are right, Cristiano. That is human nature. But you cannot say it in public; or you can, but not like that.

He went from victim to culprit.

Incidentally, the second part of his speech hardly got any attention: 'Before matches referees say they're going to protect the most skilful players, but when I play, they don't protect me at all. You can't touch some players, while I have to take a beating [for a foul to be given]. I don't understand it, I don't understand it.'

José Mourinho blamed the communications department for failing to stop him, for not showing enough authority to prevent him talking to the press.

The upshot was that Ronaldo had vented his spleen.

Soon, however, he realised the error of his ways. Nevertheless, Mendes informed the club that, despite his remorse, there was an underlying issue that needed dealing with. Both Ronaldo and his agent were convinced that the club was not doing enough to look after the player, both on the pitch and in the media. His reactions were being judged more harshly than the situations which provoked them; his outbursts were being talked about more than his performance.

The club's take was different. José Ángel Sánchez told Mario Torrejón as much in the latter's biography of Ronaldo: 'It had to do with the change of country, of fan cultures and so on, an emotional environment that Cristiano took a while to adapt to.'[13] In England he did not have to prove his greatness and he managed to convince everyone of it. In Spain he had to prove it constantly because it was questioned by people almost daily. And, for once, he seemed to be tired of trying.

'It's hard to accept that after scoring so many goals and winning so much, he is still criticised,' says his friend Hugo Pina. 'He was aware that the reactions weren't about the way he played, but about other stuff, but he didn't take it very well. He suffers a lot because of such things.'

■ ■ ■

That rant took place in September 2011, early on in the season.

Despite the limited changes to the squad (Fábio Coentrão, Nuri Sahin, José Callejón, Hamit Altintop and Raphaël Varane had come in), or maybe because of it, Real Madrid were continuing the progress they had shown in the previous campaign. They had ventured to try out a different style against Barcelona in the Spanish Super Cup a month before (during which Mourinho infamously poked Tito Vilanova in the eye): the team had played with more intensity and a higher defensive line. Ronaldo had scored his first goal at the Camp Nou and his 100th in his two and a bit seasons at Real Madrid. Despite the defeat in the first competition of the campaign, there was a sense of optimism.

Real Madrid went into the first league *clásico* of the season, in December, out ahead statistically, with more goals and more points than Barcelona. When they took the lead after twenty-two seconds, this seemed to confirm that it might be Mourinho's men's year, but Barcelona turned the game around and eventually sealed a deserved 3–1 away win.

This was *AS*'s take on the stars' respective contributions:

If we turn our attention to the battle between Messi and Cristiano, the comparison doesn't hold up. The Portuguese has nothing to press his claim: he was once again obsessed with trying to stand out, dominated by the anxiety of wanting to decide the *clásico* in every move. He missed two gilt-edged chances at pivotal moments [one of them to put Real Madrid 2–0 up]. He wasn't up to scratch and that is nothing new in Real Madrid–Barça games. Messi, on the contrary, made the difference again.[28]

The Bernabéu faithful singled out Ronaldo as one of those responsible for the latest painful loss against their arch-rivals and made their feelings known in the following matches at home. First against Málaga in the Copa del Rey (Real Madrid won 3–2, but he was not on the scoresheet) and subsequently against Granada in La Liga, a game which ended in a 5–1 victory, with Ronaldo netting the fifth in the dying stages. He was booed on both occasions.

Rather than understanding that Real Madrid were up against possibly the greatest team in history, the fans blamed the player with the €94 million price tag.

■ ■ ■

In November Ronaldo was presented with the European Golden Shoe, recognising the top league goalscorer in Europe, for the second time. He had this to say: 'If God can't make everyone love him, how could I?'

And this: 'It's better to play at the same time as Messi than not to. I like competing, that way we can know who's really the best.'

Cristiano went to the Ballon d'Or ceremony in January 2012, where Messi picked up the accolade for the third time in a row.

■ ■ ■

Having sensed a certain weariness between the Barcelona squad and Guardiola, Mourinho set about rubbing salt in the wound.

He did so through his comments and off-the-record briefings sent out from the club, as well as roping in his players to do the same at press conferences.

The work put in on the training ground and in front of the microphones paid off.

The 2011–12 season, despite the fans' doubts, was marked by stellar contributions from Cristiano Ronaldo in big matches. As well as bagging two hat-tricks against Atlético (the second in April, shortly before the title was clinched), he filled his boots against Sevilla, Athletic Bilbao, Betis, Valencia and Málaga. Real Madrid lost two and drew three of the eleven games in which he failed to score.

In the thirty-fifth game of the season, Real Madrid visited the Camp Nou.

With the sides locked at 1–1, Cristiano scored to make it 2–1 in the seventy-second minute and celebrated by gesturing at the crowd to calm down.

That strike would be the winner. Ronaldo had finally claimed three points at the Camp Nou, something Real Madrid had not done for four years.

The most hotly contested La Liga title in some time was almost in the bag.

■ ■ ■

Real Madrid fell to Bayern Munich in the Champions League semi-finals. Cristiano scored twice in the second leg at the Bernabéu, including once from the spot, but Arjen Robben levelled the tie with a penalty of his own and it went to a shootout. Ronaldo was the first taker and went for the opposite side of the goal to what he had done during normal time. Manuel Neuer guessed correctly and made the save.

In spite of the European disappointment and the occasional differences with the fans, it was a record-breaking season. Real Madrid racked up 100 points to finish nine ahead of Barcelona, and the Portuguese, who seemed to have reached the peak of his powers at the age of twenty-seven, scored forty-six league goals.

There was also a moment that, though it will not go down in the history books, will have been particularly gratifying for Ronaldo. As Xabi Alonso puts it, 'In the face of so much criticism, he must have thought, "The best way to earn respect is on the pitch, not by doing easy things or playing to the gallery, but through goals and performances; I'll win them over in the end."'

Cristiano finally received his first standing ovation at the Bernabéu on 21 January 2012, two and a half years after he had been unveiled to a packed house. It was during the game against Zaragoza, who took the lead. Kaká equalised and then Ronaldo put Real Madrid ahead in the forty-ninth minute.

The fans showed their appreciation for the goal, but, much more importantly, for his commitment in a match in which he fought for the cause, demanding the ball, running to win back possession, making tackles and interceptions, and pressing the opposition.

Was this enough, though? Did Ronaldo feel that it was enough?

■ ■ ■

During the 2012 European Championship in Poland and Ukraine, Ronaldo was subjected to the treatment that had been shown, time and time again, to unsettle him. The Danish fans chanted 'Messi, Messi' whenever he touched the ball or missed a chance. Asked about it at the end of the match, he replied, 'Do you know where Messi was this time last year? He was getting knocked out of the Copa América in his own country. I think that's worse, don't you?'

All of that was true, but did he really have to say it?

Portugal, coached by Paulo Bento, came very close to reaching the final, only to be defeated by Spain on penalties in the semi-finals. It was a very evenly matched encounter and the Portuguese had the eventual winners of the tournament on the back foot. But Ronaldo failed to make a mark. He kept himself back to take his team's fifth spot-kick, but never got to do so because Vicente del Bosque's side had sealed victory by that point.

The Portuguese press, growing impatient at Cristiano not displaying his best form for his country, was tough on him, perhaps for the first time. Well-known sports journalist Bruno Prata suggested he see a psychologist: 'When he's less fixated on winning, goals and himself, it will all be much easier.' As for him being down to take the fifth penalty, this was interpreted as an act of vanity, as if he wanted to be the hero to take Portugal back into a European final.

Ronaldo seemed to be fair game for everyone, including a country that needed him.

■ ■ ■

Despite winning La Liga, despite getting his first ovation at the Bernabéu, something was troubling him. Something that was stopping him from loving what he was doing.

The following pre-season, in the United States, Ronaldo was distant towards the squad, including his group of friends in the dressing room. He would react angrily when he had to sign autographs and kept himself to himself, not talking about what was going on.

Cristiano did not seem himself in the first few months of the 2012–13 season either. Real Madrid were not exactly flying and fell five points adrift of Barcelona after the second game of the season. Personal issues had come to a head in the dressing room between players and coach, and among the players themselves, and training under Mourinho had become a struggle.

Cristiano took his misery into another public arena. Both in August, when he was present to see Andrés Iniesta given the UEFA Best Player in Europe Award, and a few months later, when Messi won his fourth Ballon d'Or, Ronaldo was seen clapping apathetically and disdainfully, even grimacing.

In his biography of Ronaldo, Diego Torres says that, 'For years, Mourinho and his agent had repeatedly told Cristiano that the Argentinian was no match for him. They called him "midget" and poked fun at his shortcomings. The coach assured him that Messi's influence was down to Barcelona's political power.'[26]

All this was not enough to console Cristiano, though.

What was bothering him?

■ ■ ■

A balanced squad is an unquantifiable factor in a player's happiness. Even for the fringe players, if there is a widespread sense that the decisions made are fair, if there is clear, universally accepted leadership, if woes and victories alike are shared, this creates the ideal atmosphere for everyone to contribute – and to enjoy their work on a day-to-day basis.

From very early on, however, José Mourinho's Real Madrid had a serious problem relating to balance and leadership. And it affected Cristiano Ronaldo, who struggled to find his place in the group.

Xabi Alonso believes that Ronaldo leads by example, while also speaking up when necessary. 'He knows that he's a touchstone even if he's not a captain,' Alonso said. 'He's not the sort to look the other way; when there's been an issue, he's confronted it. And his dedication is an example for everyone, especially the younger lads.'

This is all true, but it overlooks the crisis that has undermined the harmony in the Real Madrid dressing room since Raúl's departure.

Truth be told, Real Madrid have been missing a leader since the legendary number seven signed for Schalke 04 in 2010. They have had cliques and factions, or affinity groups, but the club's biggest deficiency in recent times has been the lack of a voice that commands authority. Iker Casillas was supposed to perform that role, but he is a quiet figure and not a born leader, so he never seemed to feel comfortable as captain.

On joining the club, Mourinho tried to make Casillas the example to follow. A whole host of disputes later, he ended up shouting in front of everyone, 'This guy [Casillas] is never playing for me again!' The goalkeeper, meanwhile, saw enemies in the dressing room: Sergio Ramos (at the beginning), 'that Portuguese' (Ronaldo) . . .

As Casillas gradually abandoned the role, Ramos began to stake his claim. In the dressing room they joked that he was in such a hurry to be the leader, especially after winning the World Cup, that one day he was going to rip the armband off the keeper's arm.

The veterans found it hard to recognise Ronaldo's authority. Xabi Alonso has said that Ronaldo was a leader 'more for what he does on the pitch' than in the dressing room. He is the player who makes the difference and helps the team win games, and he he has opinions and shares them sometimes, but more often than not he is a bit of a loner, dancing to his own tune and sometimes isolating himself of his own accord.

Faced with this clear leadership vacuum, Mourinho steadily took over power and responsibility both in the dressing room and in the offices. He felt a need to show the way and would demand that people do anything he believed was necessary for the team.

As the months went by, both for tactical reasons and because of a personality clash, Cristiano and Mourinho increasingly pulled in opposite directions.

Jorge Mendes says that you have to take care of Ronaldo, while Mourinho takes care of himself. Mourinho told Mendes over and over again that he was wrong, that he had to cut the umbilical cord, to let Cristiano stand on his own two feet and grow.

There were disagreements, big and small, anywhere and everywhere you turned in the dressing room.

Something had to give.

■ ■ ■

'I'm sad and they know why inside the club.'

Ronaldo could not hold it in any longer. After scoring twice in the victory over Granada and not celebrating either goal, despite taking his tally to the club for 150, this is what he had to say in the mixed zone at the Bernabéu.

It was September 2012.

The beginning of his fourth season at the club.

■ ■ ■

'It's for professional reasons,' he added.

'The people here know why I'm not celebrating goals. I don't when I'm sad,' he told reporters, a solemn expression on his face.

It was not because Iniesta had just been given the UEFA Best Player of the Year Award. Or because of the injury that had forced him off after an hour.

It was not all about his friend Marcelo coming out and saying that Casillas deserved the Ballon d'Or and that Messi was the best player in the world.

Or the lack of support he felt from the club and his team-mates.

Or the rift between him and the Spanish members of the squad. Or him and Mourinho.

Or the memory of the Bernabéu jeering him, which had happened again – briefly – during the game against Granada, when he over-elaborated in a move and lost the ball.

Or the new contract he had been negotiating for several months, complete with a wage hike, which the club seemed in no hurry to finalise.

It was not a ploy triggered by interest from Manchester United, PSG and Russian club Anzhi.

It was none of these things and it was all of them at once.

■ ■ ■

Around that time, Ronaldo refused to swap shirts with an Israeli player following a Portugal match in Tel Aviv. We do not know if this was because his side had been held to a draw or because he sympathises with the Palestinian cause – a theory that was reported in some circles, with some websites going as far as to say that he 'wouldn't swap shirts with murderers'. A rumour also did the rounds according to which he had donated the €1.5 million he had received from winning the 2011 European Golden Shoe to an organisation dedicated to helping children in Palestine.

Shortly after, the model Andressa Urach stated that CR7 was a good lover but did not treat her well after their tryst.

Cristiano often pays tribute to someone who helped him get as far as he has in football, even dedicating several of his trophies to this individual. You will probably have heard the story, but I will let the player tell it in his words:

'I have to thank my old friend Albert Fantrau for my success. We played together for the same youth team. When scouts from Sporting came to see us in a game, they said that whoever scored the most goals would earn a scholarship at their academy.

'We won that match 3–0. I scored the first goal, then Albert scored the second with a great header. But it was the third goal that astonished everyone. Albert was one-on-one with the goalkeeper, I was running alongside him, and he passed to me so that I could score. In the end I was accepted into the academy. After the match I went to him and asked him why he had done what he did. Albert replied, "Because you are better than me."'[29]

Years later, a journalist went to Fantrau's house and asked him if the story was true. He said it was, going on to reveal that his footballing career had come to an end after the game and that he was unemployed. The journalist asked him, 'How can you live in such a big house, with several cars. You look like a rich person. On top of that, you provide for your family. Where does all this come from?' To which Albert proudly replied, 'All this comes from Cristiano.'

Some people say that they saw the pair hugging during the *La Décima* celebrations at the Estádio da Luz.

Speaking of hugging, Cristiano had also made a pact with his brother Hugo: if he stopped drinking, Ronaldo would dedicate *La Décima* to him. This explains their euphoric embrace at the end of the game.

The star could have had a much more productive 2014 World Cup in Brazil had a Ghanaian witch doctor not hexed him (placing a special potion in front of a photograph of the forward) to prevent him playing against Ghana. In interviews with international newspapers, the sorcerer claimed that Ronaldo's knee problems were 'spiritual'.

You may remember that Cristiano sported a new look, with zigzagging lines shaved into his hair representing the scar that Erik Ortiz Cruz, a Spanish boy born with cortical dysplasia, was left with after an operation to remove a brain tumour.

In May 2015, the French magazine *So Foot* reported that the player had donated £5 million to the charity Save the Children to help their emergency response efforts following the earthquake in Nepal.

All of the above has been published.

And it is all lies.

■ ■ ■

It is all too easy to become a scriptwriter in the drama that makes up the lives of the Ronaldos of this world. This stems from the lack of rigour among the gutter press and the desire to know everything about celebrities, down to the smallest detail. Even if it is not true.

Whenever he is asked about Cristiano, Jorge Mendes insists that we do not know the real him, that away from the spotlight he is a lovely guy. That he likes to laugh at himself and is deeply loyal to his nearest and dearest. So on and so forth.

But Mendes has not allowed us to get to know him either. All interviews with Ronaldo are steered in a particular direction; if someone comes along who wants to write openly about his environment and try to find out what made him what he is today, they may find some doors closed to them.

He has spent his whole life in a cage. He is the first Portugal captain not to give his phone number to the country's top reporters.

Instead of letting other people write Ronaldo's story, Mendes decided it was time for the player to put on a nice-guy act, because his unstable public image was denying him the affection he craved, as well as costing him votes for individual awards and money in commercial deals.

This process had been ongoing for some time, but Cristiano's comments in Zagreb had interrupted it.

The charm offensive had to be resumed.

■ ■ ■

Extract from an interview with Pedro Pinto for CNN in November 2012:

'The Ballon d'Or is around the corner. Be honest with me: how much do you want to win it?'

'A lot . . . This would mean a lot to me.'

'Do you think that sometimes you're a victim of your own image?'

'I don't want to cry about that, but sometimes I do think I am. It's a question for which I can never give the 100 per cent right answer, because sometimes I honestly don't know . . . I have to agree that sometimes I end up sending a bad image of myself on the pitch, because I'm always very serious when I play. But if you really know me, if you are a friend of mine, if you have the opportunity to live under the same roof with me or if you share a day with me, you will know that it's just a sign of my nature, since I hate to lose!'

'So when they say you're arrogant, for example, what does that make you feel?'

'I would like to have the chance to sit down with most of those people who call me arrogant one day and to simply have a chat with them, so they could see I'm not an arrogant person. I think they have to sit with me and to speak with me, in order to know who is the real Cristiano . . .'

'Who is the real Cristiano Ronaldo?'

'Well, I would describe myself as a good friend of whoever is also my friend; I hate to lose; I'm honest and a direct person . . .'

'So do you think you're paying the price for being too honest then?'

'Yes, sometimes I do . . . definitely yes. But who I am is part of my education.'

'This is a picture of your mum, your son, your girlfriend, some of the important people in your life at the Santiago Bernabéu, and I have to ask you about being a father. How is Cristiano the father?'

'I'm not bad at being a dad. I'm still learning but the best thing in life is to have a kid. It's like living a dream. To wake up each morning and hear him say "Daddy, daddy . . ." I love it.'

'So you do wish sometimes that you could go out and no one would recognise you?'

'Oh yes. I'd pay for that if it were possible.'

■ ■ ■

'I was wrong to say that people were jealous of me . . . I'm not perfect, I make mistakes too and when I say something that's not right, I apologise.'

Cristiano Ronaldo, speaking to the press

At the end of 2012, coinciding with his notorious 'sad' period, efforts to polish up Ronaldo's image were stepped up. Highly regarded journalist Pedro Pinto, CR7's fellow countryman and now in the Communications Department at UEFA, had been telling Jorge Mendes for years that things were not being done in the right way. His interview revealed a more relaxed Ronaldo, inviting us into his home and admitting his mistakes.

Social media became a platform for Ronaldo to interact more with fans and show a more human side, and soon he became the most followed footballer on Facebook, Twitter and Instagram.

'He used to be reluctant to stop and sign autographs,' recalled Nuno Luz, a journalist who has close ties with the Ronaldo camp. 'From then on, he began to stop. He always makes himself available to everyone when he gets off the coach; he understood that to be the best in the world and win the Ballon d'Or, he had to reach people.'

It was essential that this shift not be merely superficial, so as well as continuing to lobby the media – passing on inside information and putting pressure on journalists who did not support the player enough – Mendes found Cristiano an image consultant. And a psychologist.

For a while, both roles were performed by a Portuguese specialist who would accompany the star to many training sessions and have dinner with him after matches. The idea was clear: to try to control his impulsive side and understand what was behind his need to constantly show his greatness.

Ronaldo was urged to calm down, rein in his emotions and accept that the abuse he received was the result of him being feared and was intended to provoke him. He had heard all these things during his time at Manchester United, but had to be reminded.

Zinedine Zidane's advice helped him a great deal, too. The French legend repeated the same message to him again and again, worded in a hundred different ways: 'You have to think of the team.' If he did a little bit less for himself and more for his team-mates, the team would flourish and so would he. This is very much a logical equation, but it can sometimes be difficult to solve. The pair had long chats at the end of sessions at the Valdebebas training ground, during which Zidane asked Cristiano to put himself in his team-mates' shoes. If he could understand their fears and ambitions, he could repress the instinct to condescendingly remind them that they weren't as good as him. The Frenchman told him that he had to accept the idea that his team-mates did not see things the way he did.

■ ■ ■

Cristiano Jr was two when the 2012–13 season kicked off. The child's father had a steady partner in model Irina Shayk. Suddenly his life had taken on a semblance of normalcy.

This settled personal life did not curb his competitiveness. He still had one obstacle that he had to overcome to achieve his goals: Leo Messi.

This battle drove Ronaldo on. As a well-known coach told him, 'If you didn't have a player to compete with, you could take it easy. Instead, today you wake up with an objective. Messi is your permanent challenge.'

During a long chat with *Marca* editor Óscar Campillo, he told me about a conversation he'd had with Cristiano, one that he had never told anyone else about:

'He asked me why people loved Messi and not him. I told him that it was because Messi was much smarter than him. They may be equally arrogant on the pitch, but Leo always had kind words for his team-mates, always credited them for his success and normally celebrated goals, whether they were scored by him or someone else in the team, whether he liked it or not. Cristiano was the opposite: he always pointed to himself or his muscles, he seemed to celebrate his team-mates' goals grudgingly and yet went really over the top when celebrating his own.

'I thought that he would get angry when he heard all this.

'Actually, though, he paused for a little while, eight to ten seconds, to digest it. Then he said to me, "I'll have to do some thinking. Maybe we'll talk about this again one day." It hasn't happened yet, though.'

Rio Ferdinand believes that 'deep down', Cristiano is obsessed with Messi: 'He won't admit it now, but in time, when he retires, he'll admit it.'

He has not admitted it yet.

Anyway, what represents a bigger obsession, Ronaldo's constant references to Messi or the constant questions about their rivalry? It is the public and the media that have fuelled this most absurd of debates about who is the best.

Or is it?

'I am the first, second and third best player in the world.' (*O Estado de Sao Paulo*, 2008)[30]

'I'm happy to be the most expensive player in the world.' (Real Madrid press conference, July 2009)

'Am I better than Messi? You know full well that I'm not going to answer that.' (Antena 3 interview, 2011)

'Chanting "Messi, Messi" at me is the sort of thing a moron would do. Anyone who likes football likes watching Cristiano Ronaldo.' (Press conference, October 2011)

'It's part of my life now. It's only normal for people to compare us, just like they compare Ferrari and Mercedes in Formula 1. It comes with the territory and I'm used to it.' (*Marca*, 2014)[31]

'We're colleagues. We're work friends, so to speak, and so, obviously, we don't have a relationship outside the world of football . . . I hope we end up laughing about all this when we look back on it together in a few years.' (*Marca*, 2014)[31]

'I think that I'm the best in my profession and I work hard to that end. But if that's not possible, in my head I'll always think I'm the best.' (*AS*, 2014)[32]

'Of course competition helps me to be a better player. But not only competition with Messi, also with other top-class players like those I see in the Premier League and in other leagues, such as Luis Suárez, Andrés Iniesta, Neymar, Gareth Bale, Diego Costa and Radamel Falcao. They improve the level they play at and because of this I'm also going to improve. Messi and I both want to be the best and we help each other to better ourselves.' (TVI of Portugal, 2014)

How I would love to sit down and chat with Ronaldo and Messi together in ten years' time.

■ ■ ■

In recent times, the Spanish press have begun to reflect the increasing drama of the Real Madrid–Barça rivalry, which at times has taken on an unprecedented virulence. There were three highly intense years towards the end of the 1950s, when Helenio Herrera, Di Stéfano and László Kubala were around, but the drama was not the same. The current period has dragged on for an unprecedented number of years.

Cristiano arrived in Spain with one Ballon d'Or under his belt. He has won a further two in a Real Madrid shirt, while Messi has captured four. Between them, they have cleaned up over the last seven years. And they play in the same league; it is almost as if Real Madrid and Barça face off every day in Spain. If Cristiano puts three goals past Celta and Messi does the same against Almería, Real Madrid and Barça are not playing against one another, but it seems as if they are. Since we take for granted that Real Madrid will beat Celta and Barça will beat Almería, we count how many goals Cristiano and Messi score. It is the new pastime.

And we are lucky to enjoy it up close.

Jorge Valdano said in an interview for the popular Spanish radio show *El Larguero*: 'Messi owes his mum and dad far more than Cristiano does'. This may possibly be the case, but they have had similar roads to the top.

What separates them is their attitudes to performing in front of the public. This is the football world's perception of their respective visions of the game: 'The difference, I would say, is that Ronaldo likes the occasion,' said René Meulensteen, Alex Ferguson's former assistant. 'Let's put it this way: we've got Ronaldo playing in one stadium, and Messi playing in the other. Suddenly all the lights go out and everything disappears. Messi would go and play in a lit park with his friends.'

Nevertheless, football professionals place a lot of stock on something that is often overlooked: Messi wins trophies with a Barcelona side which has been playing with a similar philosophy throughout his time there. Ronaldo has had to adapt to new cities, countries, languages, cultures and clubs, which on paper would seem to be a bigger challenge.

Former Manchester United goalkeeper Peter Schmeichel has often claimed that Ronaldo could shine in a bad team, whereas Messi needs a Xavi or an Iniesta alongside him. What happens with the Argentinian national team could be cited as evidence of this.

AS editor Alfredo Relaño has spent the last decade debating the duo's credentials with a friend. 'For years someone very close to Cristiano kept telling me that he was much better than Messi. I would disagree with him. He argued that Messi played in a great Barça team, who were in a sense the world champions at club level, or the closest thing to it. Whereas Cristiano played surrounded by disarray and yet still scored fifty-plus goals a season. He'd say that if Cristiano played for Barça, he'd score a hundred goals. I would refute that point by saying that if Cristiano played for Barça, the team's style of football wouldn't be the same and there would be no telling what might happen. That's how the conversation would usually end.'

And maybe this is where we should leave it. 'It's one of the greatest individual battles of all time,' Jorge Valdano wrote in *Soho*.[25] 'When we talk about the top players in history, we always refer to Di Stéfano, Pelé, Cruyff and Maradona. They each embody an era, but on this occasion, there are two truly extraordinary players who encapsulate this era.'

Messi and Ronaldo's first meeting came in the Champions League semi-finals, a tie in which neither of them scored and Manchester United knocked out Barcelona. Aged twenty and twenty-three respectively, neither of them could envisage at the time just how large a bearing they would have on each other's careers. Ronaldo won the Ballon d'Or that year. The next encounter came in the 2009 Champions League final, with Barcelona running out 2–0 winners and Messi scoring one of the goals. Ronaldo bid his team-mates farewell that night: he was about to sign for Real Madrid.

Since then, this clash of the titans has mostly been played out in the same two rings. To begin with, Messi dominated at both the Camp Nou and the Bernabéu, collecting Ballons d'Or despite Ronaldo avoiding voting for him (and vice versa). Things have started balancing out since Ronaldo scored the winner in the Copa del Rey final in April 2011.

In the Real Madrid dressing room, that 2010–12 period is considered the height of the pair's rivalry. 'You could tell what the Barcelona score had been or whether Messi had played well by watching Ronaldo train,' revealed a Real Madrid source who prefers to remain anonymous. What Messi did gave Cristiano's efforts an extra edge: you could see it in his face, in the time he spent in the gym, in his determination.

One evening AS Monaco's then director of football, Tor-Kristian Karlsen, had dinner with Jorge Mendes, with Cristiano Ronaldo also in attendance. The Barcelona v. Atlético de Madrid match was on in the background: Falcao opened the scoring, but *Los Azulgranas* roared back and ended up romping to victory largely thanks to a sublime second-half display from Messi, including two goals. 'I'm not going to say exactly what was heard at the table,' Karlsen noted, 'but I certainly got the impression that there was "a bit" of rivalry between the two players.'

When Ronaldo spoke about Messi in insulting terms during those months, I am convinced he did so to demonstrate his own strength to others, rather than out of a genuine lack of respect.

No one in Spanish football had ever scored more than fifty goals in a single season before Cristiano arrived; the Portuguese has now done so five times to Messi's four. Incredibly, they both average over a goal a game since Ronaldo joined Real Madrid. 'You used to be a good goalscorer if you scored one in two. Not any more!' remarked Gary Neville. 'They've impacted on football beyond their own careers. We have to enjoy what we're witnessing.'

In 2012 the picture began to change. Though Messi won his fourth consecutive Ballon d'Or, he did so with the debate about who was at the pinnacle raging. Ronaldo was instrumental in Real Madrid lifting the 2012 La Liga title, not just being prolific but also bagging some hugely important goals: in six *clásicos*, he scored six times to Messi's three. Leo's stranglehold was loosening and only Cristiano could prevent the Argentinian from clinching a fifth Ballon d'Or.

'Sure, you can conjure up factors to mitigate their success,' wrote the brilliant journalist Gabriele Marcotti:

They both play for talented, attack-minded teams that score plenty of goals and are not reluctant to run up the score. Both have stellar supporting casts that are happy to cede the limelight and work hard for their respective superstars. And both benefit from the fact that star players receive more protection from match officials, unlike a few years ago, when they might have been kicked black, blue and purple.

But the fact remains that we're witnessing two men who are pushing the limits of their sport – two superstars who, technically

and stylistically, are very much the product of this era yet
somehow manage to transcend it, too.[33]

Do the pair see the game the same way? Since their La Liga rivalry
kicked off, Messi has supplied 30 per cent more assists than Ronaldo,
as well as completing more dribbles. It remains to be seen in what
ways and how successfully they will evolve when their legs start
flagging. And what shortcomings could be exposed when their
bodies slow down. Will they be unable to come to terms with this
change and adapt? We will return to this later.

A quick aside: even the television commentators in Portugal
support Real Madrid because of Ronaldo. Messi is not exactly
highly admired there; he was even booed when he featured in
Deco's testimonial in Porto.

As you would expect.

■ ■ ■

Where does all this leave Pelé, Maradona and Di Stéfano?

'When people would ask me,' Alfredo Relaño explained, 'I'd
always say that I'd take Pelé for a final and Di Stéfano for a championship, for a league campaign. But Ronaldo and Messi are good
for both.'

The old-timers at the Bernabéu have not forgotten that Alfredo
Di Stéfano won five European Cups, but most would admit that
Ronaldo is a better player, or more complete. Nevertheless, one
big distinction must be drawn between them, as the point was
recently made at a special event for Real Madrid fans who have been
members for more than thirty years: Di Stéfano was a team-builder.

The club wanted to get rid of Paco Gento and the Argentinian
told them not to because the team needed his speed. Then they
signed Héctor Rial, a playmaker, based on the following thought

process from Di Stéfano: 'If I pass the ball to Gento, I won't be able to finish it off; if we sign a playmaker, Gento can pass to him and I'll have enough time to get in there and score.' Real Madrid also brought in Pachín from Osasuna on Di Stéfano's advice. In the first half of a game between the two clubs, the centre-half was tasked with marking Gento, but could not get anywhere near him. Gento was a rocket and so Pachín's inability to contain him was no real measure of his own pace. In the second half, though, he stuck to La Saeta Rubia, who found it very difficult to shake him off. After the final whistle, Di Stéfano asked the defender what his contractual situation was because Real Madrid played a very high line and so could do with a quick centre-back.

This idea is bound to be repeated in Cristiano's advancing years: he may be a lethal goalscorer, one of the greatest in history, but perhaps he is not on a par with the likes of Di Stéfano in terms of his understanding of the game.

■ ■ ■

While Ronaldo was expressing his sadness in the mixed zone at the Bernabéu after the 3–0 win over Granada, insisting that the club (Florentino Pérez) knew exactly what was bothering him, Mourinho was giving a press conference criticising the team's 'lack of ambition and intensity', despite the scoreline. He was also unhappy with how the players were training. His words proved a harbinger of what was to come in the remainder of the 2012–13 season.

The statistics show that Ronaldo's goalscoring form went up a notch with José Mourinho in the dugout; he chalked up fifty-three goals in 2010–11 and sixty the following campaign. However, in truth the Portuguese duo's honeymoon period lasted just a few months. The coach had relieved the star of his defensive duties, but they did not have the father–son relationship that many imagined.

In fact, Ronaldo was the first player to rebel against Mourinho during that tense Champions League first leg against Barcelona.

Now Ronaldo was on edge, as he told reporters in the mixed zone that night in September 2012.

And he had his fair share of reasons.

SEVEN

REAL MADRID

A ROLLERCOASTER

I received an email from Tor-Kristian Karlsen of AS Monaco about that dinner with Jorge Mendes mentioned earlier. The agent is a good friend of the Monegasque outfit, which has taken on many of his clients in recent years: Ricardo Carvalho, James Rodríguez and Falcao, to name but a few. The Monaco vice-president Vadim Vasilyev recently admitted that they also sounded out Cristiano. This was one of the first attempts:

'As he [Ronaldo] popped by to meet Jorge Mendes after the game [Real Madrid v. Espanyol, 16 December 2012] in a restaurant near the Santiago Bernabéu, he ended up staying for dinner. He was very pleasant and good company. Upon learning my nationality he instantly asked if I knew Ole Gunnar – and greeted me "good evening" ["god kveld"] in Norwegian, which I found a very classy and highly unexpected touch. Though he had scored a brilliant goal, he was genuinely annoyed and agitated by Espanyol's late equaliser, it really played on his mind. Such was his frustration that he even apologised on behalf of the team – I thought that was very impressive. As I left the restaurant I jokingly said to Cristiano, "Why don't you join us at Monaco?" I can't quite remember what he answered – I believe he paid some compliments about the beauty of the Principality – but his expression was one of amusement.'

This offers a nice little window on how he acts in front of an influential man but in private and without a big audience.

And just after a disappointment.

■ ■ ■

José Mourinho decided to clean up his squad for the 2012–13 season by cutting out some of the 'dead wood' (Nuri Sahin, Lassana Diarra, Pedro León, Hamit Altintop, Fernando Gago and Dani Carvajal). The summer transfer saga involved the signing of Luka Modrić for €30 million plus an extra €5 million in add-ons. The team lost ground on Tito Vilanova's Barcelona, however, with internal battles coming to the fore and some key alliances shattered.

In fact, very early in the season, the foundations of the Real Madrid first team had been shaken to the core over four cataclysmic days.

On 30 August 2012, Spanish football received a tribute in the shape of Andrés Iniesta's 2011–12 UEFA Best Player in Europe Award, ahead of Messi and Cristiano. The Spanish midfielder landed in Monte Carlo, supported by Barcelona president Sandro Rosell and director of football Andoni Zubizarreta. Real Madrid had sent third vice-president Pedro López and Emilio Butragueño, the director of the club's institutional relations.

The club's weak (or inferior) representation enraged Ronaldo.

In the Portuguese's eyes, it was further proof of Florentino's limited appreciation of him and how the club undervalued his contribution. Why had the president decided to ignore protocol and attend a meeting of his company ACS instead? Nothing could make Cristiano see sense. He blew a fuse.

According to the Spanish press, Cristiano Ronaldo wanted to leave Real Madrid.

With Cristiano, it never rains but it pours. Unlike at Manchester United where his contract was never a major issue, except for his first renewal, at Real Madrid there seemed to be no compelling desire to improve his deal despite his goalscoring record (more than one a game) and importance to the club.

He had two years remaining on his contract and Real Madrid had to decide if it was time to begin the global hunt for a new Cristiano, or if, for another six or seven years, the Portuguese had enough value to help keep or improve commercial deals with Adidas and other multinationals, and bring income via television rights.

On 1 September, two days after the UEFA awards, a Real Madrid TV camera recorded a seemingly innocent clip in the corridors of power. It was a hug between Michael Essien, who was penning a one-year loan deal with *Los Blancos* and was due to be unveiled that day, and a very serious Ronaldo who was heading to the president's office.

Florentino was at the Bernabéu for the Ghanaian's presentation and had not planned to see Ronaldo. When he was told that the player had something to say to him, he asked him to visit his office.

This is how the conversation went, according to a *Marca* article published six days later on 7 December 2012:

- Mr President, I have to tell you something. I'm not happy here and I want to leave.
- If you want to go, bring me enough money to sign Messi.
- If it's a matter of money, tomorrow I'll come back with €100 million.
- It's not a hundred, your release clause is one billion.[34]

Jorge Mendes had told his client that there were interested parties who could stump up €100 million for his signature, another potential world record: PSG, Manchester City and Manchester United.

Ronaldo had more to say. He asked the club to see through some supposed verbal agreements about image rights and the odd contractual matter, but the president seemed distant.

The player did not feel the club was being contemptuous but, rather, and perhaps more painful, indifferent. Florentino Pérez told Mario Torrejón as much in the latter's biography on Ronaldo: 'He knew he couldn't leave, the transfer window had already closed. It was impossible.'[13]

That was true, but that is where the relationship between the president and the club's talisman broke down.

■ ■ ■

The very same source who told a handful of journalists about the exchange, then swiftly retracted it, having realised that it was too harsh on Cristiano: 'No, no, that wasn't the sentence [about Messi], it was more like, "Well, bring me a billion euros and it's done."' However, the Portuguese's camp confirmed that Leo was mentioned which hurt Ronaldo more than anything else.

Radio programme *El Larguero* revealed some details of the conversation on the very night of the disagreement. According to their sources, Ronaldo told the president that things were not going well in the dressing room, contradicting what he had told the captains: he did not feel supported by the squad, he was alone. The Portuguese had just had an argument with one of his best friends, Marcelo, after hearing him tout Casillas for the Ballon d'Or. The matter was put to bed a few weeks later, but it reinforced the feeling of unhappiness that had beleaguered him in the previous campaign.

According to what José Ángel Sánchez told Mario Torrejón, it was 'an episode of mutual lack of understanding. Players and clubs have ups and downs. I think he wanted to tell us that he wasn't right emotionally.'

Real Madrid played Granada at home on the following day, 2 September. Ronaldo did not celebrate either of his two goals and dropped a bombshell in the mixed zone.

'I'm sad and they know why inside the club.'

According to my sources, the funny thing was, Cristiano did not mean to say 'sad'.

The word just popped out unbidden. He had wanted to utter a different one and toe the party line for the team: what he really meant was 'disappointed'.

In any case, a war that would last an entire year was beginning.

■ ■ ■

Mourinho did not share or want to understand Ronaldo's 'sadness'. He considered it an untimely, inappropriate remark. Journalist Diego Torres told how, following that Ronaldo statement, the coaching staff took to referring to him as 'Tristano' (a Spanish amalgamation of *triste*, meaning sad, and Cristiano).

The club captains, who had been marching to the beat of their own drums just a few months earlier, tried to close ranks to rally round their team-mate. 'When he said that, we were worried,' admitted Xabi Alonso. 'We spoke to him: "Listen, Cris, we want to do everything we can so that you're happy, you're a very important player for us."' Casillas and Ramos had a meeting with the Madeiran who told them it was not a dressing-room problem and it was not even linked to Mourinho, from whom he had distanced himself.

The main source of his irritation was Florentino Pérez.

Such high-profile confrontations (between the ideologist and the main star) are rarely kept out of the spotlight for very long. The press, allegedly the cause of so much upheaval for footballers, comes in useful when it is time to reveal why someone (or a friend of a brother's brother) is sad. Or why he should not be.

Knowing that the battle was about to become a media free-for-all, the club did not waste any time in taking action. Not only did they try to explain their version of events off the record, but also let slip the name of a possible replacement for the Portuguese: Neymar, with whom negotiations were under way.

■ ■ ■

Ronaldo believed that he had put the ball in Real Madrid's court with his statements after the Granada match. It was not merely a ploy to negotiate a new contract. His threat to jump ship was real, despite his nearest and dearest insisting that, at the age of twenty-six, it could not get any better than being at one of the biggest clubs in the world. They told him he could go to a different one, but he would not be as happy, nor would he win as much.

Meanwhile, Real Madrid, after an intense but far from extensive internal debate, had decided that he was worth keeping, especially bearing in mind Barcelona had well and truly tied Neymar down (well, they had definitely tied him down, but how well is up for debate, considering the suspicious contracts that later emerged). Incidentally, we had exclusively reported on the Neymar deal on Sky Sports' weekly Spanish football round-up programme *Revista de la Liga* a year earlier.

A possibility entered the discussions. Perhaps, it was heard said in the Ronaldo camp, it would be a good idea to let the contract run until its end in 2015 when the player would be thirty.

Mendes and Ronaldo decided that would be the strategy from September 2012 onwards: to wait. The agent had spent months demanding a renewal and would have accepted a salary of €10 million net, but he suddenly started rejecting all proposals at the boardroom table.

Surprise and impatience at the star's reaction were engulfing the upper echelons of the Bernabéu.

Meanwhile, a more relaxed Cristiano was trying to avoid the president. Both men were invited to a small VIP room which would lead them to the stage for a *Marca* awards ceremony. On learning Florentino had already arrived, the Portuguese asked his guide, a representative of the newspaper, if they could stay outside. 'Cristiano, we're at a public event, go inside, this is nonsense,' he was told. But he would not budge. He was eventually told that the president of the Portuguese football association was also present and decided to go in, but only to converse with his countryman.

It seemed he had no intention of appeasing anyone, no matter how public the occasion.

■ ■ ■

During that inconsistent campaign for *Los Blancos*, Barcelona were trying to find a new hymn sheet, new styles of attacking football and renewed motivation under Tito Vilanova's stewardship, following Pep Guardiola's departure.

In the Real Madrid dressing room, Mourinho and Ronaldo, two men incapable of sharing the limelight, had been approaching the point of no return after their conflict during the Champions League semi-final the previous season when Cristiano publicly and privately criticised his coach's decisions.

Both were jostling for position in the club as well as in Portugal. 'They're both winners,' explained João Nuno Coelho. 'But Ronaldo enjoys far greater popularity in Portugal. Now he's the national team's talisman, Mourinho is much further behind in terms of public appreciation.'[24]

Mourinho uses his authority to mould consciences and create a state of tension and division – within the club and beyond – which can only last so long. He attracted a group of fervent supporters who blindly accepted his leadership (the reasons for this are worthy of another book) and managed to make the star neither Florentino nor Cristiano, but himself.

And Ronaldo does not like obeying anyone.

Mourinho loves to provoke ('And you say he's your friend? Look at all his theatrics', he told Pepe, according to one of my sources, trying to get a reaction), which Ronaldo falls for very easily. He does not see it as motivational when it comes from someone whom he expects to show him affection.

The players like how Mourinho tries to protect them from the media, but are not so fond of how he looks for guilty parties in his press conferences while rarely accepting that the blame sometimes lies with him.

The coach seeks out soldiers that can blindly carry out his orders, but the Real Madrid dressing room was filled with World Cup winners and one of the best players in the history of the game. They all demanded someone who would attempt to win them over rather than an overbearing, absolute ruler, which is how some of the key players started to view their boss.

Ronaldo had a further thought on his fellow countryman's leadership technique that he kept for his circle. He believed that turning the best Barcelona side in history into public enemy number one was necessary, but should have been done on the field. Fierce rivalries can spur on a team's development. The hatred between the two that was generated from the dugout was a mistake. Ronaldo wanted to start separating competitions from feelings that did not belong in the sporting arena.

What also separated them deep down was a footballing matter: they have a different understanding of the beautiful game.

■ ■ ■

The group stage clashes against Borussia Dortmund provided telling evidence of the widening separation between the footballing vision championed by the coach and the squad's heavyweights, including Ronaldo. The German outfit wanted to go blow-for-blow, while *Los Blancos*, who did not feel inferior to their opponents, felt frustrated by Mourinho's conservative approach.

Real Madrid progressed to the knockout stages, but were still lagging behind Barcelona in La Liga.

The tension was reaching breaking point in the Real dressing room. They faced Valencia in the Copa del Rey quarter-finals in January 2013 and, in the last stages of the first leg, Mourinho's side were winning 2–0.

With ten minutes remaining, the coach, gesturing emphatically, very pointedly told Ronaldo to track back. He also reprimanded him for hurriedly taking a throw-in that Özil was unable to control, allowing Valencia to break on the counter and provide the final fright of the match.

What follows is the version of someone who was there, someone who prefers to remain anonymous but still feels surprised about the turn of events.

Mourinho, whose blood was no longer boiling by the time he reached the dressing room, reminded Cristiano of the reason for the instruction on the pitch: '. . . if they get a goal against us . . .' And the player, who was unable to contain his fury, got up from the bench where he was changing and began shouting, 'After everything I've done for you, this is how you treat me! How dare you say that to me?!'

The dressing room turned deadly silent.

Mourinho tried to remain calm. 'I was saying it for the team, because the team needed you to track back.' As he could see Cristiano had no intention of calming down, he gradually retreated. Soon after, he approached the forward again to resume the conversation with less tension. But Ronaldo fired back angrily.

Mourinho was unable to contain himself any longer. 'Just so you know,' he shouted for everybody to hear, 'many think like me here, but don't dare say it, they don't have the balls to tell you.'

Many of the players who witnessed the scene had demanded on several occasions that Mourinho, either directly or through the coaching staff, ask Ronaldo to defend more.

The situation escalated to the point where Cristiano had to be held back (some sources say by Casillas, others say by Arbeloa and Khedira, or even Sergio Ramos) to prevent the pair from coming to blows.

Ronaldo took what should have been understood as a tactical comment as a personal attack.

The relationship between Mourinho and Ronaldo would never be the same again after that night in the Spanish capital.

■ ■ ■

Jorge Mendes had to choose between the frying pan and the fire. Despite Mourinho telling him that he was overly spoiling the player, the agent remained in charge of Cristiano's affairs, always taking his side. He did so when the Madeiran was not included against Zaragoza and once again after the latest scuffle.

As the months went by, even Mourinho's assistants noted that the situation was beyond repair; they had felt for a while that the player saw them merely as workers under the 'enemy' coach who deserved no loyalty as the distance between them grew.

But every cloud has a silver lining. Sergio Ramos's defence against a common enemy (the Spanish centre-back did not share many of Mourinho's tactical ideas) brought them together again.

■ ■ ■

Soon after the Valencia clash, Real Madrid met Manchester United in the Champions League round of sixteen. After the 1–1 draw in the first leg at the Bernabéu, Ronaldo went into United's dressing room.

Ian Buckingham (kitman): 'The first leg was over and the first thing he did was ask for Sir Alex and come straight into our changing room. That's even before we've done a team talk or anything. He sat there for a good half-hour chatting to everyone. He'd missed them.'

At the end of the return leg at Old Trafford (that Real Madrid won 2–1 with a Ronaldo goal that he refused to celebrate as the team progressed safely to the quarter-finals), the scene was repeated. Ferguson was watching a replay of Nani's controversial sending-off for a tackle on Arbeloa. Ronaldo thought, as did most of his team-mates, that it was an absurd decision.

Sir Alex said to him after a hug: 'If you'd celebrated the goal, I'd have throttled you!'

■ ■ ■

Mourinho looked for conflicts great and small, and his players saw it as a means of moving towards his inevitable exit that would see him reignite his love affair with Chelsea. He knew that he had lost the dressing room and clashed with Iker Casillas, Sergio Ramos, Cristiano, Pepe and even Di María.

With La Liga out of the question, the coach reasoned that the club was 'sad' as a whole at the start of the campaign which led to 'dropped points', conveniently forgetting that Ronaldo netted a brace on the day of his famous declaration.

In reality, though, his analysis was spot on: the team had made a jittery start to the season and was unable to recover. The coach kept rubbing salt in the wound, however, by mentioning 'losing a Champions League semi-final on penalties, when your best penalty taker, who you have complete faith in to score the first one, misses

. . . That frustration never disappears.' A year had passed since Ronaldo's miss against Neuer.

'*Foda-se!*' (Fuck you!) Cristiano seemed to shout as he angrily pointed at his badge and then at the ground after scoring his 200th goal for *Los Blancos* against Málaga. There was no doubt who it was aimed at.

'It was a type of fight between alpha males,' analysed Alfredo Relaño. 'It ended as they all do: with the coach leaving. No matter how good he is, he can't get you fifty goals a season.'

Real Madrid were knocked out of the 2013 Champions League semi-finals by a boisterous Borussia Dortmund side. Ronaldo was carrying an injury in the second leg.

Los Blancos also lost the Copa del Rey final against Atlético de Madrid (2–1). Ronaldo scored and hit the post, but was a peripheral figure during extra-time and when Simeone's side were ahead with four minutes left on the clock, he was given his marching orders for kicking Gabi in the face after a late tackle.

Mourinho stated in the post-match press conference that he had 'failed this season, the worst of my career'.

Tito Vilanova's Barcelona won La Liga at a canter, leaving their arch-rivals eleven points behind.

Despite being down at the start of the season and tension with the coaching staff, Ronaldo scored fifty-five goals in the same number of games.

Mourinho had known for some time that he had reached the end of the road at Real Madrid. Meanwhile, given his manager's stubbornness and lack of dressing-room support, Florentino realised that a change of direction was the only solution.

■ ■ ■

Since then, the soundtrack to the Mourinho v. Cristiano relationship has been:

Ronaldo: 'Out of all my coaches, the only one I've had a friendship with is Alex Ferguson, nobody else.' (TVI of Portugal, August 2014)

Mourinho: 'I just had one problem with him, a very simple and basic one which is when a coach criticises a player from a tactical standpoint to try to improve him and he doesn't take it well, maybe it's because he thinks he knows it all. If that's the case, the coach can't help him develop further.' (Reuters, June 2013)

Ronaldo: '[In the Mourinho era] there was a bad atmosphere and it was a complicated period in personal terms for me and for the club. There were situations going on with other players and the fans, too.' (TVI of Portugal, August 2014)

Mourinho: 'Cristiano had three fantastic seasons with me . . . I think we created a fantastic tactical situation so that he could express all his potential and turn it into records and goals.' (Europa Press Agency, 5 June 2013)

Mourinho knows that his words are never taken as innocent comments.

Mourinho: 'I've coached the best players, Ronaldo, for example. Not this one, the real one, the Brazilian one.' (ESPN, 3 August 2013)

Ronaldo (responding to the previous statement at a press conference): 'There are things in life that deserve no comment and this is one more of them for obvious reasons . . . I don't spit on the plate that feeds me and I don't speak about people who speak ill of me.'

Mourinho, according to Spanish broadcaster Paco Gonzalez: 'I needed to have real players again, like the ones I have at Chelsea.'

They are not on speaking terms nowadays, although a truce was declared through Mendes. And this is the sound of the ceasefire: Mourinho included Ronaldo in his best eleven of players that he has coached. Özil is the only other name from his time at Real Madrid who made the cut.

But the possibility of the odd jibe is impossible to resist for the mischievous Mourinho. Real Madrid's appointment of Rafa Benítez to the managerial post was another opportunity for him to show that side of himself in summer 2015.

Mourinho: 'Ronaldo was fantastic the season before, he scored an incredible number of goals, but I don't like players or coaches who win individual awards without the team . . . Players must understand that the team comes first.'

To be continued . . .

■ ■ ■

Let's go back to the end of the 2012–13 season, Mourinho's last at the helm. Before going on holiday, Cristiano received an offer from the club that would take his gross annual salary close to €30 million. It met many of the player's demands and could have been signed in June, but Ronaldo played a waiting game.

There was no rush.

It was not until 15 September 2013 that he finally put pen to paper on a five-year deal, making him the best-paid player in the world: €10 million net with add-ons that could easily become €21 million net per year.

His release clause remained at €1 billion.

■ ■ ■

Without Mourinho's counterbalance, the whole club shifted to Ronaldo's side. It was now at the mercy of its mercurial number seven. Florentino Pérez always attends award ceremonies involving his star, even if they are not football-related. If Jorge Mendes has a book launch, the president is there. If Cristiano scores his 300th goal, a commemorative shirt is made and presented to the player by the president while photos are taken.

If somebody wants to write a book about Ronaldo and speak to the Real Madrid directors, it has to be negotiated with Jorge Mendes beforehand.

It went from one extreme to the other, with a certain level of indifference replaced by exaggerated subservience. 'The club existed before and will exist after Cristiano,' stated Relaño. 'There's no need to be constantly at the beck and call of the man of the moment. Real Madrid have had an essence and a global vision for over a century.'

The fans, in part thanks to their topsy-turvy relationship with the Portuguese, seemed better equipped to embody the club's soul and since day one they have understood that Cristiano is just passing through. He is part of the club and may even be the best player by a distance, but opinion surveys in the sports press suggest that if he wants to leave one day, the fans will gladly show him the door.

They regard the club's deference towards him as unhealthy and unnecessary.

■ ■ ■

Summer 2013 signalled the arrival of a new coach who applied one of my favourite footballing theories, a Charly Rexach gem. Put some uncooked beans on a plate, some are on top of others, right? But if you give the plate a shake, the beans gradually move into place. It applies to matches and squads; everyone finds their place in the world in the end. Former AC Milan, Chelsea and PSG boss Carlo Ancelotti had already dealt with big-name presidents and stars and knew how to manage them; he had learnt how to shake the plate of beans. His appointment was logical – he was a kind of anti-Mourinho figure, but above all a winner.

Asier Illarramendi (Real Sociedad), Dani Carvajal (Bayer Leverkusen) and Isco (Málaga) also joined the club that summer while Álvaro Morata was promoted to the first team.

On 1 September, the Premier League's best player, Gareth Bale, the new *galáctico*, signed from Tottenham after an intense period of negotiations.

Florentino won the elections as the only candidate once again. He had just one goal: after three consecutive Champions League semi-finals, they had to win *La Décima*. The players were all on the same page: they wanted to prove they were top footballers who could also win without Mourinho's divisive and cautious approach.

Cristiano Ronaldo hit top form in November, just in time for the play-offs to determine who would reach the World Cup in Brazil. Zlatan Ibrahimović's Sweden stood in Portugal's way.

Maybe it was the tie that even his biggest sceptics were waiting for in order to be convinced. He needed to perform at the key moment.

His impact would turn out to be tremendously telling.

In the first leg, his header in the eighty-second minute was the only goal of the game and it left the tie finely poised. The return in Stockholm saw the Madeiran unleash his talent and power. Not even chants of 'Messi, Messi' that greeted his arrival at the stadium could silence him.

He was all the more prepared for a hostile atmosphere and the challenge at hand.

He managed to find space, time his runs in behind to perfection, drive forward with pace and precision, correctly identify Sweden's weak spots and strike the ball at the right moment. He had twelve shots on goal.

A stunning second-half hat-trick in just half an hour was a counter-attacking masterclass.

It was one of those performances that defines a generation. Having already overtaken Eusébio, this hat-trick took Ronaldo level with Pauleta as Portugal's all-time leading goalscorer.

He was at the peak of his footballing powers.

Poor Franck Ribéry, who believed he was in with a shot of winning the Ballon d'Or after Bayern Munich's historic league, cup and Champions League winning campaign, must have seen his chances go up in flames there and then.

■ ■ ■

I watched that 3–2 win that sealed Portugal's place at the 2014 World Cup in a bar in the medina of Essaouira, a seaside town in Morocco. The locals who packed it out sided with Sweden due to their loyalty towards Messi, who they identify with, to the surprise of three lost Swedes who had turned up to watch the game.

Every close-up of Ronaldo was greeted with a general boo. Ibrahimović's two goals were joyously celebrated by Moroccans and the three Swedes, who remained flabbergasted by the communal passion for their country. Perhaps it was down to general anti-Ronaldo feeling, as he plays for Real, the richest club in the world. It seems as though Ronaldo and the club he plays for are often seen as the antithesis to the victimised FC Barcelona and to Messi, a player from a poor background whom they can identify with. What a fascinating but confusing state of affairs, particularly as Ronaldo comes from a poor background himself.

By the end of it, Cristiano had shut them up, too.

■ ■ ■

The debate over whether the Frenchman could win the Ballon d'Or was a perfectly rational one. But given that the other two candidates were Ronaldo and Messi . . . well . . . you might as well pack up and go home. Furthermore, in December 2013 there were a number of incidents that swayed many people towards the Portuguese.

'I've been nervous for a few weeks. Everyone was speaking about the Ballon d'Or. If I would win it, if I would not, if it would be Ribéry . . . Even my mother was regularly asking me, "Are you going to win?"'[35] The Ballon d'Or had become a sort of obsession for Cristiano, especially after Leo Messi's four in a row and thousands of hours on the training ground.

The Portuguese's 2013 tally of sixty-nine goals (twenty-two more than Messi) made him favourite in many people's eyes, although he had not won any major silverware (Barcelona won La Liga). The Argentinian was prevented from hitting top form by injury, which suited Ronaldo down to the ground, but the debate remained alive.

FIFA president Sepp Blatter decided to get up from his seat during a conference at the Oxford Union two months before the vote and march like a soldier 'onto the field of play'. The gesture was immediately interpreted as caricaturing Ronaldo. Real Madrid demanded an apology, the Portuguese took offence and responded in his own way: by scoring a hat-trick in his next match, breaking Puskás's goalscoring record in La Liga, and celebrating with a military salute. His return over the next five games was a whopping ten goals.

The balance was swinging in his favour, boosted by FIFA's decision to delay the voting date for captains, national team coaches and journalists in order to include the World Cup play-offs, in which both Ribéry and Ronaldo would feature.

The Portuguese, who had threatened not to attend the FIFA ceremony, flew to Zurich on 13 January 2014 with Irina, his mother Dolores, his son, his siblings and Jorge Mendes, among others. And Florentino Pérez.

Ronaldo and Messi exchanged a look of mutual understanding, the odd joke and public words of respect.

Then the moment came.

Pelé opened the envelope and announced that the Ballon d'Or winner was . . . Cristiano Ronaldo!

Five years later, he was once again being recognised as the best in the world. I have the impression he thinks that nobody is better than him but wants the world to share that belief. That award put paid to the debate, for the time being at least.

Cristiano hugged Pelé. He knew what he wanted to say, he had rehearsed. And suddenly . . .

His son jumped onstage, having never previously seen his father win that award.

Cristiano picked him up.

And he began his speech: 'Good evening. There are no words to describe this moment . . .' And he could not go on. The audience encouraged him with a round of applause.

He was crying. His mother was crying. Irina, too. Florentino had a lump in his throat. Almost everyone did.

'Thank you to my team-mates at Real Madrid and in the national team . . .'

His words were barely coming out as he sobbed.

'Thank you to my agent, my people, my mother, my son who's here for the first time . . .' He also mentioned the name of Eusébio, the Portugal legend having recently passed away.

'Everything exploded within me,' Ronaldo admitted weeks later. 'Not just because of the prize, but for so many years of battling to be the best. I deserved it.'

There was still time for another moment of affection. Ronaldo's mother, alongside Katia and Elma, went up to Messi. She politely asked him if they could have a photo together. Leo recognised them and was surprised, but smilingly accepted.

Incidentally, Ribéry came third.

■ ■ ■

Ronaldo shook the FIFA president's hand during the ceremony. The image campaign was working, his maturity seemed confirmed.

Everyone chanted Ronaldo's name on the flight back to Madrid, president included, and had photos taken with the trophy. He was welcomed back to training with a standing ovation and Cristiano told his team-mates that the award was for them, too.

Nobody doubted Cristiano's importance on the pitch, but he now had a better attitude in matches. He would smile, complain less (against the opposition or after a bad decision by a team-mate) and avoid provocation. He would sometimes do what they call 'a run for the cameras', that ineffectual sprint after a lost cause that the Bernabéu faithful appreciates so much as a sign of commitment. And furthermore, club directors claimed that he was increasingly involved in the day-to-day goings-on at the club.

'[From a distance] I noticed a big change in Ronaldo's behaviour,' wrote Jerzy Dudek in his autobiography. 'He worked very hard for the team, he'd win the ball back and create chances for his team-mates. And he stopped those irritating gestures.'[23]

Ronaldo understood that the match no longer belonged solely to him and acted accordingly.

'When I was at Benfica,' admitted Ángel Di María, 'I saw him as an egocentric and self-centred person. But afterwards, when I met him, that couldn't have been further from the truth. He's a normal, simple and very caring person.'

The Portuguese knew that the world was his oyster. He had conquered them all, just like in his dreams.

'Maybe when he arrived he was a bit more irrational, but he gradually matured,' stated Xabi Alonso.

'He's gone from having technical leadership based on his quality, to mature leadership,' added Jorge Valdano. 'Now he has things to say and says them.'

Various dinners took place between Ronaldo, Sergio Ramos – who the Madeiran identifies as the essence of the club – and Casillas in which they discussed personal matters linked to the team and the squad. Although he was not a captain, he was invited to be part of the leadership team.

When Di María was offered a pitiful new deal, Cristiano made an effort for him to stay. 'He always treated me very well and was there in the most difficult times,' recalled the Argentinian. 'He even spoke to the president about my contract.'

His accepted ascendency within the group was accompanied by further public recognition. *Time* magazine listed him among the 100 most influential people in the world in their list from April 2014. Only three other sportsmen and women were included: Richard Sherman (NFL), tennis star Serena Williams and golfer Lydia Ko.

The Anxious One had left his angst behind. Would it be for ever?

■ ■ ■

'Carlo Ancelotti knows that the first law of football is that the players are the most important component,' said Óscar Campillo, *Marca* director. Real Madrid's stars initially confused his laid-back attitude and humility with a lack of knowledge and authority. They soon realised that his subtle interventions are aimed at finding a balance in the most natural way possible: he made demands on everyone based on their ability and offered each player what he needed. Well, with the odd exception, such as Ronaldo.

'When we arrived, Carlo wanted to play him as a central striker so that he wouldn't have so many defensive duties,' explained the

Italian's assistant at the time, Paul Clement. 'We tried it, but the player didn't feel comfortable. The coach spoke to him and he told Carlo his point of view.'

That conversation defined what would follow.

'I prefer to receive the ball down the left and attack from the wing. I grew up playing like that,' he told Ancelotti, according to a member of Real's technical staff.

And so they needed to work out a defensive solution because Cristiano could not get back and cover the wing. Ángel Di María, who was willing to run all match long, would be his protector on the left.

'We found a very coachable Cristiano', continued Clement. 'He knew he couldn't do it all himself.'

Cristiano felt comfortable in the 4-3-3 formation that the Italian proposed, which gave him the freedom of the left wing to attack as he wished, accompanied up front by Benzema in a dynamic number-nine role, which was adapted to Cristiano's needs, and by Gareth Bale, who accepted a spot down the right without kicking up a fuss, simply happy to have reached the zenith of his career.

The Portuguese, who was effectively a second striker, lifted his head more, performed better (or as more of a team player) and made more of dragging defenders out of position to play more balls in behind and increase his assist tally: he endeavoured to be more than a goalscorer. Opponents had to contend with the concept of Ronaldo both starting attacks and finishing them off.

Did Bale have something to do with that transformation? Was Ronaldo reacting to the signing of a new *galáctico* who, incidentally, was not a natural in terms of the defensive side of the game either? Or was he showing his best side because he had managed to prove his value to the whole world? Was it Ancelotti's doing, demonstrating that he knew how to fit the pieces together and understood how to treat Cristiano, with whom he developed an excellent mutual understanding?

'Every season is a new challenge for me,' explained Ronaldo on Fifa.com soon after Ancelotti's arrival. 'It's about being predisposed to learn.'

Or maybe, on the verge of thirty, Cristiano was trying to adapt to the limits that his body was starting to impose on him? During Ancelotti's first season in charge, he had a patellar tendon problem that persisted from April until June, affecting the business part of the season and the World Cup in Brazil.

The team, meanwhile, coped with the star's troubles admirably.

■ ■ ■

La Liga would go right down to the wire with everything hinging on a pivotal clash at the Camp Nou between an inconsistent Barcelona and surprise-package Atlético de Madrid. It ended 1–1, meaning the visitors clinched their first league title in eighteen years. Real Madrid, whose unbalanced squad prevented them from going the distance in the league, had devoted all their energy to the two cups, reaching both finals. The Copa del Rey final against Barça was played in Valencia, although Ronaldo could only look on from the stands as he decided not to gamble on a hamstring problem caused by his recurrent patellar tendonitis.

At the end of a contest that was 1–1 till Gareth Bale made a barn-storming sprint and cool finish with five minutes left on the clock, Leo Messi was standing hands on hips as he stared at the ground. Cristiano, dressed in a smart, tight-fitting black suit, black tie, white shirt and black cap, went up to the Argentinian and put an arm around him.

Leo looked up and tapped him on the stomach. Ronaldo lowered his neck to get closer to the Argentinian to utter some comforting words that restored a smile to his arch-rival's face.

Ronaldo seemed to grasp it better than ever. It was as though he no longer saw Leo as simply his nemesis after years of suffering (and enjoying?) from trying to keep up the level that would bring him closer to 'the Flea' and surpass him. His second Ballon d'Or and an excellent chance of a third one if the Champions League final and World Cup went well made him see his rival as a fellow professional who also suffered from injuries, received criticism and won more than he lost, but he did lose, too.

A guy who had followed a very similar path. A partner for the road.

The emotional hug was an acknowledgement that despite the rivalry beloved of the media, these two men, each in their own way, were the living embodiment of the sheer power of human will to triumph over all odds.

■ ■ ■

Real Madrid reached the Champions League final in Lisbon after eliminating Schalke 04 in the last sixteen and Borussia Dortmund in the quarter-finals, followed by a rout of Bayern Munich in the semi-finals, who were beaten 1–0 at the Bernabéu (Ronaldo played seventy-three minutes) and 4–0 in Munich with the Portuguese scoring twice.

Both Bayern Munich legs were extraordinary.

Guardiola's injury-plagued Bayern knew that Xabi Alonso was key to Real Madrid's defensive solidity and counter-attacks as he accurately and regularly released the 'three beasts' upfront, as the Catalan coach described Bale, Benzema and Ronaldo in Martí Perarnau's fascinating book *Herr Pep*. He also noted that Cristiano would not drop back to defend and so he wanted to stretch the Real Madrid defence and try to find space in behind the Portuguese.

It certainly worked in the first leg – it was a 'Bayern exhibition' in Pep's words. Ronaldo spurned a gilt-edged opportunity which was the focus of the media attention alongside a Di María miss and Benzema's goal, but the visitors were the dominant side in the 1–0 Real Madrid victory.

In the return leg, however, Pep betrayed his own footballing ideals and consequently suffered the worst defeat of his career and Bayern's heaviest mauling in Europe. His 4-2-4 formation, which he had refused to use all season long, was influenced by an overly confident atmosphere. The system filled Bayern's team with strikers who left 'a meadow of metres' between themselves and the defence.

It was Ronaldo's ideal stage.

After two Sergio Ramos headers, Cristiano, who expertly exploited the space available thanks to Pep's tactical error, scored his first from a ruthless four-pass counter-attack after Ribéry was dispossessed. Later on the Portuguese completed the scoring with a low free-kick that crept under the wall: 4–0.

'I was itching to reach the final,' explained a jubilant Cristiano after the match. 'Ancelotti has to take all the credit. He's changed everything, including the players' mentality.'

■ ■ ■

Real Madrid stayed at the Tivoli Hotel on central Lisbon's Avenida da Liberdade for the Champions League final where they were welcomed by 400 fans.

Including José Pereira.

The owner of the Don José hostel just 300 metres from the Tivoli wanted to witness the arrival of the boy who had stayed in one of the modest twin rooms in his establishment for a few months as a sixteen-year-old. It was there, while watching a communal television, that he told his friends, other Sporting Lisbon starlets, that he would one day wear the white of Real Madrid.

When the players got off the team coach, José jumped up to try to get a glimpse of what that boy had become.

He did not manage to see him, yet was unable to remove the melancholic smile from his face as he walked back to the hostel.

■ ■ ■

The Champions League final was played on 24 May 2014. Real Madrid were up against city rivals Atlético de Madrid.

Xabi Alonso: 'For him, just like for the rest of us, after five years chasing *La Décima*, having fallen against Barça, Dortmund and Bayern, the Champions League had become a type of obsession. It was the match of his life, of all our lives.'

Ronaldo's patellar tendon had been playing up before the Lisbon final. In fact, the Portuguese had been unable to free himself of the niggle since April.

Xabi Alonso: 'Cristiano missed many matches knowing that we were going to be in the final. He had special preparations in order to be ready.'

The final contained more emotion than quality. It was a gargantuan physical and mental effort by both sides in a derby that had the lot: Diego Costa went off injured after nine minutes, both teams sat deep for fear of opposition counter-attacks, Cristiano had a minimal influence on the first half, Diego Godín's goal in the thirty-fifth minute seemed decisive, the Portuguese had three unsuccessful efforts on goal around the fifty-five-minute mark, the Atlético troops were gradually running out of steam . . .

And in the ninety-third minute, up popped Sergio Ramos above everyone else to head home a corner and force extra-time.

With penalties just ten minutes away, Courtois was only able to parry a Di María shot towards Bale who put Real Madrid ahead. Marcelo's goal to allay any doubts followed soon after against a crushed Atlético. Gabi felled Cristiano for a penalty which the Portuguese tucked away during the dying embers of extra-time.

The final score was 4–1.

After twelve years of frustration, Real Madrid had won *La Décima*. Ronaldo once again tasted Champions League glory six years after winning it at Manchester United.

He played without having made a complete recovery from the injury that blighted the final three months of his campaign, but incredibly he had notched seventeen Champions League goals, breaking his own previous record by one goal.

'I got my goal,' he told me in the mixed zone at the Estádio da Luz, just as he had done in every other final for Real Madrid: two in each of the Copa del Rey and Spanish Super Cup.

Xabi Alonso: 'Those of us who'd been here for a while knew what we had pent up and what *La Décima* meant, we'd been chasing it for so long . . . It's as if you've just been passing through if you haven't won the Champions League during your time at Real Madrid. People like Sergio Ramos who hadn't won a Champions League after so many years here, or Cristiano, or Karim, or me! We had gone through so much, so many good things and bad things, too. I think everything is reflected very well in Cris celebration after scoring the goal, isn't it? It was like a weight off his shoulders.'

Ah, the celebration.

■ ■ ■

'Now he is seen as a part of Real Madrid, but still has the odd excessive touch of a prima donna that might irritate the most traditional onlookers. In any case, they are less and less frequent,' Alfredo Relaño summed up. 'Take the final goal in the European Cup final, for example. He gave off a message of, "Look at me, I've scored a goal in a final." Yet it was just a penalty which is nothing to write home about.'

Ronaldo, who picked up the ball as soon as the official awarded the spot-kick against Gabi, successfully converted to make it 4–1 before running towards the corner while ripping off his shirt. He let out a roar with his arms outstretched.

In that moment only he existed with his audience. Him and his world. His team-mates quickly arrived to make him snap out of that trance in order to share the glory, jumping together in a huddle.

A topless Cristiano suddenly separated himself from the group, turned to the stands with hands on hips, lips forming an O shape and tensed his whole body like a proud bodybuilder. You could take in (and admire) every muscle in his well-defined body.

Ronaldo was very aware of the symbolism and iconic relevance of the moment.

The gesture did not go down well with the Atlético players; it incensed opposition supporters and left a sour taste in neutrals' mouths.

Some pointed out that he did not celebrate Ramos's ninety-fourth-minute goal in the same way. In fact, after the last-gasp equaliser, Ronaldo headed back to the centre-circle without joining the group celebrations. Only he and Casillas, who, in his defence, had a long way to go, did not partake in the festivities.

The Hulk/Ronaldo was the real Cristiano, others said, not the lovely guy who had been created by GestiFute over the previous two years. It was written that the gesture was to be included in the documentary that he was having recorded (incidentally it came out in autumn 2015 as a new attempt to create the 'right' image).

The *AS* director added in his editorial : 'I couldn't help but notice the contrast with the memory of Casillas at the end of the Euro

2012 final when Spain were 4–0 up against Italy and he told the assistant referee to bring the contest to a merciful end.'[36]

Madeira's *Diário de Notícias* was unsure which of the four stand-out options would make for the best front cover. The majority of the Spanish and Portuguese daily newspapers chose the 'Incredible Hulk' look. In Madeira, they eventually opted for a photograph with the trophy, believing the other one was an unfair representation that was unworthy of Ronaldo's story and image.

Will that picture go down in history above many other achievements? Will it be the gesture that defines him?

Let's imagine that, as Rio Ferdinand said, Cristiano 'let his emotions get the better of him', in what was a celebration of overcoming obstacles, as Xabi Alonso stated. Watching the video again, a question occurred to me. Could it be that Cristiano was not in love with football, but with his battle to be the best? And is that why he preferred to celebrate his penalty with much more gusto than the equaliser or second goal, as he considered it a milestone on his personal path? I consulted a Portuguese psychologist, Sidónio Serpa. 'I agree. Football is a tool for self-improvement. Why football? Because it's what was closest to him. If his father had worked at a swimming club, maybe he'd be a world champion swimmer. The desire to better yourself and fight is intrinsic, football is circumstantial.'

By the way, Ronaldo bought each of his team-mates a Bulgari Diagono PRO watch made in Italy with the player's name and *La Décima* engraved on it. Estimated price: €8,200.

Their affection, priceless.

■ ■ ■

'I was injured in the Champions League final, I had to sit it out for two weeks before it because of the pain I had. I could've asked my national coach not to call me up and go on holiday; that would've been the easy option . . . But I prefer to face things head on.'

Cristiano Ronaldo, January 2015, on the FIFA website

The Real Madrid medical team asked him to take some time off, but he wanted to take the risk. His limited impact on the World Cup in Brazil, one of his few remaining challenges, was very simple to explain: he was not fit to play.

After losing against Germany and drawing with the United States, Portugal had a chance to get through if they beat Ghana in Brasilia and the Germany v. United States result went in their favour.

I travelled to the Estádio Nacional to watch that match; Ronaldo did not try to beat a single opponent during the first forty minutes. Here are my notes from that point onwards:

44 min: Nani tries a shot from distance that flies over the bar. Ronaldo had got into space down the wing. He crosses his arms and turns his back on Nani, shaking his head in disapproval.

Germany are winning 1–0 in the other game after a Müller goal. Now Portugal [who were drawing 1–1] have to win by four goals.

Ronaldo has taken up an attacking midfielder role, a number nine, second striker, almost never as a winger. Almost never with any vigour.

73 min: He runs with the ball, he stops in the area looking for a penalty. His left knee hurts him, he falls to the ground. He limps. He bends over. He needs four minutes to walk normally.

77 min: Defender Mensah puts an arm around Ronaldo's waist and he accepts the gesture of support.

78 min: He goes on a run to save a ball from going out and ends up limping again. He is not enjoying it. Now he seems scared.

80 min: A poorly defended ball in the area by goalkeeper Dauda sees the ball land at the feet of Ronaldo who scores with his left foot and does not celebrate. He is still limping.

84 min: Ronaldo bends over and tells his knee that's enough and it should behave. He shouts at it.

87 min: He can take no more, he bends over, hands on knees. He asks for water, speaks to Leonel Pontes and assistant Paulo Bento while Ghana get ready to take a free-kick. Hands on hips, he shakes his head which is dripping with water. He covers his face. He seems to be on the verge of tears. He wants it all to be over. But he still goes on another run down the right and asks for the ball . . . The match comes to an end. He removes his captain's armband.

Portugal has just been knocked out of the group stage at the World Cup in Brazil.

The Ghana players come over to greet him. Michael Essien hugs him. Ronaldo puts his head on his former Real Madrid team-mate's shoulder.

He turns towards the pitch. He is alone. He walks towards the middle of the field of play, he joins the rest of the group. He thanks the officials. He is now surrounded by players, but seems light years ahead of his team-mates.

Ronaldo is named man of the match and fans respond by booing.

In the mixed zone, he said, 'Portugal were never favourites and I never thought we could be world champions. To be honest, all you needed to do was look at the difficulties we had in the play-off against Sweden . . . We have to be humble and realise we aren't at the same level as the best.'

■ ■ ■

And he said this to me, too:

'Yes, we'll speak.'

'I have a year to write the book,' I explained.

'OK, so there's time. Don't worry, we'll see each other.'

In the end, it was not possible.

■ ■ ■

Ronaldo rested that summer and had treatment on his troublesome knee. He knew that he had pushed his body to its limit. 'I risked my future for Real Madrid and my national team,' he would later admit.

The injury, as indicated, was patellar tendonitis, an inflammation of the patellar tendon – the one that effectively ended Brazilian Ronaldo's career. If not treated properly, it can become a chronic condition, even requiring surgery in 10 per cent of cases. Despite this, most athletes tend to ignore the issue and keep competing, thinking it is no big deal.

The Real Madrid doctors believed that Ronaldo had hidden his problems in order not to miss the end of the season. After discovering how severely the tendon was inflamed, they had asked him to take a break, but Cristiano paid no heed to their advice and ultimately lost faith in them. For months he played through the pain, which was especially excruciating when he took shots. The extra strain produced calcification in the tendon, in turn triggering a chain reaction that caused niggles in other muscles.

Cristiano and Jorge Mendes sought solutions outside the club. The star was treated by Dr Noronha, a fellow countryman and a member of Mendes's trusted circle; by Dr Mikel Sánchez, who had helped Ronaldo's friend, Rafa Nadal, with the same injury and is known to use stem-cell and platelet-rich therapies; and even by then Bayern Munich club doctor Hans-Wilhelm Muller-Wohlfahrt. He also tried out ozone therapy.

For months Ronaldo woke up in the morning in serious discomfort. But, as he admits, he 'can't remember a pain-free day' in his career.

■ ■ ■

As well as the 2013 Ballon d'Or, Ronaldo also subsequently won another Pichichi and European Golden Shoe in recognition of his goalscoring exploits. In other words, he scooped a total of six trophies and individual accolades in five months.

On their return from the summer holidays, Real Madrid lifted the UEFA Super Cup, beating Sevilla 2–0. Cristiano got both goals and was named man of the match.

As a result of these conquests in his outstanding 2014, he would be named the UEFA Best Player in Europe and, months later, win his second Ballon d'Or in a row and the third of his career.

And yet the alarm signals his body was sending him made Cristiano uneasy.

■ ■ ■

The 2014–15 season was Carlo Ancelotti's second in charge. After Nuri Sahin made his move back to Borussia Dortmund permanent and Álvaro Morata left for Juventus, they were followed out of the door by two heroes of Real's *La Décima*-winning campaign: Xabi Alonso, who joined Bayern Munich, and Ángel Di María, who went to Manchester United.

Toni Kroos, Keylor Navas and 'Chicharito' Hernández came in, as did Colombian star James Rodríguez, fresh from finishing top scorer at the World Cup.

After a loss to Real Sociedad before August was out, Ronaldo voiced his disagreement with the transfers: 'If I were in charge, perhaps I would've done things differently, but everyone has their opinion and is entitled to say what they think.'

A week after winning the UEFA Super Cup, he had to come off at the break in the first leg of the Spanish Super Cup against Atlético de Madrid. He was only able to feature in the second half of the return leg, in which Real Madrid's local rivals claimed the title.

Despite the treatment he had undergone over the summer, his aches and pains would just not go away.

In December, the team lifted the Club World Cup in Morocco, beating San Lorenzo to secure Real Madrid's eighteenth international trophy. Though he did not score in the competition, it represented another milestone for Ronaldo: in five years at the club, he had now won every piece of silverware going.

This was a fitting ending to an extraordinary 2014 for the star. Not only had Real Madrid won four trophies out of a possible six (the Copa del Rey, Champions League, UEFA Super Cup and the Club World Cup), the first time the club had won a quadruple since being founded 112 years earlier, but he had netted sixty-one goals in sixty appearances over the twelve months. On top of that, he had become the top scorer in European Championship history with twenty-three goals between qualifying and tournament matches.

The victory over San Lorenzo in Morocco was the twenty-second on the bounce for a team that looked unstoppable.

But there is no such thing as unstoppable.

■ ■ ■

Here are a few comments about Ronaldo's third Ballon d'Or, received on 12 January 2015.

As previously noted, for the first time in Real Madrid's history the club's entire communication operation was given over to its star player: in November, a statement was published on the club's website arguing why Ronaldo deserved the award and criticising Michel Platini for having expressed a preference for a German being awarded the prize on the strength of having won the World Cup.

When Leo Messi turned up on the red carpet at the Kongresshaus in Zurich, some fans chanted 'Ronaldo, Ronaldo'. The times seemed to be changing.

Before the ceremony, Ronaldo told Leo that his son was a big fan, admitting to the Argentinian, 'He talks about you.' Then, up on stage, looking out towards his biggest rival, he blurted out his desire to 'catch Messi' by matching his four Ballons d'Or.

That roused Leo from his lethargy. 'Is that so?' he seemed to say in the following months. 'We'll see about that.'

Perhaps Platini's comments were at the root of the roar Ronaldo let out at the end of his acceptance speech, that '*Siiiiiiii!*', which, he subsequently explained, was intended as an affectionate nod to his team-mates, among whom it had become a celebratory ritual. At the end of the day, though basic and primitive, it is the type of thing that bonds people together beyond words.

The origins of this coded cry date back to summer 2011. It was first heard in pre-season in Los Angeles and since then had been performed regularly by individual players or groups after victories in training matches, extraordinary pieces of skill and special goals.

Whatever the case may be, it came across as a gesture of defiance aimed at the authorities and his doubters.

And it seemed very inappropriate.

We once again got the impression that, with no one setting the limits for him, Ronaldo becomes his own judge, jury and executioner. With all that this implies. For instance, was the statue of him unveiled in Madeira a month earlier really necessary? Did no one suggest to him that such things could wait?

Irina Shayk was conspicuous by her absence. The explanation given was that she was at the beach celebrating her birthday.

That Ballon d'Or capped a one-and-a-half-year purple patch paved with success and records.

However, for various reasons, the mistakes would start to pile up again.

■ ■ ■

The team and Cristiano himself began to run out of steam after the Club World Cup triumph. Prior to the winter break, the Portuguese had scored twenty-five goals in four months of league action, but from January to mid-May he only added another seventeen. Messi bagged ten more goals than him in that period. Ronaldo's aim was off: only 40 per cent of his shots were hitting the target, compared to 74 per cent the previous year.

What had knocked him off his stride?

'After dating for five years, my relationship with Irina Shayk has come to an end,' Ronaldo announced in a statement on 20 January 2015.

The word from the dressing room was that he was 'messed up' from the moment Shayk told him she did not want to be with him any more.

Although Irina may not have been a conventional girlfriend, Ronaldo had got into a routine which fulfilled him and conferred the aura of normalcy he needed to go about his daily life on auto-pilot. They only saw each other sporadically; Cristiano spent his holidays with friends and in the last months before they went their separate ways, the model had been staying at a hotel on Paseo de la Castellana whenever she came to Madrid. Suddenly, though, Ronaldo's small, inner circle had shrunk.

Irina's manager claimed that the break-up had nothing to do with Dolores Aveiro. Rumours remained rife, however: for example, that the model had decided not to go to the surprise party the star had organised for his mother's sixtieth birthday; that the Russian's relationship with Dolores and Cristiano's sisters was tense; that Ronaldo had cheated on her, which had driven her to despair.

'I think a woman feels ugly when she's got the wrong man at her side. I've felt ugly and insecure,' Irina would say months later.

In Elma Aveiro's words, meanwhile, the split was 'like a death' for his brother.

■ ■ ■

During a game away to Córdoba, two weeks after collecting the Ballon d'Or, the crowd rattled the Portuguese with a constant stream of abuse and imitations of the now famous '*Siiiiiii*'.

The dressing-room ritual had boomeranged back at him.

He was eventually sent off after kicking out at and slapping defender Edimar. The home fans gloated by screaming the '*Siiiiiii*' in unison, which provoked an irate reaction from Cristiano, who 'dusted off' the Club World Cup winners' badge on his shirt. However, on the way back to Madrid, he posted the following message on social media: 'I apologise to everyone, and especially Edimar, for my thoughtless actions.'

To date, Ronaldo has been shown nine red cards in his career, five of which have come with Real Madrid – and, of those nine, five followed acts of aggression towards an opposition player.

Cristiano's histrionics and unpleasant gestures towards his team-mates returned, unable at times of confusion to quell the fire in his belly, a monster that has accompanied him since childhood and which he cannot always seem to control.

His state of uncertainty had placed the 'other Ronaldo', who had never truly gone away, back in the spotlight. However much he tries to hide it, the platform created by a dysfunctional childhood has shaped and will continue to shape his choices, and though he is learning to contain this factor, at moments of weakness it re-emerges, as persistent as a cold at the end of a tough season.

Doubts were once more cast internally on his leadership. I never fully bought the worship of Ronaldo in the dressing room, which seemed unwavering when things were going well. His influence off the pitch had certainly grown, but there was always a question mark against it. He has swung towards and then away from his team-mates, pendulum-like, at different periods. As the defeats came, so the tension and accusations ('Cristiano does his own thing' and 'Ronaldo doesn't run' were among the gripes heard in the group) flared up again.

'I don't see him as a leader,' Ángel Di María told me, a comment in no way intended as a criticism. 'I think he's just another squad member, like everyone else, except we all know that he's one of the best players in the world.' This is exactly the view of Ronaldo in the dressing room.

In any case, he had not yet hit rock bottom for the season. He was tarnishing the image that GestiFute had so painstakingly crafted, and his maturity was drawn into question, despite evidence of progress.

■ ■ ■

In the second half of the season, Real Madrid would succumb to key losses by Valencia, Athletic Bilbao and Barcelona, who leap-frogged them at the top of the table. They were also destroyed 4–0 by Atlético on 7 February, with Ronaldo failing to register a single shot on goal.

After that match, the Portuguese was asked about what had happened in Córdoba. This may or may not have been a provoca-tion, but either way it was enough to bait Ronaldo, who was already at boiling point. 'For fuck's sake! Do you want to talk about today or about Córdoba? That was three months ago now! An intelligent journalist would ask me about today, about our poor performance, so you're not intelligent then. Sorry.'

From the Calderón, the star went to *#lafiestadeladeshonra* (the party of shame), as it was dubbed on Twitter, where it trended throughout the following day.

Ronaldo had organised a big bash to celebrate his birthday after the game; he had turned thirty two days earlier, but had not wanted anything to distract from the derby preparations. He had invited 150 people from all over the world to In Zalacaín, an exclusive venue he had booked two months previously. The entire Real Madrid squad were on the guest list, but few of them attended. A tacit code of conduct made it impossible for them to go to a party after a major defeat in the Madrid derby.

Some were fearful of a backlash from the fans if word got out, while some had other engagements: Iker Casillas went to his wife's birthday party and Florentino went to that of board member Nicolás Martín Sanz.

The musical entertainment at In Zalacaín was provided by Colombian singer Kevin Roldán, who made the 'mistake' of posting photos of the event on social media, including some featuring Ronaldo looking extremely merry and wearing a top hat. A video also did the rounds of the Portuguese singing up on stage alongside Roldán, drink in hand.

The public reaction verged on hysteria, while the response within the club was as expected: Cristiano's behaviour was condemned. Jorge Mendes went on the radio to defend his client: 'People spent the first two hours cheering him up [because of the defeat].'

Yeah, right.

Ten days later, after a rollercoaster encounter against Schalke 04, he announced: 'I'm not going to speak again until the end of the season.' He seemed more bothered by having been 'caught' (he was livid with Roldán) than by his own decision not to cancel the party.

The events of that match against the Germans, the Champions League last-sixteen second leg, aptly reflected the mood of the squad and Ronaldo alike.

Cristiano scored two vital goals, but his constant dialogue with the crowd revealed the frayed nerves on show.

It should have been a straightforward enough game following the 2–0 win in the first leg, but the midfield was unable to dictate proceedings and Schalke took the lead after nineteen minutes. The frontmen were doing nothing in defence and Arbeloa had a go at the Portuguese who, agitated, got into an argument with Gareth Bale.

Ronaldo equalised, but celebrated by raising his arm furiously as if chiding the crowd, who duly erupted and began jeering him. When he later made it 2–2, he went back to a more traditional celebration, jumping with his arms outstretched and pointing to the ground, but something was clearly still eating away at him.

Real Madrid threw away a 3–2 lead to go 4–3 down and the fans railed against the shambolic display. Just before the end, Cristiano could be seen mouthing, 'What a disgrace, what a disgrace' while staring into space. When Casillas forced him to stand in the centre circle and endure the supporters' wrath following the defeat, his face betrayed a thousand different emotions, none of them pleasant.

A few days later, with ten minutes to go in a league clash with Levante, the fans once again booed the team. Ronaldo responded by glaring at the crowd defiantly and crying out '*Foda-se*' ('Fucking hell' in this context) while shaking his head.

This time, despite the pleadings of Ancelotti's assistant, Fernando Hierro, he did not stick around on the pitch after the final whistle.

■ ■ ■

The Champions League semi-finals pitted Real Madrid against Juventus, who were considered the weakest of their potential opponents.

At half-time in the first leg in Turin, with the teams drawing 1–1, Sergio Ramos had a go at Cristiano – who had scored – for failing to track Andrea Pirlo, as he and Bale had been instructed to do (the Welshman was doing his bit). After being told that he couldn't just score his goal and forget about the rest, Ronaldo stormed out of the dressing room and decided to wait in the tunnel until the restart. *Los Blancos* ended up losing 2–1.

Ronaldo hit the net again in the second leg, this time with a penalty, but the final scoreline of 1–1 meant the Italians went through to face Barça in the final in Berlin.

A distraught Ronaldo rushed to the dressing room and, alone, burst into tears.

■ ■ ■

Over the course of the 2014–15 season, Ronaldo notched seven hat-tricks and a total of sixty-one goals in fifty-four matches, beating his personal best by a single strike. He was crowned La Liga's top scorer for the second consecutive year and received the European Golden Shoe for a fourth time, despite his strike rate dropping to 0.85 goals a game in 2015 from 1.28 in the first half of the season. He also finished as the Champions League's leading marksman for the fourth time, with ten goals, which left him and Messi level as the competition's all-time top scorers on seventy-seven goals.

His status as a legendary goalscorer was in no doubt.

Meanwhile, Carlo Ancelotti suspected that his days at the Bernabéu were numbered after the debacle that had seen Real Madrid conclude the campaign empty-handed except for the two trophies clinched before Christmas (the UEFA Super Cup and Club World Cup).

Ronaldo, none too impressed by what he saw as the club's irra-tional decisions, wanted the Italian to stay, as did several of the other dressing-room heavyweights. He made his feelings plain with an Instagram post: 'Great coach and amazing person. Hope we work together next season.'

Talk about a paradox: the club's flagship player was publicly backing the coach who was about to walk the plank.

By now Cristiano harboured real doubts about the path chosen by Florentino, who continued to get rid of figures who had helped the team to succeed. He could not see why Iker Casillas was being forced out – including through a smear campaign that even the goalkeeper's family attributed to the club's top brass – and why Sergio Ramos, who toyed with the idea of signing for Manchester United, had not been tied down to a new contract a long time ago.

All this despite the fact that he had once more had his differences with both men. On one occasion the centre-back said to Ronaldo, 'You want to be the best in the world, but why can't it be me?!' questioning, without a hint of irony, the need to afford the Portuguese special treatment. Once again, though, they seemed to be on good terms in the summer of 2015.

Cristiano realised nobody was safe if that was the way players who had spent sixteen and ten years respectively at the club were treated.

The incredible individual statistics Ronaldo had put together over his six years at the club had not translated into trophies. A haul of 313 goals in 300 appearances as of summer 2015, giving him the best strike rate of the club's leading scorers, had only yielded one La Liga and Champions League title apiece – not even the addition of the two Spanish Cups and the Club World Cup would bring this honours list up to scratch.

Like a recurring nightmare, a sense of not being backed up was setting in again.

Ronaldo sent messages to a former team-mate asking if he would be coming back to Real Madrid. More than anything, this was a sign of frustration, after witnessing the exits of players like Özil, Di María and Xabi Alonso – who provided him with assists and would have maintained the status quo that Cristiano stood for, with himself as the centrepiece.

He broke his self-imposed media blackout with a video posted on social networks on 5 June featuring a clear message: 'Leave me alone.'

It was the same story as two years earlier. If things did not turn out the way he thought they should, he could not prevent an emotional storm from brewing.

Something was clearly amiss.

Might the problem be him? Could it be that he could never be fully happy because he had picked a sport in which he had to suppress his ego? Or that he was reaching a point at which his presence hindered his team, with his obsession with goals becoming detrimental to the collective endeavour? Had his team begun to miss him at key moments of matches? Had he started to become less influential?

He was playing like a number nine, touching the ball less often, closer to the opposition goal and at the end of crosses more than ever, but still not performing his defensive duties often enough. Was that imbalance somehow making the team less competitive in the important matches of the season?

The epilogue to this book seeks to answer these questions from a statistical point of view, but ex-Liverpool manager Brendan Rodgers, for one, believed that Ronaldo was the world's top hitman, telling Mario Balotelli as much and trying to teach him the art of being a modern centre-forward with a twenty-minute video of Cristiano in action. These clips show a player who does not need time on the ball, who outpaces all defenders in his path, who ghosts into the area unmarked and easily finds space in what Rodgers calls the 'goal zones'.

Jorge Valdano's view on this change of style, which tentatively began when Ancelotti arrived, is positive: 'It's normal in football that with age one has to drop deeper and deeper. Ronaldo is exceptional in all respects, even this.'

And yet the question in summer 2015 was whether the 'new Ronaldo' was an evolution prompted by a body on the wane, the upshot of the type of signings Real Madrid were making (a lot of attack-minded players and not many defensive midfielders) or a move that was always destined to happen in the twilight of his career.

Only after digging deep in order to understand the needs of a player now in his thirties could everyone concerned (the club, new coach Rafa Benítez, his team-mates and Ronaldo himself) look ahead to the new season.

For example, what was his relationship with Gareth Bale like?

■ ■ ■

During the Welshman's first season, Real Madrid were losing to Sevilla at the Sánchez Pizjuán and were awarded a late free-kick in a dangerous area. This gave rise to one of those moments of subtle gestures and revelatory glances whose outcome affects the entire balance of a team.

Ronaldo set the ball down but, while he was gearing himself up, Bale walked over and asked permission to take it. The Portuguese, who would end the season with five goals from direct free-kicks, gave a 'whatever you want' which seemed to mean anything but. Bale did not need a second invitation and trained his eyes on the opposition goal. Cristiano twice tried to make him change his mind, even looking over to the dugout for support, but Ancelotti left them to sort it out among themselves. The Portuguese protested about the wall moving as Bale ran up to unleash his strike, which sailed just over the bar.

Cristiano turned towards the bench again, pulling faces and gesticulating wildly.

The next season, 2014–15, Bale took a few more free-kicks, especially from the edge of the area on the right-hand side (the goalkeeper's left), but not too many – even though the numbers backed the Welshman's case. The Portuguese had infamously become one of the worst free-kick takers in La Liga, failing to score one in a year and missing fifty-six consecutive attempts (41 per cent of these hit the wall).

The Champions League semi-final first leg against Juventus in Turin offered up some intriguing statistical evidence of an imbalance. In the first half, Bale touched the ball just fourteen times in the first half (only Casillas got fewer touches), completed a mere eighteen passes (fewer than anyone else) and did not have a shot on goal.

This was not normal, but it reflected the Welshman's lack of clout in the squad. He had not kicked on in his second season after a first that could be considered successful, having made his presence felt by scoring in the cup and Champions League finals against Barcelona and Atlético, respectively.

Bale was struggling to integrate: he did not speak Spanish and only had one good friend in the squad, Luka Modrić. Efforts were made to bring him together with other people (particularly Toni Kroos and his partner), but Gareth and his wife, who are both extremely shy, preferred to stay at home.

The pressure to be the team's next big star discomfited the Welshman because it did not seem to translate into freedom on the pitch: he had not been signed to be a winger with major defensive obligations. However, Ancelotti did not believe that the team could carry two Ronaldos, two players who were influential on the ball, but unwilling to graft too much off it.

Bale had been given a lesser part as Ronaldo's sidekick – operating as a wide man with a focus on making runs into the box – and he did not enjoy it. As a result, he made wrong decisions. And making wrong decisions meant that he could not earn himself a more important role (for example, as a playmaker). It was a catch-22 situation.

But in summer 2015 he would rebel. In a manner of speaking.

Ronaldo, meanwhile, had not helped Bale to develop. He and the Welshman did not get along; there was no chemistry between them. Cristiano had spent the whole season fighting to protect his territory. Although his influence on the game – if not in front of goal – had declined, he had more allies than Bale, whom only Modrić sought out with any regularity.

There are two types of leaders: those who sit you on their laps and look after you, and those who trample on you. Ronaldo had no intention of handing the mantle to Bale.

'No player gets better alongside him,' stated the Mexican writer Juan Villoro in an article for Colombian magazine *Soho*, one of the most vicious hatchet jobs on Ronaldo ever written. 'Supremely egotistical, the notion of a partnership is beyond him . . . The pariahs [*sic*] who conquered this earth go by the names of Maradona, Di Stéfano, Puskás, Cruyff and Pelé . . . None of these virtuosos depended on their strength or speed and they all made their team-mates better . . . Though there is room for magic in his trade, Cristiano Ronaldo is but another footballer.'[37]

Nevertheless, the fact of the matter is that the rest of the squad had a hard time accepting the Welshman as Ronaldo's successor as club icon, as Florentino Pérez had earmarked him to be. They did not believe that he had the footballing understanding to warrant such a status.

And yet when the Welshman played for his country he was a different proposition: he had an extra yard of pace and more energy, was always at the heart of everything, and had freedom to roam around while remaining a team player. He knew he was the leader, had no tactical constraints and always picked the right option, whether that was to pass, dribble, shoot or make a run.

Having been made aware of interest from Manchester United, Bale was convinced by his representatives that they had to press his case to Florentino Pérez that summer of 2015, and also that he had to give himself and Real Madrid one last chance.

Once the season was over, the Real Madrid president met with Jorge Mendes who, mindful of the precarious harmony in the dressing room, wanted to confirm that Ronaldo remained central to the club's plans. 'That's right,' he was told.

A week later, Bale's agent, Jonathan Barnett, sat down with the club.

The message he wanted to send was clear. If it was true that Bale had been brought in as a forward, then he had to be played there. The team were not using his strengths, which were what had led Real Madrid to sign him in the first place. What about playing him as a number ten, for example, with Ronaldo perhaps as a number nine?

'Bale is the future,' was the response from the club, who assured Bale's representative that he would be given more influence in the team.

Whatever way you look at it, this was a shot across the bows for Ronaldo.

Similarly, the sacking of Ancelotti, who had deferred to Cristiano's role, did not go down badly with Bale's camp. In two years under the Italian, the former Tottenham star had felt compelled to do extra training to stay in peak physical condition and improve his understanding of Real Madrid's style of play.

Shortly after his appointment was confirmed, Rafa Benítez paid the Wales squad a visit to meet Bale. Ronaldo's camp let it be known that the team's star had not received the same treatment.

The first voices were heard suggesting something that not long before would have seemed heretical: maybe it was time to sell Ronaldo.

Real Madrid did not contemplate that idea. Not for the summer of 2015.

The 2015–16 season would define the duo's roles and futures.

■ ■ ■

It is irrelevant who the next Real Madrid coach is, as the business model comes well before whomever is in the dugout. It is not by chance that the club has not enjoyed any long periods of stability over the last six years.

In any case, the contrast between Cristiano and Benítez, a staunch advocate of collective effort with and without the ball, could not be greater. And so every training session, press conference and glance was analysed to confirm what had been taken for granted: the lack of rapport between the pair.

This is how the story played out:

Despite being teed up by the media in the first press conference of the pre-season, Benítez neglected to say that Ronaldo was the best in the world, though he did do so the next time.

Ronaldo flew off the handle in one training session, telling Benítez that he only penalised the Portuguese players. In another, he complained about how often the coach interrupted proceedings.

Meanwhile, Bale was given a free role in the first few matches of the US tour.

Against this backdrop, Manchester United put the word out, perhaps to counter Real Madrid's interest in David de Gea and because of their struggle to strike a deal for Sergio Ramos, intimating that they would be willing to pay whatever it took to re-sign Ronaldo.

Benítez believed that he could tame Ronaldo's somewhat distant attitude in training. However, he very soon discovered that the 'best in the world' was a complex individual beset by emotional swings, who knew what he wanted, but was unwilling to see his standing diminished even an inch during the difficult transition to what was next for him.

What *was* next, though? Where was Ronaldo heading?

■ ■ ■

Does Ronaldo know what kind of player he is? I know that he has always said that he likes to start moves on the left and cut inside, but what is his actual position? He may operate on the left flank, but he is not an orthodox winger, a number eleven. Equally, when he goes up front and scores lots of goals, that does not make him a proper number nine. And although he sometimes plays in the hole, he is not a number ten either.

So, what *is* Cristiano?

He is a deadly finisher, an assassin in front of goal. He is a player who cannot be pinned down, a little like Messi. Leo is the more gifted footballer, while Cristiano is more powerful and has less influence on games, but fundamentally they are both deadly finishers.

Messi is able to create goals, score them and make a team tick. Ronaldo has never set out to do all this, instead simply wishing to be recognised as the focal point of his team's play, from the beginning to the end of every attack.

The key to getting the best out of the Portuguese (and the Argentinian) is understanding that you have to surround him with players who are suited to his strengths. That is what happened when Real Madrid had Benzema buzzing around Ronaldo, Di María on the wing, and both Khedira and Xabi Alonso further back, cutting off opposition attacks and launching counter-attacks.

Ronaldo's needs have changed hand in hand with the shift in his game. In his first year at the Bernabéu, his goals were mainly solo efforts starting out wide – some after dribbling at speed – and strikes from outside the area. Over time, as we have noted, he has drifted closer and closer to the goalkeeper.

As far as I am concerned, this is not an evolution: rather, his game has lost something. Cristiano has gone from being a player who drove at opposition defences from deep to one who affects the game much closer to goal. He has reduced the sphere of his influence.

Cristiano has replaced his almost unstoppable surges with the ball from the halfway line into the box with different types of runs off the ball because he has more trouble going past defenders. And these contributions have always stemmed from individual initiative, never from a collective approach.

That is not the case with Ronaldo. The Portuguese always plays for himself. He takes more or less the same number of shots now as ever and, though he may pass the ball a little more, this is only because, I think, of his physical limitations.

Having said that, he is in a team that has consistently required flashes of genius to settle matches and paper over the cracks of the fact that often it seemed like two teams in one, or at least one that was understaffed in defence. Since Ronaldo arrived at the club, during Florentino Pérez's tenure, Real Madrid teams have had moments of solidity, but they have not lasted long. Perhaps the 2011–12 vintage with José Mourinho came closer to a collective model, but simmering beneath the surface was a series of personal and ideological differences that ultimately led to the manager's exit.

This is where another doubt arises, one which will only be cleared up at the end of his career. In the period since he joined Real Madrid, teams that have favoured a collective approach have captured the biggest trophies: we can cite Inter, Barcelona, Bayern Munich or even Roberto Di Matteo's Chelsea. In all of these sides, the star man has been subordinate to the group or, in the exceptional case of

Messi, the second, third and fourth best players in the squad have bowed to the Argentinian's reign, something that has not always occurred with Ronaldo at Real Madrid.

The *galáctico* philosophy certainly makes it difficult to prioritise a team ethos, but might Cristiano's obsession with scoring goals have affected the team's performances in such a way (by hardly contributing in defence and preferring to play with a striker who acts as his foil, like Benzema) as to hinder their chances in long competitions? I am reminded here of the other Ronaldo: an extraordinary goalscorer who topped the domestic scoring charts with PSV, Barcelona and Real Madrid (he netted 104 times in 177 matches for *Los Blancos*), and notched 59 in 99 for Inter, yet won just one league title in thirteen years at these clubs.

EIGHT

ANOTHER COACH BITES THE DUST

When he arrived at Real Madrid, Benítez knew he would be unable to influence the club's philosophy and would have limited authority. In particular, he would be unable to mould the team to his requirements. (For example, his request that they sign a centre forward fell on deaf ears.) His mission statement, meanwhile, revolved around striking a balance between Ronaldo's desire to continue taking centre stage and the team's needs.

Benítez understood why things hadn't worked for Real Madrid and Cristiano the previous season (2014–15). You cannot compete at the highest level with a midfield of Kroos, Modrić, James Rodríguez and Isco. With such talented players in their ranks, the team had won matches in sparkling fashion but had lost many others through being ground down or outmuscled, because this quartet were out of their element when off the ball. This was a combination that was not sustainable when the matches came thick and fast. Conscious of this, the team naturally ended up focusing their minds on the shorter cup competitions.

This was why Real Madrid won *La Décima* but finished third in the league. Not because of a lack of quality, but because of their inability to maintain the form required to compete in the longer competitions. It was true that injuries affected the side, but this was very much a chicken-and-egg situation: forcing such players to play out of position meant that they overexerted themselves, in turn leading to injuries and taking a toll on the team's performances.

There was one other stumbling block that made a successful Benítez reign not just impossible, but unthinkable.

The former Liverpool manager was aware that several players who were no longer around, but who had been high-profile members of the squad (internationals, big-name flair players), had attempted to torpedo his candidacy for the Bernabéu hot seat because they thought he was not a good fit. And if the Real Madrid players have it in their heads that the newly appointed coach is not the right man for the club, or for them, it won't take long for it to become a huge problem. The volcano will remain dormant while things go well, but there will be a risk of an eruption at any time.

That is exactly how it played out.

Benítez had his work cut out to convince Cristiano of the benefits of his methods, because the Portuguese had his misgivings, suspicious that it was a ploy on the club's part to thrust Bale to the fore. Florentino Pérez *had* in fact instructed the coach to do just that, tasking him with getting more out of Bale and giving him a more central role in the team. That meant shifting Cristiano.

Bale wanted to play the way he had done for Wales, with the licence to roam anywhere and everywhere, but that was not possible in Benítez's system: with Cristiano having no intention of mucking in much off the ball, the team would have ended up with more holes than a colander when defending. The introduction of a box-to-box central midfielder like Casemiro, who was brought back following his loan spell at Porto, might have been a solution, but Pérez preferred Isco, James, Kroos and Modrić to all play.

In short, it was mission impossible for Benítez.

Bale and Ronaldo were both gunning for glory, and their relationship was condemned to an uneasy balancing act as a result of the club's intentions. On the one hand, Real Madrid had gone out of their way to appease the Portuguese – for example, by claiming that Bale had cost less than him (something that *AS* never bought and which *Football Leaks* later refuted by releasing the Welshman's contract) – but on the other, they were paving the way for a passing of the torch by elevating his heir apparent, Bale.

Real Madrid set Benítez up for a fall by forcing him, for political reasons, to do something he should never have had to do: giving one player precedence over another without them having earned it out on the pitch. Bale had not earned it yet. There was an inevitable consequence to relegating the guy who scored the lion's share of the goals to second in the pecking order, and that was the team's collapse.

The tension between the two forwards had been palpable during Ancelotti's last season, and from the moment that Benítez tipped the scales in Bale's favour, deploying him as a number ten, Cristiano was unforgiving.

Benítez's short-lived tenure could be predicted easily enough. The squad's imbalances were destined to be accentuated, and when that happened the weakest link in the chain would be broken: the coach.

The ball never stops rolling in football and nature should be allowed to run its course. Benítez would pay the price for pursuing his dream of going to Real Madrid without gauging that he was doing so at a bad time. A very bad time. Firstly, because of Barcelona's explosiveness and attacking potential, which remained unparalleled. Secondly, and more pertinently, because it fell to him to contend with the beginning of Cristiano's decline.

■ ■ ■

ANOTHER COACH BITES THE DUST

Before Benítez had been introduced to his squad, the coach – whose family house is near the Welsh border – paid Bale a visit at a Wales training camp. The pair spoke about Bale's mooted change of position, or at least a new attacking set-up, which would allow him to drift across the front line rather than being frustratingly stuck out on the right wing. Photos were published and Cristiano took it as a sign of where the club's priorities lay.

'It's hard to say who's the best. I think Cristiano, Bale, Benzema and James are up there . . .' Benítez would go on to say in his first press conference during the club's tour of Australia. Certain journalists followed that up by seemingly inviting him to bow down to the Portuguese star, peppering the coach with questions about Ronaldo and his greatness.

Benítez was left 'bemused', as he admitted to the *Daily Mail* a few months later, when he came under scrutiny from the press and the board for referring to Ronaldo as only 'one of the best players in the world', because behind the scenes 'senior Madrid executives had talked often about Lionel Messi being the best in the world'.

Nevertheless, the warning he was issued by a club director – 'Don't forget, Ronaldo can get us all sacked' – must surely have rung in his ears.

After just a week of training, Cristiano began to distance himself from the coach, telling him that everything was fine to his face but questioning his methods behind his back. He could be seen grimacing when Benítez pointed out possible improvements, and even when the cameras were rolling he made no effort to hide his disdain for some of the drills run by the tactician.

■ ■ ■

At times Benítez swapped Ancelotti's 4-4-3 for a 4-2-3-1 or 4-4-2 that moved Bale into the middle behind Ronaldo, who operated as a centre forward, the position from which he had scored 64 per cent of his goals the previous campaign (compared to 47 per cent and 49 per cent the two seasons before that). Yet in the first pre-season friendly, against Roma, Ronaldo rebuked the Welshman for not passing him the ball on a couple of occasions, and in August the Portuguese finally made it clear to the coach that he did not want to play as a number nine and preferred being able to cut in from the left flank.

Benítez responded by asking his forwards to play with freedom, but also to listen to him in order to raise their and the team's games. But Cristiano did not feel he had much to learn from Benítez.

■ ■ ■

An assistant gave Ronaldo a USB drive with selected footage to help him find more space when making runs off the ball. According to *El País*, Cristiano rebuffed him with the following retort: 'Tell Benítez that I'm going to give him a pen drive with all my goals so that he can study them.'

A slightly different version of events was on offer from the coach's camp: 'Ronaldo told Benítez that, instead of him being sent videos, his team-mates should be sent one featuring his goals so that they could see how goals are scored.'

I'll let you decide.

■ ■ ■

In October, Benítez sought to draw a line under the debate about Ronaldo's importance: 'I always praise my players. This Real Madrid squad is the best I've had. In any case, I've made up my mind: when I'm asked if Cristiano is the best player I've coached, I'll say yes, yes, yes.'

It was too little, too late where the Portuguese was concerned. By that point, the rift could not be mended. Indeed, around that time

Ronaldo made his feelings plain by waxing lyrical to *ESPN* about his old boss, Carlo Ancelotti, calling him a 'fantastic guy' and a 'fantastic coach' and expressing the desire to work with him again. 'I miss him a lot,' he added.

■ ■ ■

An alarming trend was in evidence early in the season. Cristiano was less clinical and more profligate than at any other time since joining Real Madrid, and his goals were largely coming against easier opposition (he put fourteen past Malmö and Espanyol combined) and at the Bernabéu. Had he lost his mojo? Or was he having trouble making the difference because other teams knew him so well and his body no longer offered him the necessary explosiveness?

In December 2015, Cristiano set forth his own explanation: 'I've been a bit below par, but I've also had some issues, some personal problems. They're things I prefer to keep to myself; I don't like sharing them with anyone. I'm in a better place now, physically and mentally too, and I hope it'll stay that way through to the end of the season.'

He was referring to his patellar tendon, and about the sense of instability that had resulted from his break-up with Irina.

The pain in his left knee just would not subside. The tendon had forced him to take a month off in March 2014, and he paid no heed to the Portuguese football association doctors' suggestion in September that he spend a couple of months on the sidelines.

His mounting frustration may have been behind the five instances of violent conduct on the pitch of which he was accused during the first five months of the season: he kicked out at Las Palmas's David Simón, Sporting Gijón's Nacho Cases and Betis's Francisco Molinero off the ball, swung an arm at Grzegorz Krychowiak after the Sevilla player pulled him back during a counter-attack and caught Barcelona's Dani Alves with his elbow while the pair tussled.

■ ■ ■

Yet Cristiano kept his shoulder to the wheel on the training ground, putting in long hours in the gym and doing prep work with the physios. His life beyond Valdebebas, on the other hand, had been unhinged somewhat after Irina had left. Needing to blow off some steam, he discovered a taste for fine wine (after many years without drinking so much as a drop of alcohol) and regularly hopped on his private jet to Morocco in search of anonymity and friends, like kick-boxing champion Badr Hari. 'Just married hahahaha. Always there to pick you up bro,' Badr said in one Instagram post as the caption to a photo of him holding Ronaldo in his arms. But his partying became less and less discreet and people began to congregate outside the mansions and villas where they were staged, phones in hand to record his every move.

Some Portuguese media outlets linked him with Miss Bahamas (Toria Nichole Penn), and when he was asked about his love life on a British TV show he replied that he'd been playing the field with several women, while noting that having normal relationships wasn't easy for famous people. 'I think I'm a confident guy, I'm tall, I have [my] own teeth, I have a nice body,' he went on.

■ ■ ■

The first defeat of the season came against Sevilla in November 2015. The tension in the air grew and the criticism became louder. Cristiano, who had gone nine matches without a goal and was particularly out of sorts in Seville, came in for some heavy flak. His camp reacted by intimating that he was not being helped by the central position in which Benítez was playing him, in spite of his protests.

■ ■ ■

Ronaldo, a documentary about Cristiano's life, was released on 9 November, the day after his poor performance at the Sánchez Pizjuán. Produced by the people behind the magnificent *Senna* and *Amy*, and distributed by Universal, one of Hollywood's 'Big Six' studios, it enjoyed a no-expenses-spared world premiere – complete with red carpet – in Leicester Square. In the wake of a loss to Sevilla that had left Real Madrid three points adrift of Barcelona after eleven games, Ronaldo jetted off to London, where Gary Neville interviewed him in front of the audience. José Mourinho was in attendance at the event, having been invited by Jorge Mendes, but kept a distinctly low profile, sitting at the back of the theatre.

The film, which packs fourteen months of following the Portuguese into just over an hour, culminates with the iconic image of his celebrations in the Champions League final in Lisbon in May 2014. With disarming innocence, Ronaldo gives us a privileged glimpse of his ego and his odd, highly masculine (his mother is practically the only female presence) and deeply lonely world, in which his friendships are not based on equality: Ronaldo is the axis around which his planet revolves. Strangely, there is more talk about Leo Messi in the documentary than about the achievement of winning *La Décima*.

'My aim with this documentary is to be myself and show my fans who I am objectively. I think people will love seeing it because it's not fictitious or manipulated, it's something real.'

No, Cristiano. It is a version of reality staged for the cameras. A documentary can never be real, whether it's about you or Gandhi. It is only your truth, the one you want to put out there and that can be controlled. That is not to say that what it shows is not you, though. It's like this book: a layer (yet another one) of your multi-faceted personality.

As Juanma Trueba wrote in *AS*: 'Cristiano is the sole star of his documentary . . . In the intimacy of his home, with his son, lifting weights, doing press-ups in his living room and in other everyday scenes . . . his goals, his celebrations . . . Cristiano comes across as an arrogant guy with his gestures and it's very possible that he isn't one. That is the film I'd like to see – I've already seen all the other stuff.'

No Real Madrid officials attended the premiere.

■ ■ ■

The camera follows Dolores when she picks up a prescription for tranquilisers, as she is unable to remain calm while watching her son play on TV. We see Ronaldo telephone her from Brazil, where he is playing in the World Cup, to ask her if she has taken her sedatives. He does this regularly. If she cannot stand the tension, she leaves the family watching the game, slips on her flip-flops and goes for a walk around the neighbourhood, as shown at one point in the film. Accompanying this sequence is a voice-over from Dolores in which she recalls the day many moons ago when she let Cristiano go at a very young age. This is the only mention of what is arguably the most important moment in his life.

Her voice wobbles and Dolores cries as if it had all happened yesterday. As if she is still haunted by the consequences of that decision and will be for ever.

■ ■ ■

With his lack of clear role models, Ronaldo continues to search for an identity beyond simply being a successful, famous footballer. Meanwhile, he continually projects his son as a smaller version of himself. In one passage in the film, Cristiano asks Cristiano Jr which car is missing in his garage. The Porsche is there, as are the Rolls-Royce, the Mercedes, the Ferrari . . . 'The Lamborghini!' exclaims the child.

'I'm going to be a goalkeeper. OK, Dad?' his son says on another occasion. 'No, that's not what I want,' the footballer replies. 'But I do.' 'A goalkeeper? Are you joking?' concludes the star.

'I want to be the best possible father,' explains Ronaldo. 'When a kid grows up in a house with everything they could ever want . . . it's complicated, because I didn't grow up that way. It might be a bit difficult for him to see the real world, but I feel comfortable with giving him everything.'

In another scene, Cristiano has breakfast with his son, who is seated to his right. In silence. On the left we see a simple portrait of his father, Dinis.

The trinity. A picture full of symbolic resonance.

■ ■ ■

I was recently told that, years back, the night before a game, Cristiano was following a Barcelona match while eating dinner with the Real Madrid squad. The sight of Messi scoring a brace drove him to despair and he threw his serviette, sprang loudly out of his chair and stormed off to his room, scowling.

But Messi, the film confirmed, was no longer an enemy for Cristiano, but rather a mere rival, a fellow athlete who had trodden a similar path. 'To see Messi win four Ballons d'Or in a row was difficult for me. After he won the second or third I thought to myself, "I'm not coming here again,"' he confessed to the documentary's director, Anthony Wonke.

Before being presented with the penultimate Ballon d'Or, his third, Cristiano admitted to Leo that his son was a fan of the Argentinian. Meanwhile, at the ceremony where Messi picked up his fifth Ballon d'Or, Neymar took any possible sting out of the atmosphere with a string of jokes. In the words of a Barcelona official, 'It was his [Neymar's] first time at the gala and he was very nice to the Portuguese, whom he looks up to for footballing reasons. Cristiano saw that, relaxed and it was all more cordial than in other years.'

'Before the gala,' Ronaldo explained, 'up on the stage, I translated for Neymar and Messi. Afterwards I told them they'd have to pay me.'

■ ■ ■

CR7 had invited us into his house in La Finca (Pozuelo de Alarcón), both in the film and on social media. His bedroom, his dining room, his garden, his jacuzzi, his swimming pool. He had shown us his business ventures – his underwear and headphones lines – and partly opened up his heart to us. One got the impression that he was increasingly mapping out his future life and gradually getting ready to retire.

■ ■ ■

I came face-to-face with both Jorge Mendes and Cristiano at the premiere. I was greeted by a 'We need to talk' by Jorge and by a crooked smile from Ronaldo.

'Facadita, facadita . . .'

Stabbed in the back. That was the way he felt – and he said as much in Portuguese – about me having revealed in *Messi* the nickname by which he used to refer to Leo.

■ ■ ■

Or was it something else? Maybe it was his reaction to the fact that I had written a book (good or bad) about him that had depicted him as a human being, not an icon. I suppose that this must also have represented a form of betrayal to him.

ANOTHER COACH BITES THE DUST

■ ■ ■

Real Madrid's displays under Benítez did not convince, although the coach was adamant that the results were good enough. It was true that the team's attacking statistics were similar to those in Ancelotti's last season, but something was amiss. The players looked shackled and as if they were not enjoying themselves.

Following the aforementioned loss to Sevilla, TV channel Cuatro engaged in a spot of lip-reading and claimed that Cristiano had told Sergio Ramos, 'Playing this way, we're not going to win anything.' Ronaldo had scored thirteen times in fifteen appearances, but his goals had come in just six of those matches. His erratic form was the biggest difference compared to the team's numbers under Ancelotti. But were they struggling on account of a lack of bravery in their approach, as some squad members insinuated in private? Real Madrid were the highest scoring side in Europe and Cristiano was the most prolific shot-taker, but the Portuguese insisted that the game plan was overly defensive, while the coaching staff reminded him that if he failed to track back, the team would suffer. Two different languages were being spoken in the dressing room.

Benítez steadily fell further out of favour with the star, who stopped listening to him. When the coach suggested a few tweaks to his game in a couple of training sessions, Cristiano took to the press to complain about 'corrections'. But if you had under your stewardship a gymnast who performed a double flip, wouldn't you teach them to do a triple? Isn't that a coach's job?

What's more, Ronaldo had begun the season thinking that it might be his last at Real Madrid – he had been entertaining over-tures from other clubs and was unsure where his future lay, which is always an unsettling factor.

November's *clásico* would bring things to a head, as these fixtures so often do.

Several Spanish media outlets reported that ahead of the game against Barcelona the Real Madrid captain (Ramos) and two of the three vice-captains (Ronaldo and Marcelo – Pepe was away on international duty at the time) held a twenty-minute meeting with Benítez to ask him to set up the team to attack against Barça. The triggers for these talks were the lacklustre showing against PSG, when *Los Blancos* could count themselves lucky to prevail 1–0, and the reverse against Sevilla. According to the articles, Benítez agreed with their assessment but reminded them that the club's injury crisis prevented him from being able to unleash the team's full firepower.

The fact is that no such meeting ever occurred. Sergio Ramos was only around in the morning on the day when it supposedly took place, while the rest of the squad reported for duty in the evening.

El Confidencial, meanwhile, leaked a conversation in which Ronaldo purportedly reiterated his dim view of Benítez to Florentino Pérez. 'We're not going to win anything with this coach,' he was quoted as saying. The following day, both Cristiano and the president issued denials to the squad and coach.

With no access to the players in the run-up to the *clásico*, the media accepted rumours – however flimsy they sounded – in order to fill column inches. Yet something else seemed to be going on: a parallel story, centred on run-ins and the coach's weakness, was being written which only had one possible ending. But did all the problems really stem from the dugout?

. . .

Benítez had two options for the *clásico*: he could stick with his original plans (by fielding Casemiro, Isco or Lucas Vázquez, for example) or bow to Florentino's pressure and put out a team packed full of *galácticos*. The latter move could, of course, be construed as an attempt to go for victory, but it might also be a way of making a statement about these players' real worth, or indeed their limitations.

He chose the second option.

Los Blancos lined up as follows: Keylor Navas, Danilo, Raphaël Varane, Sergio Ramos, Marcelo; Toni Kroos, Luka Modrić, James Rodríguez; Gareth Bale, Karim Benzema and Cristiano Ronaldo.

Ronaldo had felt uncomfortable playing as a number nine throughout the season to date, but he'd had no choice but to perform that role while Benzema was out injured. He had not enjoyed waiting for the ball with his back to the goal, or making the runs that centre forwards have to. The Portuguese had expressed his unhappiness with his duties on the pitch on several occasions over the course of the campaign. He felt angry with Benítez, but also with the president, who had refused to buy a striker in the summer. His relationship with Florentino was hitting rock bottom.

Against Barcelona, though, Benzema would be back by his side. The Frenchman would play one-twos with him and keep the centre-backs occupied. Cristiano, who had never had the guile to thrive in tight spaces, needed someone to distract defenders. And Benzema provided both that extra intelligence and a focal point for his team-mates.

But the alarming signs that the team had exhibited against other top sides were confirmed in the *clásico*. Real Madrid were emphatically thrashed 4–0 at the Bernabéu. It was Ronaldo's twelfth loss in twenty-four meetings with Barcelona, compared to just six victories.

'Maybe the 4–0 in the *clásico* was a good wake-up call,' Cristiano later said. 'When you lose, you always have to make changes.'

The wheels had been set in motion for the inevitable change in the hot seat.

■ ■ ■

Rafa received a suggestion from the club's hierarchy: 'Benítez, if you have to bench Cristiano, do it.'

That was never taken up because it would have been a case of the cure being worse than the disease.

■ ■ ■

A match against Rayo Vallecano at the Bernabéu on 20 December 2015 resulted in what was the final straw as far as Ronaldo was concerned. As well as for Florentino and the home fans.

Real Madrid went ahead, but by the quarter-hour mark a dominant Rayo side had turned the game around and led 2-1. With the threat of an upset, deafening jeers and whistles rang around the stadium. The crowd called for Benítez's resignation, although they were really voicing their discontent with the president – a month earlier he had come out in defence of the coach, who was under widespread fire, but the boo boys felt the problems with the team were not so much on the bench but in the VIP seats. An increasing portion of the fans were getting tired of Pérez's way of running the club.

The fans' reaction did not go down well with Cristiano, who wagged his finger at them, signalling that he felt they were in the wrong. This lit a fuse among the crowd, who duly responded by hitting him with quite possibly the fiercest and most sustained chorus of booing to which he had ever been subjected during his time at the club.

But the dialogue with the supporters did not end there.

Before a Rayo corner Ronaldo repeatedly shook his head and gesticulated reproachingly with his right hand. *TVE* caught him on camera telling the fans to get stuffed, to put it mildly, while raising his arm in a chiding gesture.

After scoring the first of his two goals, his side's third of the encounter (Real Madrid eventually ran out 10-2 winners after

Rayo had two men sent off), Cristiano neglected to celebrate. He did not go through the mixed zone after the match either. In fact, in the dressing room after the game, Ronaldo threatened to leave the club, according to the radio programme *El Larguero*.

Although no one told him as much, some people at the club disapproved of the Portuguese adopting this sort of attitude towards the supporters. Either way, with the atmosphere growing all the more toxic, Rafa Benítez saw his breathing room steadily diminishing.

■ ■ ■

Around that period, I ran into a journalist from TV channel *La Sexta* and he told me something that surprised me. Apparently, they had opted against airing some videos of Ronaldo because audience research had shown that many viewers changed channel when the Portuguese appeared on the screen. People were either bored by Ronaldo, the leading goalscorer in the world of the previous three years (2013 to 2015), or found him a turn-off. At least in Spain.

■ ■ ■

Real Madrid's first fixture of the new year, on 3 January 2016, was a 2–2 draw with Valencia at the Mestalla, further denting their title hopes. They languished two points behind Barcelona and four adrift of Atlético.

But even before then, the die was cast.

Prior to that game, Florentino Pérez had made moves to bring Benítez's regime to an end. Taking advantage of the players' disaffection, convinced that Rafa could not stay at the club any longer because the crowd were up in arms and trying to avoid getting swept up by the groundswell, Pérez met with Sergio Ramos and Ronaldo separately. He offered them the coach's head and, as both had been hankering after him, told them that Zinedine Zidane would be installed as the replacement. In exchange, he asked them to put things in order in the dressing room and to stop travelling so often to Seville and Morocco respectively.

Although Florentino felt that many of the team's problems (their inability to compete over the long haul, for instance) could be laid at the door of the squad's only two clear leaders, at that moment he deemed it wise to hand the captains the keys to the dressing room.

Why Zidane? Because the players had been calling for a coach of that ilk, someone less demanding and more attack-minded who would give the stars greater freedom. But also because Pérez reckoned that the fans would be pleased by the appointment of a club legend and would place any further scrutiny on the players. Florentino even went as far as to tell his two leaders that they better pull their socks up or all hell was about to break loose at the Bernabéu.

■ ■ ■

A few weeks after Rafa Benítez's sacking, announced on 4 January, the *Daily Mail* published a story about his tenure in the *Los Blancos* hot seat. In this piece, a member of his backroom staff likened his time at Real Madrid to 'trying to be father in a big house with Pérez playing the role of a patriarchal grandfather and [the] players being like twenty-five grandchildren, who would all go running to their grandad when there was a problem'.

■ ■ ■

Months later, Ronaldo granted an interview to Josep Pedrerol in which he spoke about Benítez. 'You can always learn new things from coaches. Some things you can learn and other things you can't. Under him, I saw some things which were different to other coaches, but obviously there are things that no one can teach you.

You've either got it, or you haven't. He [Benítez] didn't just talk about [how to improve my] free-kick taking, but also ball-striking and dribbling too, but that's their prerogative . . . I'd just say, "OK." There are some things you can't have a debate about because the other person thinks so differently that you just say thanks and that's the end of it.'

NINE

ONE SUPERHERO UNDER THE TUTELAGE OF ANOTHER

4 JANUARY 2016. Real Madrid announced that Zinedine Zidane – whose experience was limited to the Real Madrid B dugout – was taking over the reins. Florentino Pérez had sounded out the possibility of recruiting José Mourinho, who was out of work after leaving Chelsea. The Portuguese coach, who was so admired in the Bernabéu offices, stated later that he was the one who turned Real Madrid down. Florentino – who liked the way Mourinho kept the dressing room in line, although he was fearful of the manager's desire for authority – leaked the name to journalists and opinion polls, but the majority of people did not think it was a good idea to give him a second chance. Mourinho wanted Ramos and Ronaldo out, and maybe Pepe, too.

Zidane gave his first press conference the day after the announcement, following an inaugural training session in which the coach was seen doing running drills with the players, and he confirmed that Benzema, Bale and Ronaldo would play whenever they were fit.

8 JANUARY. Zidane spoke about Ronaldo ahead of his first match against Deportivo at the Bernabéu. 'He's the soul of Real Madrid. He isn't for sale.' It was still not yet clear where Cristiano

would play: in a free role, out wide, as a number nine? Would he have defensive duties?

9 JANUARY. Real Madrid thrashed Depor 5–0, with Bale grabbing a hat-trick and Benzema a brace. Ronaldo, who had ten efforts on goal, three of which were on target, started on the left, but popped up on the right and in the box. Zidane gave his attacking trio freedom.

18 JANUARY. Ronaldo: 'Zidane has really boosted the team. You get on better with some coaches than others. I worked hard under Benítez, I took it seriously and thought about the club's best interests, regardless of the person who was in charge. I've never had a negative opinion about Rafa, he always did his best for Real Madrid. He sees football differently from Zizou. Don't ask me why, but the players feel more empathy towards Zizou.'

19 JANUARY. Zidane jokingly showed Cristiano how to take a direct free-kick. It was clear to everyone that Zidane was giving Ronaldo the affection that he did not feel he got from Benítez. The coach was not opposed to the player's position of leadership in the team and had faith in him. Cristiano, who prior to then had at best a cordial attitude towards his coaches, responded well to the emotional treatment. Zidane was not renowned for his team talks, ability to analyse the opposition or even for opening his players' eyes to the small details. He employed an emotional approach and hardly intervened in the team's tactics beyond selecting the players.

13 FEBRUARY. After thumping Sporting 5–1 and Espanyol 6–0, including a Ronaldo hat-trick as he racked up an extraordinary eight goals in two league games against the Catalan side, Real Madrid beat Athletic Bilbao 4–2, with the Portuguese grabbing a brace in the team's fifth win in six games after sharing the spoils against Betis. At the end of the match, Zidane analysed Cristiano's change in position (against Athletic), with him spending a bit more

time out wide: 'Cristiano is very important on the wing, when he takes players on, when he uses his pace and when he tries one-on-ones. That's where he is very good. We asked Cristiano to stick to the left to receive the ball when we broke and that's how the first goal came about.'

17 FEBRUARY. Rafa Benítez had steered the team through the Champions League group stages with two wins apiece over Shakhtar Donetsk and Malmö, and four points against PSG. Ronaldo scored eleven goals, all of which came against the first two clubs. Roma awaited in the last sixteen. The first leg was in Italy and Cristiano opened the scoring an hour into the tie with a powerful shot after cutting in following a long run. The goal was similar to those he'd often scored a year or two earlier. Cristiano, who once again felt comfortable and physically fit after an inconsistent start to the season, went over to celebrate with Zidane. Real Madrid ran out 2–0 winners.

27 FEBRUARY. Zidane's first big test came at home to fellow title challengers Atlético de Madrid in La Liga. Bale and Pepe were injured. Ronaldo insinuated after the 1–0 defeat that the club's pre-season schedule, which had included a tiring tour of Australia and China, was to blame for the plague of injuries: 'The situation was already worrying before the derby'. He also had words for those who doubted him: 'Everyone says I'm not doing well, but I look at the seasons the players they say are the best are having, and I think I'm close to them. I can't see anyone close to me in the Champions League. It bothers me because I seem to be persecuted. They say that as my level has gone down, Real Madrid's level has gone down. If everyone were at my level [in the team], maybe we'd be top! The press treats me unfairly. Always. My value is brought into question here in Spain. It's as if I'm shit! But the truth is the statistics don't lie. Look at the statistics!'

Ronaldo contacted *AS* that evening to clarify what he meant. 'I wasn't saying I'm better than the rest. I was referring to the physical side of the game and injuries . . . I completely respect my team-mates and never wanted to offend them. I don't think I'm better than anyone else.' He also spoke to the squad, not just to apologise, but also to explain himself. He told his team-mates that he was referring to the problems that the players had with the medical staff, whom barely anyone seemed to trust.

8 MARCH. Roma could have shocked Real Madrid at the Bernabéu. They had chances to take the lead but ended up losing 2–0. Ronaldo played as a number nine and converted a Lucas Vázquez cross to open the scoring. 'He looked good to me!' stated Zidane in the press conference. 'At the start Cristiano was in the middle, but the idea was to mix it up. He can start in any position . . . The most important thing is to be organised defensively. When we defended, Cristiano had to move into the middle and James and Bale had to close down the wide areas.' That was the unspoken deal they had struck: if he operated as a number nine, he did not have to defend. Ronaldo did not enjoy playing as a number nine, however. He prefered Benzema to play in that role. When the Frenchman played alongside him, it made his life easier. When he had to play as the main striker, as his movement was not that good and he did not have support nearby, his influence on the game dwindled. Ronaldo is a finisher who struggles to create play.

19 APRIL. According to *France Football*, Cristiano had a meeting with PSG president Nasser Al-Khelaïfi in Paris (he took a private jet from Borrejón to Le Bourget, Al-Khelaïfi's chauffeur picked him up and they met at Hotel Costes). It was at least the fifth meeting between the pair over the previous few months. It was in both party's interests for the meeting to come to light. Constant flirting took place all season long because PSG were on the hunt for a

replacement for Ibrahimović and Ronaldo was seriously considering leaving Real Madrid. In November, at the end of the match against PSG at the Bernabéu, Ronaldo went up to French coach Laurent Blanc and said something in his ear (he thanked him for speaking so kindly about him in public, as Cristiano clarified a few weeks later). He warmly greeted Al-Khelaïfi in the mixed zone with the cameras watching. The rumour mill was in overdrive. Over the following few days, Florentino reprimanded him for saying in an interview with *Kicker*, 'Will I finish my career at Real Madrid? Right now I play for Real Madrid, but you never know. Nobody knows what might happen tomorrow. Can I see myself saying goodbye to Madrid? Why not? You have to do what makes you happy.' A few days later, Jorge Mendes had dinner with Al-Khelaïfi.

A poll by Forza Football revealed that 36 per cent of Real Madrid fans were willing to sell him that summer. A month later, a similar poll increased the figure to 80 per cent if someone paid €100 million.

2–6 APRIL. It was a crucial week for a lucky Real Madrid, who drew a weak Wolfsburg in the Champions League quarter-final. *El clásico* was on 2 April at the Camp Nou, with Barcelona ten points ahead and Atlético just one point better off in the table. Real Madrid recovered from Piqué's goal, with Benzema and Ronaldo scoring to change the dynamic of that season: Barcelona doubted themselves and Real Madrid started to grow in confidence, although performances were still inconsistent. In the Champions League, Zidane's troops were turned over 2–0 by Wolfsburg in the quarter-final first leg after a limp display.

12 APRIL. A red-hot Ronaldo, who led from the front, sealed the club's sixth consecutive Champions League semi-final berth with a hat-trick to complete the 3–0 comeback over the Germans. 'It's not bad for a bad season,' he ironically said in the press conference. 'I get criticised, criticised and criticised . . . but I'm always there. It's

like that in Spain. I'm not a boy and these things can't affect me. I'm used to it. I want to thank my team-mates for their performance. I don't want to be rested in La Liga on Saturday at Getafe. If I'm fit. Why would I stop? I love playing!'

18 APRIL. Gareth Bale picked up an injury ahead of the semi-final against Manchester City. Ronaldo was seen approaching Bale when he picked an injury during a game, looking worried and discussing the muscle problem. The Portuguese had shown greater respect for the Welshman during the season. Bale was looking for more responsibility and his influence was growing, but Ronaldo needed him to achieve the big target for the season – the Champions League – and furthermore, he is very sensitive to injuries, sustained by him and by others.

'Pain? I feel it every day. But other players would give the same answer,' he explained in an interview. 'I'm not going to make the same mistakes from the past. After a match, at twenty-two I'd go out for dinner until three in the morning. Now I avoid that: I go home, I recover and maybe I go the following day. These small details make an enormous difference at the end of the season.'

20 APRIL. Cristiano left the pitch without informing Zidane seconds before the end of the 3–0 victory against Villarreal. He attempted a bicycle kick in stoppage time and felt a twinge. Zidane said in the press conference, 'I think it was more of a fright than anything serious.' The Frenchman also blamed himself for not resting the player. In the previous five campaigns, he had racked up 4,000 minutes of action and had only missed three games in the previous two seasons. A few hours later, Cristiano wrote on his Instagram account, 'All good.'

23 APRIL. Zidane did without Ronaldo against Rayo to give him time to recover ahead of the semi-final against Manchester City. The press stated that the scan confirmed there was no muscle tear,

but there was a strain in his right thigh. 'Pending progress,' was the message from the club. Zidane was asked if any players other than Cristiano were untouchable. 'He is because he deserves to be, because of his figures. He rests when he doesn't play, but when he does he is bloody brilliant.'

26 APRIL. Ronaldo did not get changed and was left out of the squad to face Manchester City at the Etihad. The club insisted that there was no muscle tear, but without an official medical report, doubts lingered. Ronaldo revealed in private that the scar from the injury was 'rather tender' and needed more time to recover. A nil–nil draw meant the tie would be settled at the Bernabéu.

4 MAY. In the days leading up to the return leg, Ronaldo took part in intense recovery sessions with his trusted physiotherapist Joaquín Juan, with whom he had worked on his patellar tendon before the World Cup in Brazil. The Portuguese ended up starting the match. Manchester City seemed devoid of belief, while Ronaldo started out wide but ended up playing as a number nine and had seven attempts on goal, none of which went in. The tie, which was bereft of quality, was decided by a Fernando own goal after twenty minutes.

Four months after Zidane's arrival, and with a record nine-teen wins and just two defeats, Real Madrid had qualified for the Champions League final. In that period, Ronaldo had notched twenty-two goals in twenty-two games. Barcelona's spectacular drop in form left Real Madrid just a point adrift of Atlético and *Los Culés* with just two league games remaining: Valencia at home and Depor away.

8 MAY. The match against Valencia. Movistar+'s *El Día Después* show captured how Cristiano made Zidane change his mind about a substitution: instead of bringing Jesé on for James, he advised the coach to withdraw Lucas Vázquez. The footage also showed how

Cristiano went over to the dugout and Zidane consulted him about being replaced. Ronaldo looked surprised and shrugged his shoulders. Soon after, Zidane decided to send Arbeloa on for Ronaldo, but not without asking the Portuguese first. On this occasion, Ronaldo did allow himself to be taken off for the first time all season. Real Madrid ran out 3–2 winners over Valencia with a Cristiano brace, Atlético fell to a shock defeat at the hands of Levante and Barcelona demolished Espanyol 5–0 at home. With one league game to go, Luis Enrique's side sat a point above *Los Blancos* with a superior head-to-head record.

14 MAY. Real Madrid approached the final two games of the season with the chance to win two major trophies. First up were Depor in La Liga and two weeks later it would be Atlético de Madrid in the Champions League final. Ronaldo scored both goals to beat Deportivo, but Barcelona did not slip up. Second place in La Liga was treated as a partial success. The biggest stage of all remained, the one where Ronaldo and Real Madrid have always been so at ease.

■ ■ ■

Ronaldo was one step from his third Champions League title. And probably a fourth Ballon d'Or. He ended the season in exceptional form, despite the ups and downs, and had a promising European Championships on the horizon.

His legacy, which he had been so worried about in recent years, seemed to be as solid as his CV. 'I know that I have my place in the history of this sport,' he told *FIFA* magazine after winning the 2014 Ballon d'Or. 'I know there'll be a page dedicated to me next to the very greatest and that makes me happy.' Cristiano feels the need to be everlasting. 'I have plenty to keep me busy. You build for the future while young. I've been developing my own fashion line since I was twenty-seven and I want my brand to keep growing because football will be over in five, six, seven, ten years. There's another life afterwards. I think I'll find it hard initially, but if you ask me now if I want to be a coach, I'll say no. Nor a club director or president.'

How do players who have relied on their physique react psychologically when their body falters? Naturally it depends on other factors, such as what projects they have outside sport. If they dedicated themselves entirely to sport without developing other plans – or forming a family, for example – they risk losing everything. Whether or not they descend into inner conflict depends on the circumstances of their 'retirement', the people around them and how they have prepared for the moment.

'Sport should only be part of a bigger life plan,' according to psychologist Sidónio Serpa. 'The drama comes when sporting ambitions are the entire life plan, because when these are accomplished, they [sports people] have nothing left to do, there is nothing left in their lives. And any sporting failure becomes a failure in life.'

In mid-December 2015 Cristiano signed an agreement to be a partner in and the face of hotel group Pestana, owned by Dionísio Pestana from Madeira, with whom he will open four establishments in Funchal, Lisbon, Madrid and New York. The first of them, Pestana CR7, was opened in Praça do Mar in the Madeiran capital in June 2016 and is part of a complex that houses the footballer's bronze statue as well as the museum that now has three times as much space (1,400 square metres) as the previous location. Madeira Airport has been rechristened the Cristiano Ronaldo Airport.

In a promotional interview, Cristiano was asked if he would take part in a Hollywood film. 'Why not? I've had a few invitations . . . I'm sure it'll happen someday,' he answered. 'I'm a happy person because my projects are growing more and more, and I can say that after football I have an idea about what I'll do. I want my brand to keep growing in different project areas: shoes, trousers, shirts, boxers, headphones, films, etc., and the name Cristiano Ronaldo to be eternal.'

One day he would have to hang up his boots, which the media often reminded him. 'In some way it motivates me to keep working hard, improve and to continue in my field which is football. The more time I spend at the highest level, the better for my future because I will provide more in terms of contracts and everything.'

At that time, his footballing future was at Real Madrid and subsequently in the MLS, where big businessmen were trying to convince Cristiano and Messi to reproduce their rivalry in the United States.

'You never know what'll happen in the future,' repeated Cristiano over the first few months of the 2015–16 season. Word from the dressing room was that he often seemed restless, as if he did not know which way to turn. He put himself in the shop window and was playing against the backdrop of the rumours linked to his departure, but neither PSG nor Manchester United made serious attempts to sign him, although conversations were had with both clubs. It was too much money (a €25 million annual salary and at least a €70 million transfer fee) for a player who had reached his physical peak and was suffering from knee problems.

Real Madrid always said in private that PSG did not want him and never made an offer. The French club flirted with a possible deal but never made the necessary effort. In fact, Al-Khelaïfi told Florentino in late 2015 that he would not be signing Cristiano. United were debating whether to keep Van Gaal or appoint Mourinho, but neither needed the Portuguese star. Although Sir Alex had been toying with the idea of bringing him back to Manchester for many years, the 2016 Ronaldo would be the typical player that the Scot would ditch if he were the Real Madrid coach.

When it became clear in February that the Portuguese's future options were dwindling, Jorge Mendes opened talks with the Real Madrid board about a contract renewal. FIFA then punished the club with a transfer embargo, covering two windows, for infringing regulations linked to the recruiting of minors. Despite Florentino having opened the doors to a possible exit, he needed to keep the team's spine together until 2017 and accepted that Ronaldo had to be offered a new contract, possibly until 2020 or 2021, established as €20 million net per year after many months of negotiations. 'I want him to stay here for the rest of his life because he's one of the club's pillars and is part of our history. Real Madrid with Cristiano defines an era,' stated the president who has always expressed his discontent at the excessive level of authority of players in modern football.

Ronaldo also changed his tune. 'This is the best league in the world, although I've also played in the Premier League. It's incredible, competitive and great players play here. It's a privilege to leave my mark on it. I want to stay for another two years and we'll see about the future. The two years I'm speaking about are the two in my contract . . . Maybe I'll finish my career here at Real Madrid.'

■ ■ ■

During an interview with journalist Josep Pedrerol on 26 May, he revealed that the renewal was practically sealed, although some of the finer details were still to be ironed out. 'I think it would be a wise move by Real Madrid [to extend my deal]. I'm laughing, but it's true. If you were the president, wouldn't you renew my contract? I want to retire at Real Madrid.' On 3 June, he told *AS*, 'I'm going to retire at Real Madrid over the age of forty. I'm very happy here and I'm working hard to achieve that.'

That was Ronaldo's method of asking Florentino to accept the renewal conditions as soon as possible.

During the build-up to the Milan final, Ronaldo admitted that he felt better than he had done ahead of the Lisbon one, when the pain in his hamstrings had been almost unbearable. 'It's terrible because you know you could give more on many occasions, but you don't because your body doesn't let you,' he admitted. In reality, he was far from his very best and even sat out a training session four days before the game because of a thigh problem. He did only the essential amount of training in a bid not to worsen the pain or miss the showpiece fixture. He had reached the end of another season with scarcely enough gas left in the tank.

The team was certainly in harmony and more balanced thanks to Casemiro, whom Benítez had introduced to the first XI. The players seemed to enjoy themselves more with fewer tactical demands made of them.

The final on 28 May was tense and chances were at a premium, as expected.

'Real Madrid didn't put in a good performance,' Alfredo Relaño wrote in *AS*, 'but the way they kept going, even when half the team was struck down with cramp at the end, is worthy of praise. Atlético deserve credit, too. Two years ago they took Real Madrid all the way until the ninety-third minute. This time they lasted even longer, until the fifth penalty in the shootout.'

Real Madrid scored from a free-kick fifteen minutes into the game when Sergio Ramos opened the scoring, although he was offside. The scoreline reflected Zidane's side's dominance early on. In the second half, Atlético stepped up the pressure and were more daring in attack, with wide-man Carrasco coming on for midfielder Augusto Fernández after half-time. Griezmann missed a penalty, but Carrasco slotted home a Juanfran cross with ten minutes left on the clock – 1–1.

That is how it ended after 90 minutes.

Ronaldo was subdued and struggled to find his pace. He was doing the minimum to help out in defence and ended up exhausting his remaining energy in extra-time. In the second fifteen-minute period, he raced back to prevent an Atlético de Madrid counter-attack and spent the rest of the match recovering his strength for penalties.

Before receiving treatment ahead of the shootout, he went up to his teammates to admit that he was 'dead. My legs aren't working, they're done. I'm struggling.' He was in the majority, with a limping Bale on his last legs.

Whatever happened that night, Ronaldo would end the season as the top goalscorer in the Champions League with sixteen. For the seventh straight season he had reached the fifty-goal milestone (fifty-one in La Liga and the Champions League combined). The statistics were remarkable, but a trophy was needed to round off a campaign that had been filled with uncertainty.

Cristiano had been the only Manchester United player to miss a penalty in the 2008 shootout against Chelsea. In the semi-final against Bayern Munich in 2012 he took the first one, which they say sets the tone psychologically, and he also missed it. Yet in Milan, he had a vision and he told Zidane.

'Put me fifth in the shootout because I'm going to score the winning penalty.'

Lucas Vázquez scored the first one. The other players slotted home their efforts until Atlético's fourth taker.

Juanfran missed.

It was down to Ronaldo to win the Champions League. Some of his team-mates remembered his words just a few minutes earlier, that 'I'm dead', and deemed him to be low on confidence. But he assuredly struck his kick to Oblak's left, just as each of his team-mates had done. And it went in.

ONE SUPERHERO UNDER THE TUTELAGE OF ANOTHER

'I knew I wouldn't miss,' he said a few minutes later.

Real Madrid had just won *La Undécima*.

He sprinted off to the left, looking into the terraces as he took his shirt off and shouting.

He was celebrating another personal triumph.

TEN

VICTORY, THE SPECTACLE, THE BEGINNING OF THE END

11 OCTOBER 2014

'We were in the Stade de France dressing room and Fernando Santos spoke to us after losing 2–1 to France in a friendly in his first match as coach.'

Nani described a talk that he would not forget throughout the following months. It was not an easy time for the Portugal national team, which had just lost a Euros qualifier against Albania.

'He gathered us all together and reminded us we were a strong team and had to believe in the group. We had the chance to achieve something big for our country and could win the competition. We hadn't even qualified for it yet.

'He said we'd be back in that dressing room two years later to play in the Euros final.'

Santos remembered how the players looked at him incredulously. 'How can I say this?' he asked them. 'Because I can. Because how can I not say it?'

The message did not simply remain there and was repeated one way or another throughout the rest of the qualifying campaign, in which the team won every fixture except the aforementioned one against Albania. Portugal ended up winning the group. 'Game after game, month after month, he would repeat: "We have a target: the final and we will win it." That's how he managed to alter the group's mentality,' explained Sergio Fernández, a journalist for *Marca* who closely follows Portugal. 'Those who'd been there the longest always worked with coaches who said: "We're going to play our games, get through the group stage and then we'll see." Not even Scolari, who arrived as a World Cup winner, gave that type of team-talk.'

Santos managed to blend a group of veterans (Pepe, Nani, Bruno Alves, João Moutinho, Ricardo Carvalho, Quaresma) with a generation of youngsters who had still to fulfil their maximum potential (Raphaël Guerreiro, João Mário, William Carvalho, Renato Sanches, André Gomes), and who were all under the leadership of the coach and the main star. Their resources were suited to a gameplan based around defensive aggression and counter-attacking football, but also the ability to take control of a match when necessary, by adapting to the opponent's attributes. Santos would repeat another mantra: 'We have to stop playing ball to start playing football.' Entertaining the fans came second.

The coach liked 4-3-3, but did not have a centre-forward who could fit into the system, a Hélder Postiga or Nuno Gomes who holds the ball up and plays with his back to goal. He would try to make 4-4-2 work, which would mean Ronaldo being utilised in a position in which he was not comfortable, as a striker alongside Nani.

Santos and Ronaldo spoke about the role and the coach explained that the two forwards would have very few defensive duties (sometimes they would have to close down the centre-backs, but they did not need to do a sizeable amount of tracking back) and plenty of freedom. Santos reminded Cristiano that if he played him out wide, he would have to run towards his own goal, and so the player duly accepted his new role.

The balance in the team was being addressed once again. Ronaldo had not taken on a coach's suggestions before with such a level of approval. His relationship with Carlos Queiroz had been irreparably damaged very early on. Paulo Bento had tried to make demands on him and also give him what he wanted, but his distance from the squad and lack of experience had made his tenure one of intentions rather than accomplishments.

Santos (who at the age of sixty-one had already led nine different teams, including the big three in Portugal – Porto, Sporting and Benfica – winning titles with some of them, as well as during his stay in the Greek league) had been the Sporting coach during the pre-season when Cristiano was sold to Manchester United. They'd established a relationship of mutual respect which had survived the passing of time, even though they'd only spent a few months together. 'If I hadn't picked him, maybe Manchester United wouldn't have signed him,' joked Santos during the Euros.

Ronaldo had changed since the time when Queiroz had regularly given him the captain's armband in 2008. Back then, he'd felt like a star and wanted to be treated as such. In 2016, he just wanted to win and used his position to protect the newcomers and demand more from the veterans.

Santos was going to be the national team's leader. The father of the group. The dictator. Ronaldo would be his most important player. The captain. He would maintain order in the dressing room, despite the fact he did not fully enjoy his role on the pitch. That was the agreement between the pair.

His predecessors had good players at their disposal, but none of them had this new Ronaldo.

PORTUGAL V. ICELAND
(EURO 2016 GROUP STAGE, 14 JUNE 2016)

Santos warned that nobody was assured of a starting berth except Cristiano. Quaresma did not feature in the line-up. Nani and Ronaldo played up front in a structured 4-4-2 system, which forced the number seven to pick the ball up with his back to goal, meaning he was frequently unable to use his pace, which remained one of his strengths, despite it having dropped slightly.

Cristiano continually looked to get on the scoresheet, displaying a certain level of anxiety. He popped up on both wings and had to interchange his position with Nani. Both players linked up well, although Ronaldo complained about some of his team-mate's decisions. 'I try not to listen, because I've known him for many years now. I know how he reacts and what he's like. It's not an issue for me, because after the game we joke about it and everything is fine.' That is how Nani describes his relationship with Cristiano.

Ronaldo was carrying the team on his shoulders, but with limited effect: he had ten efforts on goal (Iceland only managed four), eight of which were in the second half, but only one was on target: a header in the eighty-fifth minute that Halldórsson parried. At 1–1 (Nani opened the scoring in the thirty-first minute, Bjarnason equalised in the fiftieth), Cristiano asked his team-mates to keep calm as they kept trying to seek him out with hurried, long balls.

After the game finished 1–1, Ronaldo let rip in the press conference: 'Iceland have a small mentality and won't go far. It's normal to encounter difficulties in the first match. It hasn't just happened to us. It's happened to Spain, France, everyone . . . I'm sure we'll win our next game and get through.' As for the Icelandic celebrations after clinching a draw, Ronaldo failed to be diplomatic: 'It was as if they'd won the Euros, it was incredible.'

In the mixed zone, Sergio Fernández, spotting a good news story, asked the player about his position. 'Well, I prefer playing out wide and using my pace more, but it's where the coach put me and I have to accept it. My favourite position is wherever they play me.'

Cristiano was angry about the draw but remained respectful towards his coach. It was certainly a new situation.

AUSTRIA V. PORTUGAL
(EURO 2016 GROUP STAGE, 18 JUNE 2016)

Santos felt that the side had passed a big test. Ronaldo accepted that he had to sacrifice himself for the team, not just by creating space for Nani, but also by defending set-pieces with grit and determination as well as occasionally pressing the centre-backs.

In private, his team-mates described how they felt he was now a real captain. Ronaldo spoke to Nani in confidence and admitted to him that he had faith in Santos and would follow his lead in whichever direction he deemed suitable. Hearing him speak in such a way after a disappointing opening game really boosted morale within the squad and it was an opinion also shared by Nani. 'We'd always chat. Sometimes we fight on the pitch, but we're very good friends. We tried to instil the youngsters with the confidence and ambition that we needed,' he explained.

Santos decided to bring the 4-3-3 formation back against Austria in search of a more potent attack with greater numbers. Quaresma was back in the side. Ronaldo would play just as he did for Real Madrid. It was a change of tactics that Santos felt was necessary to win that game.

Cristiano rightly had a header ruled out for offside and the Austria goalkeeper Robert Almer kept out one of his goal-bound missiles. Cristiano had eight goalscoring opportunities, but his pacey runs were not on display and he could not outsprint his opponents. His defensive work out wide also left plenty to be desired and he continued to take free-kicks (he had taken thirty-six in major competitions for the national team without scoring – the worst record in history) without enjoying success.

In the seventy-ninth minute, Portugal had the biggest chance of the game. Penalty. Ronaldo missed it on the day that he broke his country's record for international caps (128, one more than Figo) and appearances at the Euros (16), equalling Edwin van der Sar and Lilian Thuram.

Despite the draw and disappointing evening, he had no qualms about taking a selfie with a supporter who took to the pitch at the end of the match.

PORTUGAL V. HUNGARY
(EURO 2016 GROUP STAGE, 22 JUNE 2016)

Cristiano did not get a wink's sleep after failing from the penalty spot: 'I was one of the first to wake up and he was already up,' explained Fernando Santos. Criticism aimed at Ronaldo filled the international press. It read, 'His priority is strutting his stuff' in German newspaper *Bild*. In England, *The Sun* ridiculed his poses in team photos: 'Cristiano Ronaldo should spend more time practising penalties than poses.'

'The goals will come,' was the Portuguese press's stance regarding the player's failure to get on the scoresheet thus far.

'If we're awarded a penalty on Wednesday, Cristiano will take it and score,' stated Fernando Santos. 'Cristiano's greatest weapon is responding with goals in adversity.'

Santos admitted his tactical mistake and reverted to 4-4-2. He was not convinced by Moutinho's contribution and believed that Quaresma would have a bigger impact as a substitute than as a starter.

Cristiano's assist and brace saved the team against a plucky Hungary side in a frantic match brimming with action from the first minute until the last. Cristiano pulled it out of the bag in Portugal's worst performance of the tournament.

Renato Sanches was making a splash and needed to be accommodated in the team, coming on after the break, which required some tactful management by the coach. In a bygone era, Ronaldo would not have allowed an emerging star to eclipse him. On this occasion he dispelled any suggestions that he wasn't happy by speaking positively about the new Bayern Munich player.

Portugal had made it through to the next round without winning a game. And the 3–3 draw left them on the more favourable side of the draw, with Germany, Italy, France, England and Spain battling it out for a final berth in the other half.

Cristiano's goal against Hungary in the forty-ninth minute made him the first man to score at four European Championships (2004, 2008, 2012 and 2016) and also took him ahead of Zlatan Ibrahimović, who had scored in three tournaments.

■ ■ ■

A journalist from *Correio da Manhã* went up to Ronaldo the day after the Hungary game. Cristiano, without thinking twice, grabbed the microphone and threw it into a lake. The Portuguese media reported how the gesture was a consequence of the player's anger towards the national newspaper, which he had accused of defaming his private life for several years. A rumour was also doing the rounds after the match against Iceland that he had been rude to an Icelandic player who had asked for his shirt, which the opposition player himself denied.

Ronaldo, as always, was a profitable target for the sensationalist press.

PORTUGAL V. CROATIA
(EURO 2016 ROUND OF 16, 25 JUNE 2016)

The plan was crystal clear: sit deep, win the ball back and look to use the pace of Nani and Ronaldo, who were left isolated. But Portugal were not in control and defended their own penalty box for long periods. A frustrated Cristiano attempted to influence the tie but without success. Renato Sanches came on and brought renewed vigour to Portugal's game. It was a turgid affair with the first two efforts on target not coming until the 115th minute. The first was by Perišić, which was kept out by a combination of Rui Patrício and the crossbar. Then Ronaldo mustered up an effort at the other end, which goalkeeper Subašić only managed to parry with Quaresma on hand to tuck away the rebound. Goal. Portugal had won their first game at the Euros and secured a quarter-final place.

POLAND V. PORTUGAL
(EURO 2016 QUARTER-FINAL, 30 JUNE 2016)

New evidence confirmed that Cristiano was playing a less prominent role or at least was choosing his moments more carefully. He was less involved in press conferences but almost always made time for the fans who spent hours on end waiting for the Portuguese stars at the Marcoussis training camp. One day, with no press around, he grabbed a megaphone from a fan to say, 'We haven't won anything yet, keep calm.'

Ronaldo was in the thick of the action during the whole 120 minutes of the quarter-final. He was heavily involved in the game, completing forty out of forty-eight passes, and relentlessly endeavoured to find the back of the net, but his aim was off. Only one of his five attempts went on target, while one went wide and three were blocked. He lost the ball on fourteen occasions and created four goalscoring opportunities for his team-mates.

With the final score reading 1–1 (Poland having gone ahead through Lewandowski and Renato Sanches equalising), the tie would be decided on penalties.

Sanches explained: 'The coach asked us who wanted to take the first penalty. Ronaldo immediately said it would be him. He had missed one against Austria and hadn't scored as many goals as he would've wanted to, but he decided he would take the first one.'

Ronaldo scored his penalty.

Portugal were 4–3 up when Jakub Błaszczykowski spurned his effort and Ricardo Quaresma became the hero of the night.

Portugal were through to their fourth semi-final in the last five European Championships.

PORTUGAL V. WALES
(EURO 2016 SEMI-FINAL, 6 JULY 2016)

The press had a never-before-seen semi-final on their hands, which lent itself to an easy headline. Ronaldo against Gareth Bale. 'The two purebloods from the post-*galáctico* era,' as Manuel Jabois wrote in *El País*. Both sides were missing regular starters (Aaron Ramsey and Ben Davies for Wales, William Carvalho and Pepe for the Portugal), although Wales had a weaker squad on paper and so were hit harder by the absences.

Ronaldo struggled to get into the game, as the early stages were cagey. He headed an Adrien Silva cross over the bar just before the break in his only opening of the first half. The path for both sides was clear: Wales were waiting for a Portugal mistake or an individual moment of magic, while their opponents did battle with the same weapons, coupled with a stronger team game.

50th minute. Portugal take a short corner and Raphaël Guerreiro's cross requires an astonishing leap by Ronaldo, who powerfully heads the ball home. He had suspended himself in the air once again. He had reached a height nobody could fathom or compete with. Goal.

Cristiano had drawn level with Platini as the top goalscorer in Euros history with nine goals and improved his tally as the top goalscorer in the national team's history with sixty-one.

Wales boss Chris Coleman admitted later that moment was crucial. His team had taken their eye off the ball for five minutes and Portugal had punished them.

A few minutes after the opening goal, Ronaldo took a shot from outside the box which Nani steered home after getting away from Collins to make it 2–0.

Portugal kept performing with the same defensive doggedness that had been on display throughout the tournament and a team spirit that has rarely been seen in their history. 'We're a team, it's clear,' stated Ronaldo a few hours later. 'I've been doing all I can for the group, not just scoring goals, but also battling and digging in. We've got this far by being united.'

At the end of the game, with the final result 2–0, Cristiano went up to Gareth Bale to give him a hug and whisper some comforting words into his ear. 'I congratulated him on a great tournament,' explained Cristiano. 'They were a surprise package. They were the stars here, a real revelation.'

It became apparent after the tournament that Bale would soon renew his Real Madrid contract, meaning he would spend many more years alongside Ronaldo. Cristiano now understood that the Welshman was a key player who deserved great respect.

There was something else to it. The Portuguese player had won the battle. In the story that he imagines he is living, Cristiano needs supporting actors who recognise him as the winning star that he is.

Portugal's opponents in the Paris final would be hosts France.

The Euros serve as a demonstration of Ronaldo's development. He played as a winger when Portugal hosted the 2004 edition. He went on sixteen dribbles, one every twenty-six minutes throughout the competition. In France he only went on three, or one every 200 minutes.

In 2004 he had to do more defending, because there were other leaders in the side, such as Deco, Figo and Rui Costa. He won the ball back every nineteen minutes back then, compared with every forty in France.

In 2004 he provided an assist every 120 minutes from the left wing, whereas it was one every 300 in 2016 from his position as a false number nine.

His two-goal tally in 2004 went up to three in 2016.

He was the only player to have also played in the Lisbon final. It was time to exorcise the demons from that painful defeat by Greece. Winning the Euros would not only represent his first major success with his country but would also be an achievement that had escaped the grasp of many other national legends.

PORTUGAL V. FRANCE
(EURO 2016 FINAL, 10 JULY 2016)

Nani shed some light on what went down in the minutes prior to kick-off: 'Santos gave us a really good team talk. He was oozing confidence, as if he knew that we were going to win. "It's going to be a tough match, but when we got here we knew what we wanted, to reach the final, and we've done that. But we don't just want to have reached the final: we want to win it. We're going to win, however confident the French are – they seem to think it's already in the bag . . ." He instilled confidence in us. And a sense of calm.'

After the coach had said his piece, Nani yelled out: 'Come on! This match is ours for the taking! We have to run more, fight more and pull together!' Cristiano was in the zone and echoed Nani's words phrase for phrase. The pair had spoken beforehand, with Ronaldo reminding his former club-mate that it was their job to look after the younger lads and that there would be moments when the team would have to dig deep, when the two of them would have to roll up their sleeves and lead by example.

This is an excerpt from my notes from the European Championship final:

Ronaldo sings the national anthem with his eyes closed. In fact, he shouts it. His eyes are closed as if he wants to shut out the outside world for once. Just for that moment. It is his moment.

4 min: Long ball through to Nani, who blazes over the bar.

France have made the better start. Sissoko and Griezmann have both fired warning shots.

7 min: Ronaldo's knee is struck by Payet's after the latter goes steaming in.

9 min: France threaten after seizing on a loose ball. Griezmann's header forces a great save from Rui Patrício. Ronaldo clutches his knee while taking his place to defend the ensuing corner.

Ronaldo eventually collapses to the ground. He is in tears. He is injured and thinks he cannot continue.

20 min: Sissoko goes on a run and has a shot from outside the area.

21 min: Ronaldo is back on the pitch. He is running, but with a distinct limp.

He raises his hand to ask to be substituted. He rips off the armband and throws it to the turf.

He is on the ground again, crying. He is loaded on to a stretcher and carried off the pitch.

The crowd applaud him.

Our favourite villain leaves the stage. We do not want to see him like this. It leaves a bad taste in the mouth. A very bad one. It reminds us that no one is indestructible. Or immortal.

The stretcher disappears down the tunnel.

It was the most important game of his life.

His body has let him down.

And he has the world's sympathy.

■ ■ ■

'I was very sad,' recounted Nani. 'It was a very special moment for us, very emotional, we were all in it together, and when I saw him fall down and cry, tears welled up in my eyes too. I realised that he was going to miss the rest of the final, the most important one of his life. I was really gutted and I grabbed the armband quickly and tried to tell him that we were going to give our all to do him proud and show what the team was made of, that we were going to fight.'

The game went flat after Cristiano's injury. But after Quaresma was brought on in his place, the Portuguese midfield seemed to come more into their own. In fact, the impression was that after the blow of losing their leader, Portugal's morale recovered and they felt capable of anything if they stuck to the formula that had got them this far: hard work and playing as a team.

'We tried to lift each other's spirits by talking to one another and shouting things like, "Come on, let's do it, it's OK, we're going to win this, we've got quality too, come on!" And as time passed and France failed to score, we grew in confidence,' Nani said.

The players came face to face with Ronaldo at half-time. 'Yes, he was looking at his knee and was disconsolate,' Nani recalled. Cristiano had cried his eyes out, but he pulled himself together in order to rally the troops. 'Lads, we're going to win 2–0. Stick together and fight to the end,' he told them.

Chances were at a premium thereafter, although France did up their game again and looked the likelier to win it. Then, with eleven minutes to go, Lille striker Éder was introduced, with Renato Sanches – rather than Nani, who was left on the pitch – making way. It was an attacking change and it slowly but surely helped Portugal even things up once more. That said, France's André-Pierre Gignac almost snatched a winner, hitting the post in stoppage time. That was the last notable action of the ninety minutes.

Before extra-time kicked off, a limping Cristiano took to the turf again, doing the rounds and geeing up all the Portugal players. He gave a particularly warm hug to Quaresma, a kindred spirit who had similarly spent many years striving to win the affections of the Portuguese people, although they had fallen somewhat out of touch. He whispered something into his ear.

Fear and the pressure seemed to get to France during extra-time, and they took a step backwards. Those tension-filled thirty minutes also witnessed the most extraordinary of scenes: the Ronaldo show, as many media outlets dubbed it the following day.

Cristiano barked out instructions from the dugout. He shouted at everyone to track back when they lost the ball, urged the centre-backs to go up for a corner and put his hands to his face when Éder went close with a header.

In the second half of extra-time, Raphaël Guerreiro hit the bar with a free-kick. And then, in the 109th minute, Éder – of all people – smashed home a fierce right-footed strike from outside the box. Football was proving Fernando Santos right: Portugal had just gone ahead.

After the final whistle, Éder revealed that Ronaldo had predicted to him that he would be the man of the moment: 'He told me that

I'd be the one to score the winner. He passed on that strength and energy that he has.'

Ronaldo, who had been standing in the technical area, celebrated the goal by shouting up at the sky while gripping his face, before walking to the left along the touchline, away from everyone. Next he turned around and slowly made his way towards the rest of the squad, who were enfolded in a group hug on the pitch. Seeking to connect with his team-mates, albeit briefly, he gave one of them a pat, before walking away alone again.

Once the action had resumed, Ronaldo took up a position behind Fernando Santos in the technical area. Initially he was tentative, seemingly aware that he was invading the coach's space, wanting to be there but knowing he shouldn't be. At one point, Santos threw up his arms and Ronaldo followed suit. After that, the player continued to 'coach' the team, with Santos ignoring him.

'During the match I looked over to the dugout and thought, "What's Ronaldo doing over there?" admitted Nani, 'But then I refocused on the game.'

Cristiano repeatedly told his team-mates not to bring the ball out from defence hastily. He rebuked the forwards for not defending. He called on the fans to get behind the team. He advised Nani to hold the ball up, spread play and keep possession. 'Don't gamble, pass it around and play it backwards!' he shouted at Nani and Éder.

The English fourth official politely asked him to return to the dugout. Ronaldo gave a little hop, like a child, indicating that he would obey. But, as we know, he has a complicated relationship with rules and this would be shown again soon enough.

Perhaps he thinks he is above the laws of the game, despite respecting and needing them just like all lovers of the sport. Without rules, it would be chaos. At the same time, he aspires to be respected as the greatest player in history, and he must feel he is so great that the rules don't apply to him.

Either way, he didn't stay seated for long. He soon got to his feet again, and he even encroached into France's technical area. A couple of minutes later, with Ronaldo again shadowing Santos, the two of them right up alongside the touchline, the fourth official told the Portuguese players to sit down. All except for Ronaldo.

Histrionic as they were, his antics seemed genuine, but they were nevertheless out of place and excessive. At one stage he put his arms around Santos, shook him and jumped up and down as if doing a pogo dance at a punk concert.

The match came to an end. Portugal had won the European Championship.

Ronaldo celebrated the moment of victory alone. Turning towards the crowd (his audience) with a skip, his arms aloft, he looked up and shouted. A member of the coaching staff hugged him, but he did not reciprocate. Then he dropped dramatically to the ground, his sidekick still hanging on to him, and lay there spreadeagled, well aware of where the cameras were pointing.

They say happiness is only real when it's shared, and if you're Ronaldo, you can share it with the whole world.

■ ■ ■

Nani: 'I only saw all of Ronaldo's shenanigans in the dugout after the match, when we were in the dressing room laughing together. We were happy and we watched the videos. He had them on his phone and showed them to me. We laughed. He said to me, "Look, look at what I did . . ."'

The sports psychologist Bill Beswick told me that at the beginning of their careers footballers fear the cameras, but once they become better players they develop a love affair with this object that embraces them, indulges them and showcases the good things that they do. And once they are stars, they get addicted to them.

It is clear that Ronaldo's upbringing and personal development, as well as his transformation into a footballing icon, have shaped an unusual, extraordinary way of being. But it is this that has enabled him to deal with the situation in which he has found himself. Everything around him (his lifestyle, friends, employees) exists to support this personality. Now put that person in a European Championship final. On the big stage. And consider what happens when his body's limitations flare up again. His reaction, logically, would have been to think about the L-word, his legacy. Perhaps not consciously, but Ronaldo must have felt that, with the spotlight shining, the action ongoing and his whole country watching on with their hopes pinned on the result, he had to do something special.

Footballers create a mental script before games. This is a sort of story detailing how the match might play out. Ronaldo would have visualised himself having a starring role. When he got injured, he wanted to continue feeling important and so decided to help the team from outside the pitch. He believed he could have an influence from the fringes, and that's why he stood just a metre from the touchline. And performed those highly theatrical gestures.

It was his moment, but it was snatched away from him on the pitch. So he did what he felt was necessary off it.

Ronaldo couldn't imagine the team winning without him.

The way he shook Santos (who all the while looked at the ground or watched the play) suggested that he did not see him as a superior. He was just the one who named the team, guided them towards the trophy and asked Cristiano to sacrifice himself. Which he did. But none of that meant that Santos outranked him.

Interestingly, when Ronaldo affectionately shoved the coach, he did not push him towards the action, but rather in the opposite direction. As if he wanted to remove him from the stage, as if Santos were stealing his limelight.

If it were a father-son relationship, that interplay, that gesture of self-assertion, might have rung truer. But they do not treat one another like father and son, so the impression was that Ronaldo was seeking to supplant the coach or, like I said before, to get him away from the stage.

Ronaldo has had some father figures, but he has also had a dearth of what psychologists call 'significant others', influential people on whom to model himself. If he had had such a guiding influence, he would have had a voice inside him telling him: 'Take it easy, you're a member of a team.' But what surrounds him is quite the opposite: his entourage need him perhaps even more than he needs them – they do not question him. For these reasons, Cristiano does not see his coach as a 'significant other' or a disciplinary presence. He cooperates with him so long as it goes well for him and suits him. But in the final, my friend . . . centre stage is reserved for Ronaldo.

This reading may seem obvious, but I've canvassed several other coaches about these events. They all agree that Ronaldo crossed the line, and in the process showed that deep down he doesn't believe that all that much separates him and his managers.

Santos ignored Cristiano. But when other players approached the coach, he pushed and shooed them away. He had enough on his hands as it was. It was one rule for Ronaldo, another for the rest.

And Ronaldo celebrated the goal on his own. The victory, too. It was as if he were saying: 'I did it even though I'm not on the pitch.'

■ ■ ■

'This is the greatest moment of my career,' Ronaldo said at the end of the game. He admitted to having cried a lot. 'Tears of anger at the injury and then joy at the triumph. It isn't the final I wanted, but I'm really happy. This trophy goes out to all the Portuguese people, all the diaspora, everyone who believed in us.'

That same night, the Real Madrid president called him to congratulate him. According to *El Confidencial*, Cristiano appreciated the gesture and took advantage of the occasion to remind Florentino of what he had told him before the Euros got underway: 'I want to retire at Real Madrid.'

As narratives are so often driven by results, it was repeatedly stated in Portugal that the team had benefited from Ronaldo's passion and leadership. But not everyone shared this view. Portuguese football legend António Simões criticised his behaviour. So did José Mourinho: 'Ronaldo lost a little emotional control. He didn't do any harm, but I don't think he helped in any way by doing that in the final few minutes of a European Championship final. It was the eleven players on the pitch who did the job, and it was the coach who led the team. I'd like to think it was just an overflow of emotion from someone who saw that there were just minutes to go to achieve an objective that everyone wanted.'

A few weeks after the final, Santos spoke out in Ronaldo's defence: 'Since I had so many instructions to give, I turned to him, just like I turned to my assistants, to tell [Ricardo] Quaresma to close down the space around Raphaël Guerreiro.' The coach claimed that he never felt his authority had been 'undermined' because Cristiano was never guilty of trying to usurp him as the manager, he had simply 'externalised' his nerves in his own way.

Talk about a gracious explanation.

■ ■ ■

And so the curtain closed on Ronaldo's most successful season, albeit not in terms of his individual statistics. The history books will show a photo of Ronaldo after his penalty in the shoot-out against Atlético de Madrid, and another of him issuing orders on the touchline in Paris, capping what had been 'Cristiano's Euros conquest'. Two iconic images that do not tell the story of the finals, but which help to perpetuate the Ronaldo image.

As well as this European Championship, Ronaldo has three Champions Leagues, two Club World Cups, two UEFA Super Cups, a La Liga title, two Copas del Rey, a Spanish Super Cup, three Premier Leagues, an FA Cup, two Community Shields and two League Cups to his name, as well as countless individual accolades, headed by his three Ballons d'Or. That number was surely set to rise to four after the victory in France. In August 2016 he picked up the UEFA Best Player in Europe Award ahead of Gareth Bale and Antoine Griezmann.

The injury sustained in the final, a sprain to the medial collateral ligament in his left knee, prevented him from kicking off the season with Real Madrid. Zinedine Zidane told him not to rush things and to make a proper recovery – and on his return to action, against Osasuna in the third game of the season, he scored and afterwards had a go at Barcelona's Xavi for suggesting Messi was a better player. The limelight had returned to him.

Since the club dared not build the team around Gareth Bale, it seemed as though it could be the start of a new chapter in the Portuguese's career: the coach ensuring he got plenty of rest during the season so that he didn't end it the way he had the previous three. Against Osasuna, Ronaldo only played 65 minutes. Only a fellow icon could get away with mooting a change of status like that. Only a superhero can speak with another on equal footing.

This brings to mind his reaction the last time we saw each other. He told me that I had betrayed him. I understand him feeling frustrated, disappointed even. But I believe there was something else behind it: talented athletes from difficult family environments turn that talent into their identity. When they become global icons, attaining universality, they struggle with being treated like a normal human being. Ronaldo needs constant reminders of why he is special, not why he isn't.

But one day he will cease being a big star. He is drawing ever nearer to a stage of his life in which his talent will no longer weigh so heavily. And without the necessary support, he could crash down to earth – or at least fail to adapt to his new circumstances. That said, I am convinced that if that happens, he will emerge from that crisis with a new identity, and victorious. As always.

■ ■ ■

All in good time. For now, he keeps going about his daily business: after dropping his son off at school, he trains for three or four hours, has lunch with his mother, and then picks him up and they have a nap together. On waking up, he does some more exercise, sometimes in the garden or with Cristiano Jr, as in a video he posted of them doing sit-ups together.

In this clip, we see Cristiano showing his son how to do a proper sit-up and counting up to ten, which is the goal set for the child, offering encouragement as he does so. When the boy finishes, his father takes him in his arms and lets out a whoop of joy.

Apparently Cristiano Jr can already strike the ball pretty well with both feet.

I do not think that Ronaldo wants his son to be another CR7. Rather, it seems that he wants to replicate what Dinis did with him: sharing training, a love of football. This is perhaps one of the few memories of his father that he feels he can recreate.

Or at least that is what I think that Cristiano thinks.

At the end of the day, as Harriet Burden says in Siri Hustvedt's wonderful novel *The Blazing World*, 'The path to the truth is doubled, masked, ironic. This is my path, not straight, but twisted!'

ELEVEN

THE NEXT STEP, A NEW CONQUEST

Cristiano Ronaldo's dedication and willingness to train harder, longer, faster than just about anyone else on this planet have never been in doubt. It was always part of his plan, a non-negotiable road he had to take if he wanted to guarantee, to himself at least, the confirmation of his status as the greatest player in the world – which was what he always aspired to be.

But, in the words of the Indian philosopher Chanakya, 'Time perfects men as well as destroying them.' We have already witnessed in Ronaldo the first part of the statement. Two years on from the win in the European Championships against the local hosts France, the inevitable second part that is beginning to unfurl in front of us could have been less pleasing to the eye. The curve of his performance levels had started to suffer a slight inclination downwards, while still winning a fourth and a fifth Ballon d'Or and showing bursts of quality at the right time which kept him rightly at the top. Four-fifths of his goals come from one touch after the right run was picked by one of his teammates, his new main asset. But in the last couple of seasons he has taken a while to take off. His quality will make him a relevant actor for years to come, but how

Cristiano deals with the inevitable ageing of his body is what will define his future.

Without warning, his appearance for only twenty-five minutes in the final of the 2016 Euros was the start of a new era. In August, he had been voted UEFA's Best Player in Europe for the second time, but he missed the first three games of the season, including Real Madrid's 2–0 win at Espanyol which secured a club-record sixteenth consecutive victory, as he was given time by Zinedine Zidane to recover from the injury he suffered in France. He returned in September to score after just six minutes against Osasuna in a game that would finish in a 5–2 win. More interestingly, he was subbed for Benzema after sixty-six minutes. It would be the start of him being used more tactically and rotated, in order that he might stay fitter, fresher and less prone to injury. The following month he added another hat-trick to his collection against Alaves, meaning he had now scored against all thirty-one teams he had faced in La Liga. When he found the net against Sporting Gijon he became the first player to score more than thirty La Liga goals in a calendar year for seven consecutive years. In doing so he also became the first player ever to score more than fifty goals for club and country in six consecutive calendar years. Stats of a legend. Of a football god.

Despite his very public flirting with PSG and Manchester United, a new contract was signed up to the end of 2021 and then came the icing on the cake – his fourth Ballon d'Or, yet another individual award for his rapidly filling museum in Madeira. He told the French newspaper *L'Equipe*: 'I know, for posterity, what a fifth Ballon d'Or would represent. It would be an achievement and something I have been working for, for the past fifteen years. Nothing happens by accident.'

There were more individual trophies in a year that seemed impossible to beat: in January 2017 he was voted FIFA's Player of the Year for 2016 by a selection of the captains and head coaches of

FIFA's 209 federations, journalists representing each of them and users of the FIFA website. By then Real Madrid had extended their unbeaten run to a Spanish record of forty matches, following a 3–3 draw against Sevilla in the Copa del Rey.

In *Diario AS* I dared to suggest, after he had scored one goal and assisted another in a match against Real Sociedad, that, more often than not, Ronaldo relied primarily on his own game, only looking for the help and assistance of his teammates when the explosiveness that had served him so well in the past was not there, and all avenues to personal success had been closed to him. It was apparent that here was a player going through a phase of reinvention. For mere mortals, for just about any other player, one goal and one assist would be enough. But not for him, I suggested, because I did not think he was ready to embody the role of occasional goal scorer, at the mercy of his teammates, dependent upon a good performance by the team. He was not ready to see himself as only a nine.

But the transition was taking place. He was far and away Real Madrid's best player when they suffered only their second league defeat of the season at Valencia. At the same time, internationally and on the European stage, he continued to confound his critics. A seventieth international goal against Hungary in a World Cup qualifier (at the time of writing Ronaldo's total stands at eighty-five, which is thirty-eight goals more than Pauleta, the next highest) was followed by hat-tricks in the Champions League, first against Bayern Munich and then against Atletico Madrid in the semi-finals, which made him the first player to score back-to-back hat-tricks and also more than 100 goals in the competition. The way Zidane managed Ronaldo's energy and impatience was working – a slow start was turned into a strong end to the campaign.

A little while earlier Ronaldo had been treated to the sight of his 'likeness' – and I use the word in the loosest sense – in the shape of a statue unveiled in his honour at Madeira Airport in Funchal. Even a cursory glance confirmed that this was surely not a commission that the player himself sat for, although because of its uncanny resemblance to another footballer, questions were certainly asked about the whereabouts of Niall Quinn during the piece's manufacture. Months later, the bronze face was replaced.

And then, another month, another record when his strike against Celta Vigo meant he became the all-time leading goal scorer in the top five European leagues with 368 goals, beating Englishman Jimmy Greaves' forty-six-year record, before rounding the league season off with a goal and the necessary victory that guaranteed that the La Liga title would be making its way back to the Santiago Bernabéu stadium for the first time since 2012.

These were truly the good times and things were just about to get a whole lot better when he scored twice in Cardiff's Millennium Stadium as Real Madrid became the first-ever team to retain the Champions League since it moved into its latest format. In the victory against Juventus he became the tournament's top goal scorer for the fifth straight season, and sixth overall, with twelve goals, while also becoming the first person to score in three finals in the Champions League era, as well as notching his 600th senior-career goal.

What on earth could go wrong?

■ ■ ■

As we have found out, Ronaldo's hunger and motivation come from a desire and determination to be the very best, and a psychological toughness that is difficult to fathom, but probably has its roots in the hard, lonely road that he trod on his way to the very top. Furthermore, he is never entirely happy with the success he has achieved. You can never have enough. But who prepares those players who have lived at the top for so long to accept their limits?

We live in a different world today. Players have more therapists, counsellors, advisers, assistants, coaches and trainers than you could shake a stick at. But when you run more than most, score more than most, win more than most, the real world just seems a game played in a small pitch away from the big one that sends you home with yet another ovation. Ronaldo is, probably mentally, and certainly financially, better prepared to deal with the pressures that will come with facing the end of the road than perhaps Gerd Muller and Jimmy Greaves were, but only time will tell us how they will cope with retirement when it comes along. Recently we have been able to gather some clues that paint some kind of picture of how Ronaldo is dealing with the transformation he is going through and that it has to do with boundaries, with physical limitations. And his innate need to overcome them.

Fans of the Portuguese megastar seemed to be hurt by the suggestion that he had declined physically. Nobody wanted to hear that and anybody suggesting it would be abused on social networks. Gods do not grow old. The chronic knee injury – and I use the word 'chronic' in its literal meaning, which describes an illness or medical condition characterised by long duration or frequent recurrence – and entering his thirty-second year in February 2017 meant that he no longer had the blistering pace that would regularly destroy defences. And he knew it.

Nobody – certainly not me – said he would stop scoring and, in fact, it was the nature of the injury that compelled him to reinvent himself as an out-and-out striker and brought him in from the flanks. He lost some of his speed, his electric bursts of pace, and replaced them with even more of what he already had in abundance – namely, a voracious hunger, an unceasing desire to be the best, and the competitiveness and dedication required for his new role. He was determined to be the greatest striker in the world.

In the process he had to admit that to become the greatest striker in the world – and in my eyes he has to be considered the best ever – he had to strive to change his body shape to make him even more lethal in and around the penalty area. At the start of the 2017–18 season, he was around three kilos lighter, had less muscle development on his top half but had increased the muscle power and strength in his legs in his transformation to becoming purely a striker. During the season that had just finished, he had for the first time realised that, as the sands of time begin to run out, then sometimes less is more. Consequently he was far more prepared to be rotated and/or occasionally substituted by Zidane, whom he clearly trusted implicitly.

The 2017–18 season began so well. The league and Champions League would not be the only double celebrated by Ronaldo in 2017; there was also the birth of the surrogate twins Eva and Mateo on 8 June. And then the taxman came calling. It was alleged that from 2011 to 2014 he had defrauded the Spanish treasury of €14.7 million in taxes by concealing income from the sale of image rights with the help of a financial structure that diverted money to a tax haven in the British Virgin Islands, via Ireland.

Cristiano's *modus operandi* both on and off the pitch, literally and metaphorically, has always favoured attack much more than defence. No surprise, then, that when facing the judge Monica Gomez Ferrer in July 2017, he was quick to play the victim card: 'It's because of who I am.' The judge did not hold back in tackling the accusation head on. She was not about to be sold this particular dummy. 'You are mistaken,' she countered. 'Plenty of anonymous people have sat where you are. You are under investigation for an alleged financial crime based on the evidence provided and upon which it is my duty to make a ruling.'

Ronaldo's response was predictable and sparked a succession of rumours and claims that would bounce around the English media and in particular the corridors at Old Trafford. Ronaldo told the judge: 'I never had a problem in England . . . that's why I would like to go back to England.'

The problems with that journey back were, of course, numerous. Firstly, there was the small matter of the contract extension that Ronaldo had signed in November 2016 and that would run through to 2021. Real Madrid's president, Florentino Perez, insisted that the club would not sell Cristiano Ronaldo for 'his weight in gold', by which he probably meant that if he were to leave the club, it would be when they said so, not when the player decided. Ronaldo, for all his greatness and for all his reputation, was not a Perez signing, and that was never forgotten by the president. Or by Cristiano.

Unlike Barcelona's handling of Lionel Messi's and Neymar's earlier tax cases, there was a suggestion that Ronaldo felt he did not receive the same support from Real Madrid, that the club was not willing to pay for his or his advisers' mistakes. It was also significant that there was a €1 billion buy-out clause in the contract, which meant the club would always have the last say. What followed during the new 2017–18 season was talk, talk and even more talk – nearly all of it coming from Ronaldo's camp.

There was talk, for instance, about the Florentino promise of a new contract just after the last Champions League win which would require a signing-on fee of about €30 million – which, 'coincidentally', many thought was the sort of figure required to keep those nasty taxmen from the Spanish treasury at bay. Unofficial figures of the new wage agreements for Messi and Neymar, now at PSG, which made Cristiano the third-best-paid player in the world, were made public: the Argentinian was 'allegedly' going to earn double the €23 million net per season that Cristiano signed for in November 2016. Ronaldo moved from being unhappy and wanting to go back to Old Trafford with a conveniently timed article in the

Portuguese newspaper *A Bola* during the summer of 2017, to being happy and not wanting anything else from Real Madrid, with the intention of keeping the talk of a new deal alive. But the club, aware that Ronaldo had no substantial offers to leave, was not in any rush to give him his wish. If a swap deal between Ronaldo and Neymar was at all possible, then Florentino would let the Portuguese go. PSG kept insisting that this was just a Perez dream.

This was not a Real Madrid ready in any way, shape or form to surrender to demands from either the player or the team he had around him. As early as 17 June 2017 an article in *Republica* that mentioned Florentino Perez, but stopped short of quoting him directly, effectively told Ronaldo and co. that any attempt to get more money out of the club by threatening to leave would be perceived by them as 'blackmail'. The article continued:

Real Madrid will not pay a single euro for any possible sanctions that might be imposed on Cristiano by the treasury. We would urge him to reconsider his position and continue with the club. If he wishes to force the situation, the club do not discount the possibility of his departure, but not at any price.

Florentino considers that the words of Cristiano and his team stating that he wishes to leave the club are tactical, orchestrated by Jorge Mendes . . . Consequently his words have been received by Madrid as a 'blackmail' containing the message 'Pay me, or I leave.'

The article concluded, however, by stating that the club retained their 'complete confidence' in the player, were fully behind him and were 'absolutely convinced' of his innocence of all charges. Madrid were asking for truce. On the field, in the summer of 2017, things were about to get worse.

Where to begin with what happened with Cristiano Ronaldo in three short minutes in the Spanish Super Cup in one of the most famous stadiums in the world (Camp Nou) in a match featuring two of the most-watched sides in the world (Barcelona and Real Madrid)?

It was a cameo appearance that began in the fifty-eighth minute, when Ronaldo was brought off the bench. Those three minutes effectively encapsulate the massive contradiction that is Cristiano Ronaldo; three minutes that fuel just about everyone's conception – and misconception – of the Portuguese.

The start was all good news for the team in white. Real Madrid looked a class above their Catalan opponents, and in the eightieth minute, on one of the biggest of football stages, Ronaldo scored a typically brilliant goal, cutting inside and curling home an unstoppable effort from the edge of the box. Off came the shirt to expose to all and sundry the muscular and immaculately toned 'six-pack'. While many might have been impressed, the referee, Ricardo de Burgos Bengoetxea, who promptly produced a yellow card, was not one of them. Just two minutes later Ronaldo went tumbling in the Barcelona box following a tackle from Samuel Umtiti, and his claims for a penalty were answered by the referee with a second yellow card, this time for diving. In the cut-and-thrust, intense, passionate world that is top-level football anything is possible, but rarely do we see footballers dismissed for two such actions. Once he'd been shown the red card, damage limitation was perhaps the order of the day. It was never going to happen. What followed was a push on the referee – admittedly, only the gentlest of touches, but certainly enough to guarantee that Cristiano Ronaldo had in three mad minutes 'cameoed' himself into a whole heap of trouble.

Brilliance, trickery, petulance and childish behaviour were the four trademark characteristics of the man from Madeira witnessed by a disbelieving world. The overriding memory of the match should have been what happened minutes later. Marco Asensio effectively killed the tie with a sensational late strike, a goal of true quality from an up-and-coming player, and it was that moment of magic that deserved to grab all the headlines. In the end it became a mere footnote to those three minutes of insanity that guaranteed once again, for better or worse, the only thing that would dominate the sports pages would be the exploits of CR7.

What followed was a five-match ban – one for the red card and four for the push on the referee. Thankfully, for both Ronaldo and Real Madrid, the ban would only apply to domestic games and not European matches. The reaction from the player was predictable. His cries of 'exaggerated and ridiculous' fell on deaf ears.

He described his 'fall' in the penalty area as 'an uncontrollable reflex'. 'Five games,' he added. 'I think it's over the top and ridiculous. This is what is called persecution.' Once again you sensed echoes of his tirade against the judge in his tax-related court case. Punished not for what he did, but for who he was. Once again he was severely mistaken. The judgement of the disciplinary committee, in accordance with Article 96 of their rulebook, imposed exactly the same punishment as had been handed out the previous season to former Las Palmas striker, Marko Livaja, and to Diego Simeone in 2014, the two most recent similar incidents. No more, no less. No one has ever doubted that Ronaldo is a special player, but the assertion that he received special treatment over this latest matter was incorrect.

He would miss the second leg of the Spanish Super Cup, and league matches against Deportivo, Valencia, Levante and Real Sociedad. Another way to look at it was that he was going to have the opportunity, just like the previous campaign, to rest during the start of it, when nobody wins or loses titles. So it was to be a blessing in disguise for all concerned. It also meant that he would be fresher for all of the upcoming Champions League games. The Spanish FA's five-match ban effectively meant Zidane would now not have to agonise about whether or not to play, or leave on the bench, or substitute Cristiano.

But as they say, cometh the hour, cometh the man, and once again, keener than ever to prove that rumours of his demise had been well and truly exaggerated, he bounced back on the European stage. His two goals in the home leg of Real's group match against Apoel helped them to a 3–0 win, and then a further brace against Borussia Dortmund in the Germans' back yard was yet another message to his critics – he seemed to delight in attempting to prove them wrong on a regular basis. 'I have to keep showing exactly who I am in every match,' he told the media after the game. Was he dealing with an invisible enemy? It is difficult to find anybody who suggested he was finished. But, not one to cope well with criticisms, he viewed as a personal affront any suggestion that he was not the player he once was.

Was he sending a message to those noisy but few fans who have whistled at him a couple of times at the Bernabéu? Or was he perhaps again directing his comments more specifically to the club itself? Was he using his success in Europe as a way of telling them, 'Look at me, this is what I can do, this is what I am capable of. Pay me accordingly.'

In the flash interview just after scoring the two goals in the away Dortmund win, and probably conscious of the fact that, at some time in the not-too-distant future, he was going to have to write out a huge cheque to the Spanish treasury, Ronaldo (who had been quiet for months in protest against the media's perception of him) hinted again that Real Madrid should perhaps take another look at his contract. When asked if he was about to renew it less than a year after his last improvement, he answered: 'That is a question the president might be able to answer better than me.' Florentino Perez said nothing.

■ ■ ■

Many, including FIFA itself, had no doubts about his value, and in October 2017 he was voted FIFA Player of the Year for the second year running, beating off the challenges of Messi and Neymar in the process. From the hallowed portals of the London Palladium, famous for being the venue for the comeback tours of the likes of Frank Sinatra, football's own comeback king – bar none – accepted the award along with his coach, Zinedine Zidane, who won the Coach of the Year award. José Feliz Diaz from *Marca* celebrated it:

King Cristiano. There is no doubt. Not at least as far as FIFA are concerned, who proclaimed him the best in the world for the second year running, ahead of Leo Messi and the rest. The London Palladium was lit up in the white of Madrid by The Best that is the Real Madrid forward. The Portuguese has been crowned as the most valuable player in the world as a result of his performances for Madrid in the past five Champions League games where he scored ten goals and helped his side to retain the title, the first time a club has achieved this in the twenty-six years of the competition . . .

The competition with Messi continues and with the Best award, the Portuguese shows that he leads the way.

More was to follow. On 7 December Cristiano Ronaldo arrived in Paris – at the foot of the Eiffel Tower, to be precise – to receive a fifth Ballon d'Or, thus equalling Lionel Messi's record. Sid Lowe in *The Guardian* summed it up perfectly when writing about the night:

> Only Lionel Messi has as many. Or should that read: only Ronaldo has as many as Messi? To some of their supporters, the order matters more than it should. The fact that parity has been reached certainly does and it feeds a debate as furious as it is often tedious yet wonderful at heart. Between them, Ronaldo and Messi, Messi and Ronaldo, have not let anyone else win this award for a decade now. This is their era: they have won seven of the past ten European Cups between them, and been the competition's top scorer for each and every one of those seasons, and the Ballon d'Or reflects that. In part it is reduced to that, yet it also goes beyond . . .
>
> At times their dominance can feel like it is partly a product of the grand narrative built around them, the rivalry itself, sometimes forced. There's an equality that may be a little false too and there is the tyranny of numbers which is sometimes a substitute for actual appreciation, but a seductive one. Voting for them can also feel like the default setting, just what you do. And while some rebel, there may be a lack of imagination. But it is also a reality, a result of the relentlessness of their talent and performance.

Sid Lowe's astute and measured analysis summed up what we all knew, although for someone like Cristiano it would have had the feel of something perhaps a little too even-handed. But the two elephants in the room, the real thorns in his side, were that the two people he had beaten to the title (Messi and Neymar) were precisely the people who were earning more money than he was. As he saw it – still does, probably – he was the best player in the world and he was receiving the short end of the stick. It wasn't about money.

At least not money *per se*, because it would be difficult for anyone to actually physically spend the amount of money being paid to Ronaldo for his activities both on and off the pitch. Once again, it was all about respect, being loved.

In an article in *El País* after Ronaldo had been presented with the award, David Álvarez also hit the nail on the head:

> In 2013, weeks before Messi received his fourth Ballon d'Or, Zlatan Ibrahimovic visited the Camp Nou with PSG, and there branded as finished Cristiano Ronaldo's quest for another win of the trophy. 'The Ballon d'Or should be renamed the Messi because he is going to win many more. The only rival he has is himself.'
>
> With it 4–1 in favour of the Argentinian, that was in effect what the whole world was thinking. Except Cristiano, that is, who yesterday made it 5–5. The way the Portuguese has conducted his career has produced two different and diverse opinions – those who love him, those who hate him. Cristiano is continually on the comeback trail.

The following day, in an interview for the magazine *France Football*, he articulated his feelings about just where he saw himself in terms of his footballing achievements. It was not his humblest hour. With just the slightest tinge of false modesty, he said, '[I] respect everyone's preferences,' before getting back on track with, 'but I don't see anyone out there better than me.' He went on:

> No footballer can do anything that I can't do, but I see that I do things that others cannot. No player is more complete than me. I am the best player in history, in both the good and the bad times. I am now part of the history of football, and not just by winning this Ballon d'Or. And I became part of it by winning

one, then two, then three, four and five... and now it is normal that I should get my place in history as the player who has won the most. I am very happy, this is a very special moment for me.

I picture Cristiano laughing, listening to himself, and seeing how seriously he was saying all those things. There is truth and also cheekiness in many of the things he says. But certainly, as sports writer Alfredo Relaño wrote, 'There is one guy chosen by God and another one that argues that choice.'

What Ronaldo went on to say next rang more true:

I never believed that I could ever catch Messi, because after I won my first Ballon d'Or he went on to win four. But football gives you the opportunity to carry on working and winning and I have lived through a marvellous period. Yesterday I broke the record when I became the first player to score in all the games in the group phase of the Champions League – what does that tell you? One of the words I hear most often in my daily life is 'bravo'.

When you hear 'bravo' it is a sign that you are doing things properly, not just in sport, but also in life,' he concluded. Those who want to find what they are made of and where their limits are should forget the make-believe character and frame these words instead.

■ ■ ■

Real Madrid, after winning the Club World Cup in UAE, started the new year as they had ended the old – badly – getting a 2–2 draw at Celta Vigo before somehow managing to lose 1–0 at home to Villarreal. Not even a 7–1 home demolition of Deportivo was enough to lift the mood of Ronaldo, who couldn't really be bothered to celebrate, even after he had scored twice. Then Leganes beat Real Madrid for the first time in their history – and in the Bernabéu, at that – to knock them out of the Copa del Rey. Not unnaturally, noises surrounding the future of Zinedine Zidane grew louder by the hour.

The mood was not good and was not helped by further declarations, albeit from Ronaldo's entourage rather than the player himself, that he wanted to move to Manchester United. In *Diario AS* Manu Sainz wrote that the player felt deceived by what he regarded as broken promises relating to the renewal of his contract. Cristiano had scored twice in Cardiff against Juventus in the match that earned the club its twelfth Champions League/European Cup triumph, after which, according to Cristiano's advisers, Florentino Perez promised to improve his contract.

After winning his fifth Ballon d'Or he announced that his desire was to remain at Madrid, adding cryptically, 'If that is possible.' His wish, he said, was to retire at Madrid, but 'It doesn't depend on me, I'm not the one in charge at the club.' And the wheel kept going round. If it wasn't bad enough that his protestations had been met with a deafening silence, to add insult to injury Real had tried to sign Monaco's Mbappé in the summer, and after the Ballon d'Or ceremony Florentino was brave enough to announce that 'Neymar would have more chances to win individual trophies at Madrid.' Heretical words in the Ronaldo world. Certainly, it was very strange timing to mention the Brazilian at such an event. They will never be forgotten by Cristiano.

Spanish journalists close to his circle wrote that apparently Ronaldo had already told various colleagues that he would be leaving in the summer and his preferred destination would be the club he had left to join Real Madrid. Manchester United, it was said, knew of his desire to re-sign for them. But, as José Mourinho would confirm a few weeks later, they were not after the player – the finances involved were too big for someone who would turn thirty-three in February 2018. Real Madrid were planning to demand around €100m transfer fee and he would want a salary of around €50m net a year.

Zidane had won eight of the ten titles he had fought for, but with the league all but lost by January 2018 in a terrible season for a Real Madrid who seemed tired of winning, the last sixteen fixture against PSG, having scored only six goals in the league half way through the season, was another opportunity to rise up from the 'dead', a fierce challenge that Christiano enjoys confronting and a source of motivation.

■ ■ ■

Some time ago, his sister Katia Aveiro launched a defence of her brother on social media. This could have been posted at any time in the last five years. It reads like the script Cristiano and his family have adhered to, the movie they have created and they live in, the one they believe describes their world.

> I just want to say this to you, Cristiano. When you arrived in Lisbon aged just twelve, filled with hopes and fears, they said you were nothing more than a kid from Madeira. Less than five years later you were playing in Sporting's first team. When you were playing your first five games against the big teams they said you were just a 'skilful tart'. A few months later you had signed for Manchester United. When you arrived in England they said you were just a prospect. In six seasons you scored 118 goals. When Madrid signed you, they said you were merely someone to sell replica shirts. Since 2009 you have scored 422 goals in 418 games and have broken just about every single club record. When you

won your first Ballon d'Or in 2008, they said that would be the only one you would ever win. Since then you have won four more. When you were made captain of Portugal they said you were a captain without charisma, without the spirit of leadership. In 2016 you became the first Portuguese footballer to lift the European trophy. Now, because you have not carried on scoring like an extraterrestrial for two or three games, they are saying that you are no more than a player at the end of his career, almost finished, on his last legs, on the downward slope. Don't worry. When you smile while holding a trophy in your hand, or when you score a decisive goal, or when you break another record, they are going to look at you very closely. And then of course they will clap. Fools, ingrates!!! It's the only thing left to them.

And what would happen when there was no more of that? What would Katia say to him? Why was there a need to constantly show his CV, his records? Why, in fact, did Katia just talk about his football when she spoke about her brother? Where was the brother in Katia's mind? Was he only a collection of awards and goals?

■ ■ ■

There is a maturity in some of the life decisions he is making. It took him two years to be seen in public with Irina Shayk, but he took his latest partner, Georgina Rodríguez, a twenty-three-year-old Spaniard, to The Best awards in January 2017, three months after meeting her. He already had his surrogate babies, Eva and Mateo, and on 12 October 2017, the daughter of Georgina and Cristiano, Alana Martina, was born in Madrid. 'Paternity,' Cristiano said, 'has shown me things about love that I never knew existed. It has made me weaker and given me a new perspective about what is important.' Any father would agree with those words and they are genuine. But they sounded unique because they came from a man who, after breaking all the boundaries, was finally discovering the edge of the world he had known until then.

■ ■ ■

By January 2018, following the club's elimination from the Copa del Rey on away goals at the hands of Leganes, and with the league effectively lost following Real Madrid's catastrophic display against nemesis Barcelona on Christmas Eve, just before the winter break, only the Champions League remained as a realistic trophy target for 'Los Blancos'.

'Nobody gets justice. People only get good luck or bad luck,' Orson Welles said once. *En route* to their third Champions League title on the bounce, their fourth in five years, and even in the final itself, Madrid got the luck they needed – and got it in spades.

Having finished 3-0 in Turin with Ronaldo scoring the first two goals, including an extraordinary overhead kick clapped in admiration by the Juventus fans too, Real Madrid were comprehensively spanked by Juventus in the second leg of the quarter final and, with the game heading into extra time, were granted a last kick of the match penalty by Michael Oliver in the eighth minute of added time. Ronaldo – who else? – converted and somehow Real progressed 4-3 into the semi-finals. Was it a penalty? Maybe, probably. If the roles had been reversed would Oliver have awarded it in favour of Juventus?

Against Bayern Munich, Sven Ulreich, for most of the season a more than capable replacement in goal for the injured Manuel Neuer, chose the second leg semi-final of the Champions League and the Santiago Bernabeu as the occasion and the venue to make what many believe was his only mistake of the campaign – an error that would effectively hand Real Madrid a place in the Champions League final. Ronaldo did not score any of his side's four goals in the double fixture.

Surely that would be the last piece of luck Real Madrid would enjoy in this European campaign? Enter Loris Karius, another German goalkeeper who would make two potentially career-defining, calamitous errors that – either side of a wonder strike from Gareth Bale – ensured Real Madrid's third title in a row after beating Liverpool 3-1. Once again Real Madrid had entered the European Cup/Champions League history books. Ronaldo and Real Madrid had won the competition four times in the last five years. Cristiano took pictures with him and the family spreading their hands. Five. Those were the Champions League trophies won by him in his career.

His joy should have been unbounded. What followed immediately after the final was very unexpected.

■ ■ ■

Demonstrations of overwhelming happiness were instead reduced to a statement by Ronaldo when he told the watching world that he and Madrid were done – on the pitch, minutes after the end of the game.

'It has been beautiful playing at Real Madrid. Over the next few days I will give an answer to the fans that have always been at my side.'

In the mixed zone after the game it was clear that, behind the scenes, there had been words. Someone – very probably Sergio Ramos – had informed Ronaldo that perhaps one of the greatest days in the club's history, the moment which showcased one of the greatest achievements in the life of a football club already full to bursting with historical, landmark, achievements was probably not the best time to announce to the world his dissatisfaction and desire to leave the club. His tone became more conciliatory with words like, 'you know me, it's just the way I am, I say it as I see it...' and so on, but the damage had been done, despite the celebrations that occurred the following day when fans implored him not to go with cries of 'Cristiano, *quedate* [Cristiano, stay]'. He told the fans he would see them next season, while a bewildered Gareth Bale lookedon in amazement in the background – it should have been his night, but it was being snatched away from him.

Cristiano kissed the badge on his shirt, much as he had done way back on 6 July 2009 when he was presented for the first time to fans crammed into a packed Bernabeu. But when the emotion of the celebrations disappeared, the desire to leave the club was as strong as it had been for three summers. There was just one small little problem. Where was he going to go?

Both Manchester United and Paris Saint Germain had been approached. Both declined. With those two major players out of the equation the options were radically reduced, not least because the signing of such a player when all things are taken into consideration amounts to around €400m – a figure that effectively alters the financial situation of any club. In addition, however fit, strong, motivated, even at his best he may feel there is one inescapable downside. Ronaldo is 33-years-old.

In the past when Ronaldo had expressed a desire to leave the club, Perez would remind him that in fact he had a €1000m buy-out clause on his contract and, if he really wanted to go, all he had to do was bring along the money that would allow the club to buy Leo Messi as his replacement. By the summer of 2018, around €100 would be enough.

Ronaldo was earning €21m a year and he claimed that Perez promised him a new contract twelve months earlier after having won the Champions League – against Juventus. Perez did not pick that promise for many months.

Then, just before the World Cup, it was agreed verbally that Ronaldo's wages would rise to €30m and that could go up to €42m – although it was very dependent on a number of bonuses – while what Ronaldo wanted was straight payments. Actually, what he really wanted was for the €32m earned by Neymar and the €40m-plus earned by Messi to be matched. For a 33-year-old man that was never going to happen. The constant irritation of the taxman knocking at his door was also getting him down, as was his under-standing – at least that was what he had been told – that they had done nothing wrong. 'Those that have done no wrong, don't have to have any fear,' he told the media during the season.

The reality was that Florentino was beginning to get fed up with his non-stop threats and his constant 'love me or lose me' protes-tations. He was also beginning to cast an avaricious eye towards Paris and the likes of Neymar and Mbappe as more than adequate replacements, although neither player was then, nor is now, about to be lost to the French club without a titanic struggle. The flirting with Mbappe in the summer of 2017 was replaced by conversations with the entourage of Neymar in 2018. But PSG was determined not to cave in. Not yet, anyway.

For Madrid enough was enough, although all along they were keen to make it look like Cristiano's departure was his decision, not the club's, and that had to be shown on every step of the way. In the words of the song, 'Oh, we don't want to lose you, but we think you ought to go.'

■ ■ ■

Before anything was decided there was the small matter of the Russia World Cup to be contested; a World Cup that would see Ronaldo captain the European champions Portugal; a World Cup that would see his country pitted in the first group match against Spain, the very country where he was currently plying his trade. Throughout his career Ronaldo has loved the big stage, the big match and the star performance. Portugal v. Spain in Sochi on 15 June was about as big as it got. If anyone hoped that Ronaldo might use the occasion to demonstrate once again to the watching world the qualities everyone knew that he had, then they were not about to be disappointed.

In the words of BBC Sport, 'Ronaldo was, well, Ronaldo.' Before this match Cristiano had scored only three times from 13 World Cup games. Ninety minutes plus later he had doubled his tally thanks to a hat-trick, and with the opening goal he became only the fourth player to score in four separate World Cups, joining Germans Miroslav Klose and Uwe Seeler, as well as Brazil legend Pelé.

No matter that the first was a dubious penalty earned and converted by him as early as the fourth minute, or that his second came following a speculative shot from outside the box that would probably have been saved by a more confident David de Gea. But somehow on this occasion the normally reliable goalkeeper let it squirm through his hands. Any thoughts that this Spanish side would have the last word – thanks to two strikes from Diego Costa and Nacho's fizzing volley from the edge of the area that crashed in off both posts – were swiftly rebuffed.

Once again, as is so often the case, it would be Ronaldo that would have the last word. If there was any suggestion of luck surrounding his first two goals, then there was nothing fortuitous about his third goal in the 88th minute: a stunning up-and-down free kick from the edge of the box following a foul from Piqué. For the record, and for anyone doubting that Ronaldo is quintessentially the man for the very biggest of occasions, it is worth noting that his third goal was his first direct free-kick goal at a major tournament for Portugal – after 45 attempts.

The Portuguese had become the first player in history to score in eight consecutive major tournaments in a streak going back to Euro 2004.

He then carried on where he had left off in the next match against Morocco, scoring the only goal of the game, as well as hitting six of the eight shots Portugal managed. While undoubtedly the star of the first week of the competition, his performance confirmed that, as good as he was, this was a poor Portugal side and neither Ronaldo – nor anyone – was ever going to win this tournament by themselves. Portugal stumbled into the knockout stages following a 1-1 draw against Iran, but Uruguay's defeat of them in the last 16 of the knockout stages exposed their limits: a side with not enough quality or imagination, far too reliant on just one player. There was to be no repeat of their European triumph. Portugal and Cristiano Ronaldo were going home.

And then on 10 July the worst-kept secret finally came out. Ronaldo was leaving Real Madrid and going to sign for Juventus.

■ ■ ■

On 7 November 2016, the whole audience clapped when, upon signing a new contract with Real Madrid, Ronaldo announced: 'I am pleased that Florentino [Perez] and the Madrid fans have a memory which is something we are not accustomed to seeing in football. This will not be my last contract here; let me make that clear.'

Less than two years later, on 10 July from Kalamakata in Greece where he was holidaying with his family, he announced that his love-hate romance with Real Madrid was over and he had signed a four-year contract with Juventus.

■ ■ ■

Many of Florentino's signings have been for him like his favourite sons. Zidane was signed after a message in a napkin. Benzema was visited at home by the chairman before agreeing to join the White House. Cristiano, rightly or wrongly, never felt like more than a stepson, with circumstances conspiring to oblige Florentino to raise him as his own.

Ronaldo was reluctantly taken to the bosom of Perez very much on the rebound. But love - true love - can play second fiddle to pragmatism and still win through because of a harmonious working together, a building of relationships, mutual trust and, of course, respect. Sometimes. But not this time. Or rather, it only 'worked' for nine years. Florentino and Ronaldo embraced many times over the years from the moment of his arrival to his eventual departure, but never, ever, you sensed, with true admiration. Cristiano was battling to win everybody's heart but never got the one of his chairman. It was unlikely to finish well, no matter how long it lasted.

■ ■ ■

While on holiday, Ronaldo announced via Madrid's webpage:

These years at Real Madrid and in the city of Madrid have been possibly the happiest of my life. I have only feelings of enormous gratitude for the club, for the fans and for the city. However, I believe that the time has come for me to start a new stage in my life and it is for that reason that I have asked the club to accept my transfer.

I have had a club and in the dressing room fabulous team-mates and have felt the passion of the incredible fans together with who we have won three Champions League in a row and four in five years.

Alongside them in an individual role, I have had the satisfaction of having won four Ballons d'Or and three Golden Boots.

In the open letter he wrote to Real fans, he announced:

I only have feelings of enormous gratitude for this club and for this city. I have had nine absolutely wonderful years at the club.

Real Madrid has conquered my heart, and that of my family, and that is why more than ever I want to say thank you: thank you to the club, the president, the directors, my colleagues, all the staff, doctors, physios and incredible people that make everything work.

He finished his letter by saying: 'Thanks to everyone and, of course, as I said that first time in our stadium nine years ago: Hala Madrid!'

Meanwhile, Real, still eager to maintain that his departure was nothing to do with them, also released a statement saying they had agreed to the transfer 'at the will and the request of the player'.

They added: 'Real Madrid would like to express its gratitude to a player who has proved to be the best in the world and who has made this one of the most brilliant times in the history of our club.

'Beyond the titles he won during these nine years at the club Cristiano Ronaldo has also been an example of dedication, work, responsibility, talent and constant improvement.'

Honour was satisfied, everyone was happy, the circle had been squared. The official story will confirm that Ronaldo left because he wanted to.

THE NEXT STEP, A NEW CONQUEST

■ ■ ■

Of course, it was never as simple as it sounds.

Earlier on 6 July Jesus Sanchez, writing in *Marca* (regarded by many as being the next best thing to Real Madrid's representative in the sporting media), stated that:

'He [Ronaldo] has decided to leave the club over a matter of respect, of what he understands to be a clear disregard for his stature.

'For the fact that the club didn't attend to what was promised by Florentino Perez while doing numbers for Neymar. The straw that broke his back was the reduction of his release clause from €1,000 to €100m, which he interpreted as an affront: a very low amount in a market that had lost its sanity after the transfer of Neymar to Paris Saint-Germain for €222m. In that scenario, Juventus appeared.'

But any notion that this was a deal hurriedly put together, and to some extent based on his World Cup exploits, could not be further from the truth.

On 5 July, before the news of Ronaldo's departure was announced, I tweeted, 'In his head, Cristiano is a Juventus player. Juve has found a financial way to pay for his wages and fee. Real Madrid willing to let him go. No offer has arrived yet to Real, but Jorge Mendes has confirmed to Real that it will. He has never been this close to leaving. Will he?'

The day before in *AS* my colleague Sergio Gomez went as far as to say that actually the move had been instigated by Ronaldo and his agent Jorge Mendes. Sergio wrote back then, 'Far from being resolved, his stand-off with the club's president, Florentino

Perez, who rowed back on his summer 2017 promise to improve the player's contract, has deepened. So much so that Real's record goalscorer is closer than ever to leaving, with Serie A champions Juventus confident of luring the Ballon d'Or holder to Turin – in a deal which, according to a report in the Italian media, Cristiano himself initiated. Premier Sport says that the Portugal captain and his agent, Jorge Mendes, met Juventus sporting director Fabio Paratici before the World Cup to offer the 33-year-old's services to the Vecchia Signora.'

Subsequent to the deal being signed, Ronaldo has been at pains to point out that his heart belongs to Juve and he has said almost non-stop all the right things in the right places to the right people about what a great club he is joining. And he is right. Juventus truly is, both now and historically, one of the great clubs and the deal brokered between Ronaldo's team and Juventus may well go on to be seen as one of the greatest pieces of footballing business ever negotiated between two parties. But that should not deflect from the reality of the situation which is that Ronaldo joined Juventus primarily because no other club with the financial wherewithal to attempt such a deal wanted him – or, to put it another way, could make the appropriate financial adjustments to accommodate him.

Jesus Sanchez at *Marca* was keen however to put a different slant on it days before the announcement. He wrote:

Cristiano, impressed by the treatment of the fans of Juventus Stadium, by the size of the Italian club and to face the challenge of making a European champion of the transalpine team, gave the yes to Andrea Agnelli. He didn't sign but gave his word, which in its concept means the same. Ronaldo doesn't need any signature to go ahead with the pre-agreement reached with the Serie A champion.

. . .Agnelli and Cristiano have begun in the best way possible. There were numerous phone calls from the president of Juve, and in Italy they suggest up to 28 times. Ronaldo was impressed with the treatment and deference of the leader, and with the desire shown when recruiting him. He was captivated by the respect, as if Juventus were a humbler club. Cristiano, and only Cristiano, was the man called to make Juve, who had been on the verge of conquering the Champions League in recent years, bigger.

After it became feasible that Ronaldo could leave Madrid for 100 million euros, other European clubs contacted Jorge Mendes to convey their interest in his availability and to address the signing. But the player had already given his word to Juventus.

Ronaldo, who was going to earn around the same that he had been earning at Madrid since 2016, did not want to listen to anyone. He had been won over by the devotion shown by Juventus, who were willing to break their salary cap and find ways to pay for his fee and wages, and even get rid of their main striker, Gonzalo Higuaín, who was not a favourite of Ronaldo at Madrid. He preferred the way Benzema adapted to the Portuguese, while the Argentinean used similar space to the one inhabited by Cristiano now. That was the message which was received by Agnelli.

Interestingly enough, Ronaldo kept wondering it there would be a change of heart from Madrid: a grand gesture, an apology and a new contract. But things took a completely new turn after the telephone conversation between his representative and Jose Angel Sanchez, the club's general director.

■ ■ ■

Believe who you will, but some things are abundantly clear following the move from Spain to Italy.

Firstly the Madrid board, and in particular Florentino Perez, ever mindful that the loss of a striker as prolific as Ronaldo could turn out to be a monumental *faux pas*, can now turn their palms skywards, shrug their shoulders and proclaim to the world, 'What could we do? He wanted to go,' although in reality they know that all they had to do to keep him was to offer him the same financial renumeration that Neymar was getting at PSG, a few million more than the agreed figure from the 2018-19 season if he had stayed in Madrid.

Strikers of the calibre of Ronaldo are not easily replaced whatever their age. Real Madrid's ill-mannered handling of their new manager Julen Lopetegui, signing from the Spanish national side, did not go down particularly well anywhere in Spain, but Madrid fans understood their club's call is hard to ignore. But after other managers had said no to Florentino (Mauricio Pochettino, Jurgen Klopp, Massimiliano Allegri), the pressure was on for Lopetegui to hit the floor running after the club decided not to strengthen the side beyond a top goalkeeper (Thibaut Courtois), a promising right back (Alvaro Odriozola), and a youngster who is touted as the new Neymar – Vinicius Junior, only 18. Real handed the responsibility of the goals to Gareth Bale, who had threatened to leave too, Benzema and Borja Mayoral.

The more experienced two front men (Bale and Benzema) had only 33 goals between them last season, 11 fewer than the Portuguese. Nor is this a one-off. In 412 games for Madrid, Benzema has scored 192 while Bale has a conversion rate of 88 in 189. But the problem is not simply that they don't have anyone in the squad who they can look to guarantee 30 to 40 goals a season, but rather that there is no one available on the open market that they particularly fancy.

Their two preferred options have vanished over the past couple of years. Firstly, Kylian Mbappe opted for PSG – as did Neymar Jr. PSG have made it crystal clear that for the time being at least they are going nowhere. Tottenham's Daniel Levy told the club that there was no chance of Harry Kane leaving for Spain, and reports that he would accept an offer of €300m were false. Mo Salah, despite reports, was not considered but in any case he renewed his contract with Liverpool in summer 2018. Of those available, only three have reached anywhere near the required tally. Robert Lewandowski has scored 41 goals for Bayern and has made it abundantly clear that he would love to join Real Madrid, while Edinson Cavani has hit 40 for PSG and has options to leave Paris. At Inter, Mauro Icardi is showing signs of growing too big for the club he scored 29 goals for last season. The reality is that the necessity to find someone to fill the departing Ronaldo's boots is as urgent as it is complex. But Real Madrid decided it was worthwhile the risk of trusting what they had, including Marco Asensio, who is expected to become one of the top players in the world in the next few years.

Lopetegui admitted – in his first two press conferences as Madrid coach during the pre-season International Champons Cups being held in the USA and Europe – that he faced a major struggle to replace Ronaldo. He was in fact rebuilding a side who needed new answers to offensive problems.

The arrival of Ronaldo had transformed Real Madrid. In nine years with him in the side, Real won four Champions League. His legacy can only be compared to Alfredo di Stefano, the man who won five European Cups in eleven years, and changed the club in the process.

You cannot replace Cristiano. So why even try.

. . .

Ronaldo meanwhile can claim that he will be at a club with a similar pedigree as his previous employers, and a club he has chosen over and above a long line of suitors, real or imagined. So what are Juventus buying? Just like a world-class boxer who, even after his legs have gone, has a knock-out punch that will put your lights out in a nano-second, his goalscoring achievements are the stuff of legend. This is a man that over nine seasons at Real Madrid has scored 450 goals in 438 games at a rate of 1.02 goals per game. The closest to him in terms of goals scored is Raul on 323 at 0.44 goals a game; while the closest to him in terms of goals per game is Ferenc Puskas, who scored 0.92 per game over 262 matches. Even di Stefano managed only 308 goals over 396 games a ratio of 0.78 goals per game. There is of course the small matter of the well-documented five Champions Leagues and Ballons d'Or (four with Real, one with Manchester United with both), plus with 116 goals he is the all-time top scorer in the Champions League.

Much has also justifiably been made of his obsessive dedication to remaining at the top of the footballing tree, and his team were keen to downplay the reality of his advancing years by leaking stories emanating from his medical at Juventus that revealed he had the physical capabilities of a 20-year-old. He also has 7 per cent body fat, which is around 3 per cent less than the average professional, as well as a muscular mass of 50 per cent, which is around 4 per cent higher than the norm for his profession. He also recorded a top speed of 33.98km (21.1mph) at the World Cup, which was the fastest clocked by any player in the tournament. Numbers suggest his influence should be bigger in the game, but his style has been defined by the limits of his body: Ronaldo, faster than most centre backs in long distances, stronger than them too, able to jump higher, is a one-touch goal machine and ideal for counterattacking football. That is what those stats tell you too.

And what are they paying? In addition to the €100m payable to Real Madrid over two payments, they will also pick up a €12m bill in the form of compensation payments to former clubs Sporting Lisbon and Manchester United, as well as other charges due to the governing bodies. Ronaldo will receive a net €30m for every year of the four seasons that he has signed up for. And this is the figure that Madrid had agreed to pay him from the new season – but still less than what Neymar gets at PSG.

And what exactly are they getting for their money?

In the financial pages of *El País*, the excellent Paz Alvarez sums up exactly what is entailed in the deal between the two mega-corporations that are Real Madrid and Juventus. According to the figure from Deloitte, Ronaldo is moving from the richest club in the world with an income of €674,6m a year to the tenth largest on €405,7m. The Italian equivalent of a PLC, the club is reputedly owned by the Agnelli family of Fiat and Ferrari fame, among others, and is quoted on the Italian stock exchange. I say 'reputedly' because according to official statistics from Exor, the Netherlands-based firm that owns 29.18% of the Fiat parent company, they also own a controlling 63.77% stake in Juventus Football Club. For more than a week, as rumours began to circulate about the expected signing of Ronaldo, shares in the football club rose by a staggering 32%. A club that a week ago had a value of €735m was eight days later – even accounting for an adjustment of 5,18% – was valued at €888m. No signing in the history of football has had such a huge impact on a club's finances.

Fernado Pons from the sporting sector of Deloitte says that Ronaldo would be a 'fountain of income' for Ronaldo's new employers. 'The impact that he can have on the Juventus brand, especially in Asia, where Real Madrid is very strong, is large.'

Quico Vidal, founder of a consultancy company, Nadie, warned of the importance of separating the emotional aspect of the Ronaldo signing with the hard business aspects of the deal. 'Cristiano is a very emotional player and we still have to see how he is going to feel playing in Italian football bearing in mind his great tie, connection and affinity with the values of Real Madrid. And within all of this his ambition, 'not so much to play beautifully, but rather to always win, especially in the Champions league'. That said, the winning achievements of a Juventus side that has won seven league titles in a row and who in the last four seasons have been Champions League finalists twice and semi-finalists once, should not be underestimated.

In the opinion of Eduardo Fernández-Cantelli, professor of the IE Business school, this is a deal where all three of the participants loses something.

Real Madrid loses the possibility of exploiting a really powerful brand, as well as risking the continued following of a number of huge markets such as Asia – which is something that could benefit Juventus who have to cope with the fact that the Italian league has fair less exposure than the Spanish, and in order to guarantee it has had to shell out a lot of money'. Ronaldo, he added, also loses out because it has been at 'Los Blancos' where his brand has been created, 'and it remains to be seen if from now his value continues to grow at the same rate'.

The Italian journalist football expert Gabriele Marcotti perhaps summed it up best. He wrote in *The Times*: 'Go big or go home. Juventus's acquisition of Cristiano Ronaldo is not about securing the Serie A title (they have won seven in a row already) or winning the Champions League again after 22 years (they reached two finals in the past four seasons). Rather, it is about going to the next level in commercial terms.'

'Thus, when the opportunity presented itself to offer Ronaldo a way out of Real, the club seized it with both hands. The Portugal forward is, of course, one of a handful of players in the world who can move the commercial needle single-handedly. When you sign Ronaldo, you are not acquiring a player, you are effectively merging with another global corporation.'

In the meantime the club's shops were doing a roaring trade.

According to the *Guardian*, the team sold 520,000 shirts bearing Ronaldo's name within just 24 hours of the merchandise being released. CNBC added that 'to put that into perspective, beIN Sports reports that the team sold just 850,000 shirts during the entirety of the 2016/2017 season. *Business Insider* estimates that these Ronaldo-related purchases translate into at least $60 million in sales, and notes that since 'typically clubs receive only 10-15 per cent of the revenue generated by the kit manufacturer [in this case, Adidas], 'the team will probably see about $6 to $9 million of that money.'

So everyone was happy... right?

The workers at Fiat Chrysler, or at least their union representatives, most certainly won't. The motor factories are run by the Agnelli family and are part-owned by Exor. One might be forgiven for thinking that the signing of Ronaldo was the first time in the history of 'La Vecchia Signora' that the club had splashed the cash in the transfer market, such was the reaction of the Fiat Chrysler unions, who on hearing details of the deal instructed their members to down tools at the Melfi plant in the south of Italy from 10 pm on 15 July, until 6 am on 17 July . Nothing could have been further from the truth. This is a club that in 2001 paid Parma €52m for Gianluigi Buffon, making him the most expensive goalkeeper of all time until 2018. In July 2016, they signed Gonzalo Higuain for €90m from Napoli, at the time the highest-ever transfer for an Italian club. Was it the crossing of the €100m psychological barrier that upset the unions so much, or was it perhaps the spending of such large amounts in times of cutbacks and talk of recession that irritated them?

In a statement the Unione Sindicale di Base (USB) explained their reasoning: It is unacceptable that while FCA and CNHI workers continue to make huge economic sacrifices, the company then spends hundreds of millions of euros on the purchase of a player,' a statement from the USB read. 'We are told it's a difficult moment, that we need to resort to social safety nets, waiting for the launch of new models that never arrive. And while the workers and their families tighten their belts more and more, the company decides to invest a lot of money on a single human resource!

Is this right? Is it normal for one person to earn millions, while thousands of families can't even get to the middle of the month? We are all employees of the same owner, but in this moment of enormous social difficulty this difference in treatment cannot and must not be accepted. The Fiat workers have made the company's fortune for at least three generations ... and in return they have only ever received a life of misery.

'The company should invest in car models that guarantee the futures of thousands of people rather than enriching only one. That should be the objective, a company that puts the interests of their employees first. If it isn't, it's because they prefer the world of games, entertainment and everything else.

It reminded many of the voices that complained in Madrid – including from religious quarters – of Ronaldo's arrival at the Bernabeu. There is a slight sense of demagogue talk here. Football is a huge business, capitalism in its truest form, and to look at the top of it for exemplary behaviour in the most unequal of systems is to ask for rain in Sardinia in August.

Whatever the feelings of the trade union leaders, Ronaldo was effectively a game-changer not just for Juventus, but for the whole of Italian soccer. But first his teammates needed to say their goodbyes.

No sooner had news of his departure been made official than an orderly queue formed to pay tribute to the Portuguese superstar. 'Cristiano, your goals, your stats and everything that we have won together speak for themselves. You deserve your place in the history of Real Madrid. The Madrid fans will always remember you. It has been a pleasure to play at your side. Good luck and a huge hug!', said Sergio Ramos on social media with a message that was accompanied by a photograph of the two players embracing after a Champions league game.

'An incredible player and a top man! It has been a pleasure to play alongside you for the past five years. Good luck for the future, my friend,' said Gareth Bale, while Nacho wrote, 'You were and still are number one. All of Madrid will remember you as a leader.'

Toni Kroos described him as a 'legend', adding that he was a 'true champion' and that his presence in the Madrid side had been crucial to winning trophies over the past years. One of his possible heirs apparent, Marco Asensio, said Ronaldo 'had been an example in every sense of the word'.

It might just have crossed Ronaldo's mind at this point that if the team, the fans, the club and the City were all going to miss him that much, then maybe everyone should have been a bit more proactive in ensuring that he stayed. Whatever he thought, what was certain is that he – perhaps uncharacteristically - announced as he was leaving that he did not want a ceremonial, all-singing, all-dancing, tearful farewell. Ronaldo may well have come to the club in a blaze of glory through the main gates, nine seasons earlier, but by his choice he was now departing via the tradesman's entrance. Anything else would have meant sharing the stage with Florentino Perez again. And there was no way that that was going to happen.

Former Real Madrid star Manolo Sanchis summed it up on Partidazo de Cope on Spanish radio station Cope: 'After Cristiano,

Madrid need someone that will be able to bring the glamour back to the squad, and they are looking for them. It was a farewell that was cold and civilised. The opportunity to do something big was lost. Certainly, sometimes it isn't easy.'

Cristiano arrived for his first training session with his new club on Monday, 30 July, flying into Turin with his family on a private jet the night before. He arrived along with other members of the squad like Paola Dybala, Juan Cuadrado, Douglas Costa and Rodrigo Bentacur, who had also been in Russia at the knock-out stages of the World Cup.

The entire Juve squad were scheduled to train together in Turin on 8 August ahead of Ronaldo's first outing in a black-and-white-striped shirt four days later, in the Serie A club's traditional season-opener at Villar Perosa – a friendly between the first team and the youths. After seven minutes he scored his first goal with the black-and-white shirt. A week later, Ronaldo made his Serie A debut at Chievo as Juve begin their search for a record eighth straight Scudetto with his first steps at the Allianz Stadium taking place seven days later when Lazio visited Turin.

The impact made by his arrival into Serie A soon became clear, not just at Juventus. Newly promoted Parma, finally back in the big time, welcomed the Turin side on the third matchday of the season on 2 September. The hunt for a ticket began in earnest very early on in the proceedings and, when demand outstrips supply, ticket prices are only ever going to fly northwards, even though large increases are very often due to secondary ticketing. The English phrase for it is 'making hay while the sun shine', a euphemism for blatant profiteering. Tuttosport examined the case of Parma and discovered that four seats in the North Curva which on the club's offical website came out at €25 each were then offered at €178. With normal website prices in brackets, seats for the East Stand were

€199 (€60), the lateral West €233 (€70) and the two sections of the Pettitot Tribune €386 (€100) and an eye watering €438 (€150). Had you decided to buy a season ticket for the North Curva, it would have cost you a total of €190 – just €12 more than what you will need to pay if you just want to see Ronaldo play in this one game.

One ice cream parlour has even invented the CR7 ice cream cone, made up of black and white colours, a Portuguese cherry liqueur and chocolate shavings. It is the creation of Leonardo La Porta, who has owned Gelateria Miretti in the heart of Turin for thirty years. The only other time he created a special flavour in someone's honour was back in 2015 when the Pope called into Turin. 'I put it on sale on the date 7/7 because it was the day it was rumored Cristiano Ronaldo would be presented,' La Porta told The Associated Press. 'I thought of it a week before . . . the research was quite intense.'

'We chose to use a typical Portuguese liquor which is the Ginja. It is a sour cherry liquor which strongly links Portugal to the Piedmont region because here too in Piedmont we have a similar cherry liquor. In Portugal this liquor is served in a chocolate cup, so this ice cream is made up of milk, cream, sugar and carob flour, with this Ginja liquor and pieces of chocolate.'

The taste is rich and flavourful, with hints of spice and fruit.

'I hope [Ronaldo] can come here to try it,' said La Porta, adding that the flavour regularly sells out. 'If not, I'm ready to go to his house to make it for him. We'll see.'

Incidentally, La Porta added that he was not a Juventus fan, and that he didn't even particularly like football. Yet another example of the irony that football is by no means the only relevant factor in matters pertaining to Ronaldo.

Cristiano had left Spain but there was one remaining issue to be resolved. On 26 July the Spanish tax authorities finally confirmed that they had reached an agreement over the ongoing tax-evasion case. The now Juventus forward would accept responsibility for four different breaches of Spanish tax laws, and an automatically suspended two-year prison sentence, and pay €18,8m to the authorities, €5,7m which is owed in taxes on his image rights and a further €13.1m in fines as interest.

It brought to an end two years of negotiations between the various parties involved. The Hacienda (tax department) prosecutors argued that Ronaldo and his advisers used a network of companies in various countries, including Ireland and the British Virgin Islands, to evade paying €14.7m in taxes due on 'image rights' income earned between 2011 and 2014.

According to ESPN: 'Observers, including KPMG's Football Benchmark group, argue that having joined Italian side Juventus this summer, Ronaldo will enjoy a more beneficial fiscal situation, paying a flat total of €100,000 tax on all image rights income earned outside of his new country of residence.

A line was finally drawn under Ronaldo's time at Real Madrid.

And when he wakes up in his new mansion at the top of the hill in San Vito, overlooking Turin and the Alps, I think a familiar thought will occur to him. The thought that travelled with him to Lisbon, to Manchester, to Madrid, and that first appeared in the hopeful and emboldened days of Funchal. 'Each morning we are born again.'

BIBLIOGRAPHY

The following sources correspond to the number markers in the text.

1. *El chiringuito de jugones* (television programme), Sexta TV, 26 January 2015
2. Ruiz, Marco, 'Este Real Madrid tiene algo de nuestro gran Milan', *AS*, 21 November 2014
3. Chadband, Ian, 'Champions League final 2014: Move over Christopher Columbus, Cristiano Ronaldo's palace is the real deal', *Daily Telegraph*, 24 May 2014
4. *CR9 vive aquí* (documentary), La Sexta, 2010
5. *Salvame de Luxe* (documentary), Tele 5, 31 May 2014
6. López, Siro, Pino, Beatriz, and Pérez, José Luis, *La sonrisa de Ronaldo* (documentary), Dirección, 2010
7. Pereira, Luis Miguel, and Gallardo, Juan Ignacio, *CR7: los secretos de la máquina*, Prime Books, 2014
8. Relea, Francesc, 'Diamante en bruto que salió de Madeira', *El País International*, 2008
9. Larcher, Christophe, 'El funambulista que surgió del arrabal', *L'Equipe*, 2008

10. Sousa, Paulo, and Aveiro, Dolores, *Mae Coragem*, Matéria Prima, 2014

11. Siguero, Santiago, *Cristiano Ronaldo, la estrella tenaz*, Al Poste Ediciones, 2013

12. Nuno Luz, *Planeta Ronaldo*, SIC, 2008

13. Torrejón, Mario, *Cristiano, el Di Stéfano de nuestro tiempo*, Al Poste Ediciones, 2014

14. 'Cristiano Ronaldo spills all to his "close friend" Jasmine about women, football, cars . . . and money', *Daily Mirror*, 2011

15. Cuesta, Miguel, and Sánchez, Jonathan, *La Clave Mendes*, La Esfera de los Libros, 2015

16. Keane, Roy, with Doyle, Roddy, *The Second Half*, Weidenfeld & Nicolson, 2014

17. Ortego, Enrique, *Sueños Cumplidos*, Everest Ediciones, 2010

18. Ferguson, Alex, *My Autobiography*, Hodder & Stoughton, 2013

19. Rooney, Wayne, *My Decade in the Premier League*, HarperSport, 2012

20. Neville, Gary, *Red: My Autobiography*, Corgi, 2012

21. Forjanes, Carlos, 'Mamá Cristiano Ronaldo manda señales al Madrid', *AS*, 22 January 2008

22. Hunter, Andy, 'Ferguson confronts Real over lack of morality and vows Ronaldo will stay', *The Guardian*, 24 May 2008

23. Dudek, Jerzy, and Kurowski, Dariusz, *NieREALna kariera* (An unreal career), Arksom Group, 2015

24. Coelho, João Nuno, 'Entre a esperança e a tormenta: futebol, identidade nacional e o Euro-2004' in Pereira, Albano, and Amado, Miguel, *Em Jogo*, Centro de Artes Visuais, 2004

25. Valdano, Jorge, 'A favor de Cristiano Ronaldo', *Soho*, 30 May 2014

26. Torres, Diego, *Prepárense para perder*, Ediciones B, 2013

27. Gallo, Ivan, 'La desalmada historia del hijo de Cristiano Ronaldo', *Las dos orillas* (blog), 28 December 2014

28. García, Óscar, 'El Barça desmonta al Madrid', *AS*, 11 December 2011

29. http://www.thisdaylive.com/articles/why-ronaldo-dedicates-la -decima-glory-to-old-friend/179586/

30. Maluf, Eduardo, 'Sou o 1º, 2º e o 3º do mundo', *O Estado de Sao Paulo*, 17 November 2008

31. Serrano, Miguel, 'Cristiano: Pronto estaré a mi mejor nivel', *Marca*, 28 August 2014

32. Redacción, 'Cristiano: ¿Rivalidad con Messi? En mi cabeza, yo soy el mejor', *AS*, 28 August 2014

33. Marcotti, Gabriele, 'The Phenomenon of Messi and Ronaldo', *Wall Street Journal*, 18 March 2012

34. Carpio, Carlos, 'Así fue la bronco de Cristiano Ronaldo y Florentino', *Marca*, 7 December 2012

35. 'FIFA Ballon d'Or C. Ronaldo: J'en veux encore plus', *France Football*, 21 January 2014

36. Relaño, Alfredo, '14 anotaciones sobre la Décima', *AS*, 26 May 2014

37. Villoro, Juan, 'En contra de Cristiano Ronaldo', *Soho*, 30 May 2014

38. Hustvedt, Siri, *The Blazing World*, Sceptre, 2014

OTHER SOURCES CITED OR CONSULTED

'Jorge Mendes interview', *Luso Football* (blog), 15 September 2006

'Wayne: I'll split him in two', *The Sun*, 3 July 2006

A Bola

Ancelotti, Carlo, *My Christmas Tree*, Rizzoli, 2013

Antena 3

Badenhausen, Kurt, 'The World's Highest-Paid Athletes 2013: Behind the Numbers', *Forbes*, 5 June 2013

Balagué, Guillem, 'Calderón tiene atado a Cristiano para el verano', *AS*, 13 January 2009

Balagué, Guillem, *Messi*, Orion, 2013

Beltrán Llera, Jésus, https://auladelenguajeupc2014.wikispaces. com/file/view/Beltran_Llera.Ensenar_a_aprender.pdf

CNN

Conn, David, 'The brightest star in Europe and £1m to a mysterious agent', *The Guardian*, 19 January 2011

Cristiano Ronaldo, a estrela merengue. A liga confidencial (documentary), Sport TV (Portugal), 2012

Cubeiro, J. C., and Gallardo, L., *Messi, Falcao y Cristiano Ronaldo*, Alienta Ed., 2013

Dalrymple, William, *Nine Lives*, Bloomsbury, 2009

Diário de Notícias

El Larguero

El programa de Ana

ESPN

Europa Press Agency

Ferdinand, Rio, and Winer, David, *2Sides: My Autobiography*, Blink Publishing, 2014

Fifa.com

Intereconomía

Lowe, Sid, *Fear and Loathing in La Liga*, Yellow Jersey, 2013

The Making of Ronaldo, Sky Sports, 2014

Memorias do melhor do mundo, Sport TV (Portugal), 2001

Ozanian, Mike, 'Real Madrid Tops Ranking of the World's Most Valuable Soccer Teams', *Forbes*, 6 May 2015

Pelé, 'Ronaldo: Portugal's game winner', *Time*, 23 April 2014

Perarnau, Martí, *Herr Pep*, Corner, 2014

Real Madrid TV

Reuters

BIBLIOGRAPHY

Revista de la Liga

Sacks, Oliver, *On the Move*, Picador, 2015

Séverac, Dominique, *l'Equipe*, 16 August 2015

The Story So Far, ITV Sports, 2012

Téléfoot

TV2 (Norway)

TVI of Portugal

de Unamuno, Miguel, *Ensayos: La envidia hispánica*, Aguilar, 1964

Valdano, Jorge, *Los 11 Poderes del Líder*, Conecta, 2013

ACKNOWLEDGEMENTS

The great thing about having a selective memory (only the good things stick in the mind) is that I will remember for ever some of the enjoyable things this project has given me: the conversations, the research, the organising, the writing, even the editing.

Right now, I might still remember the insomnia and the whole variety of sleeping disorders, the long hours watching the summer go by from my office, the heat of a very humid Barcelona, the terrible noise from 8 a.m. as the flat downstairs was being refurbished and a new hotel being built right next door. But give me a week and all that will be forgotten.

Without the backing of Alan Samson at Orion I wouldn't have written so many books. I thought I had one in me, but not four! And two more to go! So, my first thanks go to him.

I don't believe in the solitude of the writer. I love creating a mini community that helps me reach my goal, in this case the finishing (on time) of a biography of a truly unique player.

The closest team to me, the ones that I couldn't do without, happen to be my best friends. I am lucky to have managed to get them involved again. Maribel Herruzo has done, as per usual, an extraordinary job as a researcher, organiser and one thousand things more. Having Miguel García reading the final product and suggesting new avenues in our long chats is one of the privileges of doing a book. William Glasswell is my right-hand man who also had to look after Biggleswade United while proofreading this – three full-time jobs, that is. Brent Wilks was always at hand for what was needed and Peter Lockyer looked after other sides of the business as I focused all my attention on finishing this. To all of you, eternal thanks.

I wrote the book in Spanish because of disappointing translations into my own language of previous books, one in particular, so I recruited again the very talented Marc Joss to work here, and in the last stage we also used his good friend and another very precise translator, Hugo Steckelmacher.

David Luxton, as always, has been available to do some quiet negotiating on my behalf, but he must be thrilled that my excellent timing did not require him to be quite so placatory this time!

Arnaldo Cafofo was a huge help with the transcribing of all the Portuguese interviews. And Paolo Araujo was the perfect guide to the Funchal that people don't want you to see. Dariusz Kirowski very kindly sent over some extracts of the autobiography of Jerzy Dudek that he co-wrote. We had a very fruitful time (and a great meal at the end) with Dan Reston and Christian Pickwoad, the Sky Sports crew for the Ronaldo documentary.

One of the most illuminating conversations about Ronaldo I had was with the young journalist Steve Bartram, who came on board to add his point of view and information, to transcribe interviews and to share some of the ones he had done already for a similar project, which will see the the light of day soon with Ole Gunnar Solskjær, Wes Brown, John O'Shea, Alan Smith, and Edwin van der Sar.

The interviews with people that follow ended up becoming relaxed conversations that I never wanted to end. Alec Wylie, Ian Buckinham, Alfredo Relaño, Aurélio Pereira, Bernandino Rosa, Carlos Freitas, Carlos Pereira, Davide Gomes, Angel Di María, Pedro Talhinhas, Diego Torres, Enrique Ortego, Gary Neville, Hugo Pina, João Nuno Coelho, Jorge Andrade, Jorge Manuel Mendes, José Carlos Freitas, Leonel Pontes, Luis Boa Morte, Luis Lourenço, Louis Saha, Manuel Pellegrini, Martinho Fernandes, Mike Clegg, Nelio Cardoso, Nuno Aveiro, Nuno Naré, Orfeo Suárez, Oscar Campillo, Quentin Fortune, Ramón Calderón, René Meulensteen, Ricardo Alves, Jordi García, Ricardo Santos, Rio Ferdinand, Rui Alves, Ryan Giggs, Samuel, Sergio Fernández, Sidónio Serpa, Alberto Toril, Valter di Salvo, Xabi Alonso, Sam Allardyce, Pep Segura, Pako Ayestarán, Iván Campo, my cousin Angel Pérez, Esteve Calzada, Neal Ferro, James Whealer and Dr Peter Collett.

Thank you all for your time and insight!

Those of you who spoke off the record know that the next meal is on me.

At some point I have needed the advice, help, support or the ear of these friends who appeared at the right time to make sure this table had four legs: Stephen Watkinson, Manoj Kumar, Bill Beswick and Imma Puig.

So, I, like Ronaldo, also dreamt about publishing another book. And I feel like celebrating. But, perhaps like him, too, I cannot wait to start work on the next one.

Upwards and onwards.